Popular Books

LATELY PUBLISHED BY

TICKNOR, REED, AND FIELDS.

I. — FIFTEENTH EDITION.

MRS. MOWATT'S AUTOBIOGRAPHY.

Price $1.25.

FIFTEENTH THOUSAND JUST ISSUED.

From the Preface.

If one struggling sister in the great human family, while listening to the history of my life, gains courage to meet and brave severest trials; if she learns to look upon them as blessings in disguise; if she be strengthened in the performance of 'daily duties,' however 'hardly paid;' if she be inspired with faith in the power imparted to a strong *will* whose end is *good* — then I am amply rewarded for my labor. ANNA CORA MOWATT.

We have read this book through with more than the interest of a romance. The fair authoress herself is one of the rarest of heroines. Her eight years upon the stage furnish a volume of the most entertaining and instructive experience. — *New York Mirror.*

One of the few books which it is difficult to lay down till every page is read, is the Autobiography of Mrs. Mowatt. I have actually stolen the time which ought to have been appropriated to certain special demands, to look through the pages of this strange volume. To look at any chapter of contents, is sure to send you to the text; and to start with the text is to rivet your attention in spite of every extraneous call. Mrs. Mowatt's Autobiography will have a permanent place in American literature. Edition after edition will come from the press. It will be the exciting theme of book notices and even of labored reviews. — *New Covenant.*

II. – THIRD EDITION.

PASSION-FLOWERS.

BY MRS. HOWE.

One Volume, 16mo., Price 75 Cents.

WITH these words upon its title-page, and with no acknowledgment of authorship, Ticknor Reed & Fields, of Boston, have just issued a volume of poems, which, if we do not greatly mistake its character, is destined to create an interest in the literary world second only to that produced by the sudden apparition of Alexander Smith, the Glasgow poet, a few months ago. The book is not only remarkable in itself, but it indicates a latent power, a reserved force on the part of its author, which makes the present performance, great as we feel it is, seem but the prelude to something yet higher and nobler. * * * * A word to the author. Rumor corroborates the internal evidence afforded by the book itself, that its writer is the wife of a highly distinguished professional gentleman and philanthropist of Boston — a lady, whose genius and culture have been so well known to her friends, as to exempt them from any surprise at their manifestation in her 'Passion-Flowers.' — *National Era.*

WE know of no living poet of her sex with whom to compare the author of 'Passion-Flowers,' except Mrs. Browning, whom she resembles, however, only in her generous and high culture, and in the elevation and depth of her sentiments. Lovers of poetry here will feel a special interest in the history of this gifted minstrel, from the fact that it is confidentially stated that she is the daughter of a late highly esteemed citizen of New York, although a resident of a neighboring State. — *New York Evening Post.*

III. – EIGHTH EDITION.

GRACE GREENWOOD'S

HAPS AND MISHAPS OF A TOUR IN EUROPE.

One Volume, 12mo., Price $1.25.

WHEN we travel, if she can be found, we will have a companion like Grace Greenwood. * * * * On the whole, though the volume is made up of brief sketches, and covers over many countries, it is one of the most readable and sensible records of foreign travel with which we have recently met. We would trust Grace Greenwood's judgment on almost any subject of which she speaks, sooner than we would that of a far wiser person, who had become hackneyed and tamed down to the tradition standards. The flowing and sprightly narrative, the vivid and often admirable descriptions of natural scenes, and the ever ready, but by no means undiscriminating enthusiasm, must attract, as they deserve to do, many readers interested in the 'Haps and mishaps' of her journeyings. — *Christian Register.*

THIS is, altogether, the most readable, sensible, delightful book of rambles abroad that we have read for a long time. — *Saturday Courier.*

IV. — FOURTH EDITION.

SIX MONTHS IN ITALY.

BY GEORGE S. HILLARD.

2 vols. 12mo., $2.50.

No volumes of a similar character have received as much attention in the literary world for many years, as this admirable work by Mr. Hillard. Universal commendation followed its appearance from the press; and it has taken at once high rank among the useful books of our day.

The Albion closes its review thus :

'What a pleasant business it would be, this passing judgment on books, if we had many such authors to deal with. It was with listless attention that we took up the two volumes before us, notwithstanding that these Boston publishers have the knack of courting the eye by all the tricksy niceties of typography. But let no man gainsay the truth of that homely proverb which peoples oceans with as good fish as ever came out of it, or rashly asserts that Italy is an exhausted theme ! Mr. Hillard has fairly carried us with him from his first page to his last, and we must honestly avow that no modern traveller, within the scope of our pen, has looked and listened so profitably to himself, and has recorded his impressions in a manner so acceptable to his readers.

V. — THIRD EDITION.

LIGHT ON THE DARK RIVER;

OR,

MEMORIALS OF MRS. HENRIETTA A. L. HAMLIN,

MISSIONARY IN TURKEY.

BY MARGARETTE WOODS LAWRENCE.

WITH AN INTRODUCTION BY REV. E. S. STORRS.

This admirable Memoir, although but quite recently from the press, has excited great attention throughout the country. A large edition was at once exhausted and the demand continues rapidly to increase. The highest testimonials have been awarded for the fidelity and beauty with which the authoress (a daughter of Dr. Woods of Andover) has accomplished her task.

From Rev. Dr. Storrs.

'Though not personally acquainted with Mrs. Hamlin nor her family connections, and obliged, like other readers, to estimate her character by her words and works here recorded, yet the consistency and harmony of the Memoir with itself in all its parts, and its congruity with all that has been said of her, while she lived, and by those who knew her well, has created a deep and lively interest in my own mind, in the perusal of these precious memorials, — an interest increasing from the beginning to the end, even in a painful intensity.'

VI. — FOURTEENTH EDITION.

ALEXANDER SMITH'S POEMS.

1 vol. 16mo. 50 cents.

Notices from the London Press.

SINCE Tennyson, no poet has come before the public with the same promise as the author of this volume. . . . . There are many lines and sentences in these poems which must become familiar on the lips of lovers of poetry. — *Literary Gazette.*

IT is to the earlier works of Keats and Shelley alone that we can look for a counterpart, in richness of fancy and force of expression. . . . . These extracts will induce every lover of true poetry, to read the volume for himself; we do not think that, after such reading, any one will be disposed to doubt that Alexander Smith promises to be a greater poet than any emergent genius of the last few years. — *Spectator.*

THE most striking characteristic of these poems is their abundant *imagery* — fresh, vivid, concrete images actually present to the poet's mind, and thrown out with a distinctiveness and a delicacy only poets can achieve. There is not a page of this volume on which we cannot find some novel image, some Shaksperian felicity of expression, or some striking simile. — *Westminster Review.*

AN

ART-STUDENT IN MUNICH.

THERE IS THAT TO BE SEEN IN EVERY STREET AND LANE OF EVERY CITY, THAT TO BE FELT AND FOUND IN EVERY HUMAN HEART AND COUNTENANCE, THAT TO BE LOVED IN EVERY ROAD-SIDE WEED AND MOSS-GROWN WALL, WHICH, IN THE HANDS OF FAITHFUL MEN, MAY CONVEY EMOTIONS OF GLORY AND SUBLIMITY CONTINUAL AND EXALTED.

JOHN RUSKIN.

AN

ART-STUDENT IN MUNICH.

BY

ANNA MARY HOWITT.

BOSTON:
TICKNOR, REED, AND FIELDS.
MDCCCLIV.

THURSTON, TORRY, AND EMERSON, PRINTERS.

TO

MY BELOVED PARENTS,

WHOSE KEEN LOVE OF NATURE,

AND OF ALL

THAT IS PURE AND TRUE IN LIFE,

FIRST IMPLANTED

THE ARTIST'S ASPIRATION WITHIN MY SOUL,

The following Pages

ARE AFFECTIONATELY INSCRIBED.

TO

MY BELOVED PARENTS,

WHOSE KEEN LOVE OF NATURE,

AND OF ALL

THAT IS PURE AND TRUE IN LIFE,

FIRST IMPLANTED

THE ARTIST'S ASPIRATION WITHIN MY SOUL,

The following Pages

ARE AFFECTIONATELY INSCRIBED.

PREFACE.

These pages are gleanings from letters written home during a sojourn in Munich for the purpose of artistic study. They record the beautiful and happy experiences belonging to a peculiarly poetical chapter in the life of a woman studying Art. Should some readers, however, cavil at what they may deem a certain *couleur-de-rose* medium through which all objects seem to have been viewed, the writer would simply reply, that to her it appears more graceful for a Student of Art to present herself in public as the chronicler of the deep emotions of joy and of admiration called forth in her soul by great works of imagination, than as the chronicler of what in her eyes may have appeared defects and shortcomings. The sole shadow, therefore, which the writer has purposely introduced into the chronicle, is the shadow of intrinsic sternness and mournfulness pervading certain of the great works referred to.

In the personal narrative running through this volume, as a thread upon which to string certain pearls of Art, the writer has pursued a very similar line of action, feeling that although each passage of life has its peculiar prose and its peculiar pain, that to dwell, in retrospect, upon this pain and upon this prose is not only unphilosophic in itself, but ungrateful towards that Spirit of Joy and of Beauty which is ever brooding over the world.

And here the writer would add a few words as a living protest against a very common but thoughtless calumny, namely, that it is man who thwarts every effort of woman to rise to eminence in the life of Art. With a thrill of truest happiness, she must here declare, that her experience hitherto, as an Art-Student, has been the most perfect refutation of such calumny. Invariably and repeatedly, when a hand has been required to put aside the sharp stones and thorns which peculiarly beset a woman upon the path of Art, strong, manly hands have been stretched forth with noble generosity to remove them; and manly voices have uttered words of teaching, of encouragement, and of prophecy of happy achievement.

A. M. H.

London, April 16, 1853.

CONTENTS.

AN

ART-STUDENT IN MUNICH.

CHAPTER I.

SETTLING DOWN. — A RELIGIOUS PROCESSION. — THE HOF-KAPELLE. — A GREAT PAINTER'S STUDIO AND CARTOONS.

Munich, June 1st, 1850. — Here we are in Munich. These last several days have been such a confusion of excitement, delight, disappointment, joy, fatigue, and disgust, that I scarcely know where to begin my narrative. I will, however, begin with prosaic lodging-hunting. To-day, all yesterday, and part of Saturday, have we been hunting for our little home that is to be; and as yet have not found it. The fact is, Munich is very full, from the sitting of the Bavarian Parliament, and from the great number of soldiers and students here; so that it seems next to impossible to find what we want, — cleanliness, respectability, and moderate charges combined. I should think I have been in almost every street in Munich; and what queer places and people I have seen! I fancy to-night, when I fall asleep, I shall find myself in dreams standing at the corner of some old street, reading the written advertisements which are posted up in such places.

I seem to have no ideas in my brain but '2 *Zimmer zu vermiethen. Ein sehr schön moblirtes Zimmer zu vermiethen an einen soliden Herrn, und gleich zu beziehen.*' Think how old-fashioned it is here in Munich even, when a servant-girl will be sent round with a number of such advertisements, and a paste-pot, and pastes them up at the corner of the streets throughout the city: I had the amusement of seeing one perform her business. At present we remain at the Inn.

You will naturally wish to know what we have done about the most important thing of all, — our artistic arrangements: scarcely anything as yet, for all requires time and consideration. I have not yet been even to Kaulbach's atelier. I asked advice from B——, and he recommended that I should become a pupil, for the first three months at least, of a friend of his, a rising artist and pupil of De la Roche's. I, of course, was therefore anxious to see this gentleman and his works; but I am disappointed, — and, in fact, we for the present remain in a state of the greatest uncertainty. Admission into the Academy, as we had hoped, we find is impossible for women: the higher class of artists receive no pupils.

I saw, yesterday morning, when at the B——'s, a procession, or rather a number of processions, which were moving through the street. They were a sort of sequel to the grand procession of Corpus Christi Day, which we unfortunately missed seeing by a few hours. The morning was gloriously bright, the sky as cloudless and blue as an Italian sky; the streets through which the procession passed were strewn with grass and flowers; whole forests of birch-trees seemed to have been cut down to decorate the houses; they were arranged side by side against the walls, so that the procession seemed to pass through the vista of a green wood. Banners, tapestry, garlands, floated from the windows of the houses, which were often converted into shrines with burning tapers, golden crucifixes, pictures, and flowers. The air was filled with the sound of hymns and the pealing of bells ; altars were erected at the corners of the streets, at the fountains, and before the churches. Through the gay street wound the long train ; priests in their gorgeous robes, scarlet, white, and gold, under gorgeous canopies ; Franciscan monks in their grave-colored garbs ; Sisters of Mercy ; various brotherhoods in quaint picturesque attire, all with gay floating banners and silver crucifixes. Then came young girls with wreaths of myrtle on their heads, with lilies and palm-branches in their hands, or bearing books, tapers, or rosaries ; then troops and troops of little children, all in white, and their heads crowned with flowers, and all raising their pure youthful voices in hymns of praise ! It was very beautiful. My soul seemed calmed and exalted. And, at a window opposite to where I was, sate an old, old woman, watching all with the deepest devotion. I shall not soon forget her face.

Wednesday. — We are at length settled as to domestic matters. We live not far from the Palace, at a sort of old curiosity shop, which Dickens would love to describe. You go up a dark winding staircase, and ring at a little dark door ; the door opens, and you see a large room full of gilt crucifixes, picture-frames, and huge painted saints larger than life, and glittering with gold. Beyond this, at the end of a long, desolate, white-washed passage, lie our rooms, spacious and cheerful, with many windows looking out into the public street, and giving a distant view of the Palace.

June 12th. — Rejoice with us : on Monday we become pupils of —— ! Yes, next Monday we are to begin our studies in that identical little atelier where, seven years ago, when almost a child, I saw that group of young artists resting themselves at noon, and playing on the guitar, — a group which has haunted me ever since, like a glimpse into a new world of poetry, or the old world of Italian art. Yes! that little room, with its glorious cartoons, its figures sketched on the walls, its quaint window festooned with creepers, — *that* is to be our especial studio. There we stood this morning; there we showed —— our sketches; there I talked to him in the German tongue, being the mouth-piece for us both, as though he had been a grand, benevolent angel.

I told him how earnestly we longed *really to study;* how we had long loved and revered his works; how we had come to him for his advice, believing that he would give us that, if not his instruction, which we heard was impossible. I know not how it was, but I felt no *fear*, — only a reverence, a faith in him unspeakable. And what did he do? He looked at us with his clear keen eyes, and his beautiful smile, and said, — 'Come and draw here; this room is entirely at your disposal.' 'But,' said we, 'how often, and when?' He said, 'Every day, and as early as you like, and stay as long as there is day-light.'

We knew not how to thank him; we scarcely believed our ears: but he must have read our joy, our astonishment, in our countenances.

The amount of our joy may be estimated by considering what was exactly our position the evening before, — nay, indeed, at the very time when we entered the studio. The evening before, we were discouraged and disheartened to an extreme degree; our path in study seemed beset by obstacles on every hand: in fact, we asked ourselves for what had we come, — how were we better off here than in England? We talked and talked, and walked into that lovely English Garden, along the banks of the Isar; the trees rose up calmly in their rich summer foliage; all was silent in the approaching twilight; long gleams of pale flesh-colored sky gleamed through the clumps of trees in the distance; acres of rich summer grass and flowers stretched away from our feet. Behind us rose a gentle mound surmounted by a white marble pavilion, more like something on the stage than a reality; there was the scent of early mown grass, the distant hum of the city, the towers and spires of which, in the distance, rose abruptly into the evening sky, as if from a sea of wood; there was the near rush of the water, the gentle voice of a bird ever and anon. The peace of Nature sunk into our hearts: never had nature and life and art seemed so holy and beautiful to us, I believe. We talked of a thousand things; a certain cloud, a certain barrier which seemed to have existed between our hearts, melted away; for, after all, our hearts had been strangers to each other until this night.

On our return home, we still thought and thought what was to be done; we talked till it was morning, and by that time we had arranged a grand ideal plan of work, which, as far as it went, was good. We determined, if we could find no really first-rate master, to have models at our own rooms, and work from them most carefully with our anatomical books and studies beside us; that we would do all as thoroughly as we could, and help and criticise each other; that we would work out some designs in this way, studying the grand works around us, going daily to the Basilica, to the Glyptothek, to drink in strength, and inspiration, and knowledge; that we would draw also from the antique, and would take our dawings to be corrected by ——, as he had already offered. This was the scheme of the nigh.

The first thing, therefore, this morning, was our setting off boldly to him with our sketches, to ask his advice. The rest is told.

As we left the studio, I could have fallen upon my knees, and returned fervent thanks to God, so mysterious was this fulfilment of my long-cherished poetical dream. It would have been a relief to one's heart so to have done; but though one often feels such impulses, one rarely gives way to them. As we walked through the streets home, how wondrously proud did we feel! It seemed to us as though a sort of glory must surround us, as though every one ought to read instantly upon our brows — 'the happy pupils of a great master!'

June 14th. — We were yesterday morning in the Hof-Kapelle: a long, quiet morning. I had no conception how sublimely beautiful is this chapel, although it had greatly impressed me the other Sunday morning when we were present at High Mass there. The crowd of worshipping people, the strains of music, the incense, all produced an overpowering effect; but the highest enjoyment was, in the calmness of early morning, in solitude, in so perfect a silence that one could hear one's heart beat, to sit there alone steeping one's soul in the spirit of the place; being fanned, as it were, by the angelic wings, being caught up into the golden sunlight of those heavens, forgetting all but the glorious abstractions before and above one, till Christ seemed to speak as he stretched forth his benevolent arms, till the Virgin's eyes sent peace into the depths of one's soul, till the whole quire of angels, overshadowed with their azure wings, burst into one anthem of praise and rejoicing! It is not nature, at least not familiar nature such as we see in our streets and our homes; it is an abstraction, an exaltation, an ecstasy! It is prayer, — praise. It is typical; the flowers are typical;

the wings of the angels are wings nowhere to be found on earth, but are *angels'* wings; the ark, the cross, the crown, the palm-branch, the lily, all the hieroglyphics of our faith, speaking to our souls through our hearts, are there, each chanting its appropriate hymn, subordinate, yet vitally necessary to the accomplishment of the whole great song of praise. This chapel is built in the Byzantine style; the circular arches, the three domed roofs, the niches, the three altars, are all one glow of gold, of rich draperies, of angelic forms and faces, of rainbow-tinted wings, of mystical flowers and symbols. Yet, gorgeous as are the golden back-grounds and the frescoes, all is tempered by a certain simplicity of form, a sternness of composition, a deep spirit of earnestness, and also by the rich, yet almost sombre tints of the marble columns, of the marble walls, of the marble pavement, warm greys, ruddy browns, dark cool greens. Thus you have the gravity of earth contrasted with the glow of heaven.

The same marvellous contrast may be traced in the frescoes themselves. It was not, I am convinced, without deep meaning that the old masters employed *golden* back-grounds. As for instance; here is a figure of Saul, the dark, moody, miserable man; there he sits brooding over his wretchedness; the light of earthly prosperity as yet falls upon him; his figure catches the light; *but there is no golden glow of heaven beyond*,—all is dusk. But close beside him sits David; he touches his golden harp, a crown circles his brow; you feel, as yet, that it is only a visionary crown, the crown that God will descend upon him; but he sits in the glory of God already, it streams upon his figure, upon his harp, and the golden light of heavenly glory glows beyond him! This is but one of the poetical and deeply truthful effects produced by these golden grounds.

In order more fully to appreciate the grand thought of Leo v. Kenze, the architect, and of Heinrich v. Hess, the painter, I ought to observe that the entire chapel is a shadowing forth of the doctrine of the Trinity. The first cupola is dedicated to the Old Testament, with the Creator as its centre; the second to the New Testament, with Christ as its Centre; the Quire, to the Acts of the Apostles, with the Holy Ghost as its centre.

From these awful centres proceeds the divine influence, governing the world and the church through the Prophets and all the Saints. Within the altar-niche, about the high-altar, appears the Church-Triumphant; as representative of the Church, the Virgin Mary is seated upon her throne; to her right hand and her left are Peter and Paul, Moses and Elias; and rising above the Queen of Heaven, with benevolent out-stretched arms, and calm face of immortal love, is Our Lord, surrounded by a glory of Seraphim waving their rainbow-tinted wings.

The side altar on one hand shows us the Saints of the Bavarian Orders, St. George and St. Hubert, in adoration before Christ, who appears to them in the clouds. St. George gazes upwards with a noble exaltation in his strong youthful face, whilst he tramples the prostrate dragon with his mailed foot. St. Hubert, in his quaint hunter's garb, is praying quietly beside his marvellous stag.

Above the other side-altar, St. Louis and St. Theresa, the Patron Saints of the Bavarian Royal Family, kneel in prayer before the Virgin and Child; St. Theresa's meek, white face, and emaciated figure, shrouded in nun's weeds, contrasting in startling sadness with the sweet and calmly joyful Virgin, who, seated upon her throne, holds the benignant child.

A peculiar and very beautiful effect is produced in this chapel by the windows being so arranged that from below they are invisible, the light streaming down from above the golden and frescoed galleries.

Perhaps Justina will be alarmed by my earnest admiration of this peculiar path of art, and warn me against superhuman painting. But she need fear no danger. I admire it with one portion of my being — with the highest, with *my spirit*. I regard it as an ecstasy of prayer. But truly one must know what are the beauties of nature before one aspires to represent the sublimities of the supernatural.

June 17th. — Last night we busily unpacked all our paint-boxes, looked up, with delighted eagerness, porte-crayons, chalks, everything; chose out such anatomical drawings, and drawings from the antique, as we thought most worthy; laid out our twin-copies of Wilson's *Vade-Mecum*, — even scraped our chalks, and thus had everything ready for starting as soon as we had taken our coffee in the morning, and when certain paper which we had ordered to be stretched on two frames should arrive.

Most explicit orders had I given on Friday morning about this *Carton Papier*, and these frames, and had been assured that at farthest they would be ready by Sunday evening. I had forgotten our former German experience, that when you want a thing in a hurry in Germany, you must order it six months before you need it!

This morning, therefore, having lain awake nearly all night, lest I should be asleep when it was time to get up, my first anxious inquiry from Marie, who, entering my room with bare feet, and keys jingling at her side, brought in our coffee at seven o'clock, was after the stretched paper. Marie looked frightened: the '*Herr*,' said she, 'sent this morning at six o'clock to the carpenter's, and the frames would not be ready before ten!' Not before ten! I said nothing to Clare, thinking that she might as well enjoy her coffee in the belief that the frames and the paper were all ready. After breakfast, Clare said, after enumerating all the things which we had prepared— 'and the strained paper, Anna?' 'Will not be here till ten!' said I, quite savagely, considerably relieved by having unburdened my mind. To my surprise, a most lamb-like and patient expression was on Clare's face. 'I never expected,' said she, 'that they would be ready; it is no use going to ——'s with nothing to draw on.'

I, for my part, did not expect them till afternoon, or to-morrow, or next week; and an agony came into my heart at the thought of appearing careless in ——'s eyes, when he had told us to go early that morning.

But there was no good in making oneself miserable, so, with a little pang in my heart, I set about doing various little things, and, firstly, went into the town to buy two queer, picturesque, big brown jugs, from a little, stupid, old woman. These jugs were to be very important in our *ménage*, seeing that we are young ladies, who, to their present discomfort, are perplexed with the absolute necessity of living in airy rooms, and having a plentiful supply of water, and yet who are forced to breathe German stenches, and to wash in a supply of water contained in a *decanter!* These big brown jugs, therefore, were intended to be companions to two big yellow pans which we bought yesterday.

I explained most clearly to the little old woman where we lived: she seemed as dull as an owl: a good, sprightly little body passing by explained to her where the *Residenz Gasse* was; the old woman did not know, although it is only a few hundred yards from her shop: she looked asleep, yet promised to send them at seven o'clock in the evening. I did various other things in the town, hoping that when I returned I should find the strained paper all ready. I entered our room : Clare was sitting melancholy but calm, with Haydon's Anatomical Lectures open before her : no tidings had arrived about our paper! Noon approached, and we grew quite desperate, and, like a little lioness, I rushed into the old curiosity shop, and beheld a long roll of cartoon-paper reared up against a gilded Saint. I said, 'What does this mean? Is this our paper? and why is it not strained?' 'As soon as the *Herr* gets the frames it shall be done!' was the very satisfactory reply. I felt that there was nothing for it but patience, and at length, at three o'clock, after we had arranged our rooms and put all our possessions in order, the strained paper, delightfully suggestive of work, made its appearance; but by this time it rained, and rain here is worse than in London. It rains in torrents, you are wet through in no time; and the streets, which are usually deserts of white sand, are turned into seas of white mud. Well, never mind! the paper for which we had waited so long *could* not go, but *we* must. The boy with the ear-rings, Wilhelm, the youngest son of the *Haus-Herr*, must carry our things for us : and off we set, Wilhelm, like a little beast of burden, trudging behind.

We wound along all sorts of strange places, dived into narrow lanes, came out beneath crumbling old gateways, and through a field in which hay-making was going on. Even this wet afternoon, a peasant girl, in a pink boddice, with white sleeves, and a black handkerchief tied over her head, was tossing hay in the rain. As Germans do every thing contrary to English custom, I suppose the proverb is 'make hay while *the rain rains!*'

We passed between the wet trees and knocked at the studio-door. No answer. We lifted the latch and entered: there was no great painter present; there stood his grand works on their easels; there hung his furred painting-gown; there lay his cigars: — but he was not there.

We looked around on this side and on that, and presently a picturesque somebody was aroused from behind a colossal cartoon. We inquired whether Herr v. —— was there.

'No, he would not be there till the morrow!'

Good! then on the morrow we also would return to draw; meanwhile we would have a quiet study of two small cartoons placed upon easels in the centre of the large studio.

One of these cartoons is the Reconciliation of Wittikind and Charlemagne. Every one, no doubt, recollects that Charlemagne waged war against Wittikind: fortunately I remembered reading of it in Mentzel.

On a rising ground stands Charlemagne, a grand, heroic figure: with one hand he clasps a rude, huge crucifix, which is raised upon a broken Druidical idol; this crucifix is planted on the broken feet of the idol — a fine idea! with the other hand he grasps the hand of Wittikind! He grasps his hand and gazes at him with an inspired countenance; his eyes, from beneath their massive brows, seem to flash a beneficent lightning upon his reconciled enemy. Wittikind grasps his hand in turn, but gazes on the earth, awe-struck as it were. To his right, a step or two behind him, are his queen, his mother, his little daughter, — an affecting group. The queen, with a mournful, proud bearing, with head erect, yet eyes cast down, only half assents to the reconciliation; a fierce mental struggle is yet going on within her. The old mother clings to her, weeping on her shoulder in undisguised agony at her son's desertion of his religion; the little girl, with her long, heavy tresses of hair, stands meekly beside her mother, with tears rolling down from her beautiful, sad eyes. Strange, wild, stormy, yelling groups surround them: here in the foreground, in the centre of the picture, Druids are mourning over their fallen, broken idol; some bowed over it in despair, others invoking curses from their gods upon the renegade king, wild, frantic! hurling denunciations against gods and men. Here is a group of Wittikind's subjects, serfs, nobles, men, women, and children, pointing to their slain, to their broken idol, to their wounds, wild, frantic also! There are curses, taunts, jeers; a strange contrast to the calm corpses strewn around.

To the right of Charlemagne, beneath the rude crucifix — a crucifix as rude as the Christianity of that age — are marshalled the knights of Charlemagne, calm though triumphant. The four *Haymon's Kinder*, the four heroic brothers, all seated on one horse, as they are described in the old legend, are there. One, the shadow of the other, grave, stern, heroic, *awful* almost in their beauty and their sternness. The foremost slightly leaning over the neck of their pawing, snorting horse, points to two Druids who have passed over to the new faith, and who stand bound side by side, with bowed heads, and brows yet encircled by fading oak garlands, reading a passage in one of the gospels, which is held open by a triumphant bishop. Beyond this group of knights rises a Druidical temple, the demolition of which has already commenced. On its height stands a frantic Druid, hurling his imprecations against the skies. On the other hand rises a funeral pyre; a Druidical priestess burns herself in her chariot; she breaks her sacred wand, her hair flies in wild masses behind her, mingling with the smoke and flames; around her pyre lies a circle of corpses; far away stretches a savage mountainous region, on every height burns a fire of sacrifice, its long column of smoke ascending to heaven.

The whole cartoon is a wonderful embodiment of the spirit of those old times; it seems also to be an embodiment of those words of Christ, 'I come not to bring peace, but a sword.'

The next cartoon tells its story plainly enough. It is an embodiment of the spirit of the Crusades: not alone the Crusaders' first glimpse of Jerusalem, which has so often been painted, but it is the age of the Crusades which is there. A rough road, on which is cut in rude letters the word 'Golgotha,' leads through an arid, rocky region; in the distance lies Jerusalem, its flat-roofed houses, its mosques, its temples, its fortresses, its ramparts, its towers, rising into the sky. In the centre of the picture marches along this arid road a little band of youthful priests, bearing an exquisitely sculptured shrine; their calm, grave, youthful countenances raised towards the sky. You feel that they chant a hymn. Behind them, slowly, majestically, rides a king; his eyes directed heavenwards: in his upraised hands he bears his crown, an offering to Christ, who, with outspread arms, and surrounded by the Evangelists, hovers over the earthly procession. On rushes, behind the king, a host of warriors, bearing the spoil of the Pagans, jewelled coats of mail, bracelets, chains, the whole spoil of the East, borne upon their spears, which bend beneath their weight. It is a rude tumult.

The shrine and its youthful priests are preceded by old priests, prelates, cardinals seated on mules, praying, or conversing in low, grave words. They again are preceded by knights; knights spurring on their horses in frantic haste to reach the hallowed city; pilgrims of all ranks, all ages, hurrying on into the distance! You have a confused vision of prancing, madly careering horses; of arms brandishing weapons in an ecstasy of enthusiasm;

of men, of women flinging themselves on their knees, bowing their heads to the dust in a frenzy of joy, on catching from those rocky heights their first glimpse of the Holy City!

Meanwhile, in the foreground, as the shrine proceeds on its way, Peter the Hermit, two troubadours, a flagellant, applying the lash to his naked shoulders, and several other pilgrims of various characters, fling themselves on their knees, bowing their heads to the earth, or raising their countenances with joy towards Christ.

And now come two prominent groups, connecting the group of pilgrims with the distant, careering horsemen. A very beautiful woman is borne on a litter, supported by four mild-looking young savages. She, with an upraised arm, unveils a face of the most exquisite beauty, a beauty still veiled, as it were, with an awe, — an awe inspired by the presence of Christ! In her lap lies a wreath of roses; her other hand is clasped by a young Crusader, who forgets even her presence in the thought of Christ and Jerusalem; and he waves his sword and shouts praises to God. The other group is another Crusader with a beautiful Saracen lady seated behind him on his horse.

The above will give a faint idea of the subjects of these cartoons, but not of their powerful drawing, not of their beauty, their grace, and grandeur and richness of composition.

I wish you could have a glimpse of our two pretty little sister bed-rooms, opening into the sitting-room with its four windows, now that all is complete. We have taken down various prints and paintings belonging to the people of the house, and put up our own. Our bed-rooms have pale green walls, and I have fastened up my Raphael prints and my studies of color from the National Gallery, with one of Justina's lovely water-color landscapes, so that when the door of the sitting-room stands open the effect is pretty. You catch a glimpse of a writing-table, a pale green wall beyond, with a print of Raphael's upon it; an old-fashioned looking-glass in a gilt frame, hung high, in German fashion; beneath it Justina's Highland landscape, with its ruddy heathery foreground; on one side the glass hangs a palette, and somewhat below a little white porcelain vessel for holy water, a sort of shell with a praying angel above it. Our sitting-room is also arranged to the best advantage, and ornamented with sundry of our own sketches and little works of art. Clare's little bedroom presents pretty much the same appearance when the door is open, only that instead of my Raphael she has a clever copy of a Rembrandt, and a Christus Consolator instead of my Highland landscape. And then, to complete the picture, you must imagine our chairs to have very dark *pink* damask cushions, so that we get a little warm color.

Very tired we were by seven o'clock, when, returning from the studio, we took our coffee; but very thankful to have every thing, even to our clothes, in order. Very tired, I leaned on our smart window-cushion in the window, and, looking out into the wet street, saw a droll little object wrapt up in shawls, head and body, emerge from a narrow little street opposite. The figure carried two big brown jugs! It was my little old woman! She looked round and round, half asleep; she looked at every house but this; she was close upon the house; she turned her back; she stared fixedly at the house opposite; she seemed to have made up her mind to look any way but the right. We called to her; we beckoned! She could neither see nor hear! Again she gazed up and down, and again straight before her, with her back to us, and then in despair hobbled away down the narrow lane with our two brown jugs!

CHAPTER II.

THE STUDIO OF WILHELM VON KAULBACH.

THE studio of Kaulbach is situated in the St. Anna suburb, a suburb resembling rather a quaint country town than the suburb of a smart little capital. It is altogether a somewhat out-of-the-way sort of place. It is a region of stone-masons' yards, mills, and timber-yards. If you approach from the old part of Munich, you probably pass beneath some gloomy gateway, and emerging among gardens and pleasure-grounds, cross some rapidly-running branch of the Isar, which turns many a noisy mill, and is the resort of washerwomen, who, leaning over the pleasant water from low plank balconies, wash their linen, picturesquely and merrily, the whole summer through.

On bright summer mornings, these women, in their gay-colored boddices and petticoats, furnish forth a succession of beautiful pictures as they wash their linen, which shines dazzlingly white in the shower of sunshine and amid the luxuriant grass and large-leaved plants, which droop their sprays into the stream. Across a wooden bridge you see passing an old Franciscan friar. He stops and speaks to that merry group of urchins rushing away from morning school; and now he says a word to that demure little fair-haired damsel, who knits as she walks along. The Franciscan comes from that white convent with its many rows of windows, and with its church rising up in the centre, adorned with a gay figure of the Madonna, standing in a sky-blue niche, and shaded by tall poplars. Those are promegranates trained up the walls; and there is another brown monk at one of the windows. And now you find yourself in a regular little town; among houses, white, pale green, pale pink, and salmon-colored, with rows of *jalousies* thrown back, and here and there bright-colored bedding hanging out of the windows to air in the sunshine. Here the green mill-stream is choked up with pine tree trunks, which once majestically reared themselves among the Alps, and have been floated down some tributary of the Isar, and now lie prostrate giants, ready to be sawn up and stacked in the royal wood-yard close at hand. This wood-yard connects the St. Anna suburb with the beautiful English Garden.

'Is it to a stone-mason's that we are going?' exclaims some stranger-friend, whom you are conducting to the studio, as, leaving the main road, you skirt the mill-stream, and entangling yourself in a maze of stone slabs and blocks, open the crazy door of an old grey wooden fence. This old crazy door admits you into a field, where still blocks of stone, a very chaos of them, are seen in the distance, lying in wild disorder about a ruinous building, partially covered with a straggling vine. Close before you is a long, grey, desolate-looking house: you turn the corner, you stand in the field — one lovely, odorous mosaic of flowers, and deep, rich grass. Here the tall salvia rears its graceful spike of brilliantly blue flowers; clover, white and red, scents the air with its honeyed perfume; the delicate eyebright, daisies, trefoils, harebells, thyme, buglos, yellow vetch, the white powdery umbels of the wild carrot, and the large, mild-looking dog-daisies, bloom in a gay, delicious tangle; crowds of rejoicing butterflies dance and flutter unceasingly about the flower mosaic like showers of falling pear-blossom; myriads of happy little creatures, beetles, grasshoppers, lady-birds, revel among the flower-stems and blades of grass: all is joyous life; an odor, a gentle murmur — a very hymn of nature. And there, seated beneath those elder trees in full bloom, before the desolate grey house, is a group of merry, brown-eyed children, playing with a beautiful white rabbit, while a large, sagacious mastiff sleeps beside them.

And now, opposite to you, across the field, and half hidden by thickets and a group of poplars, you see the studio; two grey wings, with a higher centre. All is bowery and green, overhung with vines and creepers. Opposite the grey wooden door in the centre of the building, and lying in a thicket, you see capitals and various fragments of broken columns arranged as seats around another capital, larger than the rest, which serves as a table. Close upon the threshold of the studio stands a peacock, displaying his handsome tail, his gorgeous green and blue neck glancing in the sun. He and his wife and young ones are doing all in their power to tempt forth the artist to feed them with a loving hand, as is his wont. These peacocks are great favorites, and know it too; you may see their portraits painted in *steriochromie* upon the outer wall of the studio, beneath a window, where they are festooned with living sprays of vine. All is a pleasant, quiet dream without; green and shady, yet with glittering, dancing showers of sunshine breaking through the branches as they are stirred by a light passing breeze.

'Very untidy all this!' remarks your Englishman, recalling his trim lawn and shrubbery at home: 'a boy is wanted here to pull up these rank weeds, and a roller to roll that gravel and grass! Can't think what Kaulbach is after, to let all run so to ruin!'

But Kaulbach, and many another artist, rejoices in all these docks and darnels, in this rank growth, in this unpruned, unfettered nature. He loves his vines, his hops, his nettles and thistles, and his myriads of wild, lovely flowers and butterflies. And in winter he rejoices in the heavy snow as it lies on the branches of the trees, in the glitter of the hoar-frost, in the pure expanse of the snowy field; and in autumn in the gorgeous tints of his trees, when they glow, gold and coral; or again in spring, when their bare branches, ruddy with awakened life, are wildly tossed to and fro by bold March winds, and above, the sky is a deep blue, across which scud fleet, bright clouds.

But we linger too long in the field. Let us lift the old-fashioned latch, and enter. A handsome, large, black spaniel greets us with a loud barking, but soon recognising old acquaintance, wags his tail, and curls himself round to sleep again. The artist is not here, though the peacocks seem to await him. We glance round the room, expecting to see him, as the spirit of the place, emerge from behind some large cartoon or canvas which had concealed him from our sight; but all is silent. We are alone with his creations.

The Englishman, remembering his smooth lawn at home, has, we have seen, disparaged Kaulbach's wild field, and probably, also, blinded by the gorgeous and richly mellow tints of our English school of painting, and fascinated by the clever execution of our English pictures, may disparage Kaulbach's works.

'Is this,' he may exclaim, 'a far-famed work of art?' as he looks at a copy in oils of the Destruction of Jerusalem, which has struck his eye on entering the studio. '*This* that much-vaunted painting! compare it only with a picture of Etty's, or of —— or of ——, and see then what a figure it will make!'

Many such an exclamation of hasty judgment has probably been heard in Kaulbach's studio, from both English and French. But the Destruction of Jerusalem, and other works by the same artist, still maintain their real greatness, not, as the artist himself would be the first frankly to avow, as *pieces of painting*, but because they are *poems*, and new subjects treated in an original manner.

Unbounded imagination, philosophic thought, and studious research, are, I consider, the peculiar attributes of Kaulbach's great historical works.

'But has not this German imagination become almost a by-word with us?' asks the caviller.

No: the imagination to which I refer, that dreamy imagination which invests all nature with a tender poetry, which gives an individual life to every bud and leaf, — that imagination, half superstition, which peoples the wild regions of the country with its spirits of the Brocken, its Rübezahls, its Libussas, which, in olden times, having created legend and saga, in later days has raised up an immortal band of musicians, philosophers, and artists! — no; this imagination has never become a by-word, and it is from the possession of this high species of imagination that Kaulbach's name stands forth with a peculiar prominence even amidst a nation pre-eminently endowed with this glorious gift. Who, studying his work, does not feel that this subtle imagination at times rises into the power of a *Seer*, which, penetrating the abyss of time, calls up forms, countenances, and scenes passed away ages ago from the earth, with such a vividness of truth that your very soul is thrilled! Dead bones and ashes, buried in funeral urns, in cairns and barrows, become instinct with life; the scald, the warrior, the Amazon, clad in their wolf-skin garments, and wearing their golden ornaments, wielding their uncouth weapons of destruction, singing their death-songs; suffering, loving, and hating with a barbarous intensity of passion, astounding to us of modern days, — all are evoked by this mighty power of the seer. And ages remoter still, lying far off in the very dawn of time, are revealed; for does not imagination annihilate time and space? Loving and understanding all things, whether sublime or lowly, is it not truly a divine sympathy with all nature, a sympathy with the flower and insect as with the mountain and the tempest; a sympathy entering into the inner life of the dumb animal, as well as into the inner life of the hero and the sage?

And if, in studying the works of Kaulbach, you discover undoubted proofs of this divine gift of intense imagination and unbounded love, wherefore turn away dissatisfied with his works, because they are not as great in color as in imagination? Why, whilst admiring the vigor and grandeur of a noble oak, destroy your delight by exclaiming, 'How perfect that oak would be did it but produce roses!' May not those attributes of beauty, of which our English school of painting is so justly proud, be as foreign to the German nature as for the oak tree to bear roses? But this is a subject on which much already has, and more probably will be, written.

So many hasty judgments are passed, by English travellers, upon Kaulbach's works, that I have been led into an invective myself, desirous that these works should be, at least, regarded from a point of view nearer akin to that of the artist himself.

But now for the works: —

We will commence our survey with the Destruction of Jerusalem, which, though not the first in the chronological order of Kaulbach's great series of historical works, now executing in steriochromie at Berlin, yet is the first of his works which strikes us on entering the studio at Munich.

Above the human turmoil, agony, famine, despair, and triumph, which fill the lower portion of the picture, throned upon clouds, and dimly visible through a haze of heavenly light, sit the four great prophets, Isaiah, Jeremiah, Ezekiel, and Daniel, who prophesied in vain to the stubborn and blinded Jewish nation; again they repeat their awful warnings, pointing with solemn gestures to their open books. The seven angels of God's wrath, as described in the Revelations, descend on swift wings, and with swords of flame, like a mighty whirlwind. And now, whilst the avenging angels descend, and the prophecies are fulfilled, Titus, seated on his white snorting charger, is seen in the distance riding onward over smouldering ruins, into the doomed city; grim-visaged lictors surround him; the Roman generals, with standards and glittering spears, crowd on behind him; a multitude of soldiers, half lost in smoke and gloom, precede him, announcing their victory with triumphant music. Roman soldiers have already obtained possession of the holy altar (the centre of the picture); have planted the Roman eagle upon it; have sacrificed upon it to their She-Wolf; crowding upon it, clinging to it, they celebrate their triumph by the braying of trumpets, the clang of arms, and the shouts of war. One soldier stretches forth his robber-hands towards one of three Jewish virgins, who, shuddering, cling together; another leans from his horse, which is laden with spoil from the Temple, and with rude grasp seizes the arm of a woman, who, clasping her hands in agony, shrinks from him towards the earth. Then is fulfilled the abomination of desolation foretold by Daniel.

And now like a huge wave around the altar, driven on

by the tide of entering Romans, see a crowd of Jews passing forth beneath their upraised shields. They cast wild looks of agony and hatred towards the desecrators of their holy altar, and above them swiftly descends the whirlwind of angels. Here, round that cauldron, cowers a fearful group: one old hag sucks blood and devours the flesh of her own arm; another devours some horror no less revolting; and a young and handsome woman, frantic with hunger, slays her infant; with rabid and glazed eyes she sits gazing at the pale corpse and her blood-stained knife. And up those broad steps, leading to the Holy of Holies, fly crowds of men, women, and little children; here lies a corpse, there sits a mother, wild with alarm, seeking to screen her children, who cling to her and hide their heads in her lap. Aloft, beneath the pillars of the Temple, cold, scornful, and impassive, stands John of Gischalla and Simon, the sons of Gioras, the reckless and wicked Jewish leaders; wildly gesticulating, frantic men and women gather around them: with clenched hands raised with impotent imprecations against heaven, they curse the descending angels of God's wrath and the triumphant Roman hosts. Beyond this infuriated throng, illumined by the ruddy glare of fire, you dimly see the sacred ark supported by its cherubim, and the waving arms of more and more fugitives and supplicants.

Such is, in truth, the background of the picture, from which stand forth three remarkable and principal groups. The centre figure of the centre group is the High Priest in his robes. His dark, haggard countenance, and bloodshot eyes, are riveted upon the approaching Romans; he thrusts the keen point of a long dagger through the golden border of his sparkling breastplate; one foot is planted upon a corpse which lies on the ground wrapt in a scarlet mantle, through which you trace the features of a dead face, and beneath which you see a crown and long tresses of dark hair; his other arm presses to him and supports his dying children; the youth's pallid face yet rests upon his father's knee, though the slight form, clad in its light golden armor, slowly sinks down upon the corpse covered with the scarlet shroud. Meanwhile, the wife of the High Priest seizes his upraised and suicidal arm, and points frantically to her own breast, longing, demanding to die with him and their children. Seated, or prostrate round the High Priest and his family, you see the Levites mourning and destroying themselves amid the scattered treasures of the Temple. One young man has fallen upon his sword; an old man, with a venerable white beard, sits in a stupor of despair,—his hand listlessly grasps a long sword, and he leans against golden vases upheaped with gold, jewels, and long strings of pearls. The left group consists of the Wandering Jew, driven forth by three demons, whose livid brows are wreathed with knotted snakes, and the whips in whose hands are snakes likewise. Forth rushes he, lacerating his naked breast, a type of modern Judaism, and undying remorse: thus connecting the historical part of the Destruction of Jerusalem with the prophecy of Christ, in which the Destruction of Jerusalem is made a symbol of the Last Judgment, etc.

Three gracious angels, bearing aloft a golden chalice encircled with a glory, the mystic sign of Christian faith, conduct a group of Christians forth from the devoted city. This is the right hand group. A beautiful and gentle woman seated upon an ass, presses lovely smiling twins to her breast; a shadow of foreboding rests on her sweet face, for in her hand she bears the martyr's palm. Behind her, on the ass, sits a boy of some seven years old, and passes through her arm a little hand which holds a branch heavy with golden fruit: his large brown eyes are full of eagerness, his lips are parted, he beckons to his three little playmates, who kneel, imploring to be taken along with the Christians. Two are lovely children — a boy with curling fair locks, a girl with thick dark plaited tresses, while between them kneels a little, yellow, naked boy; all three raise beseeching hands and weeping eyes towards the departing Christians. The nearest angel waves his hand with a look of love ineffable — they shall depart also! probably also to win the martyr's crown. See those graceful youths who conduct the ass, on which rides the mother, and a second ass ridden by the father, who chants a hymn of praise to God from the book open in his hand, and by the white-headed grandfather. All bear palm branches. Yet all sing hymns of love and praise, and with firm steps and undaunted hearts they approach their doom — a joy eternal, though purchased by suffering and death.

Such is Kaulbach's poem of the Destruction of Jerusalem; — and now, opening the door of the little inner studio, let us read one still finer, on The Fall of Babel.

'So the Lord scattered the nations from thence upon the face of the earth, and they left off to build the city.'

The Book of Genesis relates, in figurative language, how, through the dispersion of races and the confusion of tongues, history took its origin. In accordance with variety of race and variety of speech, variety of opinion soon showed itself, and confusion arose in men's minds regarding God and divine things.

'"Eat of this fruit and thou wilt be like God. Heaven thy dwelling-place, Eternity thy life!" Thus spoke the tempter, through the woman's voice, to Adam, the type of undefiled humanity. And these words, echoing through ages, fell upon the ear of Nimrod, a type of fallen man, believing himself omnipotent. But the lightning of

Jehovah's wrath smote the proud tree, scattering its fragments over the earth, until, through divine compassion, the type of reconciled humanity was born of woman, and once more the tree of life arose, shooting forth fresh branches, and filling the world with peace. But now the Tree of Life was the humbled Tree of the Cross.'

Such is a condensed translation of the introduction to the artist's manuscript account of his Cartoon of the Fall of Babel. The whole manuscript reads like a sublime poem, consisting largely of passages from the Scriptures, bearing upon his view of the event.

Now let us glance towards the Cartoon.

Nimrod, 'the mighty hunter before the Lord,' the tyrant of men as well as of beasts, is seen seated upon his throne, approached by a lofty flight of steps; behind him rises in the gloom the huge tower. The throne is supported by grotesquely carved figures of dogs; on either hand arise clouds of perfume, from tall incense-burners; the throne has been surmounted by idols of the sun and moon. But Jehovah, and his avenging angels, darting forth from a cloud, keen forked lightnings have smitten the baleful forms, which, falling upon the marble steps, have slain Nimrod's two sons, who lie crushed beneath them. The curse has fallen in truth upon the tyrant. He sits there between his mutilated gods, with his dead sons at his feet, with his wife prostrate before him and them, beseeching him wildly to acknowledge the power of the unknown God, with his courtiers, priests, and minstrels on either hand, taunting, scoffing, conjuring him to renounce his idol-worship, his tyranny: but he neither hears nor sees — he only *feels* the curse. In the swollen muscles of his brawny arms and chest, in his hands clenched on his knees, in his cruel, proud, lion face, in his quivering foot, you read a dumb bewilderment!

Through his brain ring the words, 'How art thou fallen, Lucifer, son of the morning! How art thou cut down who didst weaken the nations! Thou hast said in thy heart I will ascend into heaven; I will exalt my throne above the stars of God; I will be like the Most High! Yet thou art brought down to hell, to the sides of the pit.'

The curse has fallen also upon the tower. On all sides fly the workmen, in wild haste, leaping from the scaffolding, which breaks beneath them, letting themselves drop from the steep walls of the basement. All is bewilderment, frantic confusion. A woman meeting three men yoked like beasts to a load of ponderous stone, which they are dragging up an inclined plane, urged on by a fiendish taskmaster, shouts to them the astounding doom; but the sounds of her own voice seem to appal her: her lips look petrified, her hands are raised towards her mouth in astonishment.

In one corner of the picture you see the architect, with his plan of the tower, struck down and stoned to death by two infuriated workmen. Already the tribes have began to disperse. The minstrels to the left of Nimrod's throne, holding in their hands lyres of the most primitive fashion, and admonishing the tyrant by word and gesture to acknowledge the awful God, hasten to join the race of Japhet already departing towards the west. Their wives, seated on camels, beckon wildly to their lingering husbands with beseeching hands. Far, far away, stream multitudes, on foot, on horses, on camels, away, away, across those hills out into the world! Here a strong warrior, naked except for his helmet, formed from the head of some wild horned beast and his fluttering lion-skin mantle, holding spears in his hand and with his sword girt around him, rushes madly away on a snorting horse, swift as the wind; two slim youths, — one holding his bow, his quiver slung across his shoulder, the other swinging a sling, — grasp the long mane of the horse and fly along with him. Another warrior follows madly behind them: on rushes his steed, but with averted head he watches the solemn lightning cloud which bears Jehovah.

Away, away, out into the world, fly the ancestors of the Persians, the Greeks, the Romans, the Scandinavians, the Germans, with spears and shields to battle for liberty, for beauty, for chivalry, for the noble rights of humanity!

In front of Nimrod's throne, the race of Ham, to which race belong Nimrod himself and the luckless architect, assemble themselves. A half-idiotic priest, cowering over his three-headed idol, which he presses to his breast, is seated upon a shaggy, sullen bison, its horns decorated with pondrous pendant ornaments, its back covered with a barbaric matting. Frantic worshippers surround him; one savage-looking girl, with matted elf-locks and clad in skins, seizes the robe of the priest and licks it with her tongue. A hideous old hag, the impersonation of sorcery and false prophecy, raises her hood with skinny fingers, and casts a baleful glance of malice upon the slim youth, with his bow and quiver, who rushes past her. Thus departs the race of Ham, the idolaters of Africa, the Phœnicians, the Egyptians. The curse falls immediately upon them: 'They who eat the flesh of men and drink abominable blood to do homage to Thy name! But Thou hast compassion upon all, and bearest with the sins of men. For Thou lovest all that are, and hatest none that Thou hast created; Thou sparest all! For all are Thine, Lord! Thou lover of life! and Thy Eternal Spirit is in all!'

Meanwhile, behold towards the east the departure of Shem, in the person of the venerable patriarch Peleg, mentioned by Moses. He is seated upon a low car drawn by mild oxen; he stretches forth his arms as if at once blessing and protecting his race, his noble countenance raised towards heaven with love and gratitude. In horror of the departing idolaters a youth and maiden spring to his knees, shrinking in alarm from the savage fanatics. A grave boy, holding listlessly in his one hand the reins of the oxen, in the other a crook, stands up in the low wagon on the other side of the patriarch, and half leans against him. On the neck of either ox, see, a round-limbed naked child is seated; they are twin brothers! One presses a bunch of luscious grapes to his lips, whilst his other arm rests lovingly upon the shoulder of his little brother, who leans towards him holding a long spray of vine in his chubby little hand. Their mother walks beside the yoked oxen, gazing at them with eyes of love; in one hand she bears bunches of grapes, the other supports a flat basket upon her head, in which lies, together with a distaff, a younger child, who, laughing, stretches forth his arms towards his little brothers seated on the oxen. Other women and children follow. They are surrounded by flocks and herds; you seem to hear a gentle lowing and bleating. All is peace, fruitfulness, love. They journey towards a land of promise. 'In my race shall all the nations of the earth be blessed,' spake the Lord God; 'and to you, ye nations of the earth, to you is born, in the city of David, a Saviour, which is Christ the Lord. Glory to God in the highest, and peace on earth and good-will to men!'

Opposite to the Fall of Babel, in the small studio, hangs the design for the Battle of the Huns, another of the Berlin frescoes. The subject is taken from the old legend related by Damascius in his life of Isidorus, which relates how the hatred was so intense between the Huns and Romans, that after a great battle fought before the walls of

Rome, in the time of Valentinian III., the spirits of the slain returned into the corpses, and a frenzied conflict was renewed by the phantoms in the air; a legend fraught with deep significance, and found in various ages, and among various nations, symbolizing the bitter hatred which outlives the mortal conflict!

Rome, in the distance, with its temples, palaces, and gardens, sleeps silently upon its seven hills. Between the quiet walls and the foreground of the picture are scattered groups of slain. Here, in the front, lies a heap of corpses, Romans and Huns mingled together; soldiers, Amazons, horses, and wild Hun children. The sleep of death is, however, loosening its hold upon them. A gigantic Hun, wrapt in his skin mantle, his eyes still closed, his bearded chin sunk upon his breast, draws slowly, as yet drunk with sleep, his sword forth from its scabbard. Beside him lies a yet unwakened Amazon, her stern countenance thrown back in death upon the lap of another woman, who sits gazing, full of a wild amaze, towards the sky. A third woman is gradually awaking, though her eyes are still closed and her head bending towards the earth. Sunk upon the breast of the sleeping Amazon, like the pretty bud of some flower closed for the night, lies the round head of a little Hun child. There sleeps a Roman soldier grasping his sword, his metal helmet and armor conspicuous amidst the skin garments and savage weapons of the 'Barbarians.' Women, with faces on flame, with beckoning arms and animated gestures arouse the sleepers. At the touch of that eager woman, the warrior fallen prostrate from his dead horse will awake!

And here is a group entirely of women! Roman women they seem: some, aroused only to a dim sense of agony, sit dreamily upon the ground; others, clinging together as if drawn towards the ghastly conflict waging in the air by the might of their anguish and mourning, hover above the earth. A little naked child, heavy with sleep, clings to the girdle of his mother, as, pressing her hands with convulsive agony to her brow, she rises from the ground. Here a young Roman soldier aids the ascent of a veteran towards the battle.

Up, up, they rise! Romans and wild Barbarians. At first dreamily with heavy eyelids; then comes perfect consciousness of a more than mortal hatred. The Romans rush on with spears and standards, exhibiting with defiant gestures to their foes a cross borne aloft, from which radiates celestial light. The Roman Emperor is supported on either side by a slim youth. Old Rome, now leaning for support upon his young dependencies, leads on his cohorts. Intensest hatred fills the veteran with a transient youthful vigor; his large breast heaves, his eyes flash flame, and with fierce defiance he presses on towards his adversary, the terrible Attila, who, standing on a broad shield upheld by floating Huns, brandishes a fearful weapon, a huge whip, each lash ending in a cruel *Morgenstern.* Attila, conspicuous in his loose coat of mail, his fur-trimmed widely flowing robe, and strange high cap, and wielding his many-lashed scourge with one hand, beckons forward with the other his countless hosts, who swarm behind him, bearing along with them shields, bows, spears, arrows, clubs, and slings only less wild and rude than are their own eager, savage countenances.

On, on they come, with elf-locks and skin garments floating on the wind! on, on they come, hurrying through the air from the far-distant heavens, like flocks of ominous birds! And now, on all sides, above and beneath the two terrific leaders, the ghosts close in struggling conflict, and all is one dense cloud of agony!

Let us now, returning to the large atelier, study the

colossal cartoon in progress, — the Homer, for the Grecian cycle of the Berlin frescoes.

Homer, steered in a little boat by the eldest of the Sagas, by the Sibylla, touches the shore of a small creek, where he is awaited by assembled Greece, — by her poets, her philosophers, her warriors, her priests, her Arcadian shepherds and hunters. Homer's figure is turned away from us, the modern spectators, but we catch a profile glimpse of his glorious inspired countenance as, with sightless orbs, it is directed towards the listening crowd upon the shore. He raises one hand commandingly towards heaven; the other hand touches the strings of a large lyre, which he supports upon his slightly raised knee and the curved prow of the little bark as he pours forth his immortal strains in a mighty torrent of song. The wind waves back the rich masses of hair from his noble brow, rustles the leaves of his bay-wreath, and raises the veil of Sibylla, floating it mysteriously above her melancholy dreamy countenance, which she rests upon her left hand. Her right listlessly holds an oar, as she sits low upon the deck of the little boat. An open scroll lies upon her knees; her eyes do not read its mystic words, but are sunk in wondrous dreams. Hers are eyes which have never shed a tear, — stern, sad eyes, though tearless. What a contrast between the Sibylla, and the gentle heart-broken Thetis, who to the left of Sibylla's boat rises from the waves towards heaven, bearing with devoted love the urn which holds the beloved ashes of her heroic son! An unutterable tenderness and woe speak in her lovely, plaintive, tearful, upraised face. The gentlest and tenderest of her attendant Nereides watch her as she departs, striving to detain her by their caresses and looks of love; whilst others of a sterner nature, the nymphs of storm and shipwreck, are less sympathetic, and busy themselves with their own affairs. Their hair is wreathed with coral, with reeds and sea-blossoms, and fastened up with fantastic fish-bones; necklaces of shells rest on their large, round shoulders; one young creature defends herself from the attack of a swan which, with its companion, sails boldly towards her with ruffled plumage. Another nymph gazes towards a warrior seated on the shore with an earnest, proud glance, as though a deep, passionate love had existed once between them. But he, a type of the joyous, careless, yet heroic Grecian nature, has already buried his memories of this love amid a hundred others. Love, wine, and song, are the glories of his existence; but for this moment song has predominant sway over him. His face is averted from the proud nymph, his hand rests carelessly upon the shoulder of a lovely boy who presses to his side, holding upon his knee an ivy-wreathed beaker; and he listens entranced by Homer's strains. And now stretches along the shore in a vast semi-circle the Grecian nation, represented by its various types of poets, sages, sculptors, painters, warriors, and shepherds. There are voluptuous youthful countenances whose ambrosial locks are wreathed with odorous fresh flowers; some listen, sunk in dreams; others, roused by a generous enthusiasm, stretch forth their arms, and their eyes gleam with inspiration; there you see, seated upon the rocky shore, stern, old, bearded men, who rest garlanded lyres upon their knees, whilst their old brows are shadowed by laurel, bay, and ivy. Standing beside that rock, conspicuous amid the garlanded crowd, in solemn drapery, which hangs in stern folds around his brow, you recognise a bardic-priest of the mystics, a descendant of Orpheus, who listens with a bitter scorn to the song of his mighty antagonist; a sickening hatred growing within his soul as he finds that the glory of the mystics is about to pale before the dawn of a new poetic era.

Here rises in solemn majesty a colossal statue of Achilles. A group of youths pause from their labor of chiselling it, and feed a falcon, which screams and flaps its large wings above the arm of the youth who reclines in naked beauty, like a glorious antique statue, at the feet of the Achilles. The sculptor—Phidias himself, perhaps stands, mallet in hand and shading his eyes, as a mysterious vision of beauty bursts upon him. The divinities of Greece descend towards two noble temples which rise in the background of the picture. The artists busied upon the scaffoldings which surround one temple recognise also the glorious vision, and hail the approach of the deities with extended arms, and supplicate them upon their bended knees. A rainbow spans the sky, connecting the heavenly and the earthly multitudes.

Across this rainbow sweeps the celestial train. Love leads them on, pointing with arch mien towards the temple, whither he bends his flight, whilst the lovely Graces float in an airy dance beneath him. Apollo presses on with majestic step and radiant brow, followed by the Muses; Jupiter and Juno, attended by the gorgeous peacock, with the eagle in wild flight above them, with Diana, Mercury, and Minerva, and a throng of lesser deities crowding behind them, are seen descending and throned in calm majesty, side by side, upon a cloud of smoke which curls up in vast volumes from an altar erected on the farther shore of the little creek. A band of warriors, unconscious of the full acceptance of their sacrifice, seeing alone the ascending smoke, not the spiritual forms descending upon it, encircle the altar in a mad war-dance with clashing swords and flying plumes. Yet the strains of Homer resound above the clash of arms, and echo through these warriors' souls; two already have left the war-dance and have drawn near to the margin of the bay, where they listen, with the rest of Greece, in a trance of amazement, to the mighty voice of poetry, which is here summoning as to a vast assembly the inhabitants of heaven, earth, and ocean.

And now, whilst our imaginations are still peopled with these noble creations, let us quietly pass out of the studio, cross the pleasant grass and flowers of the field, follow the windings of the mill-stream as it rushes through the royal wood-yard, and enter the bowery English Garden, beneath whose fine trees the great artist daily goes to and fro from his beautiful studio to his no less beautiful home. Here, amidst the budding trees and upspringing weeds and flowers, let our hearts thank God, not alone for His gifts of poetry and art, but also that He gives us ever and anon a transient realization of what the artist's life may become when he remains nobly true to himself, in harmony with God, his own soul, and, ennobled through his art, ennobling humanity!

Since commencing this sketch of Kaulbach's studio, a sad change has fallen upon the pleasant field in which the studio stands. King Max is turning it into a rose-garden. A *rose-garden!* This sounds very poetical, but the reality is not very attractive. At all events, the English visitor will no longer have to quarrel with docks and darnels. Straight gravel walks, formal flower-beds, and rows and rows of hot-houses, will meet his eye. The mosaic of tangled flowers, the clouds of butterflies, the blossoming elder trees, and the little clump of poplars, are now, alas! memories of the past. Depend upon it, Kaulbach, with his Hamadryads, will have to seek out some other solitude where they may once more hear alone the gentle rustle of the trees, and tread upon grass and wild flowers.

CHAPTER III.

PASSING SKETCHES.

At half past six we breakfast, and then, as early as we can, set off to our work. It is a pleasant walk along the quaint old streets, now passing beneath the Falcon Tower, a heavy round mass of stone, which tells well from different points against the deep blue sky. All is bright and joyous: peasant women, young and old, in their strange costumes, some with heavy round caps of black fur, some with black or gay-colored handkerchiefs, bound tightly across their brows, others with their little gold or silver ***Riegel Häube*** (Munich caps) sparkling in the sun, others in Tyrolean hats, all are hurrying along with baskets to the market. Sentinels are standing on duty at almost every turn, their bayonets glittering in the sunshine. We see as we go along numbers of beautiful groups and effects.

The other morning, walking along our favorite path, one of the branches of the Isar, at a turn in the road just where the stream was crossed by a little wooden bridge, we came upon a peasant woman with a sort of reaping-hook in her hand. Behind her was a background of foliage, a magnificent tangle of vines; she had a sunburnt, handsome, strong face, brawny brown arms, loose white chemise sleeves, a black handkerchief on her head, whilst over her breast was crossed an orange handkerchief, on which the sunlight fell dazzlingly in its brilliancy. Such coloring I never saw before; and beyond, above the vines, was deep blue sky, which heightened the effect wonderfully. It was a study for Etty. She looked like a wonderful bird, with a strange, brilliant orange breast.

Having crossed this same little wooden bridge, we come to a quaint little baker's shop, in which, half filling it and surrounded with heaps of pretty looking bread, and in an atmosphere oppressive with aniseed, sits a very fat old woman, from whom we buy a pennyworth of bread,—enough and to spare for our drawing, and for ourselves.

And so, crossing another bridge, a stone-mason's yard, and another busy mill, we reach the gate close to the house where live the people who look after the studio. Here we are already recognised by the old dog as belonging to the place. If we are early we ascend the steps and ask for the keys of the studio, or perhaps a little brown-eyed girl, with her hair in a net, runs to meet us with them.

Two minutes more, and we unlock the heavy door and stand in our art-temple. The high priest as yet is not there, and we have a quiet, earnest studying of his pictures, endeavoring through them to discover how he looks at nature — endeavoring to see only the beautiful, the strong and tender. This union of the strong and the tender seems to me the great characteristic of his mind. But is not that the great and difficult union which we are all striving after, whether in life or in art? Is it not that glorious union, in its perfection, which we adore in Christ? Is it not this in our noblest poets — in the *In Memoriam*, for instance, which so touches and ennobles us?

. . . . . .

We drew last week, as a refreshment when weary with harder work, a lovely branch of white lily, and became so enamored of our work that we determined to make another study of plants. We resolved to make a drawing of the most beautiful flowers growing in the beloved wilderness-field in which the studio stands, and to keep them as memories of this beautiful place, and this beautiful passage in our lives. We began, therefore, the other afternoon; and to-day, being seized with a foreboding that, as the field was now again covered with deep grass and flowers, it would shortly be mown, we determined to draw flowers from morning till evening.

The change of occupation was in itself a pleasure, and with our usual insane enthusiasm for every new kind of work, we declared, and most firmly believed at the time, that nothing in the shape of work could compare with the delight of drawing flowers, — the tracing their exquisite, delicate lines, their infinite variation of form and character, the living in spirit, like fairies as it were, among their bells and under their leaves. Then two or three times, in the course of the day, we had to make little expeditions into the field for specimens; and as it luckily happened, nobody was at the studio that day, nor even any visitors, only a group of children in the distance: we had the whole paradise to ourselves, and could go about without bonnets as if in our own garden. We sate among the flowers in the warm grass, among bladder-campion and clover, and lady's-bedstraw, and hare-bells, and thyme, and eye-bright. Above, the sky was cloudless, and so intensely blue, that to talk of Italian skies being bluer would be absurd.

As I was thus sitting, admiring, and pondering, and rejoicing, I chanced to look up, and saw a little boy coming through the flowers towards me: he was rather a miserable-looking little fellow, and worked, I fancy, at the stone-mason's: he was gathering flowers; he saw that I, also, had gathered some, which lay in my lap: he came up, and looking very shy, but with a most good-tempered smile on his countenance, offered me some clover and eye-bright with very short stalks. I was much pleased, and of course thanked him with a smile, asking him whether he did not greatly admire the field, and other small questions; to all of which he only replied *Ja!* and held his head very low, smiling very much.

I stuck his poor little flowers into my dress, and returned to my drawing. About half an hour later, when we were absorbed with our work, Clare, who was sitting on the floor near the door which opens into the wilderness, and which said door now stood open so that the sunshine might fall upon the sprays of grass and campion which she was sketching, looked up, startled by a sudden shadow falling across the threshold, and beheld the poor little lad standing beneath the branches of the vine, with a half-grown reddish spaniel at his side; and as she glanced at him he held out a little nosegay of flowers with the same quiet, shy look. It was a pretty picture. She received them also with smiles, and we called both him and the dog in: the dog obeyed most promptly; the boy seemed frightened by our invitation, accepted it reluctantly, and soon slipped off again. We thought we had seen the last of him: But no! Again he came, and this time with a dahlia in his hand; and yet again a shadow darkened the threshold, and now he brought a nosegay of lovely carnations. Why, he must certainly, after all, be a child out of Fairy-land! Where could he get those splendid garden-flowers from? But no! he was only a poor stone-cutter's lad who was wonderfully attracted by the little studio and all the strange things it contained, and by the two young ladies who had smiled and talked so kindly. I should think he came to us half a dozen times in the course of the day, with his little offerings of flowers, and his silent, shy manner. Seeing him stand and watch us draw, with his grave, bashful eyes, we asked him whether he would like to draw, or whether perhaps he did not try to draw as it was. '*Ja!*' was again his answer —'*Ja!*' and a bashful smile. We, however, could gain but very little information from him beyond his name being Ignazius. Poor little Ignazius! I could fancy a pretty art-story written about him, and how this might have been the awakening in him of the sense of beauty.

July 21*st.* — What a deal of time I have wasted in looking out of the window and watching the blue-coated postmen, as the clocks strike twelve, filing up the street from the Post-office, each with a large packet of letters in his hand. Surely *one* among *all* those letters must be for me!

A blue-coat turns in here! I wait, and wait, and wait, but no letter! No doubt it was only a letter he brought for one of the hundred and one other inhabitants of this house, — for some student or dressmaker who lives above, or for the master of the curiosity-shop, or for some of his journeymen, or for Mr. Bürgermeister Somebody, who lives on the floor beneath; for some one, perhaps, at the Tailor's, or the Jeweller's, or the Bookseller's, or perhaps for the Under-Secretary Wagner, who has such numbers of letters and official documents brought to him. At all events, the letter is not for me! '*Paatience! paatience! paatience!*' as our friend L—— says. But how gay the street looks! Such numbers of butterfly-ladies, in gay muslins and light kid gloves, and with bright-colored parasols; such dandified young officers with their ridiculously small waists — they lace themselves up as tightly as the silliest of girls; such clean *Bürger-Leute;* such picturesque groups of students, their hair so glossy from its Sunday brushing, their scarlet caps set so jauntily on their heads, their gay corps-bands displayed over their snowy shirt-fronts; such a pleasant sound of voices and trampling of feet along the sunny pavements. I'm quite inspired to put on all my Sunday apparel and look as gay as the best: I quite long to descend into my unusual character of 'young lady,' and go abroad for a pleasant un-*exalté* afternoon; drink coffee with a gay party under green trees to the sound of music, and criticise all the faces and toilettes that pass before us. I wish Alfred were here to-day; we would for a few hours be as little in the clouds as he could wish!

I see some capital dinners going along the streets. I trust our capital dinner will soon appear; we are always ravenous about 12 o'clock. And, *à-propos* of dinners, we had anything but a ceremonious dinner the other day. We usually dine at the *Meyerischen Garten*, where they have orders when it is wet to send our dinners to the studio. Last Friday, therefore, the sky suddenly clouding over about eleven, after a most brilliant morning, when we had gone forth *sans* cloak, *sans* clogs, *sans* everything necessary for a wet day, we awaited the advent of our first studio-meal with the intensest impatience, not unmingled with a slight uneasiness as to its not appearing at all! The loud-ticking clock told quarter after quarter, till at length one o'clock arrived without the dinner, and the rain still pouring down in torrents, and we delighting in the consciousness of the thinnest of boots and muslin dresses, and a wet field of long grass to pass through before arriving at the region of *Braten* and *Mehlspeise*, were forced to summon all our philosophy, and cry, 'dinner, go hang!' Dinner, indeed! We working in the studio of a great master, and yet longing for our dinners! No, we would forget prosaic hunger, and satisfy our craving in the afternoon at home. Just having reached this point of heroism, there is a knock at the door, and enter a short, broad-built, merry brown woman, with a face not unlike a mulatto's, the resemblance even increased by her wearing a bright-colored handkerchief on her head. Ah! we know that beloved countenance — that countenance of our friend the kitchen-maid at the *Meyerischen Garten*. Beloved kitchen-maid, with thy bare feet and thy big basket, well dost thou deserve to be celebrated in verse! Would that for thy sake I were Tennyson! then should the world long since have reverenced thee with a reverence equal only to that inspired by the 'Waiter at the Cock!'

At once there was a sudden starting up from our easels; a flinging down of porte-crayons, a rushing up to the big basket, a delight and rejoicing in English and German over the contents it exhibited.

'Splendid goose!' cries Clare; '*Herrliche Mehlspeise*,' cries Anna. The magnificent kitchen-maid laughs and shows her white teeth; and we laugh and bustle about, and sweep off prints and books, boxes and flowers, from the little round table in the middle of the room. But plates! knives! spoons! Oh, thou celestial kitchen-maid, where are they? Forgotten, as mere sublunary trash! What is to be done? Oh, borrow plates, and knives and forks, from the *Hausmeisterin*. Away goes the kitchen-maid, and returns with a plate, a knife, and fork. That was all very well for the goose: — but when we came to the pudding! 'Eat it out of the dish,' suggests Clare; 'this is a pic-nic among the cartoons, instead of among trees, that's all!' And the pudding was eaten out of the dish with no lack of merriment: but most of all did our laughter increase when we came to drink our coffee, which, by the by, I ought to have said, arrived on a little green tray, all flooded with rain; the coffee in one little white-lidded jug, the milk in another, the sugar safe and dry in the basket. But again there were neither coffee-cups nor spoons! Beloved kitchen-maid! thy wits of a truth had gone wool-gathering! But that was quite a minor discomfort — a difficulty which we speedily got rid of, simply by mixing coffee, milk, and sugar, in a china jar which we keep at the studio for flowers; and then, having duly blended the ingredients, the delicious beverage was poured into the two jugs, and each drank her coffee with as much gravity as she could muster.

But why, instead of all this nonsense, have I not described last evening, with its beautiful walk down that lovely Ludwig Strasse; the long pause in the Ludwig *Kirche,* which affected us, seen in the twilight, as it never had affected us before, and our enjoyment of a glorious sunset, which we witnessed over the plain. The immensity of a plain affects one like the immensity of the ocean. Yes, I love this plain, as apparently I love everything connected with Munich! Everything, excepting the heat, the rain, the veal, and — the fleas! The greatest of all plagues! There was no plague in Egypt to compare to them! They fairly leap about the paper as I write. I have long since given up the sofa, convinced that it is stuffed with fleas instead of wool.

CHAPTER IV.

THE MIRACLE-PLAY AT OBER-AMMERGAU.

Every now and then, during the last two months, certain bright-colored placards, pasted at the corners of the streets, have greatly excited my curiosity. These placards announced that on certain days specified conveyances would depart for the accommodation of persons desirous of witnessing the performance of the Miracle-Play at Ober-Ammergau.

'A miracle-play!' I exclaimed — 'a miracle-play now-a-days!'

Numerous were my inquiries regarding the play and its performers, and various were the remarks thus called forth. From my two or three English friends, exclamations of horror; from the good Catholic people of our house, exclamations of pious delight; from our excellent friend, Doctor F., alone, the information I required. 'This play,' said he, 'is performed by the peasants of Ober-Ammergau and the neighboring villages, in fulfilment of a vow made during a terrible pestilence, in 1633. When the pestilence was at its height, the poor peasants vowed to God, that if he would stay the plague, they would perform, every ten years, in token of their deep gratitude, and (in their opinion) as a means of religious instruction to the inhabitants of the district, the whole Passion of our Saviour, from his entrance into Jerusalem to his Ascension. This miracle-play,' continued our friend, 'has been religiously performed every ten years until the present time. On the last three occasions, the music and the whole spectacle have been somewhat altered and heightened in artistic effect; and it would be difficult to meet with a more striking picture of a past age and mode of thought. Let me persuade you,' said he, 'to start with one of these *Stell-wagen* the very next time the play is performed, for you will not repent of it. Ober-Ammergau is situated in our Bavarian highlands.'

That was enough to decide us, especially as Clare's experience of mountains was confined to those pictured in our London exhibitions and panoramas, and to a certain vision of 'ethereal mountains,'—'clouds,' as she still sceptically called them—which I had triumphantly pointed out to her as 'the Alps,' on our way hither from Augsburg.

Not even rain could damp our enthusiasm, although it had rained for the whole week, pouring down in torrents, until Munich was as gloomy as London in November. Our places were duly taken in the *Stell-wagen* amid the rain; and amid the rain we rose at half-past three on Saturday morning, and after a hasty cup of tea, prepared over our spirit-lamp, and with our carpet-bags in our hands, issued forth into the wet, silent streets, under a most leaden, melancholy sky. Yet had not Doctor F. quoted to us his favorite German proverb, *Den Muthigen gehört die Welt* (The world belongs to the brave)? That was to be our maxim. Fine weather, we doubted not, as well as other fine things, would be ours, for we had long regarded ourselves as among the brave: still we were haunted by various descriptions we had heard of the Ober-Ammergau — Judas hanging himself under a red umbrella!

Outside the Sendlinger Gate, which looked particularly ruinous and dilapidated on that damp, gloomy morning, we found assembled, under an awning, a considerable number of *Stell-wagen* passengers, all provided with umbrellas, all gazing up to the sky, and all declaring, with a very doleful and hopeless expression of countenance, that they were certain it would be fine.

Do you ask to what class of people these belonged? With the exception of one jolly, rather dirty Catholic priest, and too fat little men, whom I decided were a shoemaker and a dyer, all the company in our *Stell-wagen* were women; all wearing caps, and the Munich head-dress of gold and silver thread, and not bonnets, which marked them as belonging to the lower and middle citizen class. Most of the vehicles were filled with travellers of a similar kind—jolly, beer-drinking Munich folk; not particularly refined, but very merry and good-humored.

Our especial *Stell-wagen* soon made its appearance; a long-bodied, yellow omnibus, with a large leathern hood in front (the cabriolet), before which sat the driver, dressed in a light blue jacket, ornamented with black braid, black velvet breeches, enormous black leathern boots, coming up above the knees, and a picturesque black felt hat, with a broad band around it, adorned with a huge silver buckle. You will recognise many an old acquaintance of ours in this portrait, and also in the two lean, shambling, indefatigable horses, in their high-pointed collars and rope traces, which drew us to Ammergau and back, travelling almost night and day, as though they had been machines, and not creatures of living bone and muscle.

We were soon seated under the big hood of the cabriolet, beside a quiet, pious little body, who carried in her hand a white pocket-handkerchief and two rose-buds, and who solaced herself by saying her prayers at the church of every village where she stopped, and by reading in a little religious book, and then sleeping as we journeyed onward.

The coachman cracked his long-lashed whip, at the imminent risk of blinding some unlucky tenant of the vehicle, and in a few minutes we caught once more, between the tall poplars that skirted the road, a thrilling glimpse of those cloud-like mountains, their peaks catching, even on that gloomy, grey morning, the glow of sunrise, and shining out like golden foam. On we went through village after village, being struck with two things; firstly, their may-poles, adorned to a considerable height with all manner of devices, — emblems, I believe of different trades, — little houses, flags, animals, *Brezels*, little cakes twisted like a true lover's knot, and similar fancies, all of which produced a singularly droll effect; and secondly, the gradual change from the ordinary German style of cottage architecture into that of the Tyrolean and Swiss. By the time we reached Starnberg, a favorite resort of the Munich people of all classes during the summer — from royalty, to the sickly, consumptive dressmaker, and of artists especially — we were surrounded by quaint wooden houses, under the projecting eaves of whose shingle and stone-covered roofs ran picturesque wooden balconies, all looking, as my companion observed, 'very like something on the stage.'

As we ascended the broad flight of steps leading to the handsome inn, we were struck by the beauty of the view: a blue little lake stretching away as far as the eye could reach; beyond, a wall of Alps, already stern, stony mountains, and no longer clouds, their rigid peaks cutting sharply against the sky; with a foreground of Tyrolean cottages and pleasant bowery orchards.

Attractive as was the view outside the inn, that cold July morning, the prospect inside was still more attractive.

Apparently, our fellow-travellers had thought so, for they and the late occupants of the various other *Stell-wagen,* and divers vehicles drawn up before the inn, were already regaling themselves at long tables, with beer and *Braten:* that is to say, veal. The quietest, most agreeable, and certainly the warmest place in the house being the kitchen, there we determined to stay, attracted somewhat, no doubt, by the clean hearth, upon which were stewing, and simmering, and boiling, in all indescribable sorts of pots, pans, and kettles, the favorite Bavarian dish, veal; and being, moreover, invited to do so by the smiling cook and her assistants. There we sat, and regaled ourselves on eggs and coffee, and amused ourselves with watching the activity of our gaily-attired cook and her attendants, each of whom displayed a large silver spoon in her bright-colored boddice, and with wondering at all the quaint and picturesque crockery and kitchen utensils, which were arranged round that spacious, cheerful, yet monastic-looking apartment: when, behold a discovery! Clare, in the bustle of departure, and sleepy as she was, had forgotten her purse! We had agreed the night before setting off to take each the same sum in our purses, — the one to pay going, and the other returning. But now, at the very outset, we had only *one* purse between us! So very blank and horrified did she look — so unavailingly did she feel, again and again, in bag, basket, and pocket — that I could only laugh and cheer her with the idea of strict economy for the next two days, and with the assurance that if, after all, our *one* purse did not turn out a Fortunatus's purse, as I firmly believed it would, we would throw ourselves on the mercy of some honest-looking landlord, and leave with him a ring, or even a gold chain, as a pledge, and that in any case it would only be an adventure on our journey.

But it was a long time before poor Clare could forget

what she persisted in calling 'our misfortune,' — not, indeed, until, as the *Stell-wagen* drove off, we perceived that the whole place was in a state of extraordinary excitement, an excitement not owing to the departure of our *Stell-wagen*, or to the advent of others, but to a fire — a fire in a hamlet through which we had passed some two hours before, and the news of which had just reached this place. Leaving Starnberg, we could see the distant column of black smoke rising above the trees; and the following day, on our return, we found in the hamlet, instead of a good, substantial public-house, a blackened heap of ruins. The wild excitement of Starnberg was inconceivable; nor shall I ever forget the white face of one man — the village tailor, apparently — who rushed past us bare-legged, with his long black hair streaming in the wind. Men and boys were hurrying along the street, and groups of women and children stood in the orchards, gazing in the distance. Ascending a hill from the village, we met the primitive fire-engine of the district madly descending, and drawn by a lanky, shaggy, raw-boned horse, just taken from field-labor. There was a strange mingling of the comic and the affecting in this episode of village life.

Slowly but pleasantly we journeyed on through the rest of that livelong day, drawing nearer and nearer to the Alpine chain; now catching a grand panoramic view of the mountains as we emerged from some old pine-wood, a plain dotted with innumerable villages, hamlets, and woods, lying between us and them, the tower of one of those quaint white-washed Bavarian churches, with its small, half-oriental dome rising in sharp relief against the deep indigo of the mountains, as seen under that stern sky, and making them retire in a marvellously artistic manner; and now diving again into deep woods, ever catching and again losing glimpses of those grand mountains and their glittering snowy peaks, until we arrived, in a gleam of delicious sunset, at the quiet little town of Murnau.

They call Murnau a town, but it is a marvellously small one, and would have been as still as death, but for the Ammergau visitors. So great was the overflow of strangers at the *Gast-Haus*, that it was not without difficulty we were able to secure a chamber to ourselves. The bustle and confusion, the hubbub and noise in the house, were inconceivable, and therefore, although we were to start at half-past one in the morning, and had consequently very little time for rest, the calm evening sunshine out of doors soon invited us forth. The mountains seemed fairly to close in the street of the little town, but still a plain extended from the gentle slope on which Murnau stands to the foot of the Alpine chain.

As the sun sank in a golden heaven, streaked with lilac and rose, tinting with rainbow colors the glittering peaks of the most elevated and distant snowy ridge, the nearest, and lower chain was cast into a mysterious violet gloom, and the intermediate ranges were turned to deep indigo, almost black by shadow, or copper-color and russet in the evening glow. What wonderful gradations of color! What sharp, bold, stern lines of composition! Where, after all, was the picture of Turner, or Danby, which could convey to your spirit the glory of those mountains and that sky? Even Turner's wonderful tints and magical power over atmosphere seemed cold and feeble in recollection as we gazed at this lovely vision painted for us by God's own hand! Beneath us lay the plain, golden in the evening light; long shadows cast athwart it from poplars and cherry-trees; beyond us this mountain vision, like the very gates of spirit-land; above our heads glowed an azure and pearly-tinted heaven, flecked with fantastic, gorgeous cloudlets; beneath our feet nodded, in the soft evening breeze, flowers as bright as gems, orange, deep blue, crimson, and lilac; Alpine flowers mingling with old English friends,—the lady's mantle, the graceful quaking-grass, the daisy, the mountain pink, and mountain-cistus. We sate and watched the azure shadows creeping up the mountains, and the light fading away from the snowy peaks, till they were left cold, and white, and winterly, and till a deep, stern solemnity sank down upon the whole scene and upon our hearts.

When all was grey and mysterious, and the silence of twilight had become yet more perceptible from the ceasing of the vesper-bell, which had been sounding from a distant church, we reluctantly turned our faces homewards. Stalwart women and girls, strong as men, were resting themselves at their doors, or fetching water from the fountains, as we passed up the village street. Where were the men and boys? I know not:—perhaps in the beer-houses.

It was a strange fragment of a night, that at Murnau! Throwing ourselves, half dressed, on our beds, we tried to sleep; but that was impossible; the whole town was astir, and nearly as noisy as Cheapside, with an incessant rattle of peasants' carts, *Stell-wagen*, and vehicles of all descriptions, which were jolting over the uneven pavement on their way to Ammergau, and if, by any chance, you did lose consciousness, for a moment, you were woke up again by the watchman chanting his verse, and calling out the quarters of the hour.

By one o'clock all the travellers were again astir; by half-past, having scalded their mouths with a cup of boiling coffee, and having in their sleepy haste run against each other, laden with carpet-bags and umbrellas, on dark staircases and in dimly lighted passages, all had subsided into cold and silence within the *Stell-wagen*. We again took our places in the cabriolet: Clare's sleepy head soon sunk upon my shoulder, whilst I, only too widely awake, gazed out into the starlight, and felt, rather than saw, that we were entering the mountain-gorge.

Stell-wagen after *Stell-wagen* passed us, to be re-passed by us in their turn; now an *Eil-wagen* with its four horses and postilions; now a gentleman's carriage, with its flaring lamps; now we passed groups of pedestrians; now wagon after wagon, filled with peasant women, their long rows of white draperied heads flitting along the dark road before us like strange moths, and looking in the cold, grey light of dawn, as phantom-like, almost, as the cold, white, solemn peaks, draperied with snow, above us. The roar of a mountain river accompanied us through the night; in the early dawn we were still travelling along its bank. The villages through which we passed were half choked up with heaps of timber; rafts were floating down the stream, or were moored to its banks; giant pine-trees were lying prostrate by the river's edge, ready to be converted into rafts. This lower range of mountains was clothed with pine-forests up to its very summit.

It was now four o'clock on Sunday morning, and intensely cold; we were well pleased, therefore, at the foot of the Ettalberg, to alight from our cabriolet, and commence with our fellow-passengers and numerous other pilgrims, the ascent of the mountain on foot. Cold as it was, the sun was already shining down into the pleasant birch and pine-woods, through which our road wound, and gilding the mountain peaks; a torrent was dashing and leaping over huge rocks in the gorge below us; the birds were singing, and all was fresh and joyous. The most remarkable feature of the scene, however, was the people. From the rustic inn at the foot of the mountain, to the inn at the top, where is a celebrated pilgrimage church, and all along the road, thence to Ammergau, as far as the eye could reach, was one dense stream of people! The crowd of peasants ascending the mountain was to me an affecting sight; my eyes and my heart involuntarily filled with tears. Their earnest, grave, yet cheerful countenances, told me that it was a deep religious object which they had in view: it was not curiosity and the love of pleasure which urged them up that steep ascent; it was with faith and pious hope that they pressed onward. Men, women, old and middle-aged, youths, maidens, children, family groups, neighbors and friends, all banded together to witness this outward rendering of the spirit of their creed. The variety of costume showed that the whole district for many miles round had sent out its votaries. There were groups of pure Tyroleans, with their green sugar-loaf hats adorned with golden cord and tassels, tufts of feathers or artificial flowers; there were many semi-Tyrolean dresses, and vast numbers of women wearing the queer, heavy, Tartar-looking cap of badger-skin, peculiar, I believe, to the Ober-Ammergau district; there were bodices and petticoats and head-dresses of every color of the rainbow, — red, green, and blue, being however predominant; there was a considerable sprinkling also of the swallow-tailed gold and silver Munich cap, and no lack of red umbrellas. How gay this winding multitude made the mountain, you can well imagine! Slowly and painfully behind each group ascended the poor tired horses, dragging the skeleton-like peasant's cart, *Stell-wagen* or *Ein-spann*, as it might be.

Ever and anon some frightfully deformed or diseased wretch would solicit alms, which were as freely given by the poor peasants as they were eagerly demanded by the miserable beggars. These disgusting fungi of Catholicism were a strange comment on the scene. My companion and I, in our Regent Street dresses, and with our Protestant hearts, seemed singularly out of place in a crowd of simple peasants on their way to a miracle-play; we felt out of keeping with them and their child-like faith; we drew inferences, and made comments; they went on in that earnest simplicity, and with all that primitive piety, which is one's idea of peasant life as it exists in the poems of Uhland and the tales of Auerbach.

After having refreshed their souls at the church on the summit of the mountain, and their bodies at the inn, our pilgrims mounted their various vehicles and pursued their way; the road to Ober-Ammergau becoming more animated the nearer we approached it.

The first view of Ober-Ammergau somewhat disappointed us. It lies in a smiling green valley surrounded by hills rather than mountains, and excepting for the architecture of the cottages, and certain rugged lines of peaks and cliffs, telling of Alpine origin, might have passed for a retired Derbyshire dale.

We had brought from our friend Dr. F—— a letter to the peasant, Tobias Flunger, who performed the character of Christ; and this circumstance won for us great respect amongst our fellow-travellers. The *Stell-wagen* drove up to his house, which is the second in the village, and surrounded by a gay little garden. Tobias Flunger came out to receive us; and you may imagine our surprise, when, instead of a peasant, as we had imagined, we beheld a gentleman to all appearance in a grey sort of undress coat, and with a scarlet Fez on his head. He was certainly handsome, and welcomed us with a calm yet warm-hearted courtesy. As he removed his Fez, we saw his dark, glossy hair parted above the centre of his brow, and falling in rich waves on his shoulders, and that his melancholy dark eyes, his pale brow, his emaciated features, his short black beard, all bore the most strange and startling resemblance to the heads of the Saviour as represented by the early Italian painters.

There was something to my mind almost fearful in this resemblance, and Tobias Flunger seemed to act and speak like one filled with a mysterious awe. If this be an act of worship in him, this personation of our Lord, what will be its effect upon him in after-life? There was a something so strange, so unspeakably melancholy in his emaciated countenance, that I found my imagination soon busily speculating upon the true reading of its expression.

At the door we were also met by his wife and little daughter, themselves peasants in appearance, but cheerful and kind in their welcome, as if we had been old friends. The whole cottage was in harmony with its inhabitants, bright, cheerful, and filled with traces of a simple, pious, beautiful existence. We were taken into a little room, half chamber, half study; upon the walls were several well-chosen engravings after Hess and Overbeck. An old-fashioned cabinet fronted with glass contained several quaint drinking-glasses and exquisite specimens of carvings in wood, an art greatly practised in the village. On one side of the cabinet hung a violin, and above it and another cabinet were arranged casts of hands and feet. On noticing these things to the wife, she said that her husband was a carver in wood by profession, and he had brought them with him from Munich to assist him in his art.

'He is a great carver of crucifixes and Madonnas,' she continued: 'you must see his works.'

He was an artist, then, this Tobias Flunger, with his grave, sad countenance, his air of superiority; yes, much was now explained. And, no doubt, his artist feeling had been brought into operation for the benefit of the miracle-play, in the same manner that the schoolmaster of Ober-

Ammergau had taxed his musical skill for the production of the music.

It was now seven o'clock, and as it yet wanted an hour till the commencement of the play, our kind artistic host, with that strange, awe-inspiring countenance of his, insisted upon accompanying us through the village, and showing us specimens of the wood-carving. There was plenty of time, he said, for him to prepare for the play.

The village street was thronged with people and carriages of all descriptions; all was gay and bustling, as in preparation for some great festival; the bells rang joyously from the little church tower; fantastically arrayed figures, as if stepped forth from some old sacred picture, were ever and anon seen flitting through the not less gaily-attired, but more work-a-day looking groups; and as Tobias Flunger passed on with his sad, dreamy air, a low whisper followed him, of 'There goes Christ!'

At the sound of a small cannon, the motley crowd hastened towards the theatre, which was a large, unsightly wooden enclosure, erected on a broad green meadow, within a stone's throw of the village. A few poplars growing on either side of the enclosure, no doubt mark, from one ten years to another, the precise spot. The brightly painted pediment of the proscenium rose above the rude wooden fence; crowds of people already thronged the hastily erected flights of steps leading to the different entrances. A few moments more, and we were seated in one of the boxes precisely opposite the front of the stage. A sea of heads was below us in the pit, a sea whose waves were Tyrolean hats, glittering *Riegel Häube*, ponderous badger skins, and now and then a dash of foam-like white handkerchiefs. This foam greatly increased with the heat of the sun; the women throwing over their other head-gear snowy handkerchiefs to protect them from his rays. In the boxes, on either hand, sate the gentlefolks; and very grand folk some of them were, I am sure. Could we have only known their names, we should have found a considerable sprinkling of *Grafen* and *Gräfinnen*, of *Fürsten* and *Fürstinnen*, not to speak of common *vons* and *Geheimräthe*, and *Hofräthe*, and *Professoren*.

With the first feeble notes from the orchestra, and very feeble at first they were, a dead silence sank down upon the assembled multitude; as people say, you might have heard a pin drop. All was breathless expectation. And soon, beneath the blue dome of heaven, and with God's sunlight showering down upon them, a fantastic vision passed across the stage; their white tunics glanced in the light, their crimson, violet, and azure mantles swept the ground, their plumed head-dresses waved in the breeze; they looked like some strange flight of fabulous birds. This was the chorus, attired to represent angels. Like the antique chorus, they sang the argument of the play. With waving hands and solemn music, their united voices pealed forth words of blessing—'Peace on earth and good will toward men;' they sang of God's infinite love in sending among men His Blessed Son, and their voices rose towards heaven and echoed among the hills. And whilst they thus sang, your hearts were strangely touched, and your eyes wandered away from those singular peasant-angels, and their peasant audience, up to the deep, cloudless blue sky above their heads; you heard the rustle of green trees around you, and caught glimpses of mountains, and all seemed a strange, fantastical, poetical dream.

But now the chorus retired, and the curtain slowly rose. There is a tread of feet, a hum of voices; a crowd approaches, children shout, wave palm branches, and scatter flowers. In the centre of the multitude on the stage, riding upon an ass, sits a majestic figure clothed in a long violet-colored robe, the heavy folds of a crimson mantle falling around him. His hands are laid across his breast; his face is meekly raised towards heaven with an adoring love. Behind, solemnly follows a group of grave men with staves in their hands and ample drapery sweeping the ground. You recognise the disciple John in a handsome, almost feminine youth, clothed in green and scarlet robes, and with flowing locks; and there is Peter, with his eager countenance; and that man with the brooding look, and wrapt in a flame-colored mantle—that must be Judas! The children shout and wave their palm-branches, and the procession moves on, and that fatal triumphal entry is made into Jerusalem.

Again appears that tall majestic figure in his violet robe: his features are lit up with a holy indignation; a scourge is in his hand; he overturns the tables of the money-changers, and drives before him a craven avaricious crowd. An excited assembly of aged men, with long and venerable beards falling on their breasts, their features inflamed with rage, with gestures of vengeance, horror, and contempt, plot and decide upon his death! He, meantime, sits calmly at Bethany among his friends, and a woman, with beautiful long hair falling around her, kisses his feet and anoints them with precious ointment from her alabaster vase. And now he sits at a long table, his friends on either side; John leans upon his breast; he breaks the bread; Judas, seized by his evil thought, rises from the table, wraps himself closely in his mantle, bows his head, and passes out. Again the scene changes. It is a garden. That sad, grave man gazes with disappointed love upon his sleeping friend; he turns away and prays, bowed in agony. There is a tumult! That figure wrapped in its flame-colored robe again appears!

There is an encounter, a flash of swords! and the majestic, melancholy, violet-robed figure, with meekly bowed head, is borne away! And thus ends the first act of this saddest of all tragedies.

We had come, expecting to feel our souls revolt at so material a representation of Christ, as any representation of him, we naturally imagined, must be in a peasant's miracle-play. Yet so far, strange to confess, neither horror, disgust, nor contempt was excited in our minds. Such an earnest solemnity and simplicity breathed throughout the whole of the performance, that to me at least, anything like anger, or a perception of the ludicrous, would have seemed more irreverent on my part than was this simple, child-like rendering of the sublime Christian tragedy. We felt at times as though the figures of Cimabue's, Giotto's, and Perugino's pictures had become animated, and were moving before us; there were the same simple arrangement and brilliant color of drapery, — the same earnest, quiet dignity about the heads, whilst the entire absence of all theatrical effect wonderfully increased the illusion. There were scenes and groups so extraordinarily like the early Italian pictures, that you could have declared they were the works of Giotto and Perugino, and not living men and women, had not the figures moved and spoken, and the breeze stirred their richly-colored drapery, and the sun cast long, moving shadows behind them on the stage. These effects of sunshine and shadow, and of drapery fluttered by the wind, were very striking and beautiful; one could imagine how the Greeks must have availed themselves of such striking effects in their theatres open to the sky.

Between each scene, taken from the life of Christ, was a *tableau vivant* chosen from the Old Testament, and typical of the passage which should succeed it from the New

Testament. Each *tableau* was explained by the chorus, which duly swept across the stage in all their grandeur. Those pictures from the Old Testament were singularly inferior to the rest of the spectacle, impressing you most unpleasantly with a sense of tinsel and trumpery, and so stiff and hard in their outlines that I cannot even now divest my mind of the idea that the figures were carved in wood, and were not living people. Not a limb moved, not a fold was stirred; there was nothing of the soft melting outlines of nature, none of the grace of life; they were precisely like the tawdry, hideous carved saints that one sees here in the churches. Spite of repeated assurances to the contrary, I cannot help still feeling as though these figures were an offering to the play from the wood-carvers of the village.

The performance had commenced at eight o'clock, and now it was one, and a pause therefore ensued; — the first pause of any kind during those five long hours — for *tableau*, and chorus, and acting, had succeeded each other in the most rapid, unwearied, yet wearying routine! One felt perfectly giddy and exhausted by such a ceaseless stream of music, color, and motion. Yet the actors, as if made of iron, appeared untouched by fatigue, and up to the very end of the second part, which lasted from two to five, played with the same earnest energy, and the chorus sang with the same powerful voice.

Again the little village was all astir. The bells rung; the peasants refreshed themselves beneath the trees in gay groups, or crowded into the one public-house. And what a bustle there was in that one little inn! In the lower rooms, a devouring of food and a swallowing of beer, and a cloud of smoke and a noise of tongues, and a stench indescribable and inconceivable to any who do not know what a German village inn is. Up stairs, things were scarcely less unattractive, although there sate the guests of a higher rank. The noise, and crowd, and close air of that little inn, however, were so appalling to our English nerves, that we escaped as quickly as we could to the garden, where, amidst groups of picturesque peasants, most touchingly courteous in their behavior to us foreigners, we found a comparatively quiet nook at a table. The scene was peculiar; rows of gaily attired peasants seated at long tables, laughing and drinking beer out of quaintly-shaped glasses with little pewter lids; trees waving above their heads, roses and lilies blooming around them; a background of Tyrolean roofs, covered with their large round stones and sharp jagged Alpine peaks rising closely behind the cottages into the sunny sky. Peasant girls brought bouquets of the Alpine rose to offer the strangers. Yes, we were among the Alps,—there was no doubt about that, even my dear incredulous companion was now willing to admit.

But there was no time to linger over picturesque effects or sentimental meditation, any more than over *Braten* and salad.

The cannon again sounded; the people again streamed towards the theatre. We were again in our places, and again commenced that long monotonous exhibition. But the peasant portion of the audience were as unwearying as the actors themselves; to them, indeed, the second part was the most intensely interesting of all, *eine herzrührende, angreifende Geschichte*,—whilst to us it became truly revolting and painful. There was no sparing of agony, and blood, and horror; it was our Lord's passion stripped of all its spiritual suffering,—it was the anguish of the flesh,—it was the material side of Catholicism. It was a painful, heart-rending, hurrying to and fro amid brutal soldiery and an enraged mob, of that pale, emaciated, violet-robed figure; then there was his fainting under the cross; the crowning him with thorns; the scourging, the buffeting, the spitting upon him: and the soldiers laughed, and scoffed, and derided with fierce brutality, and the people and the high priest jeered and shouted, and ever he was meek and gentle. Then came the crucifixion; and as the chorus sang of the great agony, you heard from behind the curtain the strokes of the hammer as the huge nails were driven into the cross, and, as your imagination believed, through his poor pale hands and feet; and then, as the curtain slowly rose to the dying tones of the chorus, you beheld him hanging on the cross between the two crucified thieves.

Both myself and my companion turned away from this spectacle sick with horror. They divided his garment at the foot of the cross; they pierced his side, and blood flowed apparently from the wound and from his martyred hands and feet. The Virgin and Mary Magdalene, and the disciples, lamented round the foot of the cross, in groups and attitudes such as we see in the old pictures. Then came Joseph of Arimathea; the body was taken down and laid upon white linen, and quietly, solemnly, and mournfully, followed by the weeping women, was borne to the grave. Next came the visit of the women to the sepulchre; the vision of the angels; the surprise and joy of the women; and lastly, as the grand *finale*, the Resurrection.

The miracle-play was at an end; and now the peasants began once more to breathe and to return to common life; and we most heartily rejoiced that this long, long martyrdom was over, — a martyrdom in two senses, for a more fatiguing summer's-day's work than the witnessing of this performance, which, with but one hour's pause, had lasted from eight in the morning till five in the evening, cannot be conceived. How the poor peasants managed to endure the burning rays of a July sun striking upon their heads for eight long hours, to say nothing of the heat and fatigue necessarily caused by the close pressure in the pit, I cannot imagine. In the boxes, where people were screened from the sun by awnings, many a face had for hours before began to assume a pale and jaded look, and many an attitude to betray intense fatigue.

But now all fatigue must be forgotten in the bustle of departure. There was no time allowed for a moment's refreshment; the theatre was left in ghastly emptiness in an incredibly short time. Horses were being harnessed to carts, *Stell-wagen*, and all imaginable kind of vehicles drawn up before the inn and crowding the village street. There was a cracking of whips, a jingling of horses' bells, a rushing to and fro of travellers; people were once more in their old seats in carts and carriages; there was a hum of voices, a waving of hands to departing acquaintances, mostly of that day's growth; many an anxious, hurried search after some missing umbrella or bag; and now all fairly started!

In our moment of hurried departure, however, behold the sad, pale face of Tobias Flunger bidding us adieu! He had again assumed his Fez and his grey coat, but the face was yet more gentle and dreamy, as though the shadow of the cross still lay upon it; and your eyes sought with a kind of morbid horror for the trace of the stigmata in those thin white hands, as they waved a parting signal. It was a relief to see at his side the pleasant, bright, kind faces of his wife and little daughter. There was a wholesome look of happiness and common life about them.

That we should have spoken with the personation of *Christus;* that he should have received us into his house;

should, even after the play, have hastened to take leave of us at our departure, created the greatest interest among our fellow-travellers, and inspired them with the profoundest respect for us. I was overwhelmed with questions regarding him, — questions which probably his most intimate friends could not have answered satisfactorily. But no wonder that he should have inspired so profound an interest, for throughout his conception and attempt at the embodiment of the awful, unapproachable character of Christ, there had flowed a subdued current of the deepest feeling, a sentiment of true poetry, a piety, an appreciation of the highest heroism — that heroism which shows itself in self-annihilation for the salvation of suffering humanity. We had been greatly struck by this, and by the different spirit evinced in the personation of the Virgin. The young peasant-girl who acted this character had studied her part under a well-known Munich actress, but unfortunately had brought away with her theatrical affectation and a most miserable air of conceit. This was the sole departure from that simple, earnest, unaffected dignity and truthfulness which had both astonished and delighted us in this poor peasants' play. But the play was their offering to God! what wonder, then, that it should bear the stamp of truth and fervor? for it came forth, I sincerely believe, from their very hearts' core. Let us not, therefore, call it irreverent or irreligious: depend upon it, that murmur of peasants' voices rose to heaven like the smoke of an accepted sacrifice.

There was a certain regret in the thought that though now turning our faces homewards, towards our beloved little art-city of Munich, we were, nevertheless, travelling away from those equally beloved mountains which had so long called us, as it were, with their spirit-voices, and which now glowed in the sunlight with ever-changing rainbow hues. Still, as we caught sight of the two familiar towers of the *Frauen Kirche,* we were bound to acknowledge that a city for poor civilized human beings was, after all, a fitter abode than an Alpine peak. More especially did we feel this truth when seated at our tea-table on the evening of the following day, devouring our English papers and English letters, which we so pleasantly found awaiting us.

What further? We had not a drop of rain during the whole time, and our *one* purse *did* turn out the purse of Fortunatus. Without sparing, and without borrowing, we reached Munich with yet twelve *Kreutzers* left. The forgotten purse, with its full contents of large florin pieces, lay quietly with our letters and papers to greet us on our return.

CHAPTER V.

BITS OF MUNICH LIFE.

August 8th.—This evening, Fraulein Steinhauser came in to beg us to go down stairs to see something very beautiful in their room. We of course went; and, in their strange curiosity-shop of a room, among painted saints, and gilt cabinets, and picture-frames, stood a little table, upon which was placed a very gaily-painted transparency, with queer pink angels fluttering about, and scrolls, and various extraordinary arabesques encircling a verse wishing health and happiness to the father: this being his name-day. Candles burned behind the transparency; pots of ivy and flowers were placed on either side, making a pleasant greenness; and in front lay a drawing in a gilt frame, a very grand chalk head of a boy, with a falcon on his wrist, and in a very grand frame indeed! The transparency, the drawing, and the frame, were all the work of little Wilhelm. And there he stood, as proud as could be! his black, sharp little eyes sparkling with delight; and there was his father, a tall and singularly handsome man, to-night with a smile of fatherly pride on his face, which made him look still more handsome; and there was Mrs. Steinhausen dressed all in her best, and all the little brothers and sisters, and the old grandmother with the baby in her arms, and several neighbors besides. It certainly was one of the prettiest little household festivals I ever saw.

Sometimes we send for little Wilhelm to play the 'zitter' to us. He is about twelve, has a very brown, red face, black eyes, and ear-rings in his ears. He plays very prettily. His fat little hands call forth such sweet low music from that little instrument — music, like fairy voices, sounding in solitary green spots among the mountains. There is a peculiar spirit in the zitter, and it is wonderfully adapted for Alpine melodies; for those tender, simple, peasant airs, through which ever runs such a plaintive sentiment.

These August nights are so hot and close, that after our tea, spite of its being twilight, we sometimes feel bound to take a walk. The other evening, for example, we betook ourselves along one of the old streets of Munich, a street very long and very ill-paved, the house-fronts handsome with old carving and stucco-work; a street where in the evening all the inhabitants gossip at their open windows and doors; a street much infested with bakers' shops; and where, through quaint old window-panes, you catch glimpses of queer old witch-like women, or young girls, like Faust's Margaret, sitting spinning; a street so full of detail that it would be quite a luxury to describe it graphically.

Just about the middle of this quaint old street we met a crowd, heard a hum of voices, saw banners waving, and crucifixes borne aloft. It was the return of a pilgrimage. Hot, weary, dusty, foot-sore, on they came. First walked priests with their dusty banners and crucifixes; white-robed children followed, carrying faded wreaths and garlands, their poor little heads drooping with fatigue; now a band of men, a *Brüderschaft*, dressed in their pilgrim garb, large blue cloaks with heavy capes, on which the cockle-shell showed conspicuously; then a group of young girls, many carrying bulrushes in their hands, instead of palm branches, and relics from the holy spot to which they had pilgrimed; next trooped on men — men — men, their shoes covered with white dust, their heads bare, their hands folded — old men, middle-aged men, lads; here and there a picturesque, fanatical-looking head with lank locks, and hollow cheeks, and sunken eyes, or brooding and morose-looking, with wild, bushy hair and huge growth of beard; — a strange assembly! but, nevertheless, the greater number were of the quiet, respectable citizen class; and one felt how strange it was to see such jolly-looking, every-day sort of good shop-keepers joining in a pilgrimage; they seemed so wholly opposed to everything like sentiment and enthusiasm. And all the men muttered prayers, — every now and then their hoarse voices rising into a monotonous chant of the word '*Heilige! Heilige! Heilige!*' And on they came and on! like a stream of phantoms in a bewildering dream. They rushed past in the twilight, walking fast with their dusty feet, and muttering their monotonous words, till one felt almost delirious. And now in the distance the voices of young girls and little children swelled into a solemn strain, and on came women, and women, and women — old and young, and middle-aged, and dusty also, and praying and muttering also! All, with the exception of one lady in a bonnet, a singularly gaunt and fanatical-looking woman, who walked in the middle of the procession; all, with this exception, appeared to be of the humbler class, — worn, hard-featured, suffering women: yet on they streamed, till one felt breathless. It was a striking and, someway, to me an unusually thrilling sight!

But now we were out on the quiet plain, which stretched away into an horizon of deep-blue mountain-like cloud, a pale amber sunset-streak fading away by the most delicate gradations into a lovely azure, athwart which stretched a fantastic mass of dark indigo clouds, the moon trembling above the sunset light, and here and there a dainty star twinkling in the azure and amber, whilst behind the dark mass of the Bavaria tower flashed ever and anon rose-tinted summer lightning, turning the mass of blue clouds into a range of lilac mountains, and the Bavaria building into an enchanted castle.

We were so charmed with our walk, that we resolved to go out whenever we could witness these sunsets, and then to note them down on our return home.

The next evening, therefore, we took our walk through the Triumphal Arch at the end of the Ludwig Strasse. The Ludwig Strasse looks inexpressibly beautiful in the evening: the uniformity of the Byzantine architecture, broken but not destroyed by the pale and harmonious tints employed in the various masses of building; delicate reds, and stone-colors, and greys, with here and there a mass of pure dazzling white, all brought into the most delicious harmony by the glow of evening; two white slender towers of the Ludwig church rising solemnly into the blue heavens, and surmounted each with a golden cross, which ever seems to catch the rays of the sun, and to gleam and sparkle when all else is sombre and dark. Then, in the evening and twilight, how cool and refreshing, and soothing, is the splash of the two fountains which play in the open space before the University and the Jesuits' School! I should love, were I a youth, to study in the University. That pure, solemn, calm, beautiful building, white as of the purest marble, with its long rows of round arched windows: its long band of medallions also, a medallion between each centre window, and inclosing the head of a legislator, a philosopher, or a poet. And as the western sky is lit up by the setting sun, its light streams through painted windows, and the contrast between the cool building, seen in the shadow, and those gemmed, glowing windows, is magical. There is a monastic calm about the building, which, to a studious and poetical nature, must be delicious.

The Jesuits' School is of a pale, warm, stone-color, of the same style, but by no means so beautiful. The whole effect of this square is, however, poetical and striking, and when the Triumphal Arch at the end of it is completed, will be something quite unique. The gateway is to be surmounted by a figure of Bavaria, drawn by lions, in a triumphal car: on the front and sides of the gate are very beautiful basso-relievos and statues of white marble.

The road beyond the Triumphal Arch is lined by poplars, and the entrance to Munich by this road is very impressive. For about half a mile on one side the road are scattered villas and cafés. The queen has a lovely little villa there, simple and elegant, and built in the style of domestic architecture peculiar to Munich, and which strikes me as being beautiful and appropriate.

One evening we had tickets sent us for a concert; they came late, and we had but little time for preparation. We dressed in a desperate hurry, putting off at the same time our working-dresses and our character of art-students; and attired as proper young ladies, with our tickets in our hands and our two keys (the latch-key of the house and the key of the passage leading to our rooms) in our pockets, set off across the Residenz Platz and the Odean Platz. It was a rehearsal concert of the students of the Conservatorium, and the large hall was crowded to overflowing already.

The performers were all young, and many of them very young. There was one little violinist, not more than twelve, certainly, who played splendidly, with beautiful earnestness and composure, as well as with much feeling. The applause was immense, and you felt how proud his mother and his friends must be; but he was like a little unmoved statue, his white face shaded by its dark brown hair. It was all a matter of coûrse to him.

The friends and relatives of the pupils were a marked feature of the scene; many of them quite poor people. And such numbers of little lads! We had a host of them just before us; and very amusing it was. One little fellow leaned, with all the air of a used-up man of fashion, against the balustrade of the orchestra, in the face of the whole assembly, yawning with the greatest disdain of all present, whilst he crossed his little legs and played with his little gloved hands.

There is nothing strange in our venturing to concerts and theatres by ourselves, — nothing can be easier or more comfortable. We walk quietly to the Opera in the pleasant sunshine: the theatre looking beautiful with its fresco-painted pediment, and all the square alive with a gay crowd streaming also theatre-wards. We take our places quietly in the reserved seats; and having thoroughly enjoyed ourselves at the cost of twenty-pence, walk home again equally quietly and comfortably. There is no crushing of carriages and cabs, no shouting of watermen and cab-drivers. Two or three carriages may be there, their lamps shining out like huge glow-worms at the bottom of the flight of steps; but people who have carriages get quietly into them, and there is no stir or bustle; and those who have none wend their way home singly or in groups, and the moon lights up that beautiful little square, with its palace-front, its theatre, its Pompeian-like post-office, its quaint side of old shops; or the stars look down out of a deep blue calm sky, and all is silence and poetry.

On our return yesterday from dinner at the *Meyerischen Garten*, I was informed that the lady of the ——— Ambassador had called and left an invitation for me for that evening. I was not in a visiting humor, and the idea of going quite alone to these grand people daunted me. I have courage enough for most things; I am sure I could travel to China—very easily all over America—by myself; but going alone to a ball, or even to a little party, among strangers, is my idea of desolation; and this evening I believed there was a grand party at the Ambassador's. I was in despair: it was a wet day, and I felt ill, and even if I *did* screw up my courage to the pitch of heroism, how was I to get there? how, in all this rain? Where was my carriage?—where even a cab? A cab! yes, that reminded me that I might go and return in a *fiacre*.

When, therefore, on returning home, I found that I could improvise a toilette, and when, after a cup of tea, I felt really better, and discovered that with a deal of trouble and bargaining, a driver of a *fiacre* would *condescend* (for such really was the case) to take me at the late hour of eight o'clock, (they leave their stand at seven, and go home for the night,) and then bring me back again at ten, and all for the enormous sum of two florins, not a Kreutzer less! after all this, I dressed and set out, having, of course, been inspected by the whole family of the house from doors and windows,—father, mother, daughter, little children, Wilhelm, and two apprentices with white rolled-up shirt-sleeves. What amusement the idle people could find in seeing one of the English *Fräulein* walk down stairs in a simple white dress and without her bonnet, and get into a lumbering old coach, I cannot conceive.

After a short wet drive across the Residenz and Odean Platz, and past the old *Wittelbacher Palais,* the palace where now lives the ex-King Ludwig, and which strange, red Gothic pile is guarded by two enormous stone lions, seated on either side of the gateway, into the Belgravia of Munich, we stopped at the house of the Baron von ——, a beautiful house. A tall, melancholy-looking footman, ushered me in, and to my delight there was no party. My spirits rose at once. I like Frau von ——, and I felt that it would be a charming evening.

Having been received by another tall, melancholy footman at the bottom of the stairs, and conducted through a number of pretty ante-rooms and boudoirs, I found the lady of the mansion, and a tall, aristocratic-looking man, with a very good-tempered German face, a very interesting, elegant young lady, and a lively, pretty little girl, sitting in a comfortable little drawing-room, — comfortable though splendid. The walls were hung with pictures and rich velvet draperies; the sofas and chairs were covered with crimson velvet; there was gold everywhere; mirrors and tall vases of Bohemian glass and rich china. All was very costly, but the prints, and books and pictures, and the pleasant lamp-light, and the kind, beaming faces of the group at the table, made me feel instantly at home and happy. The lovely young lady, with the calm brow, like one of Eastlake's women, and those delicate, taper fingers, loaded with rings, was a relation of the Baroness, and the gentleman was her brother. They had travelled in England and Scotland, and were well versed in English literature, of which they were very fond. We had a deal of pleasant talk, not only about old England, but about beautiful and interesting parts of Germany, with which fortunately I was acquainted; about books and pictures, and Kaulbach, whose genius we all agreed in ranking so high.

Then came in the tea on a rich silver tray, both elegant and attractive, and the little cakes were so delicate, and the tea quite strong and fragrant, like English tea. And after our rude, though most poetical life, the calmness and propriety and elegance of this artistocratic existence had an unusual charm for me. I loved to look at the glossy hair of the aristocratic little girl, — at her round arms, — at the delicate hands of the young lady so imprisoned in her rings; they were to my fancy a sort of fairy creatures who must ever live among gold and rich satin, and perfume ; and the idea of her walking in dust or mud, or in wet or darkness, was like the idea of an angel's wing being splashed with the mud of a London cab-wheel! No, there was an unusual piquancy in coming from our free, unconventional life, thus suddenly into a court-circle.

One day lately the streets were gay with people, and the sun shone down in my very heart. I longed to be among trees and fields. And was there not to be a *Kirchweih* (wakes) in the Au — the church festival of the beautiful church there? Thither would I go.

Through the gay streets accordingly I went; crowds of holiday people moving towards the Isar-gate, and over the bridge, and past the Volk's Theatre.

The Au suburb was all alive with dance-music, sounding from the public-houses and gardens. The little balconies were unusually gay with flowers; all the Madonnas had clean cambric pocket-handkerchiefs put into their hands: how comic they looked holding their handkerchiefs like fine ladies at a ball! And, by the by, in this suburb there are not a few *black* virgins, who are here regarded as peculiarly sacred. Numbers of little stalls were set out covered with *Kirchweih Nudel*, a very good sort of cold pudding. The open space in which the lovely Au church stands was very gay, and under the acacia-trees, which form an avenue along one side of the square, hundreds of people were congregated.

Two streams of people, principally peasants, were ascending the church-steps: so great indeed was the crowd that I think I must have stood twenty minutes before I could gain admittance, and when I did it was along with peasant women in their Tartar fur caps, and rosary and prayer-book in hand, and with men in red or broad-striped waistcoats and long-skirted blue coats. And then how impressive was the sight! The air was heavy with incense; the graceful, slender, white columns rose up like the clustered stems of a palm-grove! The sun shone and glowed through the gloriously painted windows. They represent the Virgin, Christ, and the Apostles moving among groves, or quiet, solemn temples and halls, or calmly rising forth against brilliant or pearly skies. In one compartment, the Virgin, a child of twelve or thirteen, is taken by her parents to the high priest. She kneels before him, and Joseph places the ring upon her finger. In another, she sits with the Infant Christ in her lap on the ass, journeying towards Egypt. And in another division she is seen ascending to heaven. I knew that these windows were very beautiful, but it was only to-day that their full beauty burst upon me. The exquisite groups stained upon them, with their correct drawing, and rich draperies, are inclosed, as it were, in jewelled shrines; the upper portions of the window being filled with Gothic work of every brilliant color, like missal pages. Pity only that too much yellow is used.

But if the windows excited my first attention, the people attracted my attention in the second place. All the seats were filled with devout peasants, and numbers stood. As the church, however, was large, there was no unpleasant crush. All was silent as death, except when, from the far end of the church, came the voices of children chanting, or you caught the murmured words of the priest, as he raised the Host before the high-altar; and then the crowd responded with one deep, sonorous voice, which could alone be compared to the hoarse, monotonous, wild sound of billows, rolling inward to the shore — not when there is a rough sea, but when all is solemn and calm.

After a time I left the church, and not being inclined to return home, and finding that all the music from the public-houses, and all the eating, and the dancing, were very inharmonious to my then state of mind, I wandered on towards the plain, and feasted my eyes on a view of the Alps, which to-day appeared fairly to have stalked towards Munich, so near did they seem, — of a tender, quiet, blue-grey, but their forms gigantic, stern, Alpine!

Another evening, after a day of industrious work, when we were in a particularly cheerful mood, I suggested to Clare that as it was so sunny and delicious, we should drink our coffee in a picturesque old orchard which I had discovered in one of my exploratory expeditions through the suburb of St. Anna. It is a pretty walk this, through the suburb to the coffee-house orchard, which joins the English Garden. You cross first the corner of a very large field, acres of which are covered with huge heaps of timber — enormous pines, which have been floated down from the Alps. The tall trees of the English Garden form a back-ground to the field; and then, passing orchards and cottages, and country houses, you arrive at the coffee-house, a bright white house, with a deal of pale sea-green paint about it, standing high, approached by a flight of steps, and having a certain Russian look. The orchard in which it stands is a grand old orchard, full of aged apple-trees, under which are some hundreds of seats.

On the former occasions when I passed it there must have been many hundreds of people drinking coffee there. On this evening, however, all was deserted; so much so, in fact, that there was no coffee to be had. After resting, therefore, a few minutes under an apple-tree, we proceeded on our way, when, turning into the English Garden, behold! another coffee-house, a very small one, peeping out from under the trees. Coffee and Wine-house of the Kingdom of Heaven, '*Zum Himmelreich*,' was painted on an arched sign over the gate. So extraordinary an appellation could not be disregarded, however contrary to our English notions.

'Let us try how coffee tastes in the Kingdom of Heaven,' said I; and in we went.

The Kingdom of Heaven, however, was also apparently deserted, except by a pair of lovers, a young girl in a white dress, and a student in a scarlet cap and black velvet coat, and by a picturesque group of old peasants, men and women, who sat on a bench before the door, and drank beer; the student also drank beer — the girl took nothing. She sate with her back turned towards him, and evidently was very unhappy. I think they must have had a quarrel: what a shame to quarrel in the Kingdom of Heaven! I went into the house, and ordered coffee from a woman whom I met with a huge coffee-mill in her hand. She said it should be ready in a minute, — fresh, capital coffee!

We seated ourselves at the end of a long verandah which was covered with vines, at the end opposite to where the lovers were, and noticed all around us, to occupy the time till the coffee appeared. Coffee at length made its appearance — vile coffee and peppery bread; and leaving the lovers still unreconciled, we bade adieu to the 'Kingdom of Heaven,' and betook ourselves home in the delicious twilight.

There is always something very picturesque in a German landscape. To-day I walked to a village which I had often passed, but never till now penetrated into. There is a picturesque little church, with a tall roof and quaint white tower, crowned with an oriental-looking red-brick dome; a row of poplars, just bordered here and there with streaks of yellow, waved quietly in front of the church, and over the low churchyard wall hung the branches of a lime which was already quite gorgeous in its autumnal livery, the richest gold and the deepest olive. I sate down upon the delicious dry grass and among dry fallen leaves beneath another row of poplars. How pleasant it was! The air was filled with an aromatic scent of leaves — not a smell of decay but of dried sap; and all was so calm. There was a certain sadness, but a peace in everything; there was not a sound, scarcely a living creature to be seen, only an old peasant woman leading a goat by a cord as it fed along the grass.

I went onward into the pleasant little village, past small cottages and farms, and quiet undulating orchards, with here and there a seat placed under some fine old apple or plum-tree, passed gardens gay with huge sunflowers, and stopped to admire a lovely little bit of color at the entrance of a gentleman's villa. Imagine the doorway festooned with crimson Virginia creeper, and opposite the open door a Madonna standing in a niche of the wall! The Madonna seemed wreathed round with crimson leaves, and shrubs turning gold and russet, and varied with every tint of green from olive to apple, were growing on either side and in front of the door. The effect was very lovely.

A desire now possessed me to walk on still further to the second church of this same village, the tall, strange-looking, *pea-green* spire of which had long attracted my curiosity. I had seen it from the road, seen it from the English Garden. On all sides it was a conspicuous object. At last I reached it; the roof was very slanting and steep, and covered with red tiles — such a strange, quiet, little church! The churchyard was crowded with graves thickly overgrown with flowers; so that what with the flowers planted on the graves and with the number of garlands hung upon the crosses, the whole churchyard resembled a flower-garden. Some of the graves were very lovely; and either suspended to the cross, which of course stands at the head of each grave, or sunk into the little flower-border of the grave itself, was a small cup containing holy water, often with a little branch or a flower in it, to sprinkle the grave with. I noticed that upon some of the graves the peasants had laid the red berries of the mountain ash, or had stuck them into the soil in form of crosses and stars. In one corner of the churchyard was a quaint little shrine, also with a steep red-tiled roof; and above the low white church-wall rose the distant woods of the English Garden, so rich in their autumnal coloring.

CHAPTER VI.

THE STUDENT'S LIGHTS AND SHADOWS.

It is a pity that P———, the frame-maker, does not know what happened to me this morning; it would give him a higher opinion of himself than ever. We wanted a couple of 'mounts' made for our groups of flowers from the studio-field, and were advised to get them made at a shop just opposite to where we live. To this little shop I carried our drawings this morning, together with one of P.'s capital mounts, which I had with me, as a pattern. I had to wait an immense time in the shop. Mr. Appleshoe — I anglicize his name — was making his toilet. At length, when my patience was completely exhausted, Appleshoe made his appearance in a tremendous hurry and bustle, as though the fate of Europe depended upon his advent in a distant quarter of the globe, and he had forgotten his appointment till the very last moment. Unlucky Appleshoe! I saw the moment was inopportune; nevertheless, as I had waited so long, I was determined I would order the mounts, — it would but detain him a moment. I had seen certain individuals in Germany, and elsewhere also, who are in a mighty bustle about trifles, and as slow as snails when a matter of importance requires haste. Appleshoe struck me decidedly as belonging to this class; therefore I had less compunction in stopping the unlucky man as he was rushing out of the shop.

With a deeply-drawn sigh, and the most piteous expression of countenance, he laid down the roll of paper he had in his hand, and condescended graciously to listen to my order.

I showed him, on the drawing, the shape of the mount we required — a rather peculiar geometric shape; but one, had he understood his business, as easy to make as an oval or circular mount. He looked greatly perplexed.

'Perhaps,' said I, 'it is not your business to do these things?'

'Oh yes, yes!' with a deep bewildered sigh; 'it was his business, but he was going out; perhaps I would call again, or leave the drawings?'

'No! I could do neither one nor the other,' was my reply: 'Could he not take the dimensions? that was but a matter of a couple of moments.'

'Well! he supposed he must *trace* the mount.'

Good heavens! only imagine P. *tracing* a mount. Would he not fly into a passion if one suggested such an insult! Well, the mount was traced at length, by Mr. Appleshoe, in a clumsy, blind-beetle sort of a fashion, but it *was* traced; and then I proceeded to explain that the lines of the mounts must be slightly curved.

'Curved? curved?' murmured Mr. Appleshoe, musingly.

'Yes, curved!' exclaimed I, growing quite impatient and exasperated: 'don't you indeed know how to curve a line? — well, I never heard such an absurd thing in my life! but if you can't do it, do what you can without the curve;' and went on to explain about a gold line, and two pencil lines that he must rule, between which we should wash in pale tint of color.

'No, that indeed I cannot do: I cannot use a pencil —

that belongs to drawing! I am a bookbinder; draw I cannot; I am a bookbinder!' said he.

I fairly laughed outright; it was too absurd.

Up towards me, at this moment, from a further part of the shop, came a great stout man, with a big, red face, and a big, white beard, and a very solemn mien; he had been listening to my discourse, and probably his national pride had been wounded by my triumphant exhibition of P.'s English 'mount' as a *chef-d'œuvre.* Up he slowly came, and slowly looking down at the drawings, whilst Mr. Appleshoe gazed up at his large countenance with a feeble appealing expression, pronounced these oracular words —

'No! Mr. Appleshoe cannot use a pencil; he cannot curve the lines; much easier draw the flowers!'

'Oh yes,' sang Appleshoe's weak voice as chorus; 'much easier draw the flowers; I cannot curve the lines!'

'Well, then, good morning to you, Mr. Appleshoe!' exclaimed I; and presently was standing before Clare, with a face, she declares, perfectly white with contempt, and a torrent of contemptuous epithets bursting from my lips.

Munich, as an art-city, is a glorious abode; but for small common-place matters it is somewhat less attractive. The apathy and dreaminess of the tradespeople often fairly astound one.

I only hope their dreaminess is not contagious! Clare persists that it is, and that Anna has caught the infection. Anna certainly, the other day, in a fit of abstraction, nearly walked into a branch of the Isar: it would have been very romantic, would it not, to have been drowned in 'the Isar rolling rapidly?' Anna too, the other day, was in a wild state of alarm about her purse, which was missing, but which, after a search of extreme anguish of mind, she discovered, most carefully wrapt up by her own hands, in a paper, and laid beside her on the tea-tray, and where Clare, with a burst of merriment, informed her she had seen her place it some half-hour before, whilst, with grave face she was discoursing upon some transcendentalism. I know also, very well, that Anna this morning boiled a tea-spoon, instead of an egg, for her breakfast! Yes, it is very alarming, this infection of dreaminess and abstraction of mind. For myself, I made an excuse for poor Anna, knowing how she supports upon her head '*the Worry-pole.*' I dare say people do not generally know what this infection is, although they themselves probably bear one always about with them, sprouting out of their brains.

Clare last night made a sketch of Anna's 'Worry-pole.' It is not a 'May-pole,' such as we see in the villages about here,—a tall pole, upon which, on either side, and running down from the tip-top till within a certain distance of the earth, are suspended little figures and ornaments, the insignia of the various village trades, and a pole that is wreathed with flowers upon a May-day,—no, it is not a merry, joyous, light-hearted May-pole, but a 'Worry-pole!'—It is a pole planted on the head of many an unlucky mortal, and though invisible to the people about him or her, he or she wanders through the world with its tremendous weight always pressing upon them: and upon this pole, from the bottom upwards, swing insignia. When I look at Clare's sketch, I don't blame Anna for boiling the tea-spoon or wrapping up her purse. At the top of the pole, behold the stern face of a great painter; he has a lowering brow, an upraised finger, and the mystic words '*Arbeit! Arbeit! Composition! Composition!*' proceed out of his lips: beneath him come casts of arms, legs, bodies, studies of draperies, the Anatomist's '*Vade-Me-*

cum,' models, compositions; then commence the domestic worries — a voluminous correspondence, typified by letters of all forms and sizes, — home-sickness in the form of certain English faces, — Munich acquaintance who have not yet found out Clare and Anna's peculiarity of never returning calls,—bills, undarned stockings, dinners, candles, 'Spiritus,' a gigantic flea, — and Clare seated, quietly drawing, in the midst of all, because, forsooth, she cannot speak or understand the delightful German tongue! And all hung upon the tall pole which sprouts out of poor little Anna's skull, whilst she wanders along painfully, with care-worn face, under her arm a portfolio, in one hand a big key, in the other a big umbrella. She is wading through a desert of dust: on one hand the Munich sun is scorching her with his rays, on the other the Munich rain is falling in torrents, and before her arise the bad stenches of Munich in the shape of venomous imps. In the far distance are seen the shores of 'Albion's Isle;' from which, in long trains, proceed many men, women, and children, — English acquaintances, who are just commencing to hook themselves on to the 'worry-pole!' Unlucky Anna! who wonders now that she boiled the tea-spoon?

But if from 'Albion's shore' proceeds the stream of acquaintance, Justina is also proceeding! Beloved Justina! before whom no 'worry-pole' ever could exist for an hour as a 'worry-pole:' her strong, fresh spirit, like a joyous sea-breeze, always driving away the worries before it, and converting the pole into a 'May-pole'; her genial hands wreathing it with the freshest, the most aromatic of flowers!

Yes, indeed, Justina will soon be here: Clare has never seen her, but they will meet as friends: Justina's name is one of our watch-words. Now we are constantly arranging what is to be done 'when Justina is here,' and wondering 'how certain things will strike Justina.'

August 30th. — Clare this week has been designing at home, and I have been alone at the studio. You know my old *penchant* for being solitary; but our days together have been so beautiful, that I began to fancy that, after all, solitude was not such an attractive thing. Still at times it is for the soul's health to be entirely alone. These long, quiet summer days have been filled with a peculiar charm and blessedness. There was a soothing, beneficial influence in the deep peacefulness of the room, unbroken except by the chiming of distant bells, or by the familiar sounds of the little suburb, breaking at intervals upon the ear, and only rendering the calmness deeper. There was the regular practising of a musician on the horn and violin, and the sound of a woman's voice calling 'Julius! Julius!' We have often wondered, Clare and I, who this Julius could be. Certainly some idle little lad, everlastingly playing in the street; the son, perhaps, of the musician, and wanted at home to practise his scales, or to fetch water, or chop wood! And as afternoon glided on, and the sunlight glided with it into the studio, flecking the red wall with quivering lights and shadows, flung from the bowery vine without, through the warm air and thick leaves have swelled the strains of music from the band playing to gay groups of idlers in the Hof Garten, Meyerischen Garten, or Englischen Garten. How calmly, how poetically unreal, has all our life risen up before me; and as my hand has mechanically and monotonously kept drawing, the hours have rolled away so beautifully, so sweetly, yet alas! so rapidly. And then, too, how pleasant has it been, after hours of quiet industry, when the mind has absorbed itself in the contemplation of bones and muscles, working problems as to their insertion, origin, and actions; and the universe seemed alone to consist of *communis digitorum*, *extensor carpi radialis longior*, and such charming individuals and abstractions; and cobwebs spun themselves over your brain, to fling open the old grey heavy door, and stand confronting the freshness and splendor of the outer world. What a flash of sunshine! what a singing of birds! what a nodding of flowers! what a rejoicing and carolling of the whole creation! God forgive me, for having for so many hours, in the darkness of the inner world, forgotten Thy glorious external world!

I cannot conceive how many of our English painters can paint in their dull London studios, where chimney-pots and lead-colored streets, and lead-colored glimpses of sky, are all with which they can externally refresh their spirits: and where, instead of the song of birds and the murmur of waters, there is the nerve-exciting and brain-deadening roar of wheels. However, much depends upon use and temperament. But the inhabitant of a town studio would indeed rejoice with an exceeding joy could he only wander forth as I — happy, privileged mortal! — did this afternoon into the sunny field, leaving care and industry behind in the studio, and with the sunshine bathing my unbonneted head, sate down upon a flowery bank behind the coppice, where I could be seen of no one; and forgetting the '*vade-mecum*' I carried in my hand, sank into the most lovely and happy of summer day-dreams.

September 1*st.* — I heard just now, rising from the street, a murmur as of many feet and voices. I looked out, and beheld a procession. Crimson and blue, orange and green banners were waving beneath me; crucifixes were wreathed with fresh leaves and flowers: there were trains of white-robed children and young girls, some bearing baskets of fruit and flowers, others, small sheaves of corn and barley. It was the Festival of Autumn. It was very poetical. There was a train of friars in their brown frocks, and of priests in their robes of gold and scarlet and white linen; there were long lines of aged men and of women. Behind came on a dense murmuring muttering crowd of all ages and of both sexes. The people in the street, as the procession passed, paused, raising their hats and caps, and joined in the muttered prayer. I watched the long procession winding through the quaint street, till it was hidden from my sight by a picturesque mass of buildings. The gay banners fluttered in the breeze, the sun glittered upon the crucifixes, and the murmur came dreamily from the distance, fraught with a strange tenderness.

CHAPTER VII.

JUSTINA'S VISIT. — A GROUP OF ART-SISTERS.

September 2d. — How delicious was my meeting with Justina yesterday! At the moment when I was sitting at a solitary breakfast — for Clare was yet asleep — with my mind full of Justina, and after having arranged and dusted everything in our rooms, to be ready for her, I heard the outer door open. I said to myself, 'Justina!' The room door opened, and she entered.

Of course the first thing we did was to cry for joy, and then to gaze at each other, to see whether really she were Justina and I were Anna. It seemed strange, dream-like, impossible, that we two could be in Munich together.

. . . . . .

Before long we set off to Kaulbach's studio — Justina, Clare, and I; but we could not resist going a little out of the way to walk down the beautiful Ludwig Strasse into the Ludwig Kirche. Many things struck her much: the rich coloring introduced into the architecture, the pervading presence of one great artistic thought throughout the city. She was more impressed than I expected her to be. I had always imagined the German school of art would not find a response in her soul; but she declared that an entirely new class of beauty, a fresh field of delight and thought, had been opened to her.

When we entered the Ludwig Kirche, I saw her form

dilate with emotion. She seemed to grow taller and grander; a rich flush came over her face; and her eyes filled with tears.

'I do not feel this,' said she, 'to be the work of man, but of nature. The arched roof produces upon me the same thrill as the sky itself!'

Then we walked through the light and shadow of the English Garden — and I pointed out to her those particular spots that had always reminded me of her landscapes; and across the timber-field and the bridge over the mill-stream, and along the side of the rushing water, till we came to the grey, wooden door opening into the studio-field, and so along the narrow path between the thick grass and flowers, in the pleasant sunshine across the field. But I was obliged to hold Justina's hand in mine, else nothing could have persuaded me that this was not one of my many dreams. We passed through the bushes; we stood under the vine; we opened the heavy grey door: we were in the little room. The clock ticked as loudly as usual; there stood the two sister easels, and a sister painting-blouse hung on each: the casts, the books, the green jug with flowers, all looked so familiar, that to set to work at once and fancy that I had only dreamed of Justina, seemed the most natural thing. But there she really stood in the body!

And having now seen what we were beginning, and having taken into her memory all the features of the beloved little room, so that she could picture our lives when she should have again vanished, we went into the other studio.

Thoroughly did she enter into the spirit of Kaulbach's works; she is worthy to understand them. She thinks, with me, that for intellect, and dramatic power and poetry, he is superior to any living artist.

We three, as it happened, had the studio all to ourselves; and we stood and sat before those grand works, in the most perfect repose and silence, and drank in the whole spirit of the place.

Justina looked grandly beautiful, with that golden hair of hers crowning her as with a halo of glory, and her whole soul looking through her eyes, and quivering on her lips as she gazed at the pictures. I longed for Kaulbach to quietly enter, and see her standing before them like a creature worthy to be immortalized by him, — an exception to the puny prosaic race of modern days, who are unworthy to live in art, — who only deserve to pass away and be forgotten.

But the sublimest intellectual emotion can, after all, last only for a time, seeing that we all, the most spiritual even, are possessed of a double nature, — body and soul. It was now half-past eleven o'clock, and we were grown very hungry, for our joy at meeting had prevented our eating much breakfast; so we betook ourselves to the Meyerischen Garten, paying the *Hausmeisterin* a visit by the way, — so that Justina might have an idea of a German kitchen with all its picturesque characteristics; might have a glimpse of her poetical little sitting-room and bed-room, made so beautiful by Kaulbach's prints and sketches; that she might see the *Hausmeisterin;* that I might have the joy of saying to the good woman, 'Here is my beloved friend out of England, the sister of my heart!'

What a pleasant dinner was ours at the Meyerischen Garten! What joy we had in all three going into the kitchen and ordering *three* portions! What a delight to see Justina's amusement at the odd look of everything! What merriment in our little bower over our dinner when it arrived! The flock of turkeys came round us as usual; all the external was the same, but the spirit was very unusual which reigned at our little dinner-table. No more 'grinding.' *Flexors* and *extensors* were forgotten; such things as anatomy, or work, or fatigue, or home-sickness, no longer existed. All was the joyous, blessed present!

Justina entered thoroughly into the spirit of our life, laughing at the want of salt-spoons and such luxuries: wiping the forks for our second course, our *Mehl-speise*, on the table-cloth, and drinking the coffee with an indescribable relish.

After this dinner, which Justina enjoyed with all the keener relish, from the contrast it made to the life she was leading, — a life of the highest respectability, a life of first-class travelling, of couriers, of the grandest hotels, of English solemnity, and aristocratic propriety. She declared again and again that there never was such a delicious, free, poetical life as ours; and she was perfectly right. I fully believe that she will in a while spend a month with us; perhaps join us in our Tyrolean trip.

Justina is gone! I am alone this evening, as Clare is out with some English friends.

Thank God that she has been here! We all agree that three such gay delightful days never before were spent by three such accordant spirits; days which we shall never forget, and out of which Justina declares that something great and good must come. She, the very embodiment of health, soul, and body, without a morbid or mean emotion ever having sullied her spirit — with freshness as of the morning, and strength as of a young oak — has had the most beneficial influence on both of us through her intense love of nature and art, through the same aims in life, yet all three so different from each other. Clare, a thorough creature of genius, born to success whether she had devoted herself to music, the drama, or painting, — an artist in the true sense of the word, with a dramatic power of expression in everything she attempts, and of a self-absorbed character by nature. I, possessing an intense devotion and love of art, of a sensitive, poetical temperament, which at times becomes somewhat morbid, yet earnest, persevering, with a constant aspiration after the spiritual, and a firmer, much firmer faith in the Unseen than either of the others. Cannot you see how great must be our usefulness to each other, — our influence upon each other? We have been all three struck by this; we have felt our peculiar individualities come out in strongest contrast.

What schemes of life have not been worked out whilst we have been together! as though this, our meeting here, were to be the germ of a beautiful sisterhood in Art, of which we have all dreamed long, and by which association we might be enabled to do noble things.

Justina, with her expansive views, and her strong feelings in favor of associated homes, talked now of an Associated Home, at some future day, for such 'sisters' as had no home of their own. She had a large scheme of what she calls the Outer and Inner Sisterhood. The Inner, to consist of the Art-sisters bound together by their one object, and which she fears may never number many in their band; the Outer Sisterhood to consist of women, all workers and all striving after a pure moral life, but belonging to any profession, any pursuit. All should be bound to help each other in such ways as were most accordant with their natures and characters. Among these would be needle-women — good Elizabeth ——'s, whose real pleasure is needle-work, whose genius lies in shaping and sewing, and whose sewing never comes undone, — the good Elizabeth! how unspeakably useful would such as thou be to the poor Art-sisters, whose stockings must be mended! Perhaps, too, there would be some one sister whose turn was preserving, and pickling, and cooking; she, too, would be a treasure every day, and very ornamental and agreeable would be her preparation of cakes and good things for the evening meetings once or twice a month. And what beautiful meetings those were to be, as we pictured them in the different studios! In fact, all has been present so clearly to my imagination, that I can hardly believe them mere castles in the air.

Justina entered our rooms on the second day of her visit, — after coming, of course, through the pestilent passage, — and exclaimed —

'You poor silly creatures! do you not know that you are killing yourselves as fast as you can by living in these close rooms and breathing this bad air?'

'Yes, we know it,' we replied.

'As for Anna,' continued the energetic Justina, 'I am angry with her; she who ought to know better, she who so thoroughly understands sanitary laws. What would the 'Pater' say if he found you here? he would soon have you away. You will grow as pale as ghosts if you stay; and you can't help either of you growing morbid; you'll paint morbid pictures if you breathe this air! Don't think that I have only just perceived it; I felt it the moment I came near your door, and I've been thinking of it ever since; and I know that it is my duty to drag you out of this place. If I saw a child with its head in a gutter or a drain I should drag it out, — and much more you.'

'Yes; but Justina, ——' we began.

'If it is the money,' continued Justina, not listening to what we had to say, 'I'll pay your month's rent myself, and you shall move to-morrow. We will set out and hunt for rooms this very day; it will be capital fun. We'll move all your things to-morrow; pack them up here, and unpack them in the new rooms: I have a surfeit of churches, and pictures, and statues upon me. It will be a delightful change; I shall not be happy else; I can't think of your living here, I can't! I shall smell that smell in Milan — Venice — everywhere. I must see you in new rooms, and know how you will be in the winter; and I shall be connected with them in your thoughts if we move in this prompt, unique sort of way.'

'But, Justina,' we now argued, 'there are now no rooms to be had: all Munich moves four times a year; we can get nothing till the end of the quarter; we have tried already, but in vain.'

Justina, however, was resolute, and we set off on our expedition.

Having confided to Justina our desire for the winter to have rooms near the studio, we commenced our search in the St. Anna suburb. I think what we saw that day both astonished and amused Justina. First we went to Mrs. ——'s friend, the miller's wife, which was at the nearest of the mills; and, after passing through a timber-yard, and then through a picturesque and really extensive garden, gay with sunflowers, we came to a long, low, white-washed house, covered with a vine. The miller's wife, instead of taking us into her house, pointed from the outside to two windows, which she said belonged to the rooms she had to let, — two southern windows, cheerful-looking from being draped with very clean white muslin curtains, and from being embowered with vine-leaves. Yes; very pleasant they looked outside; but, — Could we see the inside?

After a good deal of hesitation and mysterious consultation in a low voice with another woman, and something being said about her father who was sick, we were told that we might see the rooms if we would excuse, etc. etc.!

We were accordingly taken up a narrow staircase, and along a narrow and apparently interminable passage; a door was opened, and behold a crowd of people busied in various occupations, — sewing, eating, and heaven knows what beside; but all in a crowd and bustle, and breathing an atmosphere that took away our breath; and, seated on a bed — Oh, heavens! a sight which neither Justina, Clare, nor I, shall forget for many a day: — we saw it but for an instant, but it was daguerreotyped for ever. An old man, nearly dead! They had propped him up, and were giving him some soup: the poor skeleton legs, bare from the knees, hung down the bedside, lank and horrible, and discolored; whilst a wretched shirt barely covered his meagre shrunk chest and arms, and a whisp of a blue handkerchief was tied round his throat. One instant we saw the vision; then turned away quite sick. Poor, unhappy, neglected old man! And this was one of the rooms which was to be let! The room in itself was not amiss, if it had been cleaned and had fresh furniture, and the second opening out of it was really pretty: but could we ever get over that horrible vision, or should we like to live with people who allowed life, much more death, to be so miserable and squalid?

We saw in the garden, as we passed out, a group of respectable-looking people taking supper at a little table under some trees.

'That is the Baroness and her family,' said the miller's wife, — 'the Baroness, who lives at that house:' and she pointed to a handsome, quaint, old gabled house, which also stood in the garden. We ourselves should have enjoyed the garden very much; and when we got out among the sunflowers, and smelt the fresh evening scents, and heard the leaves rustle over our heads, we began to think whether we might not after all manage with the rooms.

But no! we had seen that which we could not forget, and we went on to search further.

Next we went to the house of a well-to-do carpenter,—but there was nothing; then to a very nice clean house, a *Wasser-Anstalt* (a Hydropathic Establishment). Such a pretty place! with a sweet fresh garden. But the people of the place,—a stately elderly man, like a character in one of Kotzebue's plays, and his wife, who was dressed as gaily as a tulip,—would, however, have nothing to do with us. It was in vain that we mentioned the most respectable of our acquaintance, male and female; they knew nothing of them. But we were well known to the Baroness von ——; naming the most aristocratic of our acquaintance. Were we indeed! It might be so; but they had no rooms to let,—that is to say, they had none to let unless we came recommended by the physician of the establishment. But, in short, they had not any rooms which would suit us!

First the man looked at us, and then the woman, and then they looked at one another; and between them both the above decision was come to. No; they had no rooms which would suit us!

Mrs. —— and I laughed heartily as we turned from the door; and Justina and Clare, neither of them understanding German, thought, good souls! that this most respectable couple had been very polite to us.

I should think we went after this to a dozen other places; and what places we saw! places to make one hang oneself, or throw oneself into the mill-stream. Lastly, when standing in the twilight on the bridge, just opposite to the shop of our fat baker-woman, out she came, waddling towards us, to ask us if we wanted anything; and on our relating to her our bootless quest, she exclaimed, her whole face lighting up at once, that she had just what would suit us. Of course we went in to see the rooms, through the hot little shop, through a still hotter little room,—a very oven,—and then *the one* room presented itself which she had to offer: 'a beautiful room, a friendly room as ever was!' she declared, good fat soul! in a coarse rough voice,—'a pretty, friendly little room, which would just suit the dear little young ladies!'

What a room it was! small almost as a coffin, underground almost, damp and hot at the same time, long and narrow; we should have died of the Munich fever in it before a month was out! But it would not have done to affront the old lady by telling her so; therefore we had a good excuse in requiring two rooms at least, and away we went.

Such was our expedition after lodgings. And when we returned home to our formerly despised abode, Justina was obliged to confess that it was really splendid, clean, and wholesome, and a very palace, after what we had seen.

CHAPTER VIII.

A BARBARIC TEMPLE BUILT IN THE IMAGINATION — A GENRE PICTURE IN THE NEW HOME.

The day that Justina left, we all paid the Bavaria a visit. I do not know how it had happened that we had never before been close to the Bavaria; but such is the case. The Bavaria stands upon a meadow outside the town, a broad green expanse, commanding a view of the distant Alps. You see a tall wooden tower flanked by two wooden wings. This tower and the wings inclose the colossal statue, and the temple which is erecting behind the statue. We had seen the sun frequently set behind this building, and the lightning flashing behind the Bavaria among the evening clouds; and yet, until this sunny morning, we had never paid her a visit.

As we drew near, above the scaffolding, towering up into the blue morning sky, we saw a gigantic, beautiful, round arm, upholding a heavy garland of oak-leaves. We stood at the foot of the statue — pigmies!

Wooden stairs ran up around her; huge scaffolding rose into the sunny, dewy air; heavy enormous folds of bronze drapery rolled to her colossal feet, which appeared formed to trample feeble human beings into dust. Ladders were placed against her large limbs; workmen in caps and aprons were busied about her; they looked human insects! And then, — her countenance! Those stern, placid, gloriously beautiful features expressed a soul large, awful, poetical, and as infinitely removed from all the pettinesses of humanity as was her form from all conventionality.

There is a power in this revelation which made me stand aghast! my spirit felt swayed involuntarily before it as though it had been a thing of life, an existence possessed of mighty power in the world, — not a mere statue of bronze: she seemed akin to the Sphynx; an awful being, a mystery, an embodiment of a spirit as yet but partially revealed to humanity.

Justina stood transfixed before the colossus. 'Of all the marvels of this marvellous Munich, truly this is the greatest!' she exclaimed.

Behind the statue, as I observed before, a temple is being erected. The walls are already raised, and so are the columns and the frieze. Workmen were busy fluting the columns. The base alone of many of the columns was fluted, — the shaft rising with a bold Egyptian kind of character, and then unfolding into the Doric capital. I heard some workmen saying to Justina's friends —

'This is to be painted in fresco!' My imagination instantly suggested that these columns, according to Egyptian and Indian taste, were to glow with the most brilliant and barbaric colors, — scarlet, green, azure, gold! I saw in fancy the long line of these strange columns supporting the marble frieze, stretching on either hand of the mighty Bavaria: the brick wall behind the pillars was knocked down — the vast green plain stretched away to the sunset! The heavens were flooded with light and glowed with hues more brilliant than the tints upon the columns, and the sinking sun cast long shadows upon the green sward from columns and statue.

Justina and I had the same vision of a barbaric temple,

— a temple belonging to the spirit of ancient India rather than to Greece. How grand, we exclaimed, is this union of apparently opposite styles of architecture! it is alone the blending of classic grandeur with a sterner, with a more barbarous age, which could harmonize with a Bavaria!

Ours was, however, but a deception of imagination. A little further on, and these shafts were fluted the entire length — their strange character had vanished. 'How is this?' I asked of the workmen: 'I thought I heard you say the columns were to be painted in fresco?'

'It is the *wall* behind the columns that is to be in fresco,' he replied.

I saw instantly what was the intention, and doubtless the Doric temple will be beautiful, as are all King Ludwig's creations; still I must regret the destruction of our ideal barbaric temple, with its vast extent of plain gleaming out beyond the gorgeously tinted columns! As yet, my imagination feels it to be infinitely grander than the correct Doric temple, with its rows of busts of great men placed within it. What have human beings to do, however great, in the presence of a Bavaria?

It is a strange ascent up into the Bavaria's head, where you sit within her face upon bronze sofas; and through a loop-hole in the rich mass of her hair can gaze out over the distant city and across the plain towards the dreamy Alpine chain. It is a strange ascent, and yet a stranger descent, by that slender iron staircase, which in the gloom at times seems lost in the rough dark chasm into which you are descending; you feel held up by an iron network in the centre of a wild cavern of volcanic rock.

Next month is to be the great Bavaria Festival.

September 22d. — It is a pity Justina cannot see our

new abode! Even she would be satisfied. We had a fresh hunt for lodgings, Clare and I: not after romantic lodgings in mills or at carpenters', — we had had enough of that with Justina — but in the neighborhood of the aristocratic Ludwig Strasse, where, now that Michaelmas is nearly arrived, and everybody flitting, lodgings may be had.

The instant we entered our present rooms, we exclaimed with one voice, 'Here is our home!' The rooms have elegant walnut furniture in them, are beautifully clean, and the situation is deliciously quiet: there is no more dirt, no more slovenliness, and there are no more bad stenches! You enter the house by a clean, airy, square passage through the regular heavy *Porte-cochère* of a German house, and ascend to the different *étages* by a beautifully clean oak staircase. On the first floor I see a Professor lives; on the second lives a Major; and on the third live we! But we do not live all alone in the little dwelling, of course. We have the rooms fronting the street; and the Frau *Rentsbeamtinn* Thekla Victoria Carolina Werff — *Anglicè*, Mrs. Tax-gatheress Thekla Victoria, &c. — and her Fräulein sister Sänchen, live at the back. The dwelling belongs to Madame Thekla, and her Fräulein sister is the servant. She was very busy scouring the day we came to look at the rooms, and she has been scouring every day since, I fancy. She has one of the most peculiar faces I ever saw — a droll face — ugly, yet agreeable: she is a character, I am certain. These two old souls have the prettiest, cleanest, little *pink*, not *white*-washed, kitchen that ever was seen, cramful of quaint pots and pans, and tubs, of every shape and description of material — copper, brass, tin, earthenware, delft, china, and wood. They have also a room opening out of the kitchen. This second room is bed-room and parlor. It is also cramful of possessions: there are, first of all, the sister-beds, with a huge crucifix hanging upon the wall between them; there are heavy chests of drawers, too, and quantities of Bohemian glass, and a portrait of the departed Mr. Tax-gatherer Werff, very smiling and wooden, in a striped buff-waistcoat and blue coat, with one hand in his waist-coat pocket; and the portrait also of the Mr. Tax-gatherer's widow when she was his young wife, some twenty years ago — a lady with eyes as black as sloes, her hair dressed in tall loops upon the very top of her head, and adorned with a brilliant tíara; she is radiant also in a green satin dress and crimson scarf. The young wife is represented, of course, slimmer than the widow now appears. Yet, as the good Madame Thekla sits knitting beside her window among her birds, perched up there, almost like a bird herself, upon that high step in the window, I can perceive a considerable resemblance between the lady with black eyes and brilliant tiara and the elderly lady in the dark blue and white striped morning gown, and with the thin black hair streaked with gray elaborately plaited low down in the neck.

Birds and clocks, one would say, were Madame Thekla's passion — at least birds are: clocks, I am assured, were the passion of the 'blessed Tax-gatherer.' Here are larks, buntings, blackbirds, — sparrows even, if I am to believe my ears and eyes; and the chirping, whistling, pecking, fluttering, in Madame Thekla's window is something inconceivable! I wonder she does not go crazy, sitting there hour after hour as she does.

The first night we slept here I feared that I myself should have gone crazy, — not from the birds but from the clocks! In the Werffs' kitchen, and in the Werffs' bed-room, there are clocks, all of which may be heard striking into our rooms; one of them is a cuckoo-clock with chimes, and in each of our rooms there is a time-piece: in Clare's room, hanging just over her sofa, is a picture of a gloomy cathedral, — it has a clock which booms forth the hours and the quarters with chimes, also! What an astonishment it was to us when the cathedral first boomed forth the time! Clare sprang up from the sofa, where she had been resting herself after the fatigue of flitting, as though she had been shot. Opposite to my bed stands a French time-piece like a small temple. Madame Thekla seems maliciously to place her clocks precisely where they may most unpleasantly remind one of the flight of time. All through that first night how those clocks did chime — hours and quarters, quarters and hours, like mad things! And as the clocks were not particularly accurate, they chimed one after another till the whole hour was a mass of chimes — booming, tinkling, striking high and low, slow and fast, till one grew frantic. I was certainly only restrained by my good angel from starting up and dashing the temple to pieces.

'Oh, Madame Thekla!' cried I, the next morning, 'we must have these clocks stopped, they drive us mad; they will kill us!'

'Don't the gracious young ladies, then, like to know how the time passes?' remarked the astonished Madame Thekla: 'but I remember, you English don't like clocks: the English gentleman who once lodged here also disliked to know how the time passed; he ran into my room, as you have done, gracious young lady, the first morning he was here, like a mad gentleman, and asked me why there was all this "Devil's music," — [*Teufels-Musik*] — yes, "Devil's music," he called it! and said if it went on, he should set off!'

'And so shall we, Madame Thekla!' cried I, much amused; 'neither can we stand the Devil's music!'

Thank heaven, the 'Devil's music' has ended in our rooms, but in Madame Thekla's it still chimes on; and this, together with the carolling of the larks, awakes me every morning betimes.

Yes; we imagine that we shall be very comfortable with these good Werffs. We only fear they may be too *fussy;* they are so very good to us, so motherly, so over-kind! How much they would delight in our being ill! Their highest delight would be wrapping us up in bed and making us drink gruel! I see their delighted, yet anxious, old faces administering the gruel! Pray heaven they may be disappointed of this pleasure. We are a regular God-send to them, I'm sure; for we are their great occupation. When they have said their prayers, and cooked their dinner, and gossiped with a neighbor, they have now the delight of caring for the two English *Fräulein.* Their astonishment at our being here 'all alone, so very, very, very far from our homes' too, as they persist in our being, is unbounded; and they persist, also, in our being 'so very young;' and this astonishment is only equalled by their astonishment over our extraordinary, inconceivable industry! and as it happens, since we have been here, we have been anything but industrious! Of course, if we are not arranging our goods and chattels, we are reading or writing, or sketching, or Clare is singing at the piano. Girls, whether English or foreign, do not usually, I imagine, sit with their hands folded quietly before them all day long. But over the reading, writing, sketching, and singing, what extraordinary exclamations there have been from the good old souls!

'*Immer so fleissig! Immer so fleissig!*'—'Always so industrious! always so industrious!' they cry, when they enter our rooms, till we grow quite nervously to dread the advent of the sisters; — and they always enter together, the one to direct, the other to execute; the one pretends to dust, the other scours.

In my eyes, Fräulein Sänchen is a much more interesting person than the widow of the Tax-gatherer: she, poor Fräulein, is always either scouring, fetching water or wood, or cooking, or waiting upon us, or brushing our shoes and dresses, or running out on errands; she is never at rest, except when she prays and sleeps for a few hours — and that is indeed only for a very few, for she is up ever so early, as soon as the lark begins his song, in order to make a cup of coffee for her '*Frau Schwester*,' as she always calls her, and then 'to make her lady sister's hair,' as she expresses it, — to dress her sister's hair in its elaborate plaits, before she attends to us. In her face I read a touching history and a touching look of humility — a look as though her inferiority to her sister in station, in riches, and in good looks, was always present to her: the same consciousness I also read in the folding of her large bony hands, which have grown coarser, and bonier, and harder, than nature made them, by all this scouring and cleaning. Poor old Fräulein! I foresee that thy lank figure, thy strange hard face, surmounted with thin black locks, and adorned with brilliant garnet ear-rings, and thy scraggy yellow neck surrounded with its garnet necklace, will become beloved objects to me. I feel, in fact, that I shall place thee in a warm corner of my heart, poor old Fräulein! Thou art one whose days have been always passed on the north side of life. I doubt whether ever a ray of sunshine fell upon thy spirit, thou good, faithful, and trusty servant!

All the sunshine has fallen upon the southern days of Madame Thekla! She is magnificent indeed, with her portly figure, her wealth in furniture, clocks, birds, gold watch big as a turnip, lying among lavendered piles of linen and stockings, and in memory of the departed loving and beloved Tax-gatherer! But it is to the despised, old servant-sister that my heart turns. Had you seen, though, how Madame Thekla took the poor English Fräulein under her maternal sway, and conveyed them to their new home, you could not have failed to like her either.

She came in gorgeous attire to the Steinhausers', accompanied by a man, a boy, and a truck to convey our trunks, baskets, cases, easels, and nondescript possessions, to our new abode. What joy beamed in her round face as she superintended the securing of boxes upon the truck: our big washing-pans filled with stray over-shoes, a coffee-pot, and 'tea-machine,' especially interested the good lady. How she scolded the Steinhausers, the man, the boy, and the truck! how she arranged, bargained, chattered! Clare and I, carrying various household gods far too precious to be consigned to the mercies of truck, man, boy, or the good widow, were, though much encumbered with our precious loads, soon far ahead of the train. Looking back, the blue bows of the big bonnet and the crimson scarf were always seen in violent gesticulation over the pausing truck.

Flittings in Germany are much more amusing than in England — and in England they are often comic enough. About the quarter-days in Munich you see the drollest groups; many things are carried by hand; soldiers are much employed, also, as porters — and this gives a peculiar character to the scene of a flitting.

The other day I saw a soldier carrying under his arm a large mirror, with a gay bonnet tied round his neck and hanging behind his back! You meet servant-girls staggering beneath huge 'ivy-tods,' the ornaments for the windows, and the children of the house carrying their toys and their mother's work-boxes, and their father's pipes. You know in Germany your neighbor's dresses by meeting the laundresses bearing them home through the streets upon tall poles, like gay pennons; and at quarter-days you become acquainted with your neighbor's furniture as it progresses along the streets also.

Our moving was, of course, very interesting to our opposite neighbors. The Appleshoes were all alive to it! So were the students, and their big white dog, who live on the other side of the Appleshoes; the young man with the fiery red beard, and the youth with the flaxen locks; — they will have lost a great amusement, I fear, now we are gone; for our goings out and comings in were apparently very interesting to them. As to the Steinhausers, they were all on the *qui vive!*

Clare and I vastly enjoyed the fun.

CHAPTER IX.

THE STUDIO AND HOUSE OF SCHWANTHALER THE SCULPTOR.

Sept. 29th. — We have just returned from Schwanthaler's studio; which is situated in a street leading out of the city towards the great Theresa Meadow, where stands the colossal Bavaria. The street was formerly called the *Lerchen Strasse,* but now it is the *Schwanthaler Strasse,* in memory of the great sculptor. Ludwig von Schwanthaler was born in Munich — was educated in Munich — worked and immortalized his name in Munich — and in Munich he died. His dwelling-house is in the same street as, and opposite to, the studio, which is a white and rather low building, standing back from the street, and forming three sides of a small court. The fourth side would be formed by the dwelling-house — a long building of one story — were it not that the studio and the house are divided by the street.

The Schwanthaler Strasse, like most of the streets in the newer quarters of Munich, spite of its gaily painted houses, with their tints of pale greens, pinks, greys, and salmon colors, their long rows of bright windows, and often their clustering vines and creepers, through which peeps forth here and there the white statue of the Madonna and Child, or a fresco of the Madonna or some saint, has a strange air of quietness, almost of desertion about it. No one is seen passing to and fro, — all is silent, as if sunk in a calm dream.

The little court-yard of Schwanthaler's studio is especially quiet, and the gravel is thickly sprinkled with small weeds. The folding-doors of the studio open, — and as we step into the long gallery, before us rise, relieving themselves against a dull red wall, the colossal figures of the *Hermann-Schlacht* or 'Battle of Arminius' — the frieze for the northern pediment of the Walhalla at Ratisbon. Hermann, in his winged helmet, grasps his terrific sword, pausing for a moment in his slaughter; his strong feet press the reeds and mosses of the morass, like the feet of a destroying angel, — his matted locks are blown back from his relentless brows, and he gazes down on the fallen and struggling foes around him. On the one hand are the Roman combatants: on the other, a bard, a female seer, with loosened hair wreathed with oak-leaves, and face raised with a wild visionary look about it, and Hermann's old dying father, — Hermann's wife, an Amazonian woman, bending over him. We stand in the very heart of the old German world, — are transported to those mighty forests inhabited by a Titantic race and by fabulous dragons. We are among beings of an elder world, large of limb, and of perfect proportions. They have had space and time to develop themselves in those primeval forests. They are not savages; it is not mere physical strength and beauty that they possess. They are endowed with a strange intellectual beauty and power that make the gazer breathless. With the grandeur and simplicity and power of the antique, the sculptor has united a fresh element — the wild mysterious poetry belonging to the mythology of the North. His gods are not Jupiters and Apollos, but Thors and Odins. They have a mystery and a grand undeveloped intellectuality about them which kindle the soul as does the rude, jagged peak of an alp, or the sound of thunder, or like the sight of a sea or of a vast plain.

This wonderful group of the *Hermann-Schlacht* stretches along one side of the gallery. At one end stands casts from three figures in the Bohemian Walhalla; one of which — Wenzell — is peculiarly beautiful, and, from the almost feminine character of the countenance turned towards heaven in an inspiration of intense love, and from the rich mediæval costume in which the figure is clothed, might readily be mistaken for Joan of Arc. The entrance to the gallery is guarded by two stern old fellows, — Huss and Ziska, — also from the Walhalla.

It would be too long a business to attempt to particularize one-tenth of the statues which enrich this wonderful studio. This gallery of which I have spoken, a corresponding gallery on the opposite side of the court-yard, and a lesser one connecting the two, and where towers the astounding head of the awful Bavaria, are crowded with works more or less successful, from the brain of this great sculptor, who died in his forty-sixth year, and the last ten years of whose life were an almost incessant martyrdom.

Schwanthaler's works may be divided into three classes: — Firstly, those belonging to the old Scandinavian world, and the age of Saga, of which the Bavaria, the Hermann, and the Libussa may be taken as the types; secondly, the mediæval; and thirdly — alas, that Schwanthaler should have succumbed to the dire necessity! — portraits. There are various colossal and illustrious dukes, electors, kings, and emperors, to whom he has certainly succeeded in giving an air of stern dignity; and there are various monuments to men illustrious in other ways, — as Goethe, Jean Paul, &c.; but all these statues are very mediocre in the presence of the Hermann, the Libussa, or the four statues of the Rivers which adorn a fountain in Vienna.

Schwanthaler revelled in the old legendary world; his

subjects are bards and seers as well as warriors and amazons. The Libussa is as unique as the old Bohemian legend itself. Once having seen that gloriously beautiful damsel, with her indescribable countenance, — in which is a strange mingling of the amazon, the enchantress, and the loving woman, — who can forget her? Yet who can describe her, as she stands there in her power and dignity, — the massive waves of hair flowing down from her shoulders, — the rich folds of her somewhat quaint drapery falling in ample abundance round her noble form, — one strong yet exquisitely moulded hand resting on her hip, whilst the other holds an unfolded scroll? Yes, precisely thus must she have stood when consulted by her future husband, then a poor knight, as to his fate in life; and when the astounding future, which she will scarcely acknowledge to herself, much less to him, has been revealed to her. Thus must she have stood, as she said, 'Wait till the evening, when, having consulted my books, I will tell thee!' And again when evening came, and she said, 'Wait till the dawn, when I shall have consulted my dream!'

There is the 'Beautiful Melusina' also, — which, however, is inferior to the Libussa; and there are a number of nymphs and river-gods all belonging to this class, full of a spirit as grand as that of the antique, but totally different. Having hastily passed through Schwanthaler's studio, — which, with his collection of casts from his principal works, he has bequeathed to the Munich Academy — let us enter his house on the other side of the street — that house where he led his dreamy, solitary, strange, fantastic life. We first enter a kind of private studio. Several casts from his works stand there; a beautiful drawing of the *Hermann-Schlacht* hangs above a long writing-table. The house appears to consist of but one suite of rooms on the ground-floor. You ascend two or three steps and find yourself in a simply furnished but elegant sitting-room,— of course with an uncarpeted floor. Various pictures hang about the walls,—none, however, of remarkable excellence; a variety of sun-pictures of his friends, and views of the Bavaria. The walls, if I remember correctly, are of a self-colored green; and the most striking feature of the room is a few statuettes placed on brackets. Above the sofa hang the sculptor's first and last sketches. The first sketch, or rather carving, is a rude, little bas-relief, in a black wooden frame; two quaint old figures drinking, and round it hangs a withered wreath of bay. The last sketch is the figure of a warrior drawn in charcoal.

A lesser room opens from this one; its character, however, is the same. Nevertheless, a few things struck me in it. Fronting the door is a shrine of mediæval character, although of modern workmanship — one of those shrines with folding-doors. The figure within it seemed to be neither a Madonna nor yet a common-place saint, but an angel with outstretched wings. Just within the shrine stood two little swans, each with a piece of money suspended by a blue ribbon from its neck — a play upon the name *Schwan-thaler*. The other thing which caught my attention was a singular drinking-cup, formed from a tree-root; its stem, curling and twisting in a strange grotesque manner, swelled out to form the cup, which was lined with gold. The lid or cover was a mass of small roots and strange knobs and deformed growths. As you looked more attentively at it, behold! you saw the figure of a knight fighting his way through those roots as through the stems of an enchanted forest: now he rested and slept, now he was hospitably entertained by a hermit in his cell. It is a strange, grotesque fancy. Schwanthaler had carved it at his leisure, and was very fond of it; he and his friends used to drink out of it on his birth-and name-days.

We next entered his bed-chamber, which opened out of this room, and was also on the ground-floor, — a quiet holy-looking little room. Some pictures were hung on the walls, and on the porcelain stove stood a statuette of Thorwaldsen's Christ. The window opens into a garden; and the branches of a vine are twined across it, so as in summer to form a lovely green blind of leaves, — which is by no means uncommon here, and the effect of which is very pretty and poetical. Here stood the bed on which the sculptor had died, — where his eyes had closed upon this world. Strange wild tales are told of his last illness, as he lay on this bed. Wild visions even then haunted his brain, which he realized around him. Sometimes he would have men brought from the studio and arrayed in quaint old armor, and whilst they fought and wrestled before him he would lie and dream of combats and tournaments. I have heard, also, that a short time before his death, on the 'name-day' of a relative and right good friend of his, he moulded in clay, as he lay on his bed, a figure of his friend, and had it laid out, I believe, as though it were dead, whilst two of his workmen from the studio, disguised as good and evil spirits, contended for the body — the evil one, much to the poor friend's consternation, bearing off the prize! Shortly after, in this very chamber, still stranger visions — visions more awful than even his imagination could conjure up — burst on him; and he himself had to pass through a more mysterious struggle than any combat in romance — the struggle of death!

The cousin of Schwanthaler, who was with us, brought out from a cabinet in this chamber two plaster masks: one, taken when the sculptor was sixteen, showed a refined delicate face, with a sensitive expression about the youthful lips; the other taken after death — the same face, but how matured by thought, labor, pain — beautiful, emaciated, and stamped with the seal of death — the face of one who had suffered intensely, but had attained to peace. I know how he looked in life, too, from a drawing made of him by Kaulbach. It is a face which from its delicacy might have been a woman's, except for a long moustache that conceals the beautiful upper lip, and for the strength of the strong man's and poet's soul which gazes out of his eyes. These are very large, and have an astonished look, as though they were ever seeing visions which were not of this world.

We now paid a visit to the *sanctum sanctorum*. We descended a narrow flight of some five or six steps from the bed-room into a queer little apartment half under ground. The walls were stone; two small windows lighted it — one of stained glass; the other, quite a little loop-hole, was covered on the outside by its vine, the leaves of which in summer would look more green and tender than ever, from their coming in such sharp contrast with the hard, gloomy stone walls. In this little cellar there was just room for a small stove, a bench on which about three people might sit — certainly no more — and a table. A shelf or two ran along the walls; and on these stood a vast variety of the quaintest old goblets and drinking-cups. Old armor and strange old swords hung upon the walls. Here Schwanthaler, his cousin said, used to sit for hours; here, too, no doubt, he saw strange visions; and here, too, he and his beloved friends — worthy and noble friends! — used to sit, and drink wine out of the queer old drinking-cup with its knight and hermit, and out of many another strange old goblet.

Such is the house of the great sculptor, and such some of the old memories that haunt it.

CHAPTER X.

THE OCTOBER 'VOLKS-FEST.'

Next Sunday, October 6th, commences the great People's Festival, and, in celebration of this, the *Enthülling* — the uncovering, the unveiling, or whatever it is called, of the great Bavaria statue takes place. Thursday, the 3d, was announced as the day of the Bavaria festival; but, strange to say, it seems next to impossible, although to-morrow is Thursday, to ascertain what really will take place. The newspapers and announcements on the walls have been contradicting one another, day after day, this week past. Neither can you discover where tickets are to be obtained for the seats erected on the meadow.

Thursday evening. — Rain! rain! and it has rained all day. There has been no festival, and people are uncertain whether there will be any to-morrow.

Saturday evening. — It rained, rained, rained all yesterday, and there was no festival. Crowds of strangers are here to witness the ceremony, and there is nothing but rain.

The King and Queen of Saxony, the King and Queen of Greece, the Duchess of Modena, King Ludwig and his Queen, King Max and his Queen, all returned for the grand day; and all is put an end to by the rain! The town is full of peasants, drawn hither several days before the commencement of their festival, in expectation of witnessing the greatest festival of all — the revealing of that august presence before whom their games and festivities henceforth are to take place.

And it rains to-day more incessantly and violently even than yesterday! It is precisely like the commencement of a second deluge; as though the idol-worshipping Bavarians were to be swept away from the face of the earth. Spite of the rains all kind of rumors are flying about. But the gloom of evening is come down, and the colossus is still awaiting her grand inauguration. There is something very fine to my imagination in the idea of that sublime, completed figure, night and day awaiting, amid the solitude of the plain and the desolation of the stormy autumn, the grand day of her honor; she so awfully calm and unmoved by all the anxiety, royal anxiety, people's anxiety, surging around her; as calm and unmoved by earthly care, by earthly glory, as the spirit of her Creator — as Schwanthaler's spirit now is! One might almost fancy that nature mourned in these clouds and rain over the absence of Schwanthaler and his friend Lazarini — his 'right-hand,' as he called him — who like him sleeps the long sleep of death.

Sunday. — Whatever may be done about the Bavaria festival, the People's festival began, as it has done for many a long year, spite of weather or anything else, on this first Sunday in October. At 12 o'clock, therefore, all Munich was in motion, — citizens and peasants all armed with umbrellas of various hues, from scarlet to the color of the most faded and decaying of autumnal leaves, from olive-green and ultramarine blue to buff and indigo; while the streets and roads were thronged with peasants' carts and vehicles of every description.

When we reached the outskirts of the town, we beheld a large wagon decked out with flags and vegetables!

The sides a mosaic of cabbages, turnips, beet-roots, carrots — a market-gardener's triumphal car. Tall, tapering, crimson beet-roots, formed elegant pinnacles at each corner, while cabbage-leaves, artichokes, and cauliflowers, were converted into the quaintest ornaments. It was like something in a pantomime, or more properly a carnival, show. Every street, every lane leading towards the meadow, swarmed with people.

The meadow itself formed, as it were, an immense theatre; temporary seats being erected, and artificial terraces formed for the convenience of the spectators: on one hand was the elevation for the orchestra, on another covered seats for people of quality; and everywhere standing places for the immense crowds. At the foot of this natural amphitheatre runs the race-course, containing within its circumference various erections for the festival. Precisely opposite the place appointed for the orchestra and decorated seats, and separated from them by the race-course, which, amid the many-colored crowd, told like a broad green ribbon, stood the royal tent on a wooden platform, a conspicuous object, striped white and blue, — the Bavarian colors, and in form not unlike a monster umbrella. The raised wooden seats were all tastefully adorned with festoons and wreaths of spruce-fir, intermixed with draperies of blue and white. Whole woods of spruce-fir must have been plundered for the occasion; for, not content with garlands and green walls, rows and rows of trees, smart, stiff, healthy fir-trees — the genuine *Tannen Bäume* of German poetry and romance, were planted about the meadow, and shaded every little wine and beer-shop. From the royal tent to the people's pump, every erection had its green spruce-fir wreaths and its waving banners.

We seated ourselves on one of the raised seats nearest

the city; consequently farthest from the Bavaria. Behind us were stalled a number of prize-horses; and behind other seats, answering to ours, but beyond the royal tent, were stalled the prize-cattle. We had an excellent view of the royal tent, and the arrival and reception of the various royalties. Lines of soldiers in their blue uniform were drawn up along the race-course on either hand of the tent; the orchestra was already filled with six military bands, amongst whom were ninety drummers! A stationary human mass met the eye everywhere, and ever and anon a gay carriage, with brilliant outriders and servants, rolled along the race-course; and halting before the pavilion, you saw ladies in delicate-colored bonnets, and gentlemen in rich uniforms alight, ascend the steps, and pass beneath the awning of white and blue. There was an undulating movement in the gay crowd as though a wind had passed over a brilliant flower-bed — a courtly dumb-show, as seen from our station, of mutual recognition; one scarlet uniform ever conspicuous as a tall red poppy; and a lady's emerald-green satin mantle giving contrast to it like a large green leaf.

Already the tent was filled with a brilliant throng, when the cannon from the walls of the *Ruhmeshalle* thundered forth that King Max was on his way; and as the smoke rolled off in white volumes, above rose that majestic hand of the Bavaria, with its oaken wreath! Again and again the cannon sounded, and King Max, accompanied by his brother, King Otho, splendidly attired in his Albanian costume, and attended by a train of cavalry, dashed up to the tent. The people shouted; two kings had arrived, but a third was yet expected — the King of Saxony, who soon, accompanied by two ladies, in a dark open carriage, with outriders and servants in green, made his appearance. All the expected royalists were now there, and the six military bands, with their ninety drummers, struck up *our* National Anthem — *their Volks-Hymne*, or People's-hymn, as the Germans call it.

The first event of the festival was the arrival of our friend, the gay vegetable-wagon, with blue and white flags flying from its beet-root pinnacles, and preceded by a procession of gardeners' daughters in broad straw hats trimmed with green ribbons, lilac boddices and full white sleeves, bearing in their hands offerings of fruits and flowers for the King and Queen, from the good gardeners of Bamberg. After the daughters came the gardeners themselves, one of them bearing with much pomp a silver cup. Wagon and procession took their stand behind the royal pavilion.

The horses, mettlesome, high-bred creatures, were now led forth, one by one, before the royal tent by what we should in England call farming-men rather than grooms, — countrified-looking fellows in short jackets of coarse blue cloth, with their legs cased in long boots of black leather, and wearing broad-brimmed beaver hats glorying in a remarkable length of nap. Behind each curveting horse walked his owner and rearer, the peasant who had gained the prizes, which he bore in his hand, a gay little flag, a small book bound in blue, with a long blue roll, containing his diploma, to which was often attached a little silver cross, hanging by a red ribbon. There was something singularly stolid and sullen in the countenances of these men, which not even their prizes, nor the small sum of money which often accompanied them, could remove. There was a long array of these prize steeds, bumpkin grooms, and discontented-looking proprietors; the monotony of the whole scene only occasionally broken by an old woman or two being kicked down, — and by a sudden shower, which led to the unfurling of some thousands of umbrellas, and which made the whole crowd resemble a garden with full-blown dome-like flowers of every hue, above which rose the white and blue monarch flower of the entire garden.

After the horses came the cattle. Monster bulls, evil-browed, with stooping heads and fettered hoofs, dun-colored and tawny, cream-colored and brown, garlanded as if for sacrifice, were led along, followed by their masters with their prizes, banners, and other gifts. Now came a young bull, less hideous and evil-looking, led by a stalwart peasant-woman; or a gentle cow and calf, also with garlanded brows and necks and with tinkling bells, telling of Alpine pastures, conducted by a Tyrolean girl. And the cattle-show was over.

Next, with much parade, and the marching about of blue and white-clad heralds, and the fluttering of prize banners, and riding about in much agitation of the Festival Committee, the race-horses were brought out before the King. A different race, truly, was this to Epsom or Newmarket. And primitive and innocent indeed must these races seem to the knowing men of the turf, when it is recollected that the owners of the racers, the grooms and jockeys, — all the racing cortège, in fact, — are obliged to attend a mass especially celebrated for them at eight o'clock in the morning; that the racers mostly belonged to farmers, and that the jockeys were not permitted to ride unless they brought certificates of good conduct and industry from the schoolmasters of their respective villages. Betting, in a small way, no doubt there was; and the excitement was considerable, as the poor little village lads, with their flying sashes, rushed again and again round the course; but a more harmless race could hardly be imagined. It was soon over. Money and banners were again distributed to the sound of music. The monarchs, and their court, returned with the sound of cannon, in a long train of gay carriages; the people shouted, and gradually dispersed themselves over the meadow for social drinking, smoking, love-making, and gossip, beneath the garlanded and fir-tree shadowed drinking booths and sheds.

Monday. — This morning, Clare and I started for the meadow early in the forenoon. The day was cold, grey and damp; the ground wet, trampled and muddy. Thousands and thousands of dead bodies covered the field — the bodies of little mice, which abound in most German land, and which live by myriads in the Theresien Wiese, darting away ever and anon from before your feet into their holes. It had been a great slaughter-field for them. Another feature in the scene was the passing along of drays heavily laden with Munich beer. As yet, however, the meadow looked desolate, damp, deserted, and particularly uncomfortable. We began our explorations by visiting a long shed behind the royal tent, where the Bamberg Triumphal Vegetable Car had taken its stand. Only imagine the disappointment of these poor Bamberg gardeners! They were to have been presented to the King; but he forgot all about them, and drove away without their grandeur having received its reward. This shed, in the centre of which glowed a crown made of gay flowers, contained the agricultural prize vegetables. A beautiful assemblage of rich foliage, ruddy roots and graceful sheaves of corn, — a very cornucopia, — the shed of Cerès, Autumnus, and Pomona. There was a tropical character in those towering spikes of Indian corn, in those large sprays of fan-like artichoke leaves, in those gigantic beet-root leaves, in their intense rich green, springing from juicy crimson stems. The Munich decorative artists might have studied them with profit. Close to this cornucopia was exhibited a mass of golden and white silk, — immense quantities of it, — the produce of silk-worms kept by a variety of Bavarian women, at the head of whom are the two Queens, and a host of Princesses and Duchesses. There is an endeavor here to introduce the silk-worm into Bavaria, and in proof of what had already been done, beautiful specimens of silks and satins were exhibited, which had been manufactured from home-grown silk. At the back of these sheds, a lottery, of prizes of six and twelve Kreutzers each (2*d.* and 3*d.*), was to take place for the benefit of the fair; and this spot, later in the day, was a place of great resort for the country people. The remainder of the erections outside the race-course, and arranged in a semi-circle, were drinking and refreshment booths, furnished with benches and tables, and all, more or less, prettily decorated with festoons of spruce-fir, bound together with the everlasting drapery of white and blue, with fluttering banners and spruce-firs, planted, as I have already said, to give shade and beauty to the space around them. One, quite a superior booth, had a regular garden fenced in with spruce fir. This we entered, and were supplied with delicious hot sausages, and excellent coffee and chocolate. The interior was very pretty with scarlet and white festooned drapery. Guests, as yet, were few, for the morning was damp and cheerless.

We saw on the meadow but one solitary 'roundabout,' such as are so common at English places of popular amusement, and among the Viennese people, and only one solitary hand-organ was to be heard. There was, however, a raised circular platform for musicians, with a heavy banner of red, black, and gold, floating over it. The whole area, including this settlement of good cheer, the refreshment booths, was marked out by spruce-firs planted at regular distances; each tree with its gay banner, and connected with its neighbor by long festoons of green wreaths; and here you caught sight of many a Teniers and Ostade group. Beyond this area, and between it and the Bavaria, a portion of the meadow was laid out in shooting-grounds, with targets and marks of various descriptions. There was a wooden stag to be shot at, as he is pulled backwards and forwards, between two clumps of fir-trees, and a bird fixed upon a high pole, looking very like a sign of the spread-eagle, holding in its beak and claws the marks at which the shooter is to aim. On the ground stand little wooden booths, from which the marksmen were to fire; with plenty of long sheds, where they might assemble, charge their pieces, and refresh themselves.

While we stood on their ground, the valiant shooters, with sound of music and much pageantry, advanced across the plain, their blue and white banners, of course, 'fluttering in the breeze,' — one grows quite weary of these banners! — the blue and white heralds of yesterday, and the scarlet trumpeters, and the queer, grotesque fellows in parti-colored slashed jerkins of black and yellow preceding them. Then came these 'Friends of Shooting,' as they call themselves — each bearing his rifle in his hand, and wearing a sort of uniform, — green Tyrolean peaked hats, as elegantly decorated with feathers, flowers, and ribbons, as a fashionable bonnet, or sometimes graced with a tuft of chamois-fur, or a staring owl's or eagle's head. Their coats were grey and loose, with green cuffs and collars. But their heads and faces were far more striking than their costume. Hard, weather-beaten men were they, with grizzled beards and snowy eyebrows; or youths, agile and active as the chamois of their native Alps, with clear, large eyes, and ruddy, healthy cheeks; others, middle-aged, black and red-bearded, men whose lives had been passed among deep woods and by sedgy lakes, looking for game — the roe and the boar. There was, as it were, a fresh mountain air blowing about them, a sylvan mountain strength, as they marched along, each shouldering his piece. Arrived at the shooting ground, they indefatigably shot and shot, out of their little booths, all the livelong day. Crowds were soon collected, and the intensest interest prevailed: but we were soon weary.

We wandered off, therefore, along the higher plain, with long, solemn stretches of pine-wood in the distance, to a picturesque and singularly interesting little church, at the feet of whose walls we found that a bloody skirmish with the Austrians had taken place. There was the mound-like grave, beneath which slept the eight hundred who had fallen. A stone chronicled their bravery, and how they fell, on Christmas Day, 1703. Autumnal shrubs and flowers shed their brilliant leaves upon the green luxuriant grass. It was a quiet, holy little grave-yard, full of crosses, and garlands, and flowers. Upon the Church wall was painted in fresco a representation of the skirmish in which an old Tyrolean and his two sons are being struck down by the Austrians; and above the tumult of the strife is their apotheosis, — Christ receives the three, who rise with garlanded brows into the pure light of heaven. As a work of art it is very feeble, but nevertheless, the *feeling* is beautiful and poetical. A group of peasants from the Festival came into the church-yard whilst we were there; muttered a prayer for the dead, and sprinkled holy water upon the green mound. When, on our return, we reached the meadow, we were again greeted by the unceasing rifle-shots, and found the booths all alive with feasting, singing, and drinking. Such was the second day of the *Volks-fest.*

Tuesday.—This afternoon the sun shone gloriously; the Alps clearly showing their snowy peaks, as though scarcely twenty miles distant, and the whole scene was really gay for the first time. The terrace-mound and seats, as well as the royal tent, now abandoned to the public, were crowded with spectators, all eager to witness the 'Olympic Games.' Ever and anon resounded the shots of those indefatigable shooters, still shooting away at their wooden butts; they, however, were no longer the objects of attraction. Tan was scattered over that part of the race-course opposite to what until to-day had been called the Royal tent, and this was the arena round which pressed an impatient crowd, kept back by green-clad gendarmes seated on prancing horses. Already a very mosaic of heads and faces lined the amphitheatre.

There was a cry 'They come! they come!' and across the plain, proceeding from the city, came a throng. Sounds of music floated on the air, banners fluttered, and now marched through the crowd, first, scarlet and gold-clad-musicians, then a band of youthful heralds, bearing the blue and white prize banners; then little girls, with their fair hair falling in ringlets on their shoulders, carrying garlands. Thus marched in six-and-twenty stalwart youths, wearing tightly-fitting canary-colored jerkins, confined round the waist by a black leathern belt; their arms, their heads, their necks bare; their legs clothed in tightly-fitting hose, and with sandals on their feet. These all were bakers' apprentices, great adepts in the art of wrestling, even from the old times, when certain valiant Munich bakers won great renown at the Battle of Mühldorf, in 1322, when Ludwig the Bavarian vanquished his rival, Philip the Handsome of Austria, and assumed the imperial crown. It is this Ludwig's triumphal entry into

Munich, after this victory, which forms the subject of the fresco on the Isar Gate.

Next after the six-and-twenty young bakers came ten sturdy young wheelwrights, in the midst of whom was borne a quaint old wheel, garlanded with wreaths of moss. Each of the ten rolled, as he came along, a gaily-painted wheel; and with their black velvet caps, their snowy shirts, gay with blue-and-white braces crossed over breast and back, and black velvet breeches and white stockings, they made a very goodly show. The quaint old wheel which was borne aloft, and around which ran a black-letter legend, is a precious heir-loom of the wheelwrights' guild. It was made in one day, some centuries ago, by a young wheelwright, and then, by him, in one day also, rolled from Augsburg to Munich, a distance of forty-one English miles.

The musicians took their place above the arena; the heralds withdrew with their banners to either side. The bakers arranged themselves in a half-circle, and the wheelwrights stood each with a hand on his wheel, and then, attended by the festival directors, all wearing blue and white rosettes, slowly proceeded along the race-course to the point whence they were to commence their race. Anon, with rapid pace, they shot past, man and wheel vying with each other. The race-course was a mile round; but it was not very long before you caught sight, in the distance, of the flying men and wheels coming on to the goal. On, on they came, three or four near together, the rest scattered at various intervals; one far behind. On, on they came! The first is here! But what a countenance! — Pale — deadly pale! livid almost! Oh, it was a fearful sight! And each panting wretch, as he neared the goal, had the same ghastly look. The first idea was that they would faint, or drop down dead. The trumpets bray forth the victor's triumph; they pause, pant, lean upon their wheels, and the wrestling commences.

I myself was quite uneasy about these poor wheelwrights, and wanted to see cloaks thrown over them. But no; there they leant upon their wheels, and remained so leaning till the end of the day, as if that had been a part of their duty.

Spite of the horror with which the wrestling inspired me, I was conscious of a strange fascination in it. There was a savage grandeur about the whole thing. That band of tawny men, girt with their black belts, glaring defiance on each other, then rushing madly together, winding together their arms, bearing each other together to the earth in a wild frenzy, looked like human tigers. You grew sick, breathless; yet look you must. And as each champion triumphed, the trumpets announced his victory!

The assembled multitude, breathless, silent thousands, added a wonderful impressiveness to the scene. And as you turned your eyes away from the fierce combatants and the eager multitude, there, along the horizon, lay that glorious, calm Alpine chain, raising its jagged peaks into the pure, tender, pale *green* sky, along which lay vast solemn stretches of cloud. It was a striking contrast.

But again the human struggle claimed our attention. It was now a trial of strength with huge stones. How fine were many of the attitudes! full of a savage poetry, which I know not well how to convey in words. It was, in fact, the *sublimity* of brute force. Then there were various war-dances, in which the repetition of the same action and sentiment by these six-and-twenty savage figures produced a singular feeling, from its very monotony. They cast javelins at a hideous giant of wood, and performed various difficult and curious athletic feats,—such as standing upon each other's arms, and shoulders, and heads, turning themselves into a human pyramid, and finally ended by a foot-race. Then to the sound of music came the distribution of prizes, which consisted of gay banners and money. Shone upon by the setting sun, the train, now worn, jaded, and soiled with dirt and blood, returned towards the city. The multitude dispersed itself across the plain; some sober souls returning home; the greater number remaining to feast and guzzle in the numerous booths. We left hundreds enjoying their seventh heaven — beer, sausages, and cheese.

CHAPTER XI.

THE BAVARIA FESTIVAL.

October 10*th.*—At length the Bavaria stands revealed in all her dignity to kings and people!

But before chronicling yesterday's proceedings, I must first add a few more words regarding the statue and its history. Of its situation I have already spoken; I have mentioned how this work of art, stupendous in its Titanic proportions, and awful in its calm majestic beauty, the result of ten years' incessant anxiety, stands on a broad meadow to the west of Munich—a portion of the great plain that stretches away to the Alps. It rests on the edge of what at first appears to be an artificial terrace, but is in fact a large step, where the plain suddenly descends into that lower plain on which stands the city of Munich. The figure of this colossal Virgin of the old German world, with her majestic lion by her side, is fifty-four feet high, and is placed upon a granite pedestal of thirty feet in height, so that the beautiful temple of the *Ruhmeshalle*, or Hall of Fame, erecting behind, seems dwarfed into strange human insignificance.

This figure, typifying the spirit of recognition and reward of all excellence and achievement whatsoever, stands with upraised wreath, as if ready to crown any Bavarian who may be worthy to enter her temple of fame. It was a grand idea of King Ludwig's, this of placing the Genius of Reward on the spot consecrated to the people and their annual meeting. It is in this meadow, as we have seen, — the Theresa Meadow, as it is called, — that the October *Volks-fest* is held; and that the king distributes prizes to the peasants. Henceforward, all successful accomplishment will be crowned in the presence of the impersonated Bavaria, — the more popular achievements alluded to as well as those of the poet, painter, musician, and philosopher. Each is to receive in the presence of his assembled country, from the hands of the monarch, the acknowledgment of merit. Such, at least, is the intention of King Ludwig.

The *Ruhmeshalle* is unfinished, — and will require for its completion at least two or three years more. It is a beautiful Doric building, of white marble from the Untersberg, — adorned with emblematical friezes by Schwanthaler. It was designed by Leo von Klenze; and the busts of all the great men of Bavaria, without regard to difference of religious belief or to origin, are to be arranged along the walls.

As I have already said, through the interior of this bronze tower-like figure ascends a winding staircase leading to a chamber in the head. This chamber is large enough to contain twenty-eight persons. But beyond the poetry of mere size, — beyond that which arises from its connecting our thoughts at once with the sublime works of antiquity, and with history and romance of modern date from the fact of its being cast out of Turkish cannon sunk in the battle of Navarino, and brought up by Greek divers — there is a yet deeper poetry in the work. This arises from reflecting on the ten years of toil — stupendous toil — mental and bodily, of its creators, — the difficulties overcome by patient industry, — the dangers endured with unflinching courage — and the melancholy truth that the final accomplishment of the mighty work is unwitnessed by the two men whose very lives seemed bound up in its success, — Schwanthaler the sculptor, and his friend Lazarini, his 'right hand,' as he called him, who modelled the colossal figure under his direction.

Though Schwanthaler was already attacked by his fatal malady at the time when he designed the Bavaria at the king's suggestion, he not only modelled a variety of designs for the Colossus, but also completed a smaller figure of the Bavaria as we now see her, thirteen feet high. When the huge wooden tower was built in the Royal Bronze Foundry, and after what may be called a gigantic wooden skeleton had been erected by a crowd of carpenters, — after tons and tons of clay had been piled together over this, so as to form a mass of material on which to work, — there, day after day, might be seen the unwearied, energetic, though physically suffering sculptor, guiding with watchfulness and love the accomplishment of his idea, which ever grew beneath the hand of his friend Lazarini and his troop of workmen.

Stiglmayer, the originator and director of the Bronze Foundry, died in 1844, just before the casting of the Bavaria began. His nephew, Ferdinand Miller, full of youth, energy, patience, and experience, was ready to succeed him. The castings took place at five different times, — commencing with the head. This was cast in 1844. In casting the bust of the figure — the largest portion — the greatest difficulty had to be encountered. It was necessary to melt for the purpose twenty tons of bronze, — five tons more than had ever before been melted in the furnace. As this immense mass of metal slowly began to fuse, it began also to cake, — thus threatening to destroy not only the casting, but the whole furnace, with untold danger to life and limb. Six men had, in spite of the oppressive heat and the ever-increasing glow of the furnace, to take it by turns night and day incessantly to stir, with long iron bars, the molten mass, lest it should adhere to the furnace walls, and so bring annihilation on all. On the evening of the fifth day of anxiety, when Ferdinand Miller for the first time sought a short repose in his chair, he was suddenly aroused by his faithful and anxious fellow-watcher, his wife, with the cry of 'Ferdinand, awake! the foundry is on fire!' It was so. The ever-increasing heat of those five days and four nights had caused fire to burst forth among the rafters. To have attempted to extinguish the fire by water, with this molten mass below, would have caused the immediate destruction of the place. All that could be done was, by means of wetted cloths, to keep down the fire. This was tried, and the melting went on as before. Amid such danger did the casting of the bust take place about midnight on the 11th of October, 1845. 'Success!' was shouted forth; a load of anxiety of many kinds fell from every breast; — and all then hastened to the complete extinguishing of the fire.

Various have been the ceremonies connected with the casting of the Bavaria. When the head was first raised out of the pit in which it had been cast, King Ludwig, and a number of distinguished persons being present, a festival was held, in which garlands, music, and illuminations played a conspicuous part. On August 7th, 1848, when the figure was complete, — all the separate portions, except the head, having already been removed to the Theresa Meadow on a carriage constructed expressly for the purpose, — the head was conveyed thither with every mark of festal rejoicing. On the following day the bell of the little church of Neuhausen tolled, — and Ferdinand Miller, the noble and courageous 'master,' accompanied by the workmen of the foundry, went to return thanks for the accomplishment of their arduous work. They had commenced their labor with prayer four years before in that little church, — and now they offered up thanksgiving, that their task was not only achieved, but achieved without loss of life or limb to a single member of their band. But Schwanthaler and Lazarini, — where were they?

And now, impressed with a sense of the poetry attaching to the statue, accompany us in the cheerful morning sun-shine, and beneath a cloudless heaven, through the streets of Munich to the Dult Platz, the square where the Munich fairs are held; for there the Bavaria procession is to assemble!

A sound of singing reaches us from various points as we walk along; all the *Sing-vereins* are vigorously practising. We pass the red Gothic palace of King Ludwig. The clumps of trees in the palace garden, and upon the Dult Platz, shine out brilliantly with their autumnal tints beneath the deep azure heaven.

It is scarcely nine o'clock; yet the square is all alive with an expectant crowd. Every one is dressed in their best. The rows of white, palely-tinted houses round the square are gay with clustered heads at every window. The garden of the English Coffee-house, and the Café itself, is all astir. From beneath the archway of the Carls-Thor streams an increasing crowd. Citizens, peasants, officers, soldiers, artists, — a motley multitude. Above the roofs of the near houses rise church steeples into the sunny air.

But, behold! what strange thing is this approaching! Higher it seems to tower than the distant church steeples. It is the Bavaria's spinning-wheel; and that is the distaff! On it moves, amid the wonder and merriment of the crowd. Gendarmes ride before to clear the way. The spinning-wheel is placed upon a low car drawn by six horses. The horses and car, as well as the spinning-wheel, are wreathed with moss and flowers.

Scarcely has your astonishment over the spinning-wheel subsided, when lo! a merry mass of leaves and flowers approaches. This is the festal car of the inn-keepers. Beneath the odorous bower formed of oak and fir-branches, sits a jovial company. Above their heads sway game of all descriptions, birds and beasts, suspended from the centre of the leafy tent. The tables are spread with the most tempting viands, — delicious pies and pasties, a boar's head, roasted fowls, pheasants and partridges! — And glasses and tankards are heaped up in artistic array among leaves and flowers; and the prettiest of Munich's *Kellnerinnen*, in their gold and silver swallow-tailed head-dresses, and with their gay-colored boddices laced up in front with silver chains, wait upon the jolly guests, and smile upon the assembled crowd, and joke and laugh. And garlanded horses, plump and sleek, slowly draw along the little inn! And now, you look around, and feel as though witnessing some poetical, yet withal most solemn, pantomime! Here stands the beautiful little Vorstadt Au Church! It has been drawn along upon a beautifully painted car, — or *illuminated* car, one might rather say. Its sides are covered with graceful Gothic tracery, amid which, here and there, upon a shield of azure, shines forth a lovely white lily; and entwining with the tracery round the car runs a scroll, on which in quaint black-letter you read the words, — 'The grateful Vorstadt Au to the illustrious founder of her Church, beloved King Ludwig I.' The horses are richly caparisoned, their trappings bearing a white lily embroidered on a deep blue ground.

And now another apparition startles you. A colossal sword, as if from the Castle of Otranto, is grasped and upheld by a colossal gauntlet of steel. A wreath of simple peaceful moss winds round the cross-like hilt and blade. The car is a mossy bank. An anvil and hammer, with various other tools belonging to a forge, show among the fresh green. Swords of every size and form, daggers and knives, from the bayonet to the minutest, are symmetrically arranged in a fan-like form, on a mossy ground, on either side of the car. This is the sword-makers' and cutlers' festal car.

Close follows a monstrous gilt lion, holding in his mouth a colossal key. He comes from the locksmiths. The carpenters have sent an idealized carpenter's shop: the masons a car bearing a garlanded church tower: the decorators and gilders a luxurious pavilion glittering with gold. Beneath that golden canopy, and shaded by those heavy curtains of Tyrian purple, you expect a vision of an enchanted sleeping beauty awaking at the kiss of the brave, handsome Fairy Prince,—that Prince so long awaited by the sleeper. But the curtains shade no Prince or beauty: it is a marble bust of King Ludwig which gleams forth from their crimson gloom.

The very butchers have idealized their trade. Their car is drawn along by four stout oxen—two black, two tawny-brown; their sturdy foreheads decked with flowers. A very pyramid of goodly brown tongues, hams, and sausages, tastefully arranged and decorated with gay ribbons and flowers and foliage, rises in the centre. The entire car is a bed of flowers and moss, amidst which, at each corner, nestles a child fantastically arrayed in scarlet and white, and holding by a cord an innocent white lamb, which gazes around with large, gentle, dark eyes. The spokes of the wheels are covered with brilliant flowers. A troop of gay young butchers follows, attired in white jackets and trowsers, with jaunty blue caps on their heads, and bearing hatchets upon their shoulders.

Each car is attended by its band of apprentices, masters, and journeymen, attired in the idealized costume of their trade. The weavers following their car, brilliant with its drapery, are attired in an Albert Durer costume.

One of the loveliest cars is that sent from the Porcelain Works. Here the most graceful vases and ewers, — many of *terra-cotta*, — are grouped with exquisite feeling; flowers garland them in thick and brilliant festoons, hanging over their round, smooth sides, passing gracefully through their handles, linking them all together in one flowery chain. And bright China-asters make brilliant necklaces round slender necks of tall ewers, or crown majestic vases as with a diadem of rainbow-tinted stars. And amidst all sits a little brown Italian child, of some seven years old, gazing out at you with large, melancholy, dark eyes, from beneath his scarlet *fez*, brilliant as a gorgeous cactus-flower.

And here is the car of the Munich Artists! Beneath a canopy of delicate foliage and flowers, upborne at the four corners of the car by plaster lions, stands the statue of King Ludwig, brought from the studio of Schwanthaler. The sun casts an especial glory upon the marble brow, as the majestic figure, in its regal robes, moves slowly through the multitude. Below the statue of the king, seated at his feet, are two female figures, — one typical of Sculpture, and bearing a model of the Bavaria in her hand; the other of Painting, with her emblematic palette and brushes. These figures on nearer inspection we find, though themselves of plaster, are draped with canvas stiffened as sculptors are in the habit of arranging draperies for study. The effect is excellent! The attendants of the car, workmen from the Bronze Foundry, form an artistic escort, being dressed in short, loose, and very full, blue velvet paletots, falling over tightly-fitting white hose. Their heads are crowned with blue velvet caps of mediæval cut, and they carry in their hands gay pennons, which display armorial bearings of scarlet and silver, orange and black, or crimson and gold.

And then the gardeners! Their cars indeed must not be forgotten or remain unchronicled. Whoever, before this day, was willing to believe that cabbages, turnips, carrots and beet-roots, might be so arranged as to form a pyramid lovely as if built of delicately tinted shells? The florists' and fruiterers' cars are perfect dreams of flowers and fruits. Regiments of gardeners and gardeneresses attend them, attired in the conventional stage costume of gardeners, and bearing in their hands rakes and hoes. Children and young girls bear fruit and flowers in picturesque baskets upon their shoulders; and in the very centre of the gardeners' train come on two stout young fellows, bearing between them, supported on a pole, an enormous bunch of grapes, as if returning from the 'Promised Land.'

But I will not attempt to particularize the wonders assembled in the Dult Platz. Suffice it to know that three-and-twenty cars appeared, each followed and preceded by its picturesque attendants; to say nothing of quaintly attired bands of musicians mounted on horseback; each one connected with the procession wearing a spray, or garland of oak.

On our way to the Theresien Wiese we encountered another marvel travelling towards the place of rendezvous: it was the brewers' car, bearing aloft its huge *Pokal* or drinking-cup. In size the drinking-cup resembled a steam-engine chimney: it was of that quaint, beautiful, half-gothic, half-rustic character, familiar to us in Neurenther's designs. In Gothic niches, around the rim, stood quaint emblematic figures,—the graceful hop, with its clusters of fruit, employed as ornament; little beer-barrels encircled the stem of the cup, forming a quaint moulding; and the lid was surmounted by an emblematic figure, gilt: such a jovial crew, too, as attended this *Pokal!* Six sleek, heavy brewers' horses slowly drew along the car, which was wreathed with sprays of hop. Men in a mediæval costume of black and yellow were mounted on every second horse, trumpeting vigorously. Men in scarlet waistcoats tightly buckled round their waists, and with brilliantly white shirt-sleeves, and green velvet caps of the Glengary form, marched along two or three abreast, bearing their various implements of brewing, garlanded with hop; two men bore aloft a huge malt-measure filled with nodding oats and barley. But their countenances were the most jovial and bacchanalian part of the show; their eyes were full of merry laughter, their faces glowed again with glee;—it was a procession to drive a tee-totaller fairly distracted.

And thus gradually all Munich proceeded, with banners, music, and a vast rejoicing, towards the Theresa Meadow. The streets and suburban lanes were swarming with the multitudes awaiting the wonderful procession. As we emerged on the plain, we saw that already the earthen steps and terraces were black with an assembled multitude, whilst streams of pedestrians and streams of carriages poured across the meadow. All previous points of attraction were now centred in the spot fronting the Bavaria; where a second royal tent had been erected,—different entirely from the white and blue umbrella of my former description, and more like a canopy supported on four slight pillars. Long ropes, stretching down from the wooden screen which concealed the Bavaria, were firmly fastened into the green turf.

About twelve o'clock, after King Ludwig, accompanied by his Queen and King Otho, had arrived, and when the whole plain, from the neighborhood of the Bavaria to the very city itself, was gay with carriages and an untold moving multitude on foot, — the fantastic procession, consisting of all the trades' offerings, gradually approached to the sound of music and amid the shoutings of the people, passing before the King and presenting their gifts. Having witnessed the arrival of the first portion of the procession in front of the royal canopy, we took our station on the sloping bank a little to the right of the Bavaria, and nearly opposite the royal party, to gaze upon the wondrous crowd of human faces turned towards the pavilion, and towards the quaint forms slowly advancing through the multitude like grotesque ships steering their course amid a human ocean — fluttering banners on long staves telling as sails and masts. Beyond this rolling sea lay a broad stretch of green plain; then the city, with its towers and pinnacles rising into the clear blue sky; and, far off, the solemn mountain chain.

When the whole procession had passed, the horses were unharnessed and the strange cars were grouped upon the meadow. A troop of singers ascended the mound, and passed behind the wooden screen, or rather screens, which concealed as yet the motive spirit of this living scene. The important event of the day was at hand! A hush fell on the expectant multitude, — the hush of intense expectation. Suddenly swelled forth the notes of the overture composed expressly for the occasion. Then came another pause. An arm was raised in signal; and through the great silence was heard the distant sound of the saw and hammer at work severing the timbers of the condemned screen. The thrill of expectation grew more intense. A rope was loosened by a small human figure, far up aloft, — the screen feel with a huge sound which the roar of the cannon repeated, and the shout of the multitude prolonged, — and the mighty Bavaria stood revealed: — awful and beautiful — of a pale, tawny gold color — the sunlight catching on her sublime brow, on her rounded shoulder, on her strong large arm, which pressed to her side a laurel-wreathed sword. It caught on the sword-hilt, and burned and glittered like a star, — a beacon far away. Then fell the lower screens; and bands of singers, with banners displayed, swarmed on either side the pedestal, and broke forth into one mighty song of triumph. In presence of that marvellous colossal Virgin their voices sounded strangely small and human.

After the song came an oration by the painter Teichlein. He looked a mere black dot standing at the foot of the statue, and his voice sounded like the voice of some booming insect. Three cheers for King Ludwig succeeded: and in a few minutes the long gay train of royal carriages was seen, amid the shouts of the crowd, rapidly returning towards Munich.

CHAPTER XII.

THE OPENING OF THE SIEGESTHOR.

THE great festivities were terminated to-day with the opening of the *Siegesthor*, or Triumphal Arch, at the end of the beautiful Ludwig Strasse. This triumphal arch, dedicated to tthe Bavarian Army, is built in imitation of the triumphal arch of Constantine in Rome, and was designed by the architect, Gärtner, in 1844. It is constructed of stone brought from the neighborhood of Regensburg, and is embellished with medallions and basso-relievos — principally from designs by Professor Wagner — executed in white marble from Carrara and the Tyrol. The masonry is said to surpass in solidity and beauty anything in Europe.

The subjects of the six medallions represent the various provinces subject to the Bavarian sway: —

1. *Upper and Lower Bavaria* — Agriculture, Cattle, and Alpine Scenery.
2. *The Palatinate* — Culture of the Vine and Fishing.
3. *Upper Palatinate* — Forging of Iron.
4. *Upper and Central Franconia* — Forging of Iron, Breeding of Cattle, and Manufactures.
5. *Lower Franconia* — Cultivation of Corn and of the Vine, and Navigation.
6. *Swabia* — Weaving.

The basso-relievos are — 1. Combat between Infantry; 2. Combat between Infantry and Cavalry; 3. Combat between Cavalry; 4. Siege of a Fortress; 5. Attack of a Fortress with Battering-ram; 6. Passage of a River. Of course all these medallions and basso-relievos are of a classical character.

Eight winged Victories, four on either side of the gate, rise grandly before the pediment. They are of the noblest forms and proportions, and are sculptured in Carrara marble. To my mind these Victories are by far the most beautiful feature of the Triumphal Arch. Often, at sunset, the red evening light catches on their tall wings and majestic forms, tinting them on one side with rose-color, while the shadow side shows a pale, cold azure. They then seem like genii keeping watch over the city. Two flying Victories, with wreaths and palms, appear over the central arch. The four pilasters which support the pediment are of the Corinthian order. The whole is to be surmounted by a figure of Bavaria, seated in a triumphal car drawn by four lions. The statue, car, and lions, to be cast in bronze, are now in progress at the foundry.

This Triumphal Arch, as may be imagined, forms a striking termination to the noble Ludwig Strasse, and a most impressive entrance to Munich. Many an evening this summer have I stopped in admiration of this noble gateway. The long, broad Ludwig Strasse, so beautiful and unique from its harmonious Byzantine architecture, widens out into a kind of square, where play two abundant fountains. On one hand stretches the solemn white mass of the University — on the other, the pale stone-colored, severe-looking Jesuits' College — behind me rise into the calm evening sky the white towers of the Ludwig Kirche, each surmounted by a gilt cross, which, catching the last rays of the evening sun, glitter like two stars. Scarcely a footstep is heard in the silent square — the only sounds being the constant fresh splash of the fountains, and the distant murmur and rustle of trees as the evening breeze passes through them. Before me rises the gateway; and as if gazing down on me, stand the grand, calm Victories, their dazzling marble whiteness catching tints of rose and azure, like snowy Alpine peaks — whilst through the three round arches of the gate I catch a long perspective of green, solemn poplars, skirting the road across the wide plain.

The effect of the *Siegesthor*, however, was not quite so poetical on the day of its opening, for it was bitterly cold. About twelve o'clock people began to collect along the Ludwig Strasse, mounted the towers of the Ludwig Kirche, and crowded windows and door-steps, — assembling in denser masses about the gate itself. The magistrates of the city were here in their best array to receive the King and Army when they should make their triumphal entry. Crowds lined the poplar-shaded road; soldiers were drawn up, — gendarmes pranced about on their horses; — all, for a full hour, pierced to the bone by a searching wind which careered across the plain from the cold Alps, and blew the leaves in myriads from the tall, noisy, shivering poplars. At length, with sounds of music, and with much pomp and brilliancy of costume, King Maximilian and his brother King Otho, followed by other princes, and escorted by several regiments, approached the gate. The ladies of the court, and two, if not three Queens, graced the procession in gay open carriages and bright summer dresses, which looked very cold and uncomfortable. Then, there was a halt of some quarter of an hour before the gateway, and a reception of the municipal authorities, and much ceremony, and a '*Lebe-Hoch!*' for King Ludwig, who was not present,—and firing of cannon; and the royalties passed through the gate,—and the *Siegesthor* was opened.

CHAPTER XIII.

SOMETHING ABOUT MUNICH DECORATION, — PUBLIC AND DOMESTIC.

October 20th. — E. has been writing to me about these new 'Tile-cottages,' of which you are talking so much in England. I imagine the effect of these tile-walls might be something like the marble stuccoing much in vogue here. The impression when you stand for the first time in the Glyptothek and Hof-Kapelle, is that the walls are built of the most splendid marbles. It is only when you reflect upon the enormous expense of such works that your reason convinces you that the walls are not marble, but stucco. The idea of stucco, I grant, is unpleasant— all my Ruskin prejudices revolted at the idea of this 'hypocrisy,' when we made this discovery; but I have reasoned with myself after this fashion: Is it not better, in one sense more beautiful, for a state possessed of but small pecuniary resources, to have expended its money upon the *art*, the creative spirit, than upon the material? And if the idea conveyed to the soul be noble and true, what matter whether the wall be of precious stones or of plaster? The regret is, that these materials are so perishable; and this painful thought presses constantly upon me, — in a couple of hundred years or so, where will be these creations? But this art, the creative soul, although fading away, will doubtless have done its work in the world by kindling the fire of love and of aspiration in fresh laborers who will carry on the work here begun with undying energy.

In speaking of the Hof-Kapelle, I have already referred to the harmonious manner in which the brilliant hues of the frescoes and the golden back-grounds are toned down by the dull reds, dull greens, pale stone-colors, chocolate browns, and tender yellows and greys. In the new Basilica the arrangement of color is in the same exquisite harmony; but there all is *real* — in looking around this beautiful new church, you can rejoice in the consciousness that each column, each slab, is marble — genuine, truthful marble! — and there is a great delight in this consciousness.

The Glyptothek, the little sculpture gallery, is in itself one of the most ideal and harmonious of the works of art in Munich. The collection of sculpture, though small, contains some statues of priceless value and world-wide fame; but it is especially their beautiful arrangement and the harmonious whole which impresses you. The walls are of this beautiful marble stucco, but here not gradated in color, each room being of some one rich tint. The sculpture is arranged chronologically. Thus, entering, the history of sculpture rises before you as you pass along, from the Egyptian Sphynx to the works of Thorwaldsen. The impression produced by this judicious arrangement is profound.

But it was about stucco walls I was writing, and in the Glyptothek their effect is very beautiful. The impression is that they are built of the richest marble or porphyry; each room is of a separate color, but contrasted or harmonized so as agreeably to affect the imagination. You stand in a room of pale-green marble; the adjoining one, seen through the broad doorway, is tender lilac, and the one beyond, dull red; and the glorious, solemn statues gleam out white and pure against these self-colored yet richly tinted walls, with a wonderfully beautiful and impressive breadth of effect.

The ceilings of this lovely little gallery are enriched with frescoes by Cornelius, and by medallions by Schwanthaler. One of these frescoes, the Destruction of Troy, has greatly impressed us. As yet it is the only work of Cornelius's in Munich which has come up to my preconceived ideas of Cornelius's genius — there is less of the overstrained and *academic* in the figures and attitudes than in the altar-piece in the Ludwig Kirche, and in the earlier of these Glyptothek frescoes — more simplicity and beauty; the sternness is grand, very grand. This Destruction of Troy gives me a feeling of what those compositions from the Campo Santo at Berlin must be, of which every one speaks in such admiration.

Beautiful and highly poetical as this Munich School of Decoration is, one sees here only too frequently the danger of its becoming commonized and over-done. I am often on the verge of being utterly weary of ornament — often am utterly weary. In fact, there are certain so-called decorations here which I avoid looking at — for instance, the Arcade of the Hof-garten; and yet one has a lingering regard for it as the commencement of the Munich revival, and at certain points seen from among the green foliage of the garden the effect of the frescoed walls is agreeable; but I always, with my strong predilection in favor of German art, feel jealous of strangers dwelling upon the Arcade as one of the *marvels* of Munich. The arabesqued ceiling seen in its long prospective always reminds me most disagreeably of a vast length of painted oil-cloth! The detail certainly is graceful when you take the trouble to study it; but the effect is tawdry, — a petty flicker of lilac, green, and pink

And in the Royal Library the other day, I was annoyed by the same thing; the ceilings of the staircase and reading-room are like embossed paper-boxes — very elegant decorations they would have been for plum-boxes, or even good patterns for a lady's shawl, — but certainly most inappropriate as *decoration* for a place of study.

And you see the contagion of this sort of thing in every ceiling of every house above the very poorest of Munich. Now and then you see a beautiful design on a ceiling, but that will be the exception: one grows weary to death of arabesque, and this rage for over-ornament I should dread in these tile-houses.

The saloon of the Von ——'s house is a beautiful specimen of domestic decoration: Kaulbach and Neureuther have united their genius to adorn this room for their friends. Lovely sprays of vine, and flowers, and flowering shrubs, display themselves upon the white walls of the room — rising in thick yet symmetrical luxuriance above the crimson silk divan which runs around it. It is as though the divan rested against a low garden-wall, above which was seen the rich foliage of the vineyard, or the tangle of the shrubbery; and from among the foliage look forth the sweet faces of the family: here is a pensive girl meditating over a book; there a fair-haired, blue-eyed, younger sister, weaving a flowery garland, or a little round-faced, flaxen-haired lad eagerly catching butterflies in his net: the portraits are by Kaulbach — the exquisite foliage by Neureuther. Neureuther's festoons of flowers link together the series of Kaulbauch's frescoes from the history of Cupid and Psyche which glow upon the walls — designs similar to those from the same legend in Duke Max's palace, but smaller in size. The effect of the whole is very lovely.

The exterior of several private houses here also strikes me as extremely agreeable, and makes me wish earnestly I could transform some of our square uncouth masses of English brick-work into forms and coloring as agreeable to the eye and imagination. I have spoken elsewhere of the general impression of the Ludwig Strasse; it is to certain detached houses I now refer. There is a house close to the Dult Platz especially agreeable, and now in autumn the crimson tints of the Virginian creeper, and the varied greens, browns, and oranges of other climbing plants trained over them, harmonize and contrast most beautifully with the pale buff tints of the brick of which they are built, with the white sculptured stone-work of the round arched windows, and with the brilliantly tinted medallions not unfrequently introduced between windows or on either side of a portico. On the front of Kaulbach's house are two medallions, the ground an intensely brilliant ultra-marine, and each containing, in relief of pale buff, a beautiful figure of a youth holding by the mane a prancing and snorting horse. Above each youth is a star.

These houses are generally built of brick of two colors —our common yellow brick, and brick of a deeper brown; with these two tints the most beautiful effects and patterns are obtained. The form of the bricks also often varies, and thus a great deal of beautiful detail is gained: there is one mass of red-brick building in the Ludwig Strasse, which, simply from the manner in which the bricks are laid and the character of the bricks themselves, is very beautiful. But there are, again, houses here in Munich where the Byzantine and Moresco taste has gone so very crazy, that one grows utterly weary of ornament.

CHAPTER XIV.

AUTUMNAL RAMBLES.

October 27. — To-day we commenced our winter campaign of work at the studio. The whole day has been one of pleasantness and beauty from beginning to end. The first beautiful thing was our walk through the English Garden to the studio. A considerable quantity of snow had fallen during the night, and lay thick and pure upon the branches of furs and pines, and upon the boughs of various trees which have not yet shed their autumnal leaves; so that heavy masses of snow lay upon the scarlet and gold, and olive-green branches, in strangest contrast. It was a singular and poetic blending of autumn and winter, full of lovely suggestions for decorative art. Upon the wall, which on one side shuts in the garden, grow tufts of grass, which formed, this morning, the most fairy-like crests of beauty; each bent and blade covered with rime, which glittered in the sunshine. Lovely, brilliant sprays dipped into the clear green waves of the mill-stream which rushes along behind the studio-field. The field was white with snow; we had our first winter's glimpse of the studio. And when we entered through the heavy grey door into our little sanctum, the air was warm with a pleasant warmth from the stove, and behold! in one corner stood a beautiful palm-tree in a green tub. It was the emblem of peace to us. It is a favorite tree of

K.'s; he has painted sprays from it in the hands of the Christians leaving Jerusalem. It had been placed in our little studio for warmth: we welcomed it with much love.

People usually call the neighborhood of Munich stupid, flat, and utterly devoid of natural beauty; they speak of the singular contrast between the beauty of the city and the barrenness and want of interest in the neighborhood. Strange to say, I shall bring away with me memories of the beauties of nature, which, in looking back to my sojourn, I almost think will outshine the memory of the beauties of art. I recall a dozen sun-set skies, that, for gorgeousness and glory, put to shame all the gold and rainbow hues of the churches. This vast plain, with its dreamy horizon of Alps, the desolate banks of the Isar, the lovely English Garden, and all the many pleasant, quiet strolls to quaint old villages, — what delicious memories shall I not carry away with me of them!

Besides this, the ground, in summer, is one mosaic of lovely flowers; and the sky is a never-ceasing delight, — so blue and clear. I often wonder whether it is owing to the atmosphere being clearer here than in England, and also to the greater beauty and freshness of coloring of the public buildings, that not a single day passes over without its presenting you with some architectural picture.

Every evening, as I cross the Ludwig Strasse, I look down it to see some new effect upon the Siegesthor. Last night the ground was sparkling with snow, the horizon the palest tint of peach-color, deepening into a warm rose, and against the sky stood forth the Siegesthor as if carved in ivory. Sometimes it glows as if carved in ruddy gold. I had no conception, till I came here, of the wonderful beauty of *color* in architecture, and how nature seems to pronounce her blessing upon it, by heightening the beauty of man's work, through her showers of sunshine and her clouds of shadow, and her glow of reflected lights. Oh, if man would only strive *with* instead of *against* nature, what a world this would be! — and will be in time. Still more so is this the case with the soul, — of which all these outward things are but types.

How lovely are our walks, to and fro, through the English Garden! The ground is covered with pure, crisp snow; the trees often sparkling with hoar-frost, till all is like a forest of enchantment; and the sun sparkles and glitters upon their branches as though they were covered with diamonds. Or, perhaps, there is no hoar-frost, only the trunks and branches are powdered with snow, and the delicate, wondrous tracery of branches relieves itself against the purest, deepest, most glowing azure sky, like a warm summer's sky — so blue and cloudless. I have no words to describe the delight which these walks are to me: the air is pure, keen, and bracing; the ground hard and crisp, and morning and evening I find some lovely, fresh picture painted for me by that most wonderful of all artists — Nature. Now it is a sky all creamy and pale amber, with early morning light, the more distant groups of trees lost in delicate haze; mist hanging about mysteriously among the glades and hollows of the garden, dropping from branches and veiling grotesque giant stems, and yet sunshine is struggling through the haze, casting long blue shadows over the snow. Now, the effect is different; ruddy sunset-light falls across the snow, turning it to rose-color, and burns upon boles and branches with a glory almost unearthly. The trees stand as of molten copper, with an azure sky behind them, and the green ice of the mill-stream, powdered with snow, looks yet more vivid in color.

Last night, as I returned, a large, calm moon was

rising out of a rose-tinted horizon, above a lawny opening in the garden. The ground was a sheet of snow, with lovely groups of trees rising here and there into the quiet, warm sky. I stopped for a moment to drink in its beauty. It was close to Prince Carl's palace, where two unlucky sentinels are always standing, often pacing to and fro this cold weather, with faces of intense misery. I always think that the placing of sentinels is a great piece of humbug; it is not an active, useful watchfulness, like that of the police — it is merely a pompous piece of man's tyranny. I felt sorry for these unlucky sentinels — one of whom passed me at this moment, pacing up and down with a blue and scarlet face. I longed to say to him, 'Look how beautiful that moon is, and how lovely the garden looks! But that would have been a very *moon-struck* action. If these poor men, however, had only eyes to see these things, they would not need so much pity.

I have spoken of our rambles in the neighborhood. One such I will describe; it was in the autumn.

As we were at work in the studio, we all at once bethought ourselves of the beautiful sunshine out of doors, and away we went for a walk, the sun shining brilliantly, and the fresh free wind roaring through the trees.

Crossing first the great Royal Wood-yard, we came to the banks of the Isar, which are very beautiful. The Isar is a broad stream, which, when swollen with rain, rushes on white and muddy; at other times it flows on smoothly among long stretches of gravelly, shoal-like portions of a shingly beach: the banks are at times very high, rising cliff-like above the river. Our side of the bank, however, was not particularly elevated, but beautified by avenues planted along it. Imagine a sort of terrace, skirted on either hand by lofty trees, sometimes poplars, sometimes elms, while sloping down to the shingly river's margin are copses of willow and undergrowth, and on the other side of the avenue, pleasant meadows, lying calmly between you and the skirts of the English Garden. Swiftly-flowing branches of the Isar rush merrily through the meadows, and turn mills, and give life and activity to this otherwise solitary and quiet scene.

The trees had almost lost their leaves; but the broad sunshine brought out all the lovely details of their stems and branches; and made us think that these avenues were now more beautiful than in summer. Long quivering shadows fell across the path, the wind rushed joyously through their branches, and the sunlight fell sparkling upon some figure approaching up the narrow avenue: now a peasant-girl, wheeling before her an old-fashioned barrow, piled up with branches or dead leaves, her white sleeves and red boddice telling as a bright focus of color in the grey landscape; or perhaps it was some grave old professor in a long dark-blue cloak, which gave him a still more solemn air.

On, and still on, we walked, until the avenue became wilder, the meadows more solitary, and the thickets between us and the river a thicker tangle of underwood and creepers. Clematis hung in rich festoons from the trees of the avenue, and here and there was a barberry bush, with its yellow leaves yet unshed; or the slender branches of the wild cherry, covered with brilliant scarlet leaves. All at once the most lovely landscape lay before us. The grey avenue lessened and lessened in a beautiful perspective, till the light at the farther end shone out like an azure star. This avenue was on the left hand of the picture; the rest of the composition was a broad stretch of river, blue as the bluest heaven, with long, white, desolate shoals, in tongues and promontories running into it; in the middle distance a group of rafts, and men busily at work on the shoals, giving life and a most picturesque animation to the scene: the further river-bank curved round in a bold sweep, overhung with a dense mass of grey trees, on which the sun shone till they looked quite hoary in the blaze of light; and a still more distant sweep of river-bank crowned with a white-washed church, the red-tiled roof and tower of which told brightly against a warm grey sky, united the two portions of the picture, the river and the avenue, by the most harmonious line of composition imaginable. And, as if to complete the picturesque effect, behold a long, long flight of birds stretching across the sky!

We stood in perfect admiration and astonishment at the artistic power of nature.

Arrived at the end of the avenue, we found that the river-bed widened out, and assumed almost a sea-shore character with its shingly shoals. On one hand was a wild sort of mainland with low brushwood, and numbers of young birch-trees rising up here and there, their delicate leaves yellow as gold, and trembling like the leaves of aspens. On a mound above the river-bank we noticed a queer little straw-hut, and beyond it a long array of what at first appeared black coffins, mounted on cars. What could they possibly be? we questioned from ourselves. And there, in that desolate solitude, stood a soldier as sentinel. Could they be cannon? No. We walked up to them, and then came to the conclusion that they were boats intended to form a bridge of boats.

We now crossed this moorland, at times up to the knees in long grass, of a coarse jungle-like character, and very soon found ourselves close to a busy manufactory of some kind. A wooden bridge, closed by heavy gates, led over a rushing branch of the Isar: long, low ranges of worshops, black and noisy, and busy-looking as if in England, were there, and tall chimneys vomiting black smoke; and there was a roar and a rattle very much out of character with the quiet moor and this primitive Germany. Smutty artisans were passing rapidly to and fro. We looked into a black, busy workshop, where blazed numbers of furnaces; there was a roar of bellows, a clank of hammers, a blaze of myriads of sparks struck from glowing masses of iron, and a crowd of black, hard-working mechanics worthy of England. Everything was black; there were heaps of iron everywhere, and the steam rushed and tumbled and boiled with an unwonted energy. This was the steam-engine manufactory.

In the court-yard behind the row of workshops, stood the house of the overlooker, with its luxuriant vine overhanging its white-washed walls, and its green shutters, as quiet and primitive as any German heart would desire. What a busy little world this seemed in the midst of that moorland solitude!

When, on our return, we reached the edge of the English Garden, the sight of a picturesque coffee-house, with its wooden galleries running round the exterior in Tyrolean fashion, over which, as it had been such a bright sunny day, quantities of bedding were hung to air, tempted us to indulge in a cup of coffee after our ramble. All looked beautiful but deserted, in the orchard, where a lanky girl, in a very short green petticoat and purple stockings, was sweeping away the heaps of fallen leaves from tables and benches. What a time we had to wait for coffee! We should have grown quite angry had it not been for the glorious sky which glowed before us, and reflected itself in the rushing stream at the bottom of the orchard. Behind us rose the dark trees of the English Garden, and before us, separated by a rapid stream, and approached by a wooden bridge, lay the quiet expanse of green meadows;

whilst all around us lay the brilliant masses of fallen autumn leaves. We thought that this was probably the last time we should take coffee in the open air, as we had so often done throughout the lovely summer, and we were patient.

At length the coffee came; but it was quite dark before we reached home.

Another day, taking our sketching materials, we went to Schwalbing, a village with two churches, just near the city; and to the first of these we directed our steps. Unlike most continental churches, it appeared to be closed, as were the gates of the church-yard. After peering about for a long time, I discovered a door leading into the church-yard. A ruinous old white building, an old spital, with the rudest of faded frescoes upon its front, was united to the church by a covered gallery, supported upon arches. This gallery, with its tiled roof, had quite an Italian character; just the kind of architectural bit which Overbeck introduces into his pictures — a capital thing, good in color and peculiar in composition, yet most simple. We regretted that it was not summer, that we might have made a careful study of it in oils.

Through these arches we passed to see another capital bit, though of another character — a covered way leading up to the porch, supported on low, grey marble pillars, very quaint! It was fit for a back-ground in some illustrations of one of Uhland's ballads. We were enchanted with our church-yard; there was no need to go farther; but first we would see the inside of the little church.

A fat, merry-looking woman, with a handkerchief, in Munich fashion, tied tightly across her forehead, and hanging down her back in long ends, had seen us, as she looked out of a house on one side of the court-yard; and she now came out with a key, and asked if we wished to go into the church. This was just what we desired, we replied; and in we went, through the low door-way. It was, like most village churches, very white from whitewash, and very tawdry with gilding and dressed-up Virgins and hideous saints, but very clean.

I inquired why the church was locked up? Was there no mass there on Sundays? — and could not people go in on week-days to pray whenever they liked?

There was no mass, she said, on Sundays, but on all saints' days; and when people wanted to pray, she was always ready to open the door for them. But had not the Holy Virgin had one of her best pocket-handkerchiefs stolen? and had not a golden heart been carried away from the altar? Ah! there were very bad people in Munich, and it was necessary to lock up the church.

She seemed an honest, good simple soul herself; for when I offered her some Kreutzers for her trouble, she would not take them, saying that she was only too proud and too happy to enter the church and show it to strangers. From her we borrowed chairs, and were soon comfortably sketching our Overbeck gallery. At twelve o'clock the woman and a little lad crossed the court-yard to ring the bell, and soon after that, our usual dinner hour arriving, we felt very hungry, and were directed by the guardianess of the place to the village inn close by. A queer, dirty place it was; but we were far too hungry to be particular. We sate waiting for our two portions of goose — everybody seems to live on goose at this season, it appears quite to have taken the place of veal — in a long dirty billiard-room. All was desolate and silent, saving that now and then a dirty, slovenly girl, or hulking ostler, came in for beer, which was brought to them from an inner room. To amuse myself I read the newspaper, which was just then full of rumors of war.

At length we had our dinner, and then went to the good

woman's in whose charge we had left our sketching materials. What a desolate place was her house! It was one of those places which astonished by their total want of everything which one is accustomed to consider a necessary of life: yet it would have done anybody's heart good to have seen the cheerful soul in her miserable room. She was so merry, and her face bespoke such habitual contentment! I think I never saw such a pair of happy, bright blue eyes in any human countenance.

To my astonishment I found the room filled with children — small children, a regular swarm — between the ages of six months and twelve years. Was it a school, or how was it? I asked.

'Oh! they are all my own,' she replied.

I looked around to see if she were not the little old woman who lived in the shoe, and who did not know what to do with her many children. But the house was not a shoe, as far as I could make out; and most certainly she seemed to know what to do with hers. Children appeared to be the only furniture to the place. I could see, besides them, only a wooden cradle, a couple of stools, a little old chest of drawers, and a long row of pegs, on which hung a whole array of tattered cloaks, and coats, and caps.

All afternoon the troop of blue-eyed, light-haired children was playing about the old church, now hiding among the old arches, now rushing out with flying locks into the bright sunshine. We heard their voices sounding merrily among the graves, and echoing back from the crumbling old walls; the place was like a pleasant poem. Throughout the afternoon, too, various peasants came to pray in the church, and the mother was constantly going backwards and forwards with her huge key in her hand; and she had ever a kind cheerful word to say to us as she passed. But we could not persuade her to take anything from us when we left.

As we returned home, the setting sun was flooding the whole plain with orange light, and turning the avenue of poplars into an avenue of dark-red gold, relieved against an indigo sky.

CHAPTER XV.

ALL SOULS DAY, AND A ROYAL CHRISTENING.

Munich, Nov. 1. — This is All Souls Day. The principal Cemetery is illuminated and decorated with flowers, garlands, and various devices, — and all Munich goes out to see it. We had heard of this grand day for weeks, and therefore were rather curious about it. We set off at two o'clock, and on our way through the Türken Strasse met King Ludwig walking alone. Spite of all the old king's failings, my heart warms to him as the generous and noble patron of Art; and as such I made him a low reverence as he passed, and received in return a gracious smile and bow. A little farther on, driving across the Maximilian Platz, we met the other king and his brother King Otho. They were in a gay carriage with outriders in blue, and their two queens were with them. They had been to the Cemetery.

The Cemetery lies outside the Sendlinger Thor, — the old and new *Gottes-Acker* lying close together. Tribes of people were streaming in the direction of the cemeteries, and all wore a holiday look. The whole day had been a holiday; mass had been performed in the churches, and the shops were closed. On the open space before the ruinous old Sendlinger gate were a number of stalls, on which were displayed wreaths of moss and ivy, and crosses covered with moss and ivy, and initial letters also formed of the same materials. As we approached the burial-ground these stalls increased in number, — on which also crucifixes were offered for sale, — and the crowd of people became quite dense; almost every peasant and burgher of the lower class carrying a rosary. There was a regular crush to get into the burial-ground. A row of frightful and diseased beggars — the halt, the blind, and the lame — men, women, and children — stood before the little church, craving alms.

A little further on, we had space to observe that every grave in this densely filled church-yard was decked out in festal array. What a singular impression is produced by seeing these gay-looking graves and the gay crowd of living people, and then to picture the equally dense crowd of the calm dead lying beneath these flowers and these busy feet! To me there was a frightful contrast between this life and this death.

There was no expression of sorrow or of reverence in the faces of the living — mere curiosity. Numbers of blue glass lamps were suspended from the crosses and monuments. There were wreaths, garlands, and festoons of moss, ivy, and everlasting; some of tawdry pink and blue artificial flowers, which were frightful. But on the whole the decorations were very tasteful, — some of them lovely. For instance, a grey marble basin for holy water, placed at the foot of a grave, would be wreathed round with myrtle and rose-buds — *real*, not artificial; while the grave would be covered with greenhouse plants in full bloom, — or the soil perhaps raked smoothly till it resembled fine black sand, so that on this black ground a mosaic of scarlet mountain-ash berries, the white waxen berries of the snowberry, and leaves and flowers in the form of crosses, initials, and various devices, would be worked; and the tall, elegantly-formed stone or iron cross at its head would be festooned with moss and ivy wreaths. On some of the graves a kind of moveable garden was placed, — a large wooden tray covered with mould, into which were stuck leaves and flowers in patterns. Cress, or some little seedling of that kind, had also frequently been sown and sprung up in patterns, in letters, or in words, variegated also with colored sands — blue, red, and white. It can scarcely be imagined how very ingenious these little gardens were; curious though, rather than pretty, — somewhat like very neat children's gardens. Every grave had its lamps or candles, and each its attendant — an old man or woman, who sate beside the cross muttering prayers with the rosary in hand. These attendants all seemed to be old. I noticed one or two very old people, — one man with a white beard, who trembled all over with age and cold.

The Old Cemetery is of considerable extent, and is quite filled with graves. A sort of cloister runs round it, beneath which were also monuments; and, of course, therefore, more flowers, and garlands, and lamps, and attendants. We now passed with the crowd into the New Cemetery. It also is inclosed by a cloister; — not, however, like the other, whitewashed, but built of rich warm brick, a yellow brown, with red bricks introduced so as to produce a fine effect. This beautiful cloister, with its numberless round arches, is very striking: — quite grand, indeed, in its simplicity. As yet there are but few graves in the inclosure. On one side, as the cloister is entered, is the monument of Gärtner, the architect of the *Siegesthor*, — and a little further on is that of Professor von Walter. On the other side of the entrance, close by the door-way, is a grey marble monument, with a bust in white marble placed on it, — an ugly, ungraceful monument. A tall American cedar was planted on either side, — a number of garlands of myrtle and bay lay at its feet. It was Schwanthaler's monument!' Had we only known that he slept there, I would have taken the loveliest garland I could have found in Munich, as a little tribute of respect to his genius. I was pleased to see the interest and respect evinced by the crowd collected round this monument. 'Yes, Schwanthaler! the great Schwanthaler!' I heard people say. I cannot conceive why King Ludwig, who erected this monument, could permit anything so common-place — nay, unsightly — to be connected with Schwanthaler's name and memory.

On our way home we noticed a crowd of people in the Maximilian Platz, — a crowd of eager people, who, with breathless interest, were watching a man mounted on a heavy ladder, or rather flight of wooden steps. He was lighting a lamp: for to-night Munich was to be illuminated, — the lamp illumination having been deferred from the opening of the *Siegesthor* till to-night. At the foot of the lamp-post stood a grave, pompous man, in a buff-colored quilted coat, trimmed with black bear's skin, holding in one hand a long pole, at the end of which burned a feeble flame inclosed in perforated tin, and in his other a little box containing a red mixture, which he stirred up from time to time with a piece of stick, — his demeanor being that of a person engaged on solemn and important duties. When, suddenly, three little flames darted up from the gas-burner, there was a perfect scream of delight from the gazing crowd below. Gas was to burn that night in the streets of Munich. There was indeed a jubilation! I smile as I contrast in my mind that huge flight of steps, and those two pompous, solemn officers, with a brisk London lamplighter. In Munich the phrase ought to be as *slow*, not as *brisk* as a lamplighter. When the lamp was lighted, the heavy ladder and the heavy men moved off, — he of the buff coat and bearskin growling '*Platz! platz!*' to the wondering crowd. At the corner of the Amalien Strasse we met other lamp-lighters, two of whom carried the ladder, and a third the light. It was, indeed, an important and formidable business this gas-lamp illumination. Looking out of my window as I write, I behold a feeble brilliancy in the streets, — and all the world out enjoying it.

Nov. 16. — Fräulein Sänchen came down to the studio yesterday, to inform us of a grand christening which was going to take place. It was the christening of 'Her Royal Highness Theresa Charlotta Marianna Augusta, daughter of his Royal Highness Prince Leutpold of Bavaria,' as the long programme which the good old creature brought in her hand expressed it. The ceremony, said Fräulein Sänchen, was to take place in the beautiful throne-room, with its white marble walls and columns, and rows of gigantic gilded statues. We thought, could we only obtain admittance, how imposing the ceremony would be in this hall. The christening would be performed at two o'clock; therefore by one we returned home, and found Madame Thekla and her friend and neighbor the 'Frau Majorin' ready to accompany us.

This 'Frau Majorin' — there are three 'Frau Majorins' in this one house! — is a fat little woman, as broad as she is long: she is a widow, and has a son, who, like her late husband, is a soldier. We have the felicity of seeing his uniform brushed just opposite our door each morning. The Frau Majorin is possessed of a remarkably high-pitched voice, in which she gossips for hours each day with good Madame Thekla. I hear the murmur and buzz of their voices through the door at this very moment; they are voices to drive one distracted!

Well, the two gossips were ready to accompany us; and off, therefore, we immediately set. We found tribes of people entering the palace, at one of the side entrances in the old portion of the palace. We followed the stream up long flights of steps and through long galleries, some hung with ugly old portraits, others ornamented with armorial bearings and various heraldic devices emblazoned on the walls, which were white-washed, and, as well as the arched ceiling, covered with stucco ornaments of the Louis Quatorze age. People had arranged themselves along the walls, to watch the procession pass to the throne-room. But we, hoping to gain admittance to the christening itself, hurried on until we ignominiously were turned back by a gendarme stationed to prevent the admission of the vulgar herd — who were without tickets.

Tall men, in a costume not unlike that of our 'Beef-eaters,' except that their livery was blue, and holding long pikes in their hands, took up their station in a long row up either side of the gallery; and behind them crushed eager spectators, looking anxiously — especially the short ones — from behind the great blue and black-striped backs and slashed sleeves, and caught snatches of the procession in considerable discomfort.

First came a number of strange-looking fellows, in splendid uniforms and court dresses. It was a curious assemblage of heads: old, withered faces, seared with worldliness till they were scarcely human — features pinched and distorted with diplomacy; they were men bowed with age, and covered with decorations, — but it was age without dignity and reverence.

Then came the Grand Master of the Ceremonies, with his rod; and now a stout lady, in full court-dress, her train borne by attendants. Upon a cushion this lady bore Her most Serene Highness the newly-born Princess Theresa Charlotta Marianna Augusta, who was covered with a pink gauze veil. The little princess certainly deserved at this moment her title of 'serene,' for she was so quiet that you never would have guessed there was an infant princess concealed by the veil, and lying upon the cushion.

It was a relief to know that this infant was a girl, and thus never could harden into quite such frightful worldliness as that of the old courtiers who had preceded her. Next followed two pretty little boys, her brothers; they were about six and seven years old, and dressed in purple velvet tunics; they carried burning tapers: they were lovely enough to have been little angels, instead of princes.

And now everybody bent as low as they could, — for the King and Queen passed by; the King wearing a uniform, and looking very gracious and spruce. He led the Queen by the hand. The Queen, I found, was rather short than tall, as I had imagined from seeing her at the theatre; she looked very handsome with her large proud eyes, and in her dress of white satin, with her long crimson velvet train borne by pages. And then there was the King of Greece, in his Albanian costume of white and gold, and he led by the hand one of his sisters, the Grand Duchess of something; and they were followed by Prince Leutpold, the father of the little serene infant, leading along another great lady. In fact, excepting the old King and Queen, all the royal family were present. There was the Duchess of Leuchtenberg, the widow of Eugene Beauharnais, who was to stand deputy godmother to the little princess, and represent the two real godmothers, the Empress Dowager of Austria and the Ex-Queen Theresa of Bavaria. And then there was the Archbishop in his lilac robes and skull-cap, and his attendant priests bearing tapers and crucifixes; and there was a long train of the diplomatic corps with their ladies, and the burgomaster and corporation of the city; and, bringing up the rear, a great number of officers.

And now, when all had passed, there was nothing for us to do but to imagine the scene in the beautiful throne-room, where, opposite the crimson velvet canopy, beneath which the King and Queen would be seated, an altar had been erected. Yes, being endowed with a tolerably vivid imagination, the whole scene was speedily conjured up, — the rows of court ladies on either side the throne, — the altar, with its gold and fine linen, burning tapers, and officiating priests, — the groups of gentlemen in uniform, and the *Te Deum* sung by choristers stationed above in a gallery, — and the whole gorgeous array visible through a perspective of marble columns and gigantic golden statues, the ancestors of the little princess now being received into the Christian Church!

CHAPTER XVI.

CONSECRATION OF THE BASILICA.

Nov. 24.—The first stone of the Basilica of St. Bonifazius was laid by King Ludwig in 1835, in celebration of his *Silberner Hochzeit*—or the twenty-fifth anniversary of his marriage. It has taken fifteen years to complete and enrich it with sculptures, arabesques, frescoes, and carving in wood. Last week the rich gold and silver vessels, the gold and silver crucifixes, the altar-cloths and splendid robes for the priests, the embroidered banners and canopies, the velvet cushions, the gorgeous carpets, thrones, and seats required by the pomp of Catholic worship, were exhibited for three days in the church to the public, who streamed thither in crowds. To-day was the consecration.

This church may be considered unique; being a revival of the Basilicas of the fifth and sixth centuries—a Roman hall of justice converted into a Christian temple. It is built entirely of beautiful dark-red brick. Adjoining it is the monastery of the Benedictine Monks, built also of brick, and with the same round-arched windows as the church—of which, indeed, it seems a portion. A portico, supported by eight noble limestone columns, runs along the front of the Basilica; and three lofty doors, rich with emblematical carvings in wood and stone, lead into the church. The interior is divided into five naves by sixty-four columns of grey marble, with exquisitely sculptured white marble capitals and bases. Entering by the middle door, the lofty centre nave stretches away before the spectator — an avenue of noble columns supporting upon rounded arches an expanse of wall glowing with arabesques and frescoes, and perforated by a long row of small round-topped windows, high up, and near the roof; which, after the manner of the old basilicas, exposes its beams and rafters to view, but gilt and ornamented, and glittering with stars on a deep azure ground. This centre nave terminates in a lofty semi-circular niche, wherein, approached by a flight of twelve steps, rises the high altar.

On the wall above the high altar, on a gold ground, and divided from each other by the typical palm-tree, stand the first teachers of Christianity in Bavaria: St. Bonifazius, St. Benedict, St. Willibald, St. Corbinian, St. Rupert, St. Gimmeran, St. Cilian, and St. Magnus. Above them floats Christ, as the head and symbol of the Church triumphant, surrounded by a glory of Cherubim and Seraphim, and with the Virgin and St. John the Baptist praying at his feet. Beneath the high altar and its flight of steps extends the crypt. Two side altars terminate the outer naves, as the high altar the principal nave. Above the side altar to the right are the Virgin and Child receiving the homage of the patron saint of the Bavarian royal family; above the one on the left is the Martyrdom of St. Stephen — the most beautiful of all the frescoes in the Basilica — the most beautiful, I am inclined to say, of all the frescoes in Munich. St. Stephen, with his meek, pale face, and with clasped hands, falls to the earth beneath the cruel stones of his assailants like a broken white lily.

These altar-pieces are, together with the other frescoes in the Basilica, painted by Hess, and his assistants. The history of St. Boniface, to whom the church is dedicated, is told in a series of frescoes which extends along either side of the centre nave, above the noble columns of which I have spoken. These represent twelve principal incidents from his life; commencing with his reception as a child among the Benedictine monks, and his departure from England to Germany upon his perilous mission — and ending with his martyrdom in Friesland, and his burial in the Abbey of Fulda. The lesser events are told in smaller designs alternating with the large frescoes, and are painted in grey on a blue ground, so managed as to suggest sky. Many of these smaller designs are peculiarly beautiful; they are in octagonal compartments, and are surrounded by graceful arabesques of crimson, green, gold, and lilac, on a deep chocolate ground. Below the frescoes illustrative of the life of St. Boniface, is a series of medallion heads of the Popes; and above the frescoes, alternating with the round-arched windows, and painted on a gold ground, are groups of saints and martyrs who lived and suffered for the propagation of Christianity in Germany. The effect of this centre nave is that of a gorgeous and solemn missal.

The walls of the church are a mosaic of rich marbles: — dark greens — dull, ruddy browns and reds — and delicate greys and lilacs. Opposite the side altars, and to the right and left as you enter the church by the side doors, are two little chapels — the chapel for baptism and the chapel for burial. A peculiar simplicity, solemnity, and dignity characterize the whole edifice.

The ceremony of consecration was to commence, we understood, at half-past seven o'clock in the morning. Long streaks of golden and pale pink light from the newly-risen sun stretched athwart a sombre grey sky, as we set out towards the church, and wonderfully enhanced the beauty of the Pinakothek and Glyptothek, which we passed on our way to the Basilica: the Basilica and the monastery attached to it being only separated by a wall from the beautiful white marble temple which faces the Glyptothek, and which is erected for the triennial exhibition of paintings here. The streets were as yet almost vacant, although the bells of the Basilica now for the first time summoned the good citizens. As we turned, however, into the street in which the church stands, we were greeted by sounds of life. The burgher-guard, preceded by their band, marched along, and all the houses were festooned with moss garlands, gay flags, carpets, and pictures hung out from the windows and balconies. Tall cedar-trees in tubs were placed within the portico of the Basilica, one on either side of the lofty carved doors. Few people, however, had as yet congregated.

The citizen-guard stationed itself before the church with much parade; and soon the crowd grew. A school of little girls, in white dresses, and each bearing her small nosegay in her hand, and a school of little boys, drew up on the steps of the portico. And now the Archbishop, in his purple robes, descended from his carriage, — was received by the priests, — was presented with the heavy golden key of the church, — and, beneath a crimson canopy which was borne above him, blessed, anointed, and sprinkled with holy water the portal of the church, previous to entering it. People then crowded into the court-yard in which stand the church and the monastery, as well as the monks' garden with its long pleached alleys and flower-beds. And now, with crucifixes borne aloft, and fluttering crimson banners, — with white and black robed priests and choristers chanting in loud voices from large missals which they bore before them, — with a train of emaciated young Jesuit scholars, — with the twelve Benedictine Brothers, in their long black gowns, — with a procession of magistrates and citizens, — with the little boys' and girls' schools, and all the scholars of the Latin school, arrayed in purple dress-coats with velvet collars, like a set of stunted little men, — came the Archbishop in his gorgeous white and golden robes, with his mitre on his head. He walked beneath a canopy of gold and crimson, his vestments borne by attendant priests; and with upraised hand, on which glittered his large amethyst ring, and with muttering lips he blessed the church. Three times the procession encircles the church; now the Archbishop sprinkles the walls with holy water from a silver vessel with a bunch of holy herbs; now he sprinkles the multitude; the choristers sing; the five bells of the Basilica, each bearing the name of a saint, and exquisitely cast, peal from the belfry; — and the outer walls are consecrated.

But, for the unlucky public collected outside the church, there now commenced a most tedious time. For two mortal hours did they wait until the church doors should be thrown open; the only incident to beguile the cold and weariness being the arrival of a carriage full of dignitaries of the Church in their violet robes, violet caps, white fur and fine linen, — and the constant, sudden, and annoying charges of the stupid burgher-guard upon the patient crowd.

At length the huge doors were swung back, and in poured the multitude, met by a fragrant breath of incense. The high altar glowed and glittered with its bevy of priests. At the foot of the twelve steps leading to it were placed crimson seats on either hand, on which was a small assemblage of gaily attired gentlemen, — a group of bright uniforms to the right, and the more soberly arrayed magistracy to the left. The railing which inclosed the high altar, the flight of steps, and the seats, were decorated with moss and lovely greenhouse plants in full bloom. Tall laurels, myrtles, and orange-trees, in huge tubs, were arranged in rows on either side of the steps, and interspersed with lovely aloes and graceful palm-like plants, which drooped their tender fresh sprays with exquisite carelessness over the balustrades.

Then commenced a bewildering succession of ceremonies. The Archbishop sprinkled the holy water; anointed the walls, the candlesticks, the crucifixes, the gold and silver vessels ; chanted, and prostrated himself before the altar ; rows of priests, young and old, with burning tapers, ascended and descended the steps ; the Archbishop was robed and disrobed ; sat upon a raised seat to the right of the altar, his head resplendent in his mitre, his amethyst ring sparkling on his gloved hand, his feet resting on a splendidly embroidered violet carpet ; the four Bishops, with long white and gold embroidered mantles covering their violet robes, kneeling around him, or seated upon low amber-colored seats at his feet ; priests knelt before him with their large open missals, out of which he chanted ; the choristers responded ; now he blesses the great golden crucifix, now the golden candlesticks of the high altar, and the altar itself. The candlesticks are borne back to their place ; young priests put tall tapers into them one by one ; they are lighted, and the whole altar is consecrated and arrayed. Gorgeous crimson carpets are unrolled and cover the steps ; the little girls in white scatter their nosegays ; the bells peal out ; the organ resounds through the vast church with its thrilling tones ; the *Te Deum* is sung ; priests and people adore ; and the glorious sunshine pours in through the many windows, glitters on the golden walls, and lights up the marble columns, but sparkles with the greatest splendor on the bright fresh leaves of the laurel, orange and myrtle-trees. Their

12

leaves burn with such a magical brilliancy and freshness, that in comparison the gorgeous hues of the walls fade into an earthly dimness.

While the sunlight thus floods the centre aisle, leaving the rest of the church with its forest of columns, in a mysterious mistiness and gloom, high mass is performed. As it terminates, the distant sound of booming cannon is heard, mingling with the pealing organ and the ringing of the bells. The Archbishop is unrobed by his attendant priests, whilst the altar is covered with fine white linen napkins. He descends the steps, and passes out of the consecrated Basilica, blessing the people; — and the ceremonies are at an end.

CHAPTER XVII.

WINTER TWILIGHT AND CHRISTMAS EVE.

December 14. — I am just returned from the station, where I have bade my dear fellow pilgrim, Clare, God-speed upon her journey. Yes, she is returning to England. It is a very sudden resolve on her part, and we have been full of regret on account of this return; but it must be. God speed the dear pilgrim!

Now commences for me a truly solitary sojourn; but solitude has always had more charms than terrors for me. There will not, however, I fear, be much solitude at present, as I perceive an incursion of condoling Werffs!

. . . . . .

These long winter nights have an additional gloom flung over them by the horrors of a strange rumor which is afloat among the Munich gossips. This rumor says that at night, in lonely places, there appears a fearful man, who suddenly draws forth a horrible weapon — a poisoned knife, or knives! concealed in a ring, with which he cuts and cruelly wounds innocent and unsuspicious individuals. Report farther states, that the man has already wounded several unhappy women, one of whom report declares to be dying! It is farther stated, that the man has vowed to destroy ninety persons! — ninety girls or women!

Some ten days ago one heard of a fresh victim daily. People one spoke with declared that they had seen the crowd which surrounded the victim, as she lay bleeding upon the ground; or had known the cousin, or mother, or sister, or brother of the victim, or of a person who knew the cousin, mother, etc., as it might be. You can scarcely imagine the panic people have been in about the 'face-cutter,' or 'man with the iron clasp,' as he is called. They say — mind, I do not vouch for the truth of the story — that a man guilty of the same crime was beheaded last year in Augsburg; others say seven years ago. Report says, also, that this terrible man has only vowed vengeance against women, — and young girls especially; and the handsomer the better, he having been 'jilted' by a beautiful young girl, and that his revenge can alone satisfy itself with the destruction of pretty faces! Is it not a history worthy of the '*Neue Pitival*' — if it were true?

Clare witnessed something at the studio a few days before her departure, which had also a dash of the interestingly terrific in it. Unluckily for me I was absent that afternoon from the studio, and lost the spectacle. Clare heard a tremendous noise in the studio-field — the shouts and screams of a man, the howls of a dog. Out rushed one gentleman, from the studio, out rushed another, and out rushed Clare, of course, after them, to see what these terrible cries could mean, and all this excitement. And there in the field, through the snow, fled a man pursued by an enormous dog: the dog sprang upon the man, tore him, shook him by the hair of his head, and dragged him along the ground; the man howling! the dog howling! Then they were up again, careering round and round the field, man and dog, like wild beasts. Clare was so much horrified that she began to cry quite hysterically. And what was her indignation to see the two gentlemen, instead of rushing to the man's assistance, quietly standing before the studio door, looking on and smiling! When they saw Clare's tears and indignation, they smiled still more! 'It is only the training of a watch-dog,' said they. 'Dogs are always trained in this way here: dogs are trained so in England, are they not?' Clare now more carefully inspected the man who had so greatly excited her compassion, and perceived that he had his head and face bound up in such a manner as to prevent the dog wounding him, — and he wore also a padded jacket; but at the first moment the bandages about his face had suggested to her the idea of terrible wounds.

Yesterday, passing through the field, I also encountered the dog-trainer, cased in his wadded jerkin and wadded helmet; he was talking with the children, and reminded me of an Esquimaux, — the terrible romance failing, as there was no dog present.

Hearing such accounts of 'face cutters,' and of fierce dogs, you might naturally imagine that Munich was a terrible place, and that one was environed by dangers dire; — but were you to see the cozy room in which I am writing, and the cheerful look of the streets as I pass to and fro from the studio morning and afternoon, you would not be much alarmed.

As I observed before, these suggestions of horror only belong to the long winter evenings, and are as much a sign of the season as the number of winter garments you meet in the streets. I wish you could have seen the long, grotesque crimson boots Clare and I met the other day! — this class of boots, though usually of untanned leather, is very much affected by the students; — or could you only have met the tall, shadowy figure of a student, arrayed in a long grey cloak, with a pointed hood standing up on his head, in a wizard or 'Mother Red-cap' style! It was a misty afternoon, just about dusk, when we came upon him at the abrupt turning of a street: he was a shadow, a creature of the mist — certainly not a man! And he had all the more a fantastic unreal air about him, as he loomed upon us close to the red Gothic palace of King Ludwig, the *Wittlesbacher Palais,* which, with its red walls and gleaming lights, glowed through the mist like a burning castle of enchantment. It certainly had a singular appearance this palace in the mist; the whole building seemed on fire, and in a dull glow.

These hooded cloaks are the rage here among the young men and lads. Youths and boys generally affect them of drab or grey, lined with crimson, blue, or scarlet. Men usually wear them of darker colors, but with the hoods equally gaily lined. Gentlemen wear, besides these hooded cloaks, cloaks with large capes, which they fling gracefully over one shoulder, draping themselves picturesquely. If a man does, in Munich, possess a great-coat, he invariably wears it cloakwise, letting the sleeves dangle uselessly at the sides, or float foolishly behind him.

The ladies' winter dress has nothing very particular about it. Of course, among the unbonneted class, with the damp, cold weather, you see a great increase of white, bound-up heads telling of tooth-ache. I must not forget either to notice the garments of boards and planks worn by all the fountains, and by the statue of the youth at the entrance of the English Garden, who all summer and autumn invites you pleasantly, with outstretched hand, to wander among the trees.

One little thing peculiar to the winter here I greatly admire, — the long rolls of fresh green moss laid inside the windows, to keep out draughts. In many houses the moss garlands are decorated with artificial flowers; but this spoils them entirely. Sometimes you see ivy leaves stuck into the moss, and that is very pretty. Peasants are constantly bringing these moss-wreaths into the city.

Speaking of these moss decorations reminds me of the way in which the Germans train ivy, which is one of the loveliest things of a small kind to be seen in Germany. We in England rarely attach an idea of decoration to ivy beyond its adornment of old houses and ruins, and of our garden-walls. Yet in England ivy flourishes uncared for with much more luxuriance than it does in Germany. But the German, perhaps, appreciating its beauty — because with him it is a rarer blessing — trains it lovingly around his dwelling, around the internal as well as the external walls. From the palace to the cottage, in Germany, there is scarcely a room to be found which does not possess its ivy-tree. As you walk through the streets, and cast your eyes upon the houses, there is hardly a window to be seen which is not twined into a very bower by the graceful and gracious festoons of ivy. Among the picturesque leaves often gleams forth a small statue of the Madonna, or of Christ. Ivy trails around the window-bars; ivy makes a pleasant green background to bouquets of flowers blooming in vases or in flower-pots.

A very pleasant little paper, I have often thought, might be written, descriptive of the windows in a German street; and the mode in which the cherished ivy was trained would play a conspicuous part in it. You may read much of the character of the inmates of the dwelling by the ivy: sometimes its leaves are dusty, and its growth is ungraceful, and its sprays untastefully trained: sometimes it grows in a gaudy flower-pot, or swings from the centre of the window in a hideously-shaped *Blumen-lamp* — flower-lamp, as it is called — a kind of swinging vessel for plants very much in vogue here; but, as a rule, the ivy is gracefully — nay, most poetically trained; its Blumen-Lamp, if it be planted in one, is often of a graceful, rustic character,—perhaps of red terra-cotta, with delicately moulded foliage of yellowish white clay meandering over it.

But it is not alone in windows that you see ivy trained. Ivy often forms a green and fresh screen across a room, being planted in boxes, and its sprays trained over rustic frame-work. Ivy often casts its pleasant shadows over a piano, so that the musician may sit before his instrument as within a little-bower—ivy may be seen adorning the shrine which hangs upon the wall, or dropping its sprays above the lady's work-table.

The staircase in the house of a great painter here is a complete little bit of fairyland,—thanks to his love of ivy, which festoons the balustrade of the polished oak stairs, and shows forth its kindly leaves among the rarer beauties of palms and myrtles which rise grove-like upon the landings! I know an apothecary's shop, which is rather like a bit of a wild wood, from its growth of ivy, than a shop of physic. I was told the other day of a studio here equally sylvan; and I know an old cobbler who could not mend his shoes without seeing his ivy-bush daily before him as he works.

CHRISTMAS.

December 15.—Last evening I heard the bell tolling from the ruinous tower of a desolate church in the old part of the city; and as I saw numbers of people entering the church, I of course followed. I went in at a side door, and found myself close to the high altar. A train of priests in their crimson and gold-embroidered robes, and little choristers in their white garments, and a number of men in black, each bearing a lighted taper in his hand, were just passing down the aisle. The church is very large and very gloomy, and it was almost twilight: crowds of people stood and knelt in the gloom, telling as dark Rembrandt masses of shadow. The one grand point of light was a side altar — one blaze of crimson satin drapery and burning tapers, which ascended in long rows out of massive silver candlesticks. The men in black extinguished their tapers; the priests knelt before the altar; the people bowed themselves. It was more like a Rembrandt effect than anything I ever saw in nature before: those singular groups of the crowd, lost in the gloom and vastness of the church; that brilliant focus of light, with lesser masses of light, here and there diffusing itself through the picture; light catching upon the shaft of a tall candlestick in the foreground, and upon an upturned white face. It was a wonderful scene altogether, and the responses of the multitude most solemn in the gloom.

On going out, I looked into a side chapel, where I perceived a crowd. There, decked out with fir-trees, was a curious erection of small cottages in the Tyrolean style; and before these cottages stood a group of large dolls dressed up in remarkably gay draperies. This group represented the arrival of Mary and Joseph at Bethlehem; Mary and Joseph in the dresses of pilgrims, with huge pilgrim hats on, and tall staves in their hands; the ass, with panniers containing Joseph's axe and carpenter's tools, following them; a man and woman in modern costume, with very mournful countenances, receive them, standing upon a very green carpet, representing turf, while cattle are grazing round them.

I understand that a series of these scenes (which are common at the same time of the year in all Catholic countries) will be thus exhibited to admiring crowds, until Christmas; there will be, no doubt, the Adoration of the Magi, the Announcement to the Shepherds, etc. The crowd seemed very much edified; and a priest stood with a money-box in his hand ready to receive alms.

On the Sunday before Christmas Eve was held what is called, in the Munich dialect, the '*Christ-Kindle-Dult*,' that is, the Little Christ-child Fair. The fair commenced at noon on Sunday; and, sinner that I am, I went and bought my little Christmas presents on that day,—which presents, be it remarked, have given such hearty satisfaction, that it was quite a delight; and when I saw poor dear old Fräulein Sänchen crying and kissing my hand with surprise and joy, I longed to have been made of money that I might have given a present to everybody.

How pretty the fair looked, that bright frosty Sunday noon! but still prettier on the Monday evening, when all was lighted up. Madame Thekla, with her face tied up in a large white handkerchief, in German fashion, *to prevent toothache*, accompanied me. She looked rather a funny figure, and I know certain people who would not have walked down Regent Street with her; but neither she nor I cared for the huge white head-gear: indeed, I thought it rather *piquant* than otherwise.

First, we walked through the principal street, to peep into the shop-windows, which were all adorned with their most tempting merchandise. Such gaudy vases, ewers, *pokals* (drinking-glasses), of variously tinted and gilded Bohemian glass, in one shop; such exquisite ball-dresses and artificial flowers in another; such tempting jewelry! But the confectioners, with all manner of devices for Christmas Trees, were perhaps the most brilliant—quite enchanted grottoes; and in each shop the counter, or a table in the middle of the floor, was festooned and decorated tastefully with the choicest articles. It would have been difficult, even in London or Paris, to find anything more beautiful. At this time the streets were deserted in comparison with what they were about four o'clock. Then there was a stir! as busy and well-dressed a throng as any West-end thoroughfare would exhibit on any bright afternoon in May. Ladies and children, all in their best, and all so happy and cheerful, and alert; such rolls and parcels as peeped out from muffs, and from beneath heavy warm cloaks! Every one, high and low, was purchasing presents; and the gentlemen were no whit behind the rest. You saw tall, aristocratic gentlemen, with their wives, busy discussing various purchases; you saw knots of students buying; you saw good fathers in toy-shops; you saw them in booksellers' shops buying Andersen's '*Marchen*,' and other favorite books; you saw even little children making their purchases. There were dandified young fellows inspecting the most elegant trinkets, evidently for ladies' wear; and I speculated as to those for whom they purchased. You saw a regular succession of gay Christmas Trees carried through the streets by maid-servants and men-servants — by poor, care-worn, yet, at all events for that one day, happy-looking mothers.

Oh! it was a sight to warm you that cold day, all this happy crowd — more than the warmest Russian furs could have done. But all this, as I said, I saw in the afternoon, and not when good Madame Thekla, with her white head-dress, and I were on our evening perambulation. Then the chief point of interest was the fair; the effect was very pretty indeed. My good companion, however, assured me, as people always do when you admire anything, that the fair was not nearly as beautiful this time as it was ten years ago, when she last saw it. Let it have been as much more splendid as it might then, it was, however, quite enough to please me now. Was there not still a pretty effect in the long vista of illuminated booths, with the strip of dark azure night-sky overhead, which, contrasting with the glare of the lamps, looked perfectly oriental — at least as I imagine an eastern sky at night? And were not those booths themselves very pretty, all lined with pale pink and blue tissue-paper, and the stalls heaped up with confectionary, drapery, or crucifixes, and really lovely statuettes of madonnas and saints, as it might be, and presided over by elegant young women in their gayest attire, or bearded men wrapped up in furs?

At all events, the students of the good University of Munich, and various young painters, recognisable by a yet longer growth of hair and beard than the ordinary student, and by a certain semi-Raphaelesque cut of cap and cloak, seemed to think the *fair* — in two senses — attractive; for they were there in crowds, considerably increasing the picturesque character of the scene, as you may imagine. And then, what groves of Christmas Trees there were, all fluttering with gay ribbons! and what heaps and heaps of gilded walnuts! and what heaps of gay dolls, with large tinsel wings to represent the Christ-child! what hideous little idols! But all was bright, and glittering, and cheery; and the keen frosty night-air added quite a zest to the whole thing. Such was the Christmas Fair.

Of the Christmas Eve itself I have not much to tell, at least as regards any Christmas Tree; for, as I had another object in view than seeing trees which are so familiar to us all, I resisted every invitation, well knowing that what I gave would be duly presented by the respective Christ-child though I were not there, as well as that every gift designed for me would reach me in time; and accordingly, after my tea, while all the world was rejoicing itself, I lay me down, and in imagination passed through all the happy homes of this blessed Eve. I saw the tree that the peasant had driven off with, in his ladder-wagon, with its long shambling horse, set up in his little cottage in a quaint old-world village, and decorated by some peasant-woman in a badger-skin cap and embroidered silk boddice. I knew exactly how the tree would look in the palace itself, and how thousands of other beautiful trees must look in their different homes — in the home of the noble — in the home of the small citizen — in the home of the painter. I was there in imagination, and seemed to hear the delighted, astonished shouts of thousands of little children, and to see the beaming looks of love from parents, and brothers and sisters, and friends throughout this great Germany! And you may be sure I did not forget dear old England, with its jolly Christmas doings, — its holly, and turkey, and roast-beef, and mince-pies and plum-puddings. I lived over many a past Christmas Eve — both beautiful and sad — many strange old ghosts came of past times, but they were more beautiful than sad. I was anything but lonely; I was surrounded, steeped, as it were, in love. And thus I sank into a delicious slumber to be woke by Fräulein Sänchen, as it seemed to be the next moment.

But it was half-past ten at night, and I must rouse myself, for had I not resisted all the joy of the Christmas Eve for this — that I might be present at the midnight mass in the *Hof-Kapelle*? Fräulein Sänchen was inexorable; I must rise, for we must set off at eleven, if we meant to secure good places in the chapel.

I never should have had strength to rouse myself out of that delicious sleep, had I not kept saying to myself 'You'll repent to-morrow morning — you'll repent to-morrow morning, if you don't hear that organ — don't see that exquisite chapel all lighted up!'

So I rose; dressed myself in great haste; drank a cup of coffee in great haste, and found myself as fresh as though it were morning, instead of approaching midnight. And when we stepped out into the cold frosty night, how beautiful it was! The crisp snow beneath our feet, and above our heads such a dark-blue frosty sky, with its myriads of glorious stars. The air was filled with the sound of bells: such holy music! And as we passed along, the trees, covered with hoar-frost, shone out like strange phantoms. There were numbers of people hurrying along the streets to various churches.

Our way lay through the courts and galleries of the palace, till we came to the *Hof-Kapelle.* Lights shone from the palace windows; the whole place seemed astir; the warm breath of incense met us as we approached the chapel. Priests were already chanting and prostrating themselves before the altar, and the organ was fitfully pealing through the chapel. The altar was one blaze of tapers; tapers fixed in all the candelabras around the walls, like tall fire-lilies, cast long glittering reflections upon the marble walls and pavement. And how grand did the prophets, saints, and martyrs appear by this brilliant, artificial light, gazing down upon you from their golden grounds!

Soon the two kings, Max and Otho, and their queens, and all the court, appeared in the golden and frescoed galleries on either side the high altar; and the archbishop, in his mitre and brocaded robes, attended by a train of priests, young and old; and a train also of young court pages, lads of from twelve to fifteen, some score of them, dressed in court suits of blue and silver, all entered by a side door near the altar, and bowing first before the altar, and then bowed before the king, and passed on. A second train of court pages also entered in the same dress, but apparently some three or four years older, and each carrying a tall waxen taper. These stood before the steps of the altar, with their burning lights, and they were, Fräulein Sänchen assured me, every one high nobility; and their fresh young faces seemed to have a vast charm for my poor old wrinkled and time-worn companion. Poor old Fräulein Sänchen! If her face appeared in that brilliant light, and contrasted with the beauty of the saints and martyrs painted on wall and ceiling, yet more old, and odd, and withered, I felt in my heart a still deeper respect and compassion for her — for her who, in the sight of God, from her touching unselfishness, her unwearying goodness in the most prosaic of lives, must have been one of the most acceptable worshippers present. I had a real joy in being with her; it was much more beautiful, in fact, than sitting up in one of the golden galleries among kings and queens.

The service lasted about an hour, and was impressive. But the sudden change from the warmth, the light, the music, the color, and the intoxicating incense within the chapel, to the silence, the snow, the frosty sky, with a brilliant rising moon without, was much more impressive.

What with the excitement of the midnight mass, the heat, the cold, and the beauty, I was so wide awake when I once more found myself in my own little room, that I did not attempt to go to bed till it was about time to get up, in an ordinary way. And then came a packet of English letters — greetings from my beloved ones: and they have been the joy of the day!

In the afternoon I went into several of the old churches of Munich, to see what was going on. High mass was performing everywhere, and there were in some of the churches extraordinary figures of the infant Jesus, decked out in golden swaddling-clothes, exhibited among burning tapers and artificial flowers, and lying in long glass cases.

In the Jesuits' Church there has been a grand exhibition this week, of the Nativity, in the style which I have already described, with wooden angels in sublime attitudes, and wooden cattle surrounding the wooden Holy Family. These '*Krippen,*' as they are called, are exhibited in various churches, and have attracted immense crowds.

CHAPTER XVIII.

AN ACT OF ROYAL MERCY. — THE FAIR OF THE THREE KINGS. — A PUBLIC BALL.

January 10. — Fräulein Sänchen went out through the deep snow this afternoon, and the terrible stormy weather, — good old creature ! — to post me a letter. She has just been in to tell me of a little thing she saw which had much interested her. Returning through the palace-square, she perceived that there was a considerable number of soldiers drawn up before the palace ; it was a regiment just returned from Holstein, and was drawn up for the King to inspect it. The King had come out of the palace, and whilst he was surveying the soldiers, a peasant, leading a little girl by the hand, pushed his way through the crowd till he stood close to the King. The peasant kissed the King's hand, and presented the child — she was blind !

'Would his Majesty,' besought the peasant, 'take compassion upon the little girl and have her admitted into the Blind Asylum ? There was so much difficulty : the King, his father, had promised that she should be admitted ; would his Majesty take compassion upon her, and see that this was done ?'

The King smiled, and laying his hand upon the child's head, gave his royal word that she should be admitted into the asylum. The poor peasant was in a rapture of joy;— and so was Fräulein Sänchen as she described the scene to me.

January 12*th.* —I wonder when there is not a fair in Munich. This, however, was *Drei Königs Dult*, or the Fair of the Three Kings. By way of amusement, I thought I would go to it; but as I could not very well go alone, I invited Madame Thekla to accompany me, with which she was very well pleased, as I promised to treat her to the shows. As far as buying and selling, and the crowds of peasants, and towns-people, and students, and soldiers, go, it was like any other fair. At a little distance from the long array of booths stood the shows — and thither we bent our steps.

The first thing we came upon was a small ladder-wagon, covered with an arched awning; and bound to one side of the wagon were tall poles, from which floated a series of ghastly pictures — hideous raw-head-and-bloody-bone pictures! There were murders, executions, beheadings in German fashion; the criminal extended on a horrid sort of rack, and his head being chopped off by a grim executioner with a sword, whilst a priest stood by in his long robes; there were houses on fire; drownings; miraculous escapes; there were tall, smirking Hussars, and weeping ladies in white — all heroes and heroines in these bloody histories!

The subjects, the hideous drawing, the hard outlines, the goggle-eyes, the blood, the knives, the fire, made you feel sick. A considerable crowd was collected, and listened breathlessly to the sounds of an organ, to which two Tyroleans sang appalling tragedies. They sang in such clear, sweet, mountain tones, that you were strangely fascinated. Mournfully sang they, in a monotonous chant, of blood, and crime, and terror, till you felt your blood creep; and, by a frightful fascination, your eyes gloated on the disgusting pictures.

What a terrible immoral influence must these exhibitions have upon such an uneducated crowd as surrounded these syrens! Why should not a *paternal* government, which guards its people from immoral books and disgusting newspapers, not guard them equally from such a disgusting sight and sound as this Tyrolean exhibition? These Tyroleans sold printed histories of the fearful crimes and calamities which were depicted on their banners. These histories are very exciting and romantic reading, as you may believe when I give some of their titles: — 'The History of the Great and Terrible Monster who cruelly murdered his Beloved, his Child, his Father, his Mother, his two Sisters, and his Brother, on the 8th of July, 1850;' 'Heroic Self-sacrifice of a Bohemian Hussar Officer, and the Punishment of his Murderers;' 'A true and dreadful History which occurred on the 14th of March, 1850, in Shopka, near Melnick, in Bohemia;' 'The Might of Mutual Love; a highly remarkable event, which occurred at Thoulon, in the year 1849;' 'The Cursed Mill, a Warning from Real Life;' 'The Temptation; the Deed; the Consequences!'

If you care to know anything of the style of these remarkable productions, I will give you a specimen. One begins thus: 'In Ross-dorf, in Hanover, lived the criminal Peter Natzer. He was by trade a glazier, his father having followed the same calling. Peter was five-and-twenty years old, and was, from his earliest youth, addicted to every species of crime. He had a sweetheart, named Lucie Braunn, a poor girl,' &c. &c.

Again: 'Silent sat the miller, Leverm, in his garden; thoughtfully gazed he into the distant valley. He was scarcely thirty years of age, but heavy cares had bowed him, and robbed him of his fresh, youthful bloom. Beside him sate his wife, who cast many an anxious but affectionate glance on her husband. How tender and lovely was this young wife! The inhabitants of the neighborhood called her "the Rose of the Valley;"' thus begins a most awful tragedy. And, not contented with these dismal histories in prose, they are also done into verse. Here is a specimen of these dismal ditties, being the rhymster's version of the heroically self-sacrificed Bohemian officer: —

I.

At Melnick in Bohemia
    There was a deed of horror done,
By wicked hands, as you shall hear,
    All in the pleasant noonday sun.
Eleven men of bad intent
Unto the mill of Melnick went,
And there five people did they kill,
All in cold blood their lives did spill!

II.

The miller he came home at eve,
    And soon beheld the dreadful sight:
And he resolved to go at once
    And seek the murderers out that night.
Unto his friend his grief he told,
And he, a captain stout and bold,
Called for his horse, and with good speed
Set out to do this righteous deed.

III.

But first I must to you make known
    That their own dog did them betray,
Which had been tied up in the mill,
    And now was tracked upon its way.

The eleven murderers thus were found
With all their booty on the ground:
The valiant captain entered in
And charged them with their heinous sin.

IV.

But ah! what could a single man
  Against eleven murderers do?
They all fell on him as he stood,
  A brave young man, and killed him too!
Just then his troop broke down the wall
And killed the cruel murderers all;
Except such few of them as fled,
Whose blood was by the headsman shed!

Of course we did not read these things in the fair. It was enough for us, there, to listen to the mournful chant of the mountaineers, till our blood was frozen in our veins. I took home with me some of these horrible printed histories, as many another simple soul did; and now, after I have read them, and been filled with horror and disgust by them, I have put them away from me as unholy things. But think of the effect they will have in many a lonely village, this winter — in many a desolate farm-house or cottage — on the wide plain, or among the mountains! These papers are productive seeds of murder and crime; of that one may be certain.

The next wonder that stopped us in the fair was a little fat man, who was shouting away at the top of his voice, whilst he briskly sharpened a knife on a long, rough board, which was smeared over with a black ointment. He was a vendor of magical strop-salve! something in the fashion of Mechi. 'Ladies and gentlemen,' shouted he, 'witness my wonderful invention! The dullest knife — stick-knife, bread-knife, clasp-knife, fruit-knife, table-knife, carving knife, shaving-knife, (*Rasirmesser*), pen-knife, pruning-knife, though dull as this knife — *though dull as this knife!*' and here he began hacking away upon the edge of a big knife with a strong piece of broken pitcher. 'Yes, though dull, dull, dull as this knife! — when subjected to my wonderful salve,' and here he smeared it with his black ointment, 'will cut a hair, or the most delicate shaving of paper — as it now does!' and with that he severed paper-shavings as if they had been nothing. If it was really the *same knife*, his was a wonderful invention, and beat Mechi hollow.

Next, I had my fortune told at three different places, for six Kreutzers, or two-pence each; and as I was promised pretty much the same fortune by all, I suppose I ought to believe in the truth of it. They foretold me lots of trouble in the way of love-crosses, false friends, and unkind relations, and such small trifles; but were equally liberal of rich lovers, and plenty of them, plenty of money, and a good husband to crown all, and good children to be the *props* of my old age: so I think I had, after all, a good sixpenny-worth.

Next we came upon a little caravan, on the steps of which vociferated a most picturesque Tyrolean, in broad-brimmed, sugar-loafed hat, adorned with chamois hair and eagles' feathers, in broad-ribbed stockings, and with a broad, gaily-embroidered band round his waist, which half covered his chest. He assured the crowd below that there was not in the whole of Bavaria anything half as interesting, half as extraordinary, half as astounding, as the singularly gifted, singularly beautiful, singularly intellectual being within; a being from another quarter of the globe — a being adapted to an entirely different mode of existence to ours — a being who could see in the dark — a being who lived upon raw meat! — a wonderful Albino who could speak the German tongue!

Of course we must see the Albino: so in we went, and some way or other I felt an unusual shock. There he sat, in a black velvet dress spangled with silver, the light coming in from the top of the caravan, and his transparent complexion, his burning, fiery eyes, like carbuncles, his long waves of white, silky hair, and his long, curling, snow-white, silky beard, gave him the appearance of some enchanted dwarf — some cobold or gnome out of a subterranean palace. He ought truly to have been seated upon an ivory or crystal throne, and with a golden gem-incrusted drinking horn in his hand, and not cramped up in a miserable caravan.

But I had not much time to lose myself in dreams about enchanted dwarfs or gnomes, for there was something else burning in the caravan besides the Albino's eyes — and that was Madame Thekla's grand silk cloak! She had come out with me in all her grandeur; and now, while we stood enchanted before the Albino, her fine silk cloak was singeing at a little iron stove that stood behind the door. Poor Madame Thekla! Out we rushed, and she revenged herself by vociferating to the crowd outside, as the Tyrolean had done just before, and by exhibiting her unlucky cloak in a sort of savage despair.

An hour afterwards, we again passed the caravan, and the Tyrolean in the ribbed stockings was once more holding forth on the steps, when, at sight of us, he interrupted his oration, and politely invited us to re-enter and complete, *free of cost*, our inspection of the Albino. But Madame Thekla, pointing with stern dignity to her cloak, declined, and marched on.

After this we went to the *Waffeln*-booths, where we ate hot-baked *Waffeln*, a kind of gofre cake; and then, resisting a wonderful elephant show, we hastened to the monkey theatre, the poor elephant's rival exhibition — the 'Grand Monkey Theatre from Paris,' in which forty-two apes and poodles, the property of M. Le Cerf, would exhibit the most wonderful and artistic feats.

We had to wait some time till the four o'clock performance was over, which unfortunately had begun before we arrived; and whilst Madame Thekla and I stood impatiently waiting in the cold, up there came a merry-faced lad of about ten, and began, in great glee, to describe to us the glorious things that were performed by those 'dear little monkeys and dogs.' He was quite eloquent in his delight; and 'Oh!' said he, 'if I had but another *Sechser* (two-penny piece), wouldn't I see it again!' 'There is another *Sechser*, then!' said I, and put one into his fat little hand. What an astonished, bright face looked up into mine; and he seized my hand in both his, and shook it almost off; and away he run up the steps for his ticket, flying down again to us, and keeping as close to us as possible, talking all the time, and fairly dancing for joy.

'You've quite bewitched that little fellow,' said Madame Thekla; and I seemed to have bewitched all the little lads in the fair, for, by a strangely mysterious power, they were drawn towards us in crowds, from all hands — little fellows in blouses, little fellows in little green and brown surtouts, little fellows in old-fashioned jackets and trowsers — and all crept bashfully towards us. Oh, the wonderful magic of a two-penny piece! Heaven only knows how the news of this munificent gift of a *Sechser* had so swiftly spread through the fair! One little lad actually had the bravery to say to me that 'children were admitted at half-price!' And was I not a cold-hearted wretch to reply, 'Oh, indeed!' just as though it were a matter of perfect indifference to me, though, in truth, it was not; but I felt rather appalled at the sight of such a crowd of little eager heads, well knowing that my purse was not full to overflowing, even with two-penny pieces!

At length we were seated in the little theatre; and, after a fearful charivari from the ochestra, the curtain drew up, and we beheld, seated at a long table, a company of monkeys! It was a *table d'hôte.* A dandified young fellow — perhaps Monsieur Le Cerf himself — in the most elegant of cravats, the most elegant white wristbands, the most elegant ring, and the most elegant moustache, performed the part of host; the waiter and waitress were monkeys. The waiter — a most drunken, good-for-nothing waiter he seemed — a fat, big ape — drank behind the backs of the guests the very wine he was serving them with; he seemed so very tipsy that he could hardly walk; he staggered backwards and forwards, and leaned against the wall for support, as he emptied the bottle he was bringing for the company. But the little waitress! She was a little darling; the tiniest of little monkeys, and she came skipping on the stage in a broad-brimmed straw hat, and a bright-colored little dress, with the daintiest of white muslin aprons on; she looked just like a little fairy. Everybody was enchanted with her. Even Monsieur Le Cerf himself caressed her, and gave her not only, every now and then, a nut, but a kiss. She behaved beautifully. But as to the guests! They quarrelled, and even fought — Monsieur Le Cerf said it was about paying the bill.

I can't pretend to tell you half the clever things the monkeys did in the way of swinging, dancing, firing off muskets, riding on a pony, etc. Wonderful things, too, were performed by the dogs — splendid spaniels and setters. One large black-and-tan creature walked on his fore-legs, in the style of what children call 'playing at a wheel-barrow,' only he himself, poor wretch, had to wheel the barrow. He walked demurely round and round the stage, carrying his two unlucky hind legs up in the air; then he walked on three legs, and then, the most difficult task of all for a dog, as we were assured, upon two legs on the same side. Another beautiful white spaniel came walking in most grandly on her hind legs, as *Madame de Pompadour*, in a long-trained dress which was borne by a tiny monkey in livery, bearing a little lantern in his hand.

The finale was the besieging of a fortress; and to see some twenty milk-white spaniels rushing up and down the stairs of a burning fortress, illumined by brilliant rose-colored, green, and blue lights, was very curious indeed. If I could have forgotten the terrible training through which these poor creatures must have gone, I should have enjoyed it much more. But I did not wonder, after seeing all their feats, that our little friend had been so enchanted. He sat behind us in the half-price seats, but for all that we continued to exchange many smiling glances during the performance. I only wished I could have seen a whole row of little fellows all equally delighted and surprised by their good fortune.

A PUBLIC BALL.

I went last night to one of the grand public balls; but not to dance, only into the gallery, to look on and enjoy the spectacle without the fatigue, or the pleasure. This ball was in the Odéon, one of the principal public buildings here, and where the Conservatorium is. The room where the ball was held was the same that I described to you once before, when a concert was given by the pupils of the Conservatorium. Myra Amsel and I mounted some dozen steep flights of stairs, and at length emerged into the gallery. We left a throng of carriages setting down ball-attired ladies and gentlemen at the principal entrance, and a throng of spectators admiring them.

Quite out of breath, from our long ascent, we found ourselves in the gallery which runs round the large hall, at an immense height from the floor. The gallery was crowded with people, all eagerly leaning, in a double row, over the railing; so that, from the ball-room below, the ceiling must have seemed adorned with a cornice of living faces. The gallery-crowd appeared to consist of friends of the ball-room company, who were anxiously watching or waiting the advent of their friends below; and of good citizens, and other people, who, not being themselves of the *haute volée*, had come to criticise and copy their betters — in rank.

It was with considerable difficulty that Myra and I found standing-room where we could see; yet it was only half-past six. When we did, we looked down upon numberless chandeliers, which, with their circles of starry lamps, illumined a very gay-looking company indeed. At the further end of the hall was a low platform, approached by a flight of steps covered with carpeting; and here stood a very fine grove of fir-trees, orange-trees, and green-house shrubs, behind which were concealed the musicians. The whole platform was in fact an elegant saloon; where stood couches, chairs, and tables, the crimson and richly-colored coverings of which looked excessively pretty among the green trees and shrubs. Tapers burned in tall, branching candlesticks upon the tables, and groups of young ladies, in clouds of white muslin, or in pink gauze, looking like rose-buds among all the green leaves, stood or moved about; whilst gentlemen in gay uniforms, or in the less brilliant civil costume, as it is called — black coat, white waistcoat, and hat in hand — crowded round them. There was no lack of more sober coloring in the dresses of the *chaperones*, in their velvets, silks, and satins. And all these gay people were scattered, not only over the aristocratic platform, but over the whole hall, a group of gentlemen clustering together in the very centre of the beautiful inlaid floor, like a swarm of bees.

Many of the grandees of Munich were either already present, or were expected. King Max himself was looked for: Prince Adelbert had already arrived, and only to be distinguished from the company by wearing a *brown* instead of a *black* coat; such being his privilege as a prince of the blood.

And now, from the concealed orchestra, sounded the first note of the polonaise, and the gentlemen hastened towards their partners, and all solemnly paraded, in stately procession, through the ball-room; and now burst forth a waltz, and away flew the dancers. It really was very tantalizing to hear that beautiful music, and to see those dancers; and to be up in that hot and close gallery, in a merino dress and overshoes! There was a painful contrast! For the first few moments I declared to Myra, that, spite of all my philosophy, which had made me decline an invitation to this very ball, I now wished I had been there, and that I *must* and *would* go to the next, if it were only for the sake of old times! But soon after came a *Française*, or, as we call it, a quadrille; and then another waltz, and then a polka, and then a *Française* again; and, by that time, I began to feel that if to look on at a ball was at first tantalizing, it became, after a while, very wearisome — 'the greatest bore under the sun!' as I remember to have heard certain unhappy victims, who did not dance, declare — but which assertion I, at the time, did not appreciate.

But soon a pleasant excitement arrived for us. Myra's mother, and her sister Ida, entered the ball-room. They came aristocratically late. How handsome they looked! Frau Amsel in black, with scarlet flowers in her hair; and Ida looking a very Hebe, in simple white muslin, with a scarlet sash and scarlet bows on her sleeves, and nothing whatever in her hair. She was the simplest, and, to my taste, the most elegantly-dressed girl in the room. Her beautiful head, with its rich, dark hair, looked quite conspicuous, from the entire absence of all artificial ornament. Standing there in the gallery, in my winter dress and overshoes, I felt really proud of them. They created quite a sensation as they entered; and as Ida stood beside an orange-tree on the platform, with all her simple beauty, in her white dress and scarlet ribbons, and with her beaming, happy face, I did not wonder at the hosts of gentlemen that made their way to her.

Myra and I, and their servant Elise, who by this time had joined us, grew quite excited. 'There,' said Myra, 'is Count R. I *know* Ida will dance with him. And there is young S.: I think she has promised him a dance! And there is that little lieutenant; and there is the student from Nuremberg; but she won't dance with *him* — of that I am sure!'

And so we watched until the dumb-show of Ida's arrival had subsided somewhat, when, leaving Mrs. Amsel quietly seated upon one of the couches among the orange-trees, we beheld Ida waltz away with a tall officer in blue uniform.

Again I began to grow desperately weary, and looked round with longing eyes for dear old Fräulein Sänchen's old-fashioned face. It seemed to me that she never would come! Fortunately a little love-making in the foreground of our gallery made me forget my fatigue for the time.

There sat just before us a very pretty girl, very young and childish looking. I caught a glimpse of a sweet, child-like brow, and long, drooping eyelashes, as she sat in the front row, with her married sister. Presently one of the gentlemen from the ball-room below made his appearance. I fancy he was a student; I did not admire his look at all. He was evidently desperately in love with the pretty girl; he forgot all about the ball, and talked most earnestly to her behind the married sister's back; she smiled and said very little, but listened, and seemed also to forget the ball. Soon, another gentleman arrived from the ball-room below; and then jealousy was added to love. The first lover turned black as a thunder-cloud, and I thought looked more unpleasant than ever; he did not go away, but stood scowling like a jealous lover in a picture of Stephanoff's; and the girl listened with the same smile and the same innocent brow to the second lover, the married sister all the time looking down into the ball-room.

This amused me for a while, and then another group also amused me. A dowager, in her velvet and grandeur, attended by a queer little old officer, a regular German Major O'Dowd — with spectacles on, and a plumed hat in his hand — brought up a beautiful young lady to speak to some dear friend in the gallery; and lots of other grandees from below found their way into our upper regions, till we also seemed all astir and gorgeous. But, O! joyful sight! amid all the grand arrivals, there was Fräulein Sänchen, with my shawl on her arm.

But the poor dear old soul was in no hurry to go, now she was once there, and I could not find in my heart to deprive her of a glimpse of the gay world, which was such a novelty to her. Besides, she was very anxious to point out to me two grand gentlemen in whom she takes great interest, a young Herr Baron and the son of a certain

Frau Geheimräthinn, who is a great lady. But I was too tired even to care about her favorites, though I have heard so much of them for the last several weeks, without having yet had the pleasure of seeing them. These two young fellows went to one of the court balls the other night: the next morning I had, however, the pleasure of seeing the mother of one of them hanging out clothes in the garden. This is truly German!

CHAPTER XIX.

THE LEUCHTENBERG GALLERY.—THE PAINTER GENELLI.

I WENT this morning to the Leuchtenberg Gallery of Pictures, which, it is said, will be removed to Russia, after the death of the old Duchess, the widow of Eugene Beauharnais. The Duke, her son (since deceased) resides in Russia, having married the daughter of the Emperor of Nicholas. These pictures were collected by Eugene Beauharnais; and there are various memories of him, of Josephine, and Napoleon, meeting you at every turn.

A picture which, on entering the room, almost immediately strikes you, is a very beautiful portrait of the Empress Josephine, by Gerard ; a portrait which satisfies you with its calm gracefulness: she is dressed in the French classic style, as one always sees Josephine represented, but it is here anything but offensive; her small, dark ringlets cluster becomingly round her noble, oval countenance; and the bare arms, unencumbered with heavy sleeves, are seen in their perfect beauty. She languidly rests one arm upon the amber-velvet cushions of a low divan on which she sits. A bouquet of beautiful flowers, gum-cistus, roses, and pansies, lies beside her. She wears a white gauze dress without a single ornament, and seems to have just entered from a garden, the flowers and trees of which peep in at you through the open window above the cushions of the divan. She sits as in a reverie, with a quiet, sombre gloom softening the rich colors of the room about her — just as if a gloomy fate cast its sobering influence over her own brilliant life. Opposite to this interesting portrait is Gerard's well-known picture of Blind Belisarius bearing the dead body of his youthful conductor in his arms. One has grown so weary of engravings from this picture that I felt quite startled by the beauty and nobility of the original painting, as though I had now felt the painter's idea for the first time. The blind old man grasping his staff, and slowly, majestically moving along in the gathering twilight; the pallid face of the corpse catching the last rays of evening, while the distant mountains and lake are glowing in dim, dusky purple and crimson, — all strike one with a fresh poetry.

This first room is filled with pictures of the modern French and German schools. I was pleasantly surprised to see the names of three women in the catalogue. One is that of Elizabeth Sirani: her picture is a Madonna and Child, and St. John; and as she lived at the commencement of the seventeenth century, her picture takes its place in the second room of the gallery devoted to the older masters. The other two paintings are in the first room: one bears the name of the Baroness Freiburg, and is also a Madonna and Child; the third, which is by far the best picture of the three, though all are very good, is by Marguerite Gerard, born in 1761. It is in fact a Madonna and Child, but of modern treatment. A beautiful young mother is holding high up in her arms and pressing to her rosy lips a fat little child, which struggles in a pretty pettishness against his mother's caresses. There are various other figures in the picture, — the father in the dim obscurity, the worst part of the picture; a nursemaid busy about preparing the child's breakfast; and a curly-headed boy playing with a couple of kittens seated upon the child's cradle. All the accessories of the picture, as well as the flesh and draperies of the principal group, are exquisitely drawn and painted, and finished with a care worthy of a Flemish painting. It is a lovely work of art.

The two pictures, however, before which I paused longest in the first room were a Winter Landscape by Henrich Bürkel, and a Tyrolean Village Scene by Peter Hess. Imagine a picturesque village church and church-yard, with its crosses and graves rising up in the centre of the picture; the church-yard is somewhat raised above the road which winds around it to the left. The church is built of warm, ruddy stone, mottled with many a weather-stain; the quaint old building, with its varied lines of roofs and low spire and dormer windows, rises sharply against the clear, pale, opal sky of a bright winter's morning. A crucifix also standing upon the brow of the hilly grave-yard to the left of the church, relieves itself clearly against the light. To the left of the church, and more in the foreground, is a group of trees, their delicate brown and ruddy branches flaked and feathered with snow and rime. Behind these trees is an old-fashioned house partly concealed by them: this is the house of the priest, who is seen advancing from its gate in his violet and white robes, preceded by a boy in white and scarlet. Peasants pause bare-headed in the snowy road as they pass; other peasants are going upwards to the church through the crisp snow. These figures are the key-note to the whole picture; their clear violets, reds, and olive-greens, in delicate gradations of opal tints, spreading themselves throughout the picture, giving warmth to that snow, and frost, and gush of winter sunshine. You follow these people in imagination into the frosty church; you hear the bell tolling through the frosty air; the voices of the choir burst forth clear and piercing; and the frozen breath rises from many an old devout peasant's lips, and from the lips of the old priest himself, —

'Like pious incense from a censer old.'

Now transport yourself to the village of Partenkirchen among the mountains of Upper Bavaria. It is sunrise, but we see neither sun nor heaven; tall peaks and jagged crags close in our picture; but amid these peaks floats mist, and slant sunbeams dart up upon crags and upon the slender spire of a church which measures itself against the mountain's sides, and rises above the clustering stone-scattered roofs of a Tyrolean village. We stand in the village street; before us is a fountain, where the girls and women are busily washing their clothes at the stone troughs which branch away from it. An old woman standing with her back to us leaning down over the water, clad in a black petticoat, rose-colored, gold-embroidered boddice, and ruddy-brown fur cap — just such an old dame as one frequently meets in these Munich streets — is the focus of color and light in the picture; the sunlight glows upon her, and catches here and there upon others of the group; but most of the street is yet in gloom, for the deep slanting roofs and heavy eaves of the cottages cast broad and dim shadows. Yet the morning sunshine is piercing and resplendent, and falls in bright showers upon many a roof and upon many a mass of luxuriant vegetation, upon the upper branches of many a tree; the village is seemingly a very Garden of Eden — such leafy trees and festoons of creepers adorn it. And forth from the dim twilight of shadow come lowing kine; the cow-herd in his scarlet jerkin winds his horn; the bells of the cattle tinkle cheerily; the women and girls laugh and gossip shrilly; there is a busy stir of life in this Alpine village, amid the early sunshine of those departing mists of night! I fairly forgot all around me, as I stood before this sweet simple idyll, and was transported into the heaven of summer amid the mountains.

The second room which we now enter is the principal portion of the Leuchtenberg Gallery; but this is of no great extent, for this collection of pictures, though choice, is but small. Along the centre of the room are arranged several groups of sculpture, among which are Canova's Graces and Magdalene. The other groups are, I think, French; with classic vases, and several antique remains; together with a beautiful carved ivory goblet or two, and some reliques of Napoleon and Eugene Beauharnais, which are placed on marble slabs around the room.

The walls are covered with pictures of the masters of the Italian, Spanish and Flemish schools, arranged in separate compartments: but I am not intending to give a catalogue *raisonné*, though there are several world-famous pictures here, — Murilloes, Titians, Leonardo da Vincis, etc.

Let us now examine a certain portrait which, as you enter, your eyes instantly rests upon with a strange feeling of curiosity. It is the portrait of a woman, life-size, and taken down to the knees: she sits with her figure fronting you, her head turned aside, so as to present the profile: she is clad in a black dress, with a closely-plaited tucker of thick muslin over her bosom, and confined at the throat with a gold button: she wears a slender gold chain round her neck, and a slender gold ring with a small dark stone upon the taper finger of one of her beautiful hands, which holds a book open upon her knees. There is a severe, strange look both about the dress and the position; there is a solemn, ashy look about the whole picture. As you see it across the room, it falls upon your heart like a spectre. It seems like the portrait of one whose soul sits in sackcloth and ashes. Look at the face. How strange ! the same stiffness, the same rigidity, the same ashiness. The features are almost as the features of a skeleton ; so thin, so sharp. The soft hair is drawn away from the brow and temples, and concealed beneath a white stiff cap formed not unlike a nautilus-shell, and which fits upon the back of her head ; over it and over her brow falls a transparent white veil of the most delicate gauze. Her large, mild, dark eye looks out beneath an arched eyebrow sharp and clear, but scarcely more than a line ; her nose is somewhat large and aquiline, but slender and almost transparent ; her lips small, and, though not narrow, fleshless,—it seems as though some strange mental anguish had worn them away, till only a sentiment of grief was left upon them — as though they could never smile more ; they have never quivered, those lips, with fretfulness or nervous weakness, but have closed themselves with a high resolve, and meek patient endurance. The cheeks are hollow, the eyes are hollow, the complexion pale and transparent with ashy shadows. It is no physical suffering, but a martyrdom of the spirit, which has worn these hollows, spread this pallor ; for the hands and form are those of a woman in sound health. No, it is some unusually mournful destiny which has inscribed such strange words upon mouth and brow, and has refined a noble, pure, spiritual woman into something scarcely of earth. So particularly strong is this refined spirituality in the strange face, that glancing from it to a Raphael's Madonna hanging near, the gentle Madonna even looks coarse and vulgar.

And who is this singular woman ? She is Petrarch's Laura ! Not the Laura as the poet saw her first kneeling in her twentieth year in the Church of St. Clara — the young wife in the heyday of her beauty, — but the Laura after years of trial and suffering of many kinds ; the Laura whose eyes followed him with such a tender gaze of anguish and foreboding, when he last saw her upon earth, that he burst into tears, reading in this strange lock, which eternally remained written in his soul, her speedy death and their final separation ! The Laura whom the Emperor Charles IV., at a splendid ball given in his honor, summoned to him, amidst all the youth and beauty of Avignon, and kissed upon eyes and brow, for the fame of Petrarch's love ! whilst a prince exclaimed, 'Is *this*, then, the wondrously beautiful Laura who bewitched Petrarch ! '

But it must have been a beauty of the soul if she resembled this picture, which, to a spirit like Petrarch's, was a thousand times more potent than all the ordinary splendor of physical beauty. It is a refinement, a purity, and noble meekness, which haunt and trouble one even at the sight of her pictured features.

It must, however, be confessed that this portrait is ideal; the costume itself is of the sixteenth rather than of the fourteenth century; probably it is copied, however, from some older portrait. Laura died in 1347, and this picture, according to the catalogue, is painted by Angelo Bronzino, who lived between 1501 and 1576. Nevertheless, it is a strange picture, which haunts and troubles the imagination.

THE PAINTER GENELLI.

The name of Genelli is not much known in England : it was quite new to me when I came here. Clare and I, soon after our arrival, saw some of his designs, which greatly pleased us. Clare admired them extremely.

To-day, therefore, having been kindly invited to do so by Mr. Genelli, I went to see his drawings. He lives outside the old walls of the city, close to the dilapidated Sendlinger Gate. Above the gloomy city wall, dark with age, rise picturesque roofs and steep gables, dotted over with little windows, and tiled with, here and there, a quaint church spire or tower. A narrow line of orchard skirts the wall: then comes a narrow moat, and then a row of houses: in one of these lives Genelli.

The wife of Genelli received me,—a handsome woman, with rich plaits of dark hair; then came the daughter, who is a young actress,—*very* pretty she is, short and round, with large, bright, beautiful blue eyes, and rich golden hair. After sitting a little while, and talking, Genelli himself came in. Going then into his little studio, he brought out a series of very clever drawings,—*very* clever indeed, and full of a wild fancy.

This one series represented the life of a wicked man,—the life of a libertine.

Several of the designs struck me much. One, where the hero of the series is seated with his wife in a boat upon a lake,—it is a broad expanse of water, with swans swimming near the boat: a peasant girl, standing on a wild rocky shore, warns, with wild gestures, the wife of her husband's wickedness, and the wife rises in a storm of indignant anger. Then there is another, equally full of passion, where he is brought before an Archbishop,—one of the military archbishops of the Middle Ages,—to answer for his crimes: the peasants have risen against him, have set his castle on fire; he is taken prisoner, and now stands, stubborn, before his judge, two soldiers endeavoring to force him on his knees. In the next design you find him in the cell of a prison: he has slain his Confessor, who lies dead, and stripped of his robe, upon the floor; the murderer has clothed himself in the monk's gown, and now hastily fastens his sandals: a burning torch reveals his haste, the corpse, and the prison door. Again you see him, asleep in a wood: he dreams a fearful dream, — lies tossed in agony; behind him you see the figures of his dream: himself, in the monk's gown, flying in haste from the infuriated Archbishop, who rides on a fiery steed. Two huntresses watch him with astonishment, whilst he tosses in his agonized sleep. Next he meets with a witch in this wood, and has his evil fate foretold. He has numerous adventures, ending at last by his being stabbed by his jealous wife.

The nature of these designs may be imagined: they are very German. The impression left on my mind, however, was painful. There were so few touches of beauty and love or nobility. Of course one should not expect this in the hero himself, but one seems to require such touches in the other characters, and as I recollect this is the case with other designs by Genelli which I have seen. All are impressed with the same character.

One set is called 'The Life of a Witch,' — and most wild and fearful it is.

CHAPTER XX.

THE SCHAFFLER DANCE AND CARNIVAL.

Jan. 26th.—I have just returned from seeing the *Schäffler Tanz.* Everybody has been saying of late—'So the *Schäffler Tanz* takes place this year.' The Munich papers have for several weeks past been announcing, that 'about the middle of the month the Schäffler would perform their interesting dance,—this being the seventh year since its last exhibition; and that having danced before the royal palace, they would take in course the various palaces and residences of the chief nobility, and so continue their dancing until Carnival time.'

According to printed authority to which I have referred, the origin of this dance is as follows. In the year 1517, a fearful plague desolated Munich. So great was the consternation which it occasioned, that people dreaded to leave their houses. All doors and windows were closed, and every man avoided his neighbor. In the midst of this universal terror and silence, all at once a troop of men, coopers by trade, came in from the country with music and fresh green garlands, and went from house to house, calling to the people with sounds of merriment to open their doors and windows. The effect of this unexpected summons was wonderful. The people came forth, and, as if in frantic joy, danced through the streets. The plague-spell was broken by the delirium of gaiety which, as if in defiance of past misery, seized on every heart. There is something strangely wild in the idea of this fearful scourge being banished by an excess of merriment scarcely less fearful, — the reaction of lacerated human souls!

Every seventh year, therefore, in commemoration of this event, is the *Schäffler Tanz* performed — and this, fortunately for me, happens to be the year.

On Monday the Coopers danced before the Palace — the royal family witnessing their performance from the windows; and this morning they have danced before the War Office — where I have seen them. An acquaintance of mine having a friend in the War Office, we were promised seats at a window; and accordingly, at the appointed hour, made our way thither — and soon found ourselves seated comfortably and gazing down on the crowd below us. But where were my antique costumes? — where was all the wild poetry of the dance, as I had imagined it? I had expected too much. This is what I saw: —

A ring of spectators, in the centre of which moved in a variety of figures in character not unlike our country dance, our Sir Roger de Coverley, or the various *tours* of the German cotillon, a score or so of young men dressed in close-fitting jackets of scarlet trimmed with silver lace, (but the jackets had a sadly modern air,) black velvet breeches, white stockings, shoes, little short yellow leathern aprons adorned with broad crimson satin ribbon fringed with gold, and on their heads modern-shaped light green caps, in which were stuck little nodding white and blue feathers. The dress was very disappointing: not to be compared in antique cut and association with the quaint, parti-colored costume in which I once saw a troop of 'English Plough-Bullocks' attired.

The dance itself, however, was very pretty; especially

from the different effects produced by garlands of fresh, green box which the dancers bore in their hands. The lively music, the bright contrast of the scarlet jackets with the fresh green of the wreaths, and the piquancy of the dance, were altogether something very pleasing to witness. The musicians were clad in the same costume; and on the ground before them stood a graceful little pyramid of some light-colored wood, on which were painted stripes of bright blue. On this stood an elegant little barrel, with a basket containing glasses, out of which wine and beer, the contents of the pyramid and the barrel, were drunk in honor of the noble Minister of War — who, of course, was witnessing the performance.

On the ground also lay hoops twisted with white and blue ribbons, which were ever and anon snatched up and used in the figures of the dance. Also there were — that I should so long have omitted to mention them! — two lively harlequins, whose business seemed rather to interrupt than to assist in the dance. Various were the antics which they played on the crowd of spectators, perhaps in traditional memory of the feats of the *Schäffler* of old. One seized on a rosy-faced girl who was quietly looking on, and twirled her away into the centre of the dance — much to the merriment of the crowd, and her own real, or apparent annoyance, for she tried in vain to hide her face in her shawl. The dance lasted perhaps three-quarters of an hour; and then, to the sound of music, the dancers marched in procession gallantly up the street.

This *Schäffler Tanz* may be almost considered as the commencement of the Carnival. We already hear on all sides of balls and masquerades; and see people in milliners', printsellers', and booksellers' shops consulting prints of costume and fancy dresses. Masks, hideous, grotesque — the masks of animals, of demons, and the black romantic half-mask — are exhibited in numberless windows in the town.

MILITIA BALL AND MASKED ACADEMY.

I saw in the little daily paper, 'The Latest News,' an announcement of a grand ball to be given in the Odeon, with a lottery, for the benefit of the old *Landwehr*, or militia. It was announced, also, that their majesties had graciously condescended to attend, and that the whole court would be there. I therefore felt a vast curiosity to go and see all that was to be seen, and especially did I want to have a good view of the young queen, of whom K. was telling the other day the most beautiful things; — how that she was the sweetest, gentlest, most amiable young creature; quite a peasant girl in simplicity; the purest, noblest being that was ever seated on a throne; a lovely innocent flower, in the midst of the temptations and intrigues of a court; — how that being too good for a queen, she was fitted only to be an angel, and that to see her with her children was the most beautiful thing in the world. After all this, was it wonderful that I longed to be in the same room with this pure, lovely, queenly flower, and to see her dancing, with all the joyousness of a peasant girl, among her admiring people?

No sooner was my determination taken than I set off to Mrs. Amsel's, to ask them if we could not go all together, not into the gallery as before, when I had watched Ida in all her glory, but into the ball-room, with the rest of the company. They agreed immediately; no time was to be lost, for the ball was that night, and the first thing that was to be done, after securing tickets, was to find out some officer who would attend us, for without a uniform no party of ladies could be admitted. No black coats were on this occasion admissible; nothing at all but uniforms; either an officer of the army, or one of the militia, must introduce us. However democratic any of us might be, we did not particularly covet the escort of one of the militia — one's confectioner, one's draper, or one's butcher; there was no fear, however, of our being reduced to this extremity, for Mrs. Amsel and her daughters were acquainted with hosts of officers; and Ida and Myra ran over a whole list of names, any of whom would only be too happy to accompany us.

I was quite easy, therefore, and left this important part of the business in their hands. I called, on my way to the studio, at a gardener's, and ordered from the gardener's consumptive daughter an ivy wreath for my hair. I described what I wanted. Oh, yes, she knew very well; she was sure she could please me, for she had often made such for the young Queen. I saw an enchanting little rose-tree, which, with its one lovely rose and its buds, seemed fitted to be an emblem of the lovely Queen herself; I bought it, therefore, out of ideal love for her, and it now stands in my window, making my room fresh and beautiful. I ordered my wreath and my rose-tree to be sent home by four o'clock, and went to my work.

Imagine me about that hour returned; my ball-dress of white, with white shoes and gloves, all laid out ready, looking suggestive of the evening's pleasure; my dinner just over, and I, lying on my sofa for half an hour's rest, when in came the Amsels, to say we could not go; they had got no tickets, they had got no one to go with us. All their officer-acquaintance were already engaged; people were rushing wildly about the town after tickets; people were already crowding into the gallery; it would be the most amusing ball of the season, but go we could not! Was it not a pity — was it not disappointing, and it would be so brilliant, so well worth seeing!

'Oh, but we must go!' said I, feeling quite desperate, 'we *can't* be disappointed; why the town is half full of uniforms! What a disgrace it is if we cannot make a uniform of use for once in a way! But I have an idea!' exclaimed I, 'a strange one, it is true; but never mind! My opposite neighbor, the Count —— is an acquaintance of yours, though he is not of mine; he goes to every ball that is given; no doubt he is going to-night; cannot you make use of him? No doubt he would be charmed to accompany you — nay, I am sure he would!'

We looked at each other and laughed heartily. It was rather a strange idea; but, nevertheless, he was an acquaintance of theirs from whom they could ask such a favor, and they said they would do so. We sent across the street to inquire; but he was out. He was an erratic mortal, of whose movements nobody could give any account; he might be back in a quarter of an hour, he might not return till midnight. A message was left with the good woman of the house for him, and the Amsels would return in an hour, when our fate must be decided, for if *he* did not return before then, go we could not.

Scarcely were they gone, when I saw the Herr Graf return, unlock the outer door, and enter with a great clatter of spur and sword, as usual. Three minutes after, the good woman of the house was in my room. The Herr Graf had not intended to go, but now he would go with the greatest pleasure — with the greatest pleasure in the world! He desired her to tell the gracious lady, Frau Amsel, that he would be immediately ready. 'Yes, Fräulein Ida!' said he, 'she is an old partner of mine; she dances beautifully — very beautifully! I know her very well; I shall be most happy to go!'

All in a hurry the Amsels came back, learned the news, rushed away to dress, and at half-past six were to call for me and my opposite neighbor, the Herr Graf, in their carriage. I dressed very comfortably, with the gardener's poor consumptive daughter acting as my maid, for which I was very thankful, as poor dear old Fräulein Sänchen my usual tire-woman's eyes being none of the best, she makes a regular botheration of the tiny hooks and eyes, a series of impotent attempts which generally end in my doing the business myself, to my great discomfort. But my little maid was charming, and the wreath so entirely to my mind, that when my toilet was completed I thought the effect very fascinating.

All this time my opposite neighbor was making his toilet; and, as I was taking a cup of chocolate, a message came that he was ready, and very impatient to be off, as he feared the gracious lady, the Frau Amsel, would not find a place to sit down in the crowded hall. At that moment the carriage stopped, and in two seconds more the Herr Graf was handing me down stairs, while poor old Fräulein Sänchen lighted us with two candles.

The Herr Graf is very young and good-looking; and it was immediately so evident that he was desperately smitten by Ida's beauty, that I was half sorry for what I had done. But never mind, thought I to myself, it is something to keep the poor lad's mind from stagnation, and Ida will have no objection to have another worshipper added to her train. These young officers are never allowed by government to marry, unless they and their bride have a certain sum of money between them — I don't know exactly what it is — and therefore the greater number of them neither marry nor even think of it.

They spend their 'young days,' as my friend S—— would have said, in a series of flirtations and hopeless passions, more or less serious; therefore I will console myself if my unlucky neighbor has had his heart wounded, for it may as well be by Ida's beautiful face and saucy tongue as by any one else's.

At last we were at the entrance of the Odeon; and as we were getting out of the carriage, there was a cry of 'The King! the King!' But this, I believe, was only a *ruse* of the crowd collected on such occasions, for their own private amusement; however, it turned all eyes on our arrival. I felt almost a shock when, on glancing up the broad staircase, I saw it lined on either side by a row of uniforms; it seemed like facing an army itself. The Odeon Hall was filled with a dense crowd, every man in regimentals. The room was beautifully decorated. First and foremost there was that cornice of human faces gazing down from the lofty gallery; secondly, a raised platform for the Court, all carpeted, and decorated with greenhouse plants, with a fountain playing before the seat intended for the Queen, the water for which said fountain, I understood, was being constantly pumped up by an unlucky man beneath the ball-room floor. This idea made the fountain, to me, rather a fatigue than a refreshment. Upon the platform, which was guarded by grim stone lions, and behind rows of crimson velvet and gilt chairs arranged for the Court, rose a tent of crimson and gold, beneath which were displayed a number of warlike trophies, flags, cannon, arms of all kinds, in picturesque array, and above them, glowed in fire, a gigantic M, the initial letter of the King's name. Armor, helmets, and breast-plates of various ages, and guns, swords, and pistols, arranged in groups, and forming columns, and stars, and wheels, as we see them in the

Armory at the Tower, flanked the tent, on either hand; tall fir-trees shadowing them, palms and tender flowers — Peace and Love, as it were — drooping over, and twining about these implements of torture and horror, in strange contrast. Quick, keen tongues of flame leapt up, ever and anon, from brazen lamps, types of destroying fire, as the weapons were of bloodshed. But both fire and sword produced a wild and poetical impression, thus used in ball-room decoration.

Thirdly, the two long sides of the rooms were rendered gay and attractive by green bowers, regular arbors of fir-tree boughs, intertwined with wreaths of artificial flowers, beneath which were throned, in each, an elegant lady and gentleman, disposing of shares in the lottery; whilst at the end of the room the prizes were displayed upon long stalls, bearing a strong resemblance to a scene in our Oxford Street Pantheon. There were numbers of capital things to be won; besides work-tables and easy-chairs, and dressing-cases, and thousands of elegant and *in*elegant knick-knacks which one would be thankful *not* to win; there was, at least if report was to be believed, a statuette, in marble, of the 'Bavaria,' by Schwanthaler himself, and sent by Queen Theresa. That *would* have been a prize!

I dare say, however, if it was there, that, by some singular freak of Fortune, it would find its way back again to Court. Such things will happen! I saw lots of capital things carried up the steps of the royal platform — gay parasols and lace handkerchiefs. As for us! — poor wretched mortals — we got nothing out of numberless chances, not one of us. But a young officer who joined our party, and who, I dare say, never swallowed half-a-dozen cups of tea in his life, won a tea-caddy! He did not seem at all to know what it was. I know fortune meant that caddy for me — it is a pity she is so blind! A tea-caddy is one of my idols; I would have one made of gold if I could! I deserved to have had that tea-caddy! — that young fellow ought to have had a beer-tankard, or a tobacco pouch! Well, Fortune certainly had her eyes well bandaged on that occasion.

The drawing of prizes continued all evening, even during the dancing. But no dancing, of course, commenced until the Court arrived.

All at once we saw some half-dozen little men in blue uniforms, with white ribbons in their button-holes, rushing through the crowd, which parted before them, like the Red Sea before the children of Israel, and on came the courtly train, two and two, — a brilliant procession of uniforms, and satins, and brocades, and diamonds. Poor King Max was ill with influenza, which is attacking everybody here, and therefore was not present. But the young Queen was there, attended, if I mistake not, by King Otho; but, as he wore his uniform, instead of his handsome Albanian dress, I did not immediately recognise him. The human wall, on either side, bowed enthusiastically, as their Royalties and their Serene Highnesses passed on, the Queen, especially, acknowledging their loyalty by her most gracious smiles. She wore a brilliant tiara of diamonds, and a rich pink satin dress, and had chains of diamonds round her neck, and her arms were loaded with bracelets. She looked rather different to my simple, peasant-like ideal; but her face was lovely and kind, and in that expression of kindness lay an infinite charm. What a study of faces was here! I read in many of them strange histories of court life and intrigue; but with that we have, now, nothing to do.

There were numbers of court ladies, young and old, all very grand, and princes and dukes in abundance; they proceeded to the platform, and took their seats, chatting among themselves, and seeming very merry. Soon they again descended, to walk the stately *polonaise* round the ball-room; the grand ladies returning, however, to their crimson chairs of state, whilst many of the gentlemen might be seen moving amongst the crowd. And soon, when a waltz began, behold Prince Adelbert dancing with a citizen's daughter, and various other of the grandees dancing away with equally plebeian partners. That was all very right — was it not? If they were the guests of the citizens, as on this occasion they were, it was right to associate with citizens. I saw the King of Greece talking to all sorts of people as merrily as could be. There was, however, very little space for dancing — just a circle for the waltzers, and that was all.

We ourselves were neither *aristocratic* enough, nor yet *plebeian* enough, to dance; therefore, we stood in a good place and looked on, and a most amusing scene we beheld.

At the first glance, from the uniforms being pretty much alike, you scarcely distinguished the prince from his butcher or his baker; but in a very short time your eye told you that there was in the room, as in the world at large, a most subtle, almost imperceptible gradation of rank, both conventional and moral! With the women it was the same; from the diamond crown of the Queen, to the silver head-gear of the citizen-maiden of the lower class. It was to me a singular, almost affecting study. But sentiment soon gave way to the intensest amusement, as one queer couple after another passed before us! There was a little fellow, in militia uniform, fairly waltzed round 'a huge whale of a wife,' in a heavy black cotton dress, gorgeous with brilliant flowers, while her head bore the silver, swallow-tailed Munich cap; here a sentimental maiden, in tawny muslin, clung to the arm of some gigantic crane in regimentals. The most extraordinary costumes presented themselves. All the cotton and stuff dresses danced, while the muslins and satins looked on. And why not? All the middle-aged, elderly, nay, *old* people danced, so at least it seemed to me, whilst the young looked on. And why not? I again asked myself — it was only my *taste*, not my *reason*, that objected. There was the feeble Appleshoe in brilliant red and blue, with spectacles on nose, and thin, buff-colored hair, dancing away with his bony but good-natured wife, in black silk. I rather admired them. I recognised, in various of the military figures, acquaintances of mine. There, from that soldier I bought my winter dress, from that ferocious little fellow a packet of charcoal that very morning, and there was the modeller of a beautiful statuette, from whom I shall make a purchase one of these days.

I told you that we stood looking on from a good place which happened to be close to one of the grim lions guarding the steps of the platform. As Prince Adelbert returned to the aristocracy, he passed us, and having danced with Ida at several balls this winter, and being a sort of acquaintance of Mrs. Amsel's, he stopped to speak to them. He seemed very good-tempered, and as he chatted about the ball, and various other things, he glanced several times towards me with a smile, as if to say — 'And who is this young lady?' Whereupon Mrs. Amsel introduced me to his Royal Highness, and his Royal Highness was very polite indeed, and we two had a little chat. I tell this in order that —— may honor me because I have exchanged words with a prince of the blood.

Once more, in the course of the evening, the Court

ladies descended from their elevation and danced a quadrille — the Queen is excessively fond of dancing, they say — after which, about ten o'clock, the whole Court again paraded the room, and then took their departure, and soon after we followed their example. Before we left, however, I saw rather a characteristic bit of Munich life, the militia and their partners regaling themselves with beer and ham in a room adjoining the ball-room; such a chaos of plumed helmets, tankards, and plates of ham as there was! And the ceiling of the room adjoining was painted with grand allegorical frescoes of Apollo and the Muses!

But I have not yet done. I must tell you of the

MASKED ACADEMY.

'Fräulein Amsel has been to ask you to go with her to the *Maskirte Academie* at the Odeon to-night!' exclaimed Madame Thekla, when I came home about half-past five last Thursday evening; 'she said you must be there at latest by six, as it will be so terribly crowded, and she wishes you to call on her.'

All this was impossible; it was then more than half-past five, and I had not yet dined, to say nothing of dressing! 'Would Madame Thekla go with me into the gallery?' I asked.

'Yes, with pleasure, as soon as she had had her beer,' the tea of most Munich women of her class.

When she had drunk her beer, and I had dined, dressed, and had a cup of coffee, away we started. The gallery was crowded to excess, although it was only just six; and if people had not been very polite to me, as a foreigner and a young lady, I should have had no place at all. However, squeezed up against a pillar and a poor little humpbacked lad, to whom of course I was very polite all the evening, for he had inconvenienced himself for me — I saw capitally.

The scene of operation was again the large hall of the Odeon. At one end was erected a stage, for the performance of a pantomime, which I soon perceived was to be the amusement of the evening. Before the proscenium were seats and music desks, then came rows and rows of chairs for the audience, filling about half the room. In the other portion of the hall were arranged card-tables.

There were very few people in the room when we first took our place in the gallery, so that for the hour preceding the performance of the pantomime, my amusement was watching the arrivals. People were to be masked; at least, such were the directions on the cards of admission: therefore I was considerably disappointed to see the ladies, with very few exceptions, without masks or masquerade dresses, only in full evening costume, perhaps, however, somewhat more brilliant in color than usual. Many children were in fancy dresses, looking excessively pretty; one little girl of about twelve, especially, who paraded about in extreme grandeur as a minute Morisco lady. The gentlemen, however, were all either in fancy dresses or dominoes, and the effect of these dominoed gentlemen was, to my eyes, remarkably comic. They swept along in scarlet, blue, orange, green and crimson dominoes, trimmed with deep white lace frills and capes, yet wearing their every-day black hats, on which were stuck their masks, and with common-place black trowsers and patent-leather boots peeping out beneath.

The court in attendance on the three kings and the two queens arrived. King Ludwig's tall, spare figure, decked out in a white and scarlet domino, looked very like that of a Catholic priest. The King of Greece wore blue, the young King of Bavaria crimson. The young Queen was dressed in a very simple mode — a crimson velvet dress, over which she wore ermine, and with a tiara of diamonds on her head. The old Queen wore black velvet, and looked so very quiet, that I never knew she was a queen till the evening was almost over. The royalties scattered themselves through the room, sitting, standing, talking, laughing, like ordinary mortals; the white and scarlet Catholic priest bowing and nodding his head about everywhere in that lively manner which instantly announced him as King Ludwig.

Every now and then small troops of regular masks entered, men evidently, most of them, dressed as women. In they came, with that queer, uncertain gait, mysterious air, and peering gaze, which masks always have. There were two mysterious, veiled, Moorish beauties; two nuns; two pink sentimental sisters; and three big-boned white ones, dressed in white bed-gowns and mob-caps. These three Amazonian dames stalked about together, distributing little papers among the crowd, which said little papers usually created much laughter and astonishment. Now a sister mysteriously drew aside a guest, and whispered something in his or her ear. Kings, queens, and courtiers, all had their turn.

Such was the fun going on before and during the pauses in the pantomime. The pantomime itself was nothing particular. Harlequin, Columbine, Pantaloon, and some half-dozen other oddly attired mortals, performed a variety of antics and practical jokes, which called forth roars of laughter from the motley audience. To me, however, they seemed poor and dull. The most amusing thing, I thought, was a dancing donkey, the legs of which you instantly recognised as youthful human legs. Pantaloon, extremely enamored of this donkey, rushes off for hay to feed it with ; but the donkey, with donkey politeness, refuses the hay each time it is offered, wheeling round, presenting his tail and his heels instead of his mouth, till poor old Pantaloon is in the last stage of astonishment and despair. The only pretty thing was a dance of children, dressed as Swiss peasants.

People, I suppose, considered this Masked Academy very amusing ; and you will ask, 'But why Masked *Academy*?' So have I asked from numbers of people, and the answer I get is, 'Oh, it is the Masked Academy!' as though everybody knew what that meant. You, therefore, must make the best of this answer, as I have done, and be content.

There are quantities of Balls just now, one of which I must mention ; it was at the beautiful house of an artist — a house exquisitely furnished in the old German style, all the decorations exquisite, and all the company artists. It was what is called here a 'picnic,' which means a party, the expense of which is divided by the company ; different friends joining and providing different portions of the entertainment. This is a custom very general here, and a very rational one, I think — but very un-English. These picnics circulate. I have heard of the officers' picnic, the students' pic-nic, and so on.

The Carnival is now approaching its end ; everybody is being merry whilst they may. In a few days comes Lent.

CHAPTER XXI.

THE BUTCHERS' LEAP IN THE FOUNTAIN. — END OF CARNIVAL.

THIS strange ceremonial, like the *Schäffler Tanz* which I lately described, is said to have its origin in the time of the plague. While the coopers danced with garlands and music through the streets, the butchers sprang into the fountain in the market-place, to show their fellow-citizens that its water was no longer to be dreaded as poisoned. Perhaps they were the Sanitary Commissioners of those days; and by bathing themselves in the water and dashing it about on the crowd, would teach the true means of putting pestilence to flight.

Though the Coopers' Dance takes place only once in seven years, the Butchers' Leap occurs annually, and always on *Fasching Montag*, — the Monday before Shrove Tuesday. I believe the ceremony is of great importance to the trade of the butchers; as certain privileges granted to them are annually renewed at this time, and in connection with the Leap. These two ceremonies — of the Coopers' Dance and the Butchers' Leap — are now almost the last remains of the picturesque and quaint customs of old Munich.

The butchers commence their proceedings by attending high mass in St. Peter's Church, — close to the Schrannen Platz, or market-place, in which the fountain is situated. It is a desolate-looking church, this St. Peter's, as seen from without, — old, decaying, and ugly: within tawdry, and, though not desolate and decaying, ugly. From staringly-white walls frown down on the spectator torture-pictures, alternating with huge gilt images of sentimental saints in clumsy drapery. The altars are masses of golden clouds and golden cherubs.

Music, as from the orchestra of a theatre rather than from the choir of a church, greeted Madame Thekla and myself as we entered. The butchers were just passing out. We caught glimpses of scarlet coats; and saw two huge silver flagons, covered with a very panoply of gold and silver medals, borne aloft by pompous officials clothed in scarlet. Having watched the procession — some half-dozen tiny butchers' sons, urchins of five and six years old, with rosy, round faces, and chubby hands, mounted on stalwart horses, and dressed in little scarlet coats, top-boots, and jaunty green velvet hats — seven butchers' apprentices, the Leapers of the day, also dressed in scarlet, and mounted on horseback — the musicians — the ample train of master-butchers and journeymen, in long dark cloaks and with huge nosegays in their hats — and the scarlet officials bearing the decorated flagons, — having watched, I say, all these good folk wend their way in long procession up the narrow street leading from the church, and seen them cross the market-place in the direction of the Palace, where they are awaited by the King, — let us look around, and notice the features of the market-place: for it is, in fact, a quaint old bit of the city, and well worth a glimpse.

If I love the Ludwig Strasse as the most beautiful portion of new Munich, I almost equally love the Schrannen Platz as about the quaintest part of old Munich. It is long and narrow as a market-place, but wide as a street. The houses are old; many of them very handsome, and rich with ornamental stucco-work, —

> 'All garlanded with carven imageries
> Of fruit and flowers, and bunches of knot-grass.'

The roofs are steep, red-tiled, and perforated with rows of little penthouse windows. The fronts of the houses are of all imaginable pale tints, — stone colors, pinks, greens, greys, and tawnies. Three of the four corners of the market-place are adorned with tall pepper-box towers, with domed roofs and innumerable narrow windows. At one end is the fountain; and in the centre a heavy, but quaint shrine, — a column supporting a gilt figure of the Madonna. The eye wanders down various picturesque streets which open into the market-place; and on one hand, above steep roofs, gaze down the two striking red-brick towers of the *Frauen Kirche* — the cathedral of Munich: those two red towers which are seen in all views of this city, and which belong as much to Munich as the dome of St. Paul's does to the City of London, — those towers which in the haze of sunset are frequently transformed into violet-tinted columns, or about which, in autumn and winter, mists cling with a strange dreariness as if they were desolate mountain peaks!

But the quaintest feature of all in the Schrannen Platz is a sort of arcade which runs around it. Here, beneath the low and massive arches, are crowded thick upon each other a host of small shops. What strange, dark cells they are, — yet how picturesque! Here is a dealer in crucifixes; next to him a woollen-draper, displaying bright striped woollen goods for the peasants; then a general dealer, with heaps and bundles, and tubs, and chests, containing everything most heterogeneous; and next to him a dealer in pipes. There are bustle and gloom always beneath these heavy low arches; but they present a glorious bit of picturesque life. There are queer wooden booths, too, along one portion of the Schrannen Platz, where it rather narrows, losing its character of market-place, and descending to that of an ordinary street. But the booths do not degenerate in their picturesque character. The earthenware booths, of which there are several, are truly delicious. Such rows and piles of dark green, orange, ruddy chocolate-brown, sea-green, pale-yellow, and deep blue and grey vessels of all forms and sizes — all quaint, all odd — jugs, flagons, pipkins, queer pots with huge lids, queer tripods, for which I know no name — things which always seem to me to come out of a witch's kitchen, but by means of which I suspect that my own dinner is cooked every day. All these heaps of crockery lie about the doors, and load the windows of the wooden booths, and line shelves and shelves within the gloom of the little shops themselves. When I first came here, these old crockery shops were a more frequent study to me than anything else in the old town.

We ascended a steep, narrow staircase leading out of this arcade into one of the houses above it, from which we were to witness the leaping into the fountain.

It was a clean, old-fashioned, dreary sort of a house, with its crucifixes surrounded with artificial flowers hanging upon the white-washed walls of the staircase, and with heavy dark oaken doors with quaint hinges and clumsy locks. One of these doors opened, and we were kindly welcomed by an old man, a carpenter, who had promised us the use of his window to see the sight.

The room was meagrely furnished, but the white-washed walls were adorned with several very tolerable prints after Raphael, — all of them religious subjects of course; there was a neat bed in one corner, a huge black earthenware stove in another, a crucifix, several pipes, and a cage containing a canary-bird hanging near the windows, which looked gay with their rolls of fresh green moss laid along the sills. At one of three windows the old carpenter was at work; he soon moved all his tools away, and brought out a singular piece of wood, which at first considerably puzzled me.

'May I ask,' said I, 'what you are making there?'

'An organ, *gnädiges Fräulein*, for my little grandson there!' pointing to a shy little lad with large blue eyes and very white hair.

'You are a musician, then?' said I, looking with still greater interest at the old man, with his thin, intelligent face.

'No, not so much of that; but that little chap is very fond of music, and I'm making this for him. I work at it all my leisure moments. I've the pipes all ready; it will turn out well, I think, and we are both very anxious about it, arn't we, Hänschen? Ah, he's a slow lad, that is, at his books, though! — a very slow lad! I've to comfort him often, *gnädiges Fräulein*, — he's so slow; he's not like his brother, who died last year — that was a quick lad! But I tell Hänschen he'll learn easier by and by — and he's a good lad, *Fräulein*, and very fond of music!'

'And Hänschen,' said I, 'you are not slow at music; of that I'm certain: are you!'

If any one could have seen the bright flush of the little fellow's face, and his large kindling eyes, they would have felt as delightful a thrill as I now do in recalling his face, and the pleased kindly countenance of the old grandfather.

Madame Thekla and the old man had a long gossip.

Hänschen whispered and tittered with a group of little lads come to see the 'Leap' — a group of 'youth,' as the old grandfather called them.

Madame Thekla soon fell into discourse with the old man. We probably might have an hour or more to wait until the commencement of the spectacle.

Sometimes I amused myself with watching the people outside; sometimes I fell into pleasant day-dreams, lulled by the droning voices of the two old gossips, and I felt astonished every now and then by their inquiring from me if I were not tired, were not impatient? Not at all! I could have sat there for hours. I found my attention, however, aroused by Madame Thekla's voice, — she was talking of birds; I think it was *à propos* of the old man's canary. She was talking of the time when her '*seliger Mann*' was alive, and when she lived near Salzburg. I always liked to hear her talk of that time, for the 'blessed husband' must have been a good husband indeed, — a kind old fellow, who, nearly twice her age, treated her not only as a beloved wife, but as a spoilt child. He was a well-to-do man, and their life near Salzburg is her Garden of Eden. And as she talked of the pigeons they had there, of the old thrush that used to hang beneath the vine, and of their tame lark, her memories seemed to mingle with my own beautiful memories of Salzburg. I wove such pleasant fancies of dewy, sunshiny mornings in a quiet, old-fashioned garden, where there was a fluttering of white-winged pigeons settling down to drink out of a stone basin in the grass, of the thrush singing beneath the vine odorous with blossoms, of the old tame lark hanging in an apricot-tree, and, above all, the glorious, craggy sides and snowy summits of the Salzburg Alps rising in glorious majesty and grandeur, that I felt quite sorry to be called away from these imaginary pictures to the reality, amusing as it was, which was going on in the market-place.

Looking out of the window on the crowd that began to collect around the fountain, I noticed the tall roofs and handsome fronts of the houses opposite, and the crowd of pigeons — scores and scores of pigeons — assembled just opposite the fountain on the edge of the steep roof which rose like a red hill-side behind them. They seemed solemnly met to witness the great festivities about to be celebrated, and sat in silent expectation brooding in the sunshine. Then I wondered what attraction the icy water could have for the children who leaned over the fountain's side, dabbling in the water as though it had been Midsummer. The crowd increased and increased, and seven new white buckets were brought and placed on a broad plank, which extended across one side of the fountain basin.

A shout from the crowd announced the arrival of the butchers. First of all came the tender butcher-infants, in scarlet coats, top-boots, and green velvet hats, borne in the arms of their fathers through the crowd in order that they might witness the fun. Then followed the scarlet officials; and then came seven of the queerest beasts man ever set eyes on. What were they, if human? Were they seven Esquimaux chiefs, or seven African mumbo-jumbos? They were the heroes of the day — the seven butcher-apprentices, clothed in fur caps and garments, — covered from shoulder to heel with hundreds of dangling calves' tails — red, white, black, dun!

You may imagine the shouts that greeted them, — the peals of laughter. Up they sprang on the broad plank, — leaping, dancing, making their tails fly round like trundled mops. The crowd roared with laughter.

A stately scarlet-clad official, a butcher (*Altgesell*), stands beside them on the plank. Ten times they drink the health of the royal family, and prosperity to the butchers' craft. The *Altgesell* then striking many blows on the shoulder of the nearest apprentice, frees him and all the remaining six from their indentures. They are henceforth full-grown butchers. Then they plunge into the very centre of the fountain with a tremendous splash. The crowd shouts; the startled pigeons wheel in wild alarm above the heads and laughter of the crowd; the seven Tritons dash torrents of water on the multitude, who fly shrieking and laughing before the deluge; — the seven buckets are plied with unwearied arms; lads are enticed within aim by showers of nuts flung by the 'Leapers,' and then are drenched to the skin. It is a bewilderment of water, flying calves' tails, pelting nuts, and shrieking urchins!

The 'Leapers' then ascend out of their bath, — shake themselves like shaggy dogs, — have white cloths pinned round their necks as though they were going to be shaved, — and have very grand medals hung round their necks suspended by gaudy ribbons.

The procession retires across the market-place to its '*Herberge*,' and the crowd disperses, — but disperses only to reassemble in various public-houses for the merriment of the afternoon and night. That night and the next day are 'the maddest, merriest of all the year.' Music is everywhere — dancing everywhere. It is the end of the Carnival. Ash-Wednesday comes, — and then, all is gloom.

CHAPTER XXII.

CONVERSATION WITH A PAINTER. — THE FRESCOES OF THE NEW PINAKOTHEK AND STERRIO-CHROMIE.

March 12th. — In conversation to-day with a Munich painter, I chanced to observe what a great charm, for me, the character of Munich had, — not alone its churches, its pictures, its galleries, its beautiful and quaint houses, but its whole poetical dreamy character: I loved the mild oxen yoked in the heavy wagons, the peasants, the villages, the Isar, the desolate plain, and the glorious chain of Alps, with a peculiar and an indefinable love.

'But,' observed he, 'there is one feature in Munich life from which you, unfortunately, as a woman, have been cut off, — the jovial, poetical, quaint life of the artists among themselves. This is a great pity, for you would have so much enjoyed it, — the life of the artists, I mean, in their *Kneips*, with their festivals and odd usages.' And then he went on to tell me how gay the artists here usually are during Carnival time, and described one of their masked balls, where all is deliciously artistic, and poetic. 'This year and last, however, people,' said he, 'have been too much dispirited by all these political troubles to have heart for such merriment. But the meetings at their Kneips! those were delightful, poetical, artistic! Then too, in May, there is the May Festival, when all the painters go forth, with their wives and children, to Starnberg, where they spend a day full of beauty and merriment upon the lake, and among the woods, and make huge bonfires by the water-side, leaping over them in memory of old pagan times.'

'Have you ever been to Schwanthaler's Castle?' asked the painter.

'No,' I replied; 'where is it?'

'It is about two *Stund* from Munich, a strange romantic little castle, a great resort of the Munich artists. On one occasion they had all gone forth,' pursued the painter, 'with music and with banners flying, a grand, jovial company, and when with sounds of music they approached the little castle, behold! a knight, clad in armor, suddenly appeared upon the battlements, and in a hoarse, sepulchral voice, demanded —

'Who are these men that, with music and jollity, have aroused me from my sleep of centuries?'

And then one of the intruders replied in a grand speech to the old knight, and there was a deal of parleying.

How thoroughly German is all this! Imagine highly intellectual, and earnest spirited men, even were they painters and poets, in England giving themselves up to such a frolic. It would be felt as childish and undignified. But here it is in keeping.

'And,' continued the painter, 'there is also another beautiful feature of our Munich artist-life which you have never yet properly enjoyed, — this is the *Schnee-Gebirg*, — those sublime mountains where we behold that poetry which we strive to work out in our pictures here in the city. The Schnee-Gebirg (the Alpine chain) is a portion of Munich art — it is our heaven. Such beauty as there is among these mountains! such grandeur! such gorgeous coloring! such flowers! such wild legends! such a primitive race of people! such remains of old times, — of the Romans, of the old Germans, of the Druids. Yes, indeed, the Tyrol is a district! Talk of Switzerland! it is modern in its feeling, it is common-place in comparison! Think only of the *Untersberg*, with old Barbarossa asleep in his enchantment beneath it, with his beard grown through the stone table upon which he leans! Think of the whole region around Salzburg; it is brimful of legends and beauty!'

Had you only heard the painter's words of enthusiasm, and seen his countenance flush with earnest love of these mountains, you would have felt, as I at the moment felt, ready to start that instant for the mountains.

Yes, at the bottom of my soul I have a pang of '*Heimweh*' whenever I look towards the Alpine chain. The ew glimpses I have had of its beauty are always haunting my imagination

I wish E—— would paint, some day, a little picture, called 'In the Tyrol.' It should be a picture of flowers. It should represent a small portion of grey-rock, covered with mosses and lichens of every tint; and flowers should droop over the rock and spring out of its crevices; flowers like the brightest gems, crimson mountain-pinks, deep azure gentians and flowers like stars of gold, and delicate, feathery grasses, and luxuriant leaves of ladies'-mantle sparkling with dew-drops; and beyond, as background, should be a pearly evening sky, streaked with rose and orange, and Alpine peaks of deepest violet, dreamy and sublime in the glow of sunset. If E——, with his exquisite love of flowers and weeds, should not be inspired to paint such a picture, I myself feel so, and must attempt it some day, setting off to the mountains and bathing my spirit in their beauty and joy.

Kaulbach is at work this spring upon his designs for the New Pinakothek, a series of frescoes illustrative of the history of modern German art: the building of the New Pinakothek being destined for the repository of works as exclusively of modern schools, as the old Pinakothek is of the old.

Seven designs for the south façade of the New Pinakothek are now complete, and the frescoes are in progress. The centre composition represents King Ludwig as descending from his throne, and receiving with a gracious welcome various artists and lovers of art, who approach him with chef-d'œuvres both ancient and modern. Classic, Egyptian, mediæval, all are welcome to enrich the galleries and palaces of his art-city.

It would seem no easy task to adapt our modern costume to the poetical necessities of colossal figures. Looking at these designs, however, one is inclined to await a happy result. Kaulbach has preserved the individual characteristics both of the men and of the age which he has portrayed, and yet there is no want of dignity.

One could have wished that the genius of so great a man as Kaulbach should have had some more congenial subject intrusted to it, for a series of great public works, in the city of his home, than the illustration of an almost personal theme; for Kaulbach's true path lies among the highest regions of the ideal.

Yet, even working upon this task, his genius has burst forth in many a beautiful and poetic touch, contrasting wonderfully with the vein of genial humor and keen satire running through the whole series; as characteristic of the man as in his spirit of tenderness, grace, and beauty.

The first in order of this series — though not the first completed — is the design upon which the painter is now at work. It is an allegorical representation of the triumph of knowledge and modern taste over the formalities and stagnation of what the Germans designate the '*Zopf-Zeit*,' or Pigtail-age. Kaulbach's peculiar spirit of humor and satire, to which I have just referred, and of which his designs to 'Reineke Fuchs' are a striking example, a spirit akin to the satire of our own Hogarth, singularly and most forcibly in this design contrasts with another element of his nature, an element as strikingly akin to Flaxman as the other is to Hogarth, — the most lovely appreciation of the antique — the most exquisite grace and simplicity in his lines of composition.

A hideous three-headed monster keeps watch and ward over a small stone cell, adorned with architectural monsters in periwigs and lace cravats. Within the cell, and clinging together on the ground, sit the imprisoned Graces. A lamp burns beside them. One holds, listlessly, an unbound wreath of flowers; another hides her face in the lap of the third. The third Grace raises her head as though a sudden hope had rushed to her heart and flushed her cheek! Sounds of rescue have reached her ear. A mighty combat is being waged without. Upborne by a low light cloud, on comes Minerva, with upraised spear and shield, to attack the Cerberus. Close upon her follows Winckelmann, who flings, with unerring aim, his ink-stand at the monster, whilst Thorwaldsen aims vigorous blows with his mighty mallet, and Karsten — the friend of our Flaxman — brandishes his sword! Up through a marsh out of the distance comes on the architect Schenkel, with a large portfolio beneath his arm. Hideous frogs are ready to meet him, with hateful croakings, on the mainland, but he cares not for them: on he comes, with calm, brave face to aid in the rescue!

The monster's death-hour is arrived; the three scaly necks writhe beneath the three elegant lace cravats; the three hideous human countenances turn livid, and are distorted by death-pangs, beneath the three powdered periwigs.

And lo! on the other side of the little cell up rushes Pegasus, carrying upon his back between his swift wings Cornelius, wielding a tremendous two-edged sword; Overbeck, with his devout countenance, bearing with love and awe a fluttering banner, upon which glows the Madonna and Child; and Veit, vigorous in his genius and youth!

Veit, like a right generous soul, lends his hand to a nameless brother painter, so that he also may mount Pegasus. Alas, poor fellow! it is time a friendly hand should raise him, for already he is growing bald, and from his pocket peeps forth a pistol, and his one foot still rests upon a tortoise. A moment more and he will be seated upon the back of Pegasus, the fourth of the '*Haimons-Kinder*' of Modern Art, ready to lend his arm to the strife.

On rushes Pegasus, and beneath his hoofs sleeps in self-contented rest,—his arm encircling a lay-figure, his ideal of grace—a withered old fellow dressed in full periwig costume, a decoration in his button-hole, a smile of the utmost self-gratulation on his lean visage.

The seventh study of color for these frescoes of the south façade is also just completed.

It represents the group of sculptors who have embellished Munich. In the centre sits the Munich sculptor *par excellence*, Schwanthaler. He is seated on a low seat, as though designing; sketches of various statues lie at his feet. A tall exquisite Gothic *Pokal* (goblet) rises from the ground beside him, and near to him also stands a quaint and hideous bust as of some demon dwarf: it is clothed in strange old crumbling armor, and to those who know the sculptor and his love of such things, and his whole life, it is full of suggestive meaning.

To the right of Schwanthaler sits, modelling a bust, Professor Halbig, celebrated for his great skill in various branches of his art, for his modelling of classic, romantic, and religious subjects, as well as of portraits and of animals. Behind Halbig stands Rauch of Berlin, busied upon the statue of Max-Joseph, which is erected on the Rese denz Platz opposite the beautiful Opera-house. Near to Rauch you see Rietschiel of Dresden and the veteran Schadow. To the left of Schwanthaler stand the sculptors Widnmann and Brugger, and grand old Thorwaldsen, with his thoughtful and serene brow shaded by its cloud of snowy locks: he wraps himself majestically in his cloak, and looks out, as with prophetic gaze, towards the great future of German art.

Beyond these figures, and various statues familiar to the inhabitant of Munich, rises the pediment of the Regensburg Walhalla. Workmen, their muscles strained, their chests heaving, place upon it the heroic figure of the Hermann with his winged helm and firmly clenched sword.

And now above the pediment, and relieved against the cloudless deep-blue Munich sky, is a lovely group! It is the poetry of the Munich people's life. Sweet round-faced girls and women and children gaze down upon all these wonders of art, and upon this busy throng of artists and workmen. Theirs is the enjoyment, the astonishment! This woman in her sparkling silver head-dress and pretty gay boddice, and silver necklace of many chains, points out the wonders to those two doubly astonished urchins who lean over the pediment. And here sits a bright, smiling '*Kellnerin*,' pouring out the intoxicating '*Bock*' into the tall, ell-long glass! How pretty she is, and how gracefully she pours! And see! here is another bright creature bearing a plate heaped up with round loaves and those odd-looking roots,—those huge radishes, said to taste so good with Munich beer! And beyond, up come peasant women! You know them by the kerchief tightly bound across their brows. How amazed that woman is! and well she may be, at that long array of golden statues of the Electors, which you just see looming out of the distance, and at the commanding Kurfurst Maximilian I., who, seated on his bronze horse, grandly waves his bronze arm against the blue sky.

This little bit of the people's life is an exquisite touch, and repeated in various phases throughout the whole series of designs, — it is the artist's link between the actual and the ideal; and though these touches are *true* to life it is a *beautiful truth.* The costume to its minutest detail is the actual every-day national costume, but through the artist's mind it has lost all that in the vulgarity of life it has gained of harsh and repulsive, — it is mellowed and purified as by a glowing and beautifying sun. If it is thus with the costume, how much more is it so in the faces and forms!

The other designs are treated in a similar manner. There is the entrance of a troop of young German painters and sculptors into Rome. Their studying also the great works of the old masters and the antique, and being summoned in the midst of their studies by a Bavarian herald. Among these students are Cornelius, Schnorr, Hess, and Schwanthaler. In the distance prophetically beckons the Bavaria with her oak-wreath.

Next in order, and the centre fresco which I have already described, is the King's reception of the artists and their works, and of the various artistic treasures with which he has stored his capital. Next follow a design of the painters busily employed on their different works, and another of the architects; and lastly come the sculptors, of which I have given you a more elaborate description.

Each design is rich to overflowing with suggestive thought and beautiful fancy.

Since writing the above, the scaffoldings have been removed from before two of the completed frescoes of the New Pinakothek, and all Munich has streamed to look at them. For my own part I greatly prefer the small cartoons and sketches of color to the finished frescoes: the coloring of the modern costume in the frescoes tells to my eye gaudy and forced. Again I must repeat, would that a different class of composition had been chosen for the exercise of Kaulbach's peculiarly exalted genius.

I hear on all sides regret expressed that these frescoes, which are exposed without the least defence against the weather upon the external walls of the building, have been executed in the old mode of fresco, and not according to the new method of sterrio-chromie, in which Kaulbach's Berlin frescoes are being painted.

Sterrio-chromie is the discovery of the celebrated chemist the *Oberbergrath* von Fuchs of Munich, and is considered by German painters one of the greatest discoveries of the age. Among its advantages over ordinary fresco and encaustic painting, are its greater durability, and the power which the painter has of retouching and *glazing*. The colors are mixed with water, and the whole picture permanently fixed by profuse sprinklings of water in which is mixed a certain proportion of *fluoric acid*.

I understand that sterrio-chromie is in fact a preserver of the wall upon which the picture is painted, by the chemical action of the solution sprinkled over the picture whilst it is in progress, and when completed the ground on which it is painted, and the colors of the picture, become one hard flinty mass, the colors themselves being converted into the hardest stone; whilst in ordinary fresco it is a mere skin of flint which preserves the painting. So hard, I am told, is a picture in sterrio-chromie that neither fire nor damp can affect it. During the last twelve years numerous experiments have been tried with this process, and it is said to have stood all tests admirably.

That Kaulbach has perfect reliance upon sterrio-chromie is proved by his employing it as the medium by which he perpetuates his great series of historical works at Berlin.

I have already referred to the Hogarthian element in Kaulbach's genius; and to one design of his in particular, belonging to the Hogarthian class, I must refer more in detail. This is his design entitled 'The Mad-House,' universally known throughout Germany, and a design which is interesting from the history of its origin as well as from its intrinsic genius. Kaulbach's childhood and early youth were a season of bitterest poverty; his is the old and affecting story of glorious genius putting forth its tender roots and germinating in an arid and rocky soil.

'The Mad-House' takes its origin from the time when Kaulbach was a lad of fifteen studying at the Düsseldorff Academy. The physician of an asylum frequently visiting the house where Kaulbach lodged, proposed to him that he and a fellow-student should decorate the church of the Asylum with frescoes from sacred subjects. They were to be paid *in food.* The youthful decorators completed their work; and then the physician, with a secret and benevolent intention in his heart, the purport of which only in later years revealed itself to the painter, proposed to show them over the Asylum. He led the two youths through the desolate wards of that house of woe, relating as he went along the mournful histories of the miserable inhabitants. He wished to recompense the boys for their labor, not alone by food for the body, but by food for deep thought and reflection; he wished to read them a deep and impressive life's lesson, and he related therefore these miserable histories to them in an extraordinarily vivid and poetic manner. The impression made by his words upon one of his listeners was profound. Those mournful histories and forms haunted young Kaulbach's imagination like ghosts for ten years; then, in order fairly to lay the phantoms, he made his design of the 'Mad-House.'

The design represents the patients as grouped together, men and women, in the desolate yard of the Mad-House: here is an awful commentary upon human life — upon the sane as well as the insane. Ambition, avarice, fanaticism, cruelty, love, over-excitement of sense and of intellect, each presents its wretched victim! With the exception of three out of the fifteen mad people which the design contains, all are absorbed in their own reflections or occupations, heedless of those around them: these three are two young women, who contend with each other about a man, and an old crone who watches the contest. The man, a wretched, sordid being, with a thin, mean face, wrinkled-up eye, and mouth drawn down, with an indescribable look of cruel hardness and meanness combined, — with a lottery ticket pinned upon his battered hat, with ear-rings in his ears, and his hands doggedly thrust within his apron, looks out unconcernedly, heedless of the women, whose arms are locked around his bull-neck; his eyes are filled with avaricious madness. The ribald shriek rings in one's ears of the woman who, with a tiger-look in her coarse face, and with her hair closely shaven, seeks with maniac violence to push back her rival, who with closely-locked hands clings round the man. Ah!

those are arms which should have clung around a kind and noble being, — that sweet feminine face should have gleamed with the sunshine of domestic joy; in that beautiful, sad countenance, veiled now with the mist of madness, and in the close, close clasp of those hands, one reads the history of a miserable, cruel marriage; it is a face that makes the heart sick to dwell upon. The old crone, wearing her quaint peasant costume, whilst her bony fingers knit busily, looks round upon this group; her old eyes also have the mist of madness in them, and from her toothless jaws proceed, you feel, coarse, horrible mumblings.

All the other maniacs are self-absorbed. Here in the centre sits, with ungartered stockings falling from his legs, and resting his fierce face upon his fists, one who believes himself a soldier; his wooden sword is slung around his shoulders. Close to him sits a king, bearing his wooden sceptre, a medal hanging round his neck, his poor, sad imbecile head crowned with a paper and tinsel diadem. There, on the other hand of the soldier, with dreamy spectacled face, an old man demonstrating to himself, with upraised hands, books laid upon his knees, and diagrams drawn upon the ground before him, a problem from Euclid. This man is a shoemaker: singularly bearing out the truth that the cobbler-craft so frequently has an inexplicable kinship with the speculative intellect. One man has bowed his head upon his knees in the utter, hopeless abandonment of despair; a letter hangs from one of his hands. A woman with anxious face hushes, as if to sleep, a piece of wood, which she has wrapped up in handkerchiefs, believing it an infant, and rocks it tenderly upon her knees. Prominent in this mass of anguish stands forth a large man; his open, frilled shirt displays a brawny breast, to which he presses a wooden cross with one hand, pointing towards himself with the other. His bold face, his partially bald head, from either side of which flies his shaggy hair, are impressed with a revolting, sneering scorn; laughter and misery, and blasphemy, contend in that dreadful countenance. Close beside him stands a youth, who clasps his rosary piously and yet fanatically to his breast; his beautiful, dreamy, sensitive countenance pleads mournfully whilst he mutters prayers. Are not these the types of the two fanaticisms — of the sceptical and the religious? A young girl, whose rich hair falls in heavy masses from her comb, and whose sweet young face, as it is caught in profile, speaks of a soul's sickness, clasps her poor hands and prays also.

The background of this group is in savage desolate harmony with it: you see a portion of the madhouse wall, a small barred window looking out of it, and a piece of door, the heavy hinges of which and the very bell-handle have a harsh, prison-like air. A piece of blank wall stretches along from this corner of the madhouse: it is crested with a few dreary tufts of weeds, and above the wall you can catch a dreary sweep of low hills, with a dreary tuft or two of bushes and a dreary stretch of sky above. The yard itself is full of weeds and stones, dreary yet more, if possible, than is the glimpse of the external world.

Two figures, which as yet I have not referred to, add strongly to the strange spirit of the scene. One is an old mad-woman pacing rapidly up and down — up and down — beside this wall; she paces like a caged beast before the bars of its den: the carriage of her stooping head, the swing of her gown, the position of her slovenly feet, tell of her restless pacings to and fro, and the lower portion of her stern old face, as it is partially revealed by her hood-like drapery, excites the imagination extraordinarily. I can scarcely account to myself for the impression always produced upon me by this especial figure, which is by far the most insignificant, as regards size, in the design. It is a vague horror, — to me she is the maddest of all the maniacs, and the most terrible in her madness.

The other figure is — *the jailer*, I was about to say — the *keeper*, though jailer would truly be the fitter term for such a man as this appears to be ; short and very stout, and hard and cruel. Would that in charity his cruelty might be pronounced madness ! There he stands, with feet doggedly planted before the door of the prison-house ; his arms are folded behind him, and in his hands he holds a great bunch of keys, the very number suggesting the many cells which he has to lock ; his hard, coarse, cruel face is turned towards the group, the eyes half concealed by a furred night-cap, which is drawn down over them, and with a pipe in his mouth he glares broodingly over his victims : and out of the pocket of his great-coat protrudes a stout whip with a keen, heavy thong.

The use of this thong is shown by a rude drawing upon the madhouse wall, where this human fiend, in coarse but striking caricature, is depicted flogging a victim, who with goggle-eyes and circular head, and circular body, such as we see in children's drawings, flings up in agony two arms like toasting-forks.

CHAPTER XXIII.

A PICTURE IN LENT. — FEET-WASHING ON GREEN THURSDAY.

In the garden of one of the churches here, there is a *Kreuz-Gang* or *Via Dolorosa*, a number of small shrines or '*Stations*' erected to commemorate the various sufferings of Christ on his way to the Cross. During Lent, prayers are read and chanted every Friday by the priests before these shrines to a considerable assembly of devotees.

I visited this *Kreuz-Gang* the other Friday, but did not observe anything very remarkable in the ceremony.

A few priests in robes of sky-blue and white, attended by a number of choristers, and with a veiled crucifix borne before them, were slowly progressing from station to station, praying and singing, whilst a crowd composed of all ranks, and principally of women, followed them, also singing and praying.

I observed a number of heads looking down into the church garden from the windows of the neighboring houses. A knot of maid-servants at one of these windows seemed especially edified by observing the actions and bearing of one of the officiating priests. I wondered within myself whether he was the priest of whom I had once heard a strange and affecting history from Fräulein Sänchen.

He was an extraordinary man, at all events — whether this sad history attached to him or not. He was singularly handsome, and knew it well enough. He marched along with the step of a soldier rather than with the step of a priest: and with his keen eagle's face gazing upon his missal, and the expression was full of a certain scorn; the crisp locks of his black hair escaping from beneath his priest's cap fell upon his priest's robes in unusual luxuriance. He was no meek follower of Christ. The carnal, not the spiritual sword belonged to that hand, the epaulette to that shoulder, not purple and fine linen. The lines of the strong passionate face told of a proud nature hardened into a bitter scorn through a mistaken vocation; it was a countenance about which to weave strange imaginary histories.

I have just witnessed the ceremony of the Feet-washing, which has been announced for this month past as one of the great sights of the season. My good friend at the *Kriegs Ministerium* kept his word faithfully, and procured tickets for us. Accordingly, Myra Amsel and I have seen the whole ceremony. At nine o'clock Myra was with me, and, early as it was, Madame Thekla advised us to set off to the Palace, as people were always wild about places, and if we came late, spite of our tickets, we should see nothing. The good old soul also accompanied us, on the plea that, as she was big and strong, she could push a way for us through the crowd, and keep our places by main force. She stood guard over us — the good creature! — for two mortal hours, and when the door at length was opened by a grand lacquey, had the satisfaction of seeing us step through the very first. But before this happy moment arrived, we had to wait, as I said, two hours; and leaving, therefore, the patient old lady as our representative before the little door which led into the gallery of the Hercules Hall, whither our tickets admitted us, and before which door no one but ourselves had yet presented themselves, Myra and I ranged along the white-washed galleries of the old portion of the Palace in which we were. Cannot you see these vistas of white-washed wall, with grim old portraits of powdered ladies and gentlemen, in hoops, ruffles, gold lace, and ermine, and framed in black frames, interspersed amid heavy wreaths and arabesques of stucco? — dazzlingly white walls, dazzlingly white arched ceilings, diminishing in long perspective! Now we came upon a strange sort of little kitchen in the thick wall, where a quaint copper kettle, standing on the now cold hearth, told of coffee made for some Royal servant some hours before; now we were before the door of some *Kammer-Jungfer;* now in a gallery with the white-wash, but without the portraits, where opposite to every door stood a large white cupboard — a goodly row of them.

And now below stairs, on passing through a doorway, you stood upon a low terrace; above your head a ceiling rich with ponderous wreaths of fruit and flowers, and other stucco ornaments which probably, once upon a time, had been gilt; faded frescoes representing gods, goddesses, and Cupids, mingling with the other ornaments. From the wall protruded, like a hideous and grotesque excrescence, a grotto-work summer-house, a perfect incrustation of pebbles and spars, and with an ugly Triton on either side the entrance, bearing a brown marble shell before him.

By a few steps you could descend into a quiet little garden, shaded by the tall palace walls on the other three sides, and where grass grew rank and brightly green around green bronze statues, and around the basin of a fountain. Old-fashioned ladies and gentlemen scattered over the grass in Watteau-like groups, would have been greatly in character with the garden — the ladies with lap-dogs and with fans. A stately *minuet* ought properly to have been danced upon the terrace by a stately lady in a hooped petticoat of white and rose color, and by a stately gentleman in blue, adorned with many knots of ribbon, and who was graced with very long legs, whilst the musician played his flute leaning against the pedestal of a Triton, with a soft and languid air.

This old part of the Royal Palace of Munich is quite a little town. We discovered also a tiny chapel, now quite forgotten in the glory of Hess's frescoes and the beauty of the new *Hof-Kapelle*. To-day this old chapel was open, hung with black cloth, and illuminated with numberless waxen tapers, and the altar verdant with shrubs and plants placed upon the altar steps. There was, however, a remarkably mouldy, cold smell in the place; but I suppose the royal procession visited this old chapel as well as the new one, on its way to the Hercules Hall. This *cortège*, with the King and his brother walking beneath a splendid canopy, and attended by priests and courtiers, went, I believe, wandering about a considerable time, to the edification of the populace; but of all this, excepting from hearsay, I cannot speak, having considered it as the wiser thing to return to Madame Thekla and our door, rather than await it.

The Hercules Hall is rather small, and certainly more ugly than beautiful, with numbers of old-fashioned chandeliers hanging from the ceiling; a gallery at each end, supported by marble pillars, with a row of tall windows on either side; a dark, inlaid floor of some brown wood; but with no sign whatever of Hercules to be seen. Suffice it to say, that having noticed all this at a glance, we observed, in the centre of the hall, a small altar covered with white linen, and bearing upon it golden candlesticks, a missal bound in crimson velvet, a veiled crucifix, and a golden ewer standing in a golden dish. On one side of the altar rose a tall reading-desk, draped with a sulphur-colored cloth, upon which lay a large open book: a row of low crimson stools stood along the hall, opposite the altar; on the other side, across the windows, ran a white and very long ottoman, raised upon a high step covered with crimson cloth, and chairs of state were arranged at either end of the hall below the galleries. The arrival of people below was gradual, although our gallery and the gallery opposite had been crowded for hours. We at length had the pleasure of seeing something commence.

The door at the further end opened, and in streamed a crowd. Then tottered in ancient representatives of the twelve 'Apostles,' clothed in long violet robes, bound round the waist with white bands striped with red, and with violet caps on their heads: on they tottered, supported on either side by some poor relative, an old peasant-woman, a stalwart man in a black velvet jacket and bright black boots reaching to the knee, or by a young, buxom girl in her holiday costume of bright apron and gay boddice. On they came, feeble, wrinkled, with white locks falling on their violet apparel, with palsied hands resting on the strong arms that supported them — the oldest being a hundred-and-one, the youngest eighty-seven years old! My eyes swam with sudden tears. There was a deal of trouble in mounting them upon their long snowy throne; that crimson step was a great mountain for their feeble feet and stiff knees to climb. But at last they were all seated, their poor friends standing behind them. A man in black marshalled them like little school-children; he saw that all sat properly, and then began pulling off a black shoe and stocking from the right foot of each. There, with drooped heads and folded withered hands, they sat meekly expectant. A group of twelve little girls, in lilac print frocks and silver swallow-tailed caps, headed by an old woman in similar lilac and silver costume, took its place to the right of the old men in a little knot; they were twelve orphans who are clothed and educated by the Queen, and who receive a present on this day.

The hall at the further end was by this time filled with bright uniforms — blue, scarlet, white, and green. In front were seen King Max and his brothers, also in their uniforms; number of ladies and children; and choristers in white robes, who flitted, cloud-like, into a small raised seat, set apart for them in a dark corner behind the uniforms. A bevy of priests in gold, violet, blue, and black robes, with burning tapers and swinging censers, enter; prostrate themselves before the King of Bavaria, and before the King of Hosts, as typified to them on the altar; they chant, murmur, and prostrate themselves again and again. Incense fills the hall with its warm, odorous breath. They present open books to the King and Princess. And now the King, ungirding his sword, which is received by an attendant gentleman, approaches the oldest 'apostle;' he receives the golden ewer, as it is handed from one brother to another; he bends himself over the old foot; he drops a few drops of water upon it; he receives a snowy napkin from the Princess, and lays it daintily over the honored foot; he again bows over the second, and so on, through the whole twelve; a priest, with a cloth bound round his loins, finishing the drying of the feet. A different scene must that have been in Jerusalem, some eighteen hundred years ago!

And now the King, with a gracious smile, hangs round the patient neck of each old man a blue and white purse, containing a small sum of money. The priests retire; the altar and reading-desk are removed. Six tables covered with snowy cloths, upon each two napkins, two small metal drinking-cups, and two sets of knives, forks, and spoons, are carried in, and joined into one long table, placed before the crimson step. In the meantime the man in black has put on the twelve stockings and the twelve shoes, and, with much ado, has helped down the twelve 'apostles,' who now sit upon the step as a seat. Enter twelve footmen in blue and white liveries, each bearing a tray, covered with a white cloth, upon which smoke six different meats, in white wooden bowls; a green soup — remember it is *green Thursday;* two baked fish; two brown somethings; a delicious-looking pudding; bright, green spinach, upon which repose a couple of tempting eggs, and a heap of stewed prunes. Each footman, with his tray, is followed by a fellow-footman, carrying a large bottle of golden-hued wine, and a huge, dark, rich-looking roll on silver waiters. The twelve footmen, with the trays, suddenly veer round, and stand in a long line opposite to the table, and each opposite to an 'apostle;' the twelve trays held before them, with their seventy-two bowls, all forming a kind of pattern — soup, fishes, spinach; soup, fishes, spinach; puddings, prunes, brown meats; puddings, prunes, brown meats, — all down the room. Behind stand the other footmen, with their twelve bottles of wine and their twelve rolls. I can assure you that, seen from the gallery above, the effect was considerably comic.

A priest, attended by two court-pages, who carry tall, burning tapers, steps forth in front of the trays and footmen, and chants a blessing. The King and his brothers again approach the 'apostles;' the choristers burst forth into a glorious chant, till the whole hall is filled with melody, and the King receives the dishes from his brothers, and places them before the old men. Again I felt a thrill rush through me; it is so graceful — though it be but a mere form, a mere shadow of the true sentiment of love — any gentle act of kindness from the strong to the weak, from the powerful to the very poor. As the King bowed himself before the feeble old man of a hundred, — though I knew it to be but a mere ceremony, — it was impossible not to recognise a poetical idea.

It took a long time before the seventy-and-two meats were all placed upon the table, and then it took a very long time before the palsied old hands could convey the soup to the old lips; some were too feeble, and were fed by the man in black. It was curious to notice the different ways in which the poor old fellows received the food from the King: some slightly bowed their heads; others sat stolidly; others seemed sunk in stupor.

The Court soon retired, and twelve new baskets were brought by servants, into which the six bowls of untasted food were placed; these, together with the napkin, knife, fork, spoon and mug, bottle of wine and bread, are carried away by the old men; or, more properly speaking, are carried away for them by their attendant relatives. Many of the poor old fellows — I see by a printed paper which was distributed about, and which contains a list of their names and ages — come from great distances; they are chosen as being the oldest poor men in Bavaria. One only is out of Munich, and he is ninety-three.

We went down into the hall to have a nearer view of the 'apostles;' but, so very decrepit did the greater number appear, on a close inspection, — their faces so sad and vacant; there was such a trembling eagerness after the food in the baskets, now hidden from their sight; such a shouting into their deaf ears; such a guiding of feeble steps, and blinded, blear eyes,—that I wished we had avoided this painful part of the spectacle.

Evening of Green Thursday.—Madame Thekla this afternoon, on her way, as she expressed it, 'to pray a little,' told me that there would be beautiful music in the Hof-Kapelle about four o'clock. And thither I went.

Glorious music pealing through the lovely chapel; now bursts of wild chanting, which hoarsely died away among the golden arches; now a voice, as of an angel gently pleading in soft, silvery tones; tapers burning before the altar, on a large dark triangle of wood; streams of warm sunshine falling down from the unseen windows, high up above the golden balconies, and resting, ere they fell to the marble floor, upon the fair curls of some little kneeling child, crowning its innocent head with celestial glory; a blessed feeling of all the beauty without the walls of the chapel and of the city, of the resurrection of nature and hope throughout the world, in the bursting of buds, in the up-springing of weeds and flowers, and in the carolling of birds—such are my memories of the 'Vesper' in the Hof-Kapelle on Green Thursday.

CHAPTER XXIV.

THE HOLY WEEK — EASTER EVE.

I HAVE to-day lived in the churches from morning till evening. At nine o'clock this lovely, bright morning — having crossed the picturesque old Schrannen Platz, where, spite of its being Good Friday, the corn-market was held as usual — I found myself in the old St. Peter's Church. Although in walking through the streets you saw no sign of a holiday, the shops being open as usual, and people going about in their ordinary clothes, yet within the church you saw that it was a day of holy significance. It was crowded to excess; and with such a restless crowd passing in and out, that I soon had my veil torn from my bonnet, and felt truly thankful that no greater misfortune befell me. All that was to be seen for a long time was a crimson canopy, which rose conspicuous above the crowd of heads, and was placed below the altar steps. A large painting of 'Christ's Agony in the Garden' had taken the place of the usual altar-piece.

Soon the most plaintive music pealed through the church — a long, mournful wail, as of the lamenting disciples. Involuntarily I found myself filled with a strange sadness, and I had come to the church with a feeling of utter disgust towards the ceremony which I was about to witness — a representation of Christ borne to the sepulchre. To the strains of this solemn dirge a long procession wound its way round the church, descending from the altar, and passing beneath the canopy. First went the choristers in their white robes — tender children and grey-headed men, blending their voices in this wild chant; then priests, and priests, and priests, two and two, in black and white robes; — in their centre, and borne upon a bier, and covered with a white veil, an effigy of our Saviour. Ever and anon, instead of the bell calling the crowd to bow before the host which was borne aloft, you heard the dead, abrupt, wooden sound of clappers which certain priests carried in their hands. After the priests came a stream of citizens, men bearing burning tapers. Then — headed by the most wan, emaciated, stunted-looking priest, who walked with folded hands laid on one side, and downcast eyes, an embodiment, it seemed to me, of the most fearful vice of priestcraft — came on a long, long train of women, women of all ages and various degrees of station, from the small tradesman's wife to the lady in her lace bonnet and elegant gloves: all were in black; all carried in one hand an open book, from which they read, and a rosary; and in the other a burning taper.

I could not but admire the progress of refinement, when I noticed the tapers carried by the women. To prevent the wax falling upon their black dresses, these tapers burned in long white sockets, which, unless minutely inspected, appeared to be wax. Every woman bore such a taper. And thus slowly proceeding round the church, the figure was laid in a sepulchre erected in a little chapel. To visit these sepulchres of the various churches is the great business of Munich on Good Friday.

The arrangement of the sepulchres is pretty much the same in all the churches, especially in the old ones. The body is generally laid among flowers in a small cave beneath the altar; sometimes the recess in the altar uncomfortably reminded me of an English fire-place in an unfinished house before the stove has been set. But generally artificial rocks surrounded the opening of the cave; a small lamp was often suspended over the corpse, and a row of tiny lamps burned upon the ground in front, not unlike foot-lights; only each burned behind a small globe filled with colored liquid — crimson, green, blue, and yellow — considerably reminding you of the ornamental bottles in chemists' windows in England. The altar itself was transformed into a very mountain of plants and flowers — arums, roses, crown-imperials, myrtles, geraniums, and a dozen other plants, all blooming in pots, which were generally artfully concealed or artificially decorated.

Lights were disposed everywhere on the altar; at the mountain's summit, the golden rays surrounding the host glittered and sparkled in the light of these many tapers. Often lower down on the mountain you would see two angels praying, their robes very fluttering, of pale pink and white drapery, their hair very yellow, and their cheeks very pink; often ivy and creeping plants were made to festoon, and gracefully shadow the opening of the cave. The steps, too, approaching the altar and sepulchre, were a mass of flowers; sometimes a steep wall of flowers and greenness rose abruptly up, and permitted you but a narrow glimpse of the interior of the cave. Tall orange-trees, in tubs, laurels, and cedars, stood in groups on either hand. To complete the general idea, you must imagine the rest of the church darkened, with daylight struggling through blinded windows, and through the doorways, as the heavy doors swung ever to and fro to admit the entrance and the departure of the restless crowd. Imagine, also, a dense multitude circulating through all these churches, and only stationary before the sepulchre; and above, the shuffle of feet and the murmur of prayers or adoration, fitful, plaintive strains of music moaning through the gloom, and the sonorous voices of the priests chanting their solemn dirge.

Such, with slight variations, was the scene in the Munich churches throughout this Good Friday. In the Basilica the sepulchre was somewhat more tasteful. There a very spacious sepulchre was erected beneath the organ loft, between two of those beautiful marble columns which are so great an ornament to this exquisite church. This, it must be remembered, was the first celebration of Good Friday in the new, beautiful Basilica. Towering shrubs rose against the marble columns, laurels, orange-trees, and myrtles; ferns, and moss, and palms shadowed the entrance of the cavern, drooping naturally from the artificial rock; there was no altar, no praying angels, only heaps and heaps of the most lovely fresh flowers; and far in the gloom of the cave reposed a figure of Christ; but this time, without any attempt to deceive you into the idea of its being a real corpse by aid of color. It was a pure statue; and how much more did it affect the imagination, by merely suggesting the poetical idea of death! This church, unlike all the others, was flooded with sunshine, which glowed on the gold and frescoes, and warmed the marble floor and columns.

Above the lofty, verdant cavern swelled the tones of the organ, mingling with the laments of the choir, fitfully and mournfully; and the circle of Benedictine monks afar off at the opposite end of the church, seated behind the stripped altar, repeated the lament, as though heaven mourned and earth responded. I sat for a long time in the warm sunshine before my favorite altar-piece, that beautiful Martyrdom of the white, meek St. Stephen, where all was quiet, and one did not see the sepulchre, or the crowd, but only heard the music, and felt the impression of the church and the day.

With the Basilica we terminated our afternoon visit of the churches. One little picturesque bit must not be omited. Madame Thekla, knowing all the by-paths in and out of the churches, led me, in leaving one old church, past the open door of the sacristy, and I of course looked in. It was a very large and lofty room ; the walls wainscotted half-way up with very dark wood, rich in panel and carving ; above the wainscot, on the white-washed wall, hung a row of old portraits of cardinals ; a sort of *dresser*, or low press, of black carved wood, ran round the wainscot of the room, and upon this lay priests' robes, violet, gold, sky-blue, and white ; and here and there were seen groups of tall candlesticks and censers, or a large brush for the sprinkling of holy water. Light fell into the solemn room from four lofty windows high up in the walls, and here and there was seen a black and white priest passing in and out; in the foreground two little choristers adjusting the sit of their white sleeves and blue petticoats.

After tea I set forth again. Soon we were at the entrance of St. Michael's Church ; crowds and crowds streamed into it. A royal carriage waited before the principal entrance — royal carriages have been seen driving about from church to church all the afternoon. In the forenoon there had been a royal ceremonial of some kind in the *Hof-Kapelle ;* but of course, as it was impossible to be in two places at once, I did not witness it. Neither did I see King Ludwig, this Good Friday night, praying among the crowd in St. Michael's Church as earnestly and as unostentatiously as the meanest beggar there, and perhaps side by side with one, as he often does ; because King Ludwig is celebrating, this year, the holiest night of the Holy Week in Rome itself.

A very ocean of human beings filled the vast church ;

dark, undulating waves of life filled the nave; heads crowded the galleries, and every possible standing-place. Above the human mass, high up, suspended in the air, beneath the boldly swelling arches of the richly ornamented roof, and casting a warm, golden light upon the nearest stone-wreaths, and angels, and glimmering in a warm, dark haze at the farthest end of the church, burned and blazed a mighty cross of fire. The effect was thrillingly beautiful; the gradual softening of the warm light upon arch and column, till it was lost in the night of the remoter portions of the church, was the most beautiful effect, in its way, conceivable;—the contrast so strong; the forms so sharp; yet the whole an imperceptible gradation from the strongest light to the intensest gloom.

Suddenly, music, wilder, sadder, than any before heard that day, burst like a whirlwind through the church; moaning, lamenting, pleading; the waves, the forests, the winds, heaven and all nature seemed to mourn, as in the old Scandinavian mythology, over the slain Balder. And the voices vibrated beneath the dim, arched roof, floated over the human ocean, and died away in long sighs. Again they arose, sadder and sadder; ceased suddenly,—and the multitude streamed forth into the streets.

I felt myself strangely affected by the whole scene; moved to the inmost soul with a vast pity and grief by that sad lament—and, no wonder, for was it not *the Miserere*?

Dear old Fräulein Sänchen! As we walked slowly back, she opened her poor old heart to me, and told me many of her sorrows. I fancied long ago that I had discovered the bitterness of her life, and I see that I was right. I did all I could to comfort and cheer her, but it was only the balm of sympathy which I could drop into her wounds, and I fear those wounds will only smart the more when she has no one to sympathize with her, no one to whom she can moan a little. Ah! it is a selfish world; and the more gentle and patient is the heart, the more it is crushed! I could only comfort her with the comfort especially belonging to Good Friday!

Crossing the Dult Platz and various streets, we saw all the confectioners' shops brilliant and crowded. Children were celebrating Good Friday by buying sugar lambs, which held little crimson and gold banners between their fore-legs, as they lay innocently reposing upon green sugar banks. Many, also, were the sugar hares, Easter hares — those fabulous creatures so dear to German children — which were also bought, though, properly, Easter had not yet arrived. But the hares and their gay crimson eggs had arrived days and days before. Would that our English children could see some of these wonderful hares! one grand one, especially, which stands life-size, of colored sugar, upon its hind legs, rejoicing over a large nest of crimson eggs, which it, of course, is supposed to have laid. There are chocolate hares, biscuit hares, and hares of common bread. You hear the words 'hares' and 'eggs' upon the lips of every child you meet; 'kreutzers to buy hares' seem strangely to be conjured out of your purse; you see everywhere crimson egg-shells, and in all the book-sellers' shops are displayed books relative to this remarkable animal, for the edification of the youthful naturalist.

Easter eggs are not alone eaten by the children, but by people of maturer growth. On Easter Sunday, Fräulein Sänchen will take a basket of eggs to be blessed by the priest, in one of the near churches. Whole baskets of eggs are carried on that day to the sacristies, to be consecrated. A consecrated egg is promised me; I am anxious about its flavor. On the Saturday between Good Friday and Easter Sunday I hear that it is the custom to carry small fagots of wood to be blessed; and this consecrated wood is, I am told, useful in various ways. Besides eggs on Easter Sunday, meat, and butter, and various kinds of food, are blessed.

The first church on Easter Eve that Madame Thekla and I visited was the Ludwig's Church. As we entered beneath the lofty portal which stood open to receive the throngs of devotees and curious, a very firmament of stars glittered towards us through the darkened church. A curtain of dead gold brocade fell from the vaulted ceiling, hiding from view Cornelius's Last Judgment, above the high altar. And from the ceiling to within but a short space of the altar gleamed a galaxy of tapers, burning in groups of six together, and so arranged as to form starry crowns.

These starry crowns appeared suspended in the air above a square inclosure of lovely shrubs and flowers, hedged in by tall burning tapers. This little garden bloomed upon the broad platform before the altar. A pale effigy of Christ reposed among these roses, tulips, stocks, myrtles, geraniums, arums, ivy, upon an odorous fresh couch.

The mournful dirge which I had heard in the old St. Peter's Church resounded also here — now dying away, now taken up by a group of priests who chanted at a side altar before tapers burning upon a triangle of wood.

The whole scene strangely recalled what one has read of dirges chanted over the dead Adonis, sleeping his last sleep upon a couch of rose and myrtle.

We were bound for the St. Michael's Church, which is situated in old Munich. On our way thither Fräulein Sänchen led me up the steps of a crumbling old building.

'You must,' said she, 'see the chapel of the Herzhog Max: sentinels watch it night and day!' This honor doubtless was owing to the chapel being a *royal* one; but a less tasteful sepulchre could not well have been imprisoned in a huge cage of twisted, rusty iron-work, guarded by two solemn guards with halberts.

'What is this strange old mass of building, Fräulein Sänchen?' I asked, as we descended the steps, and I glanced up at its gloomy windows and discolored walls: 'I hear everybody call it Herzhog Max, as though it were a man and a duke, instead of an old tumble-down building!'

'It was the Palace of the Electors,' returned my good companion; 'no one lives there now: it used to be the palace of the Dowager Queens. Old Queen Caroline died there; since then no one has lived in the Herzhog Max: Queen Theresa will have her little villa beyond the Sieges-Thor.'

It was a relief to recall that cheerful, sunny little villa, standing as we did in the twilight within the courts of this decaying palace! What a mournful dwelling was this for widowed and dethroned queens! Its tall square towers, its gloomy gate-ways, its long, long rows of dark lifeless windows, its grey discolored walls telling of former gold and fresco, its windows on the ground-floors covered in with heavy iron gratings, its heavy mouldering doors,—all breathed a mournful spirit of a stern hard time and of departed splendor. Its walls looked as if fraught with evil memories; it is a mansion whose age impresses one with a sense of evil decay: those desolate suites of rooms have no bright memories of a beautiful sunny youth. Gibbering sad ghosts flit through them of a certainty: strange faces, terrible and mournful, looking forth through those window-bars,—spiritual footsteps creaking upon the dreary stairs!

The Resurrection was celebrated in all the churches. I, however, witnessed the ceremonial only in the Ludwigs Kirche. Toward six o'clock the Ludwig Strasse was black with swarms of people hastening from the Theatine Kirche towards the Ludwigs Kirche. The church was already so full, when I entered it, that it was impossible to approach the altar. All still remained as it was on Good Friday; the starry crowns of fire suspended over the figure of Christ reposing amid the flowers and tapers. Priests first knelt, praying, before the garden. As far as I could judge, at the distance where I stood, this, for some time, was all the ceremony. Then a canopy was seen to approach the altar; there was much chanting and gesticulating. The organ and the quire burst forth into a joyous anthem. Trumpets from the near altar took up the rejoicing with their wild harmony, and a voice sang forth, amid a sudden hush, 'Christ is arisen!'

And, above the crowd, you saw a figure of Christ, clothed in white and purple garments, and bearing in his hand a small banner. Then a procession of choristers and priests, with the Host borne aloft beneath the canopy, with swinging censers, and to the sound of trumpets, kettle-drums, and little bells, which the choristers rung, passed down the centre of the church, and out beneath the beautiful portico, and through the white arches of the colonnade, into the little garden behind the church.

Although the canopy and the procession passed out into this little garden, I preferred remaining in the church; and approaching nearer the altar, saw that the figure among the flowers was now concealed by a cloth, and that above it rose the other figure with its banner. A troop of youths and young girls from the Blind Asylum also drew near, as if to *see;* they were all connected together, two and two, by a long cord, which passed between them, so as to form a sort of human team. You always see them walking along in this manner. It was strangely affecting to observe their sightless eye-balls and their white uncouth faces turn towards the figure of Christ, their hands clasped, and their lips moving.

Another thing was noticeable before the procession returned from the garden; this was the excessive delight of the children over the figure; troops and troops of children were in the church, and now that there was more open space, you saw them distinctly. Children of ten and twelve, children even of seven and eight, held up a fat little brother or sister to see the gloriously beautiful figure. There were lots of *Strassen Buben* (street lads) and little gentlemen in their smart cloaks with their pretty hoods, and smart little ladies, also all eagerness, brought by their attendants. Several little girls, who had no attendants, amused me vastly by making the lowest, lowest of courtesies before the beautiful figure, so very, very low, and with such an air of respect, as if they said, 'Oh, thou beautiful, glorious figure, in thy purple robe, how I love thee! how I will courtesy to thee!' and then down they went in the very centre of the marble pavement, with the air of little princesses. And such a troop of children rushed in before the procession, as, with its crimson banners fluttering against the cool, grey sky, it entered the glowing church! You heard the tramp and rush of little footsteps up the long church before you heard the music and the bells.

And then the people bowed reverently as the Host was borne aloft, and with music and chanting a short mass was performed, and Easter had arrived!

I passed Easter Sunday out in the country.

How tender and beautiful was the whole scene! Yet the very intensity of the fresh beauty called forth a mournfulness in the soul! Who does not know this strange mournfulness! when the luxuriance of the grass and flowers, the soft air, the perfume of unfolding buds and blossoms, the gentle hum of insects, the unearthly loveliness of awakening life, seem to swell the soul with an unutterable longing — a longing after what? Perhaps God's voice alone could give the answer! It is this longing which is so wonderfully embodied in a cast, after the antique, which stands in Kaulbach's studio — the head of Castor, the brother who was mortal. Never had I seen this longing and this mournfulness so fully expressed as in that beautiful countenance. I had walked towards my favorite old church with the pea-green tower. All was silent as a dream. I sat down amid the fresh grass for a long time. And now the clock tolled the four quarters, and then the hour — two; and through the silence the sound vibrated again and again — ever gentler and gentler — with a strange low music. The air was filled with the warm perfume of incense lingering around the little old church, and with the delicious breath of spring, which told of near beds of violets and primroses. The trees were flushed with life; some ruddy, others amber, others already faintly green. I saw them rise in thick, distant masses above the low, crumbling, white-washed wall of the church-yard. As I looked upon the fresh burnished arum, hemlock, ficary, and daisy-leaves and grass springing up around me, I felt the peculiar beauty and aptness of Keats's expression when he speaks of the year 'growing *lush* in juicy stalks.'

And now a little meek child wandered alone into the

church-yard, with large, pale oxlips wreathed into the plaits of her hair. Soon people streamed into the church for afternoon mass. And whilst the bell tolled from the tower a group of young peasant-girls came with their bright, old-fashioned costumes, and round arms, and rosy faces, and clear eyes, and wandered arm in arm round the church, sprinkling certain graves with holy water from the vessels hung to the crosses.

Soon the young girls entered the church; and sitting where I did, the voice of the priest praying came to me sweetly and distinctly. It was much more beautiful listening to the service thus than being within the church among the people! I heard the little organ peal forth, and the singing of the quire. There was one fresh young voice that sang like a very angel. This voice celebrated the Resurrection. My eyes overflowed with warm tears, and my soul responded, though I sat, a heretic and an alien, outside the walls of the little church.

Then all the peasants streamed forth; and the holy, solemn hush closed once more over the scene.

The whole was a lovely idyl, more holy and pure than any ever written, than any picture ever painted, of peasant-life. There was such a tenderness and simplicity, mingled with a certain sadness, that one could only imagine its spirit to be conveyed away from the spot by a peasant musician, who should suddenly improvise a melody which should become a *Volks Lied.*

I shall long remember that Easter Sunday as one of the loveliest bits of poetry that I have enjoyed in Munich.

Returning towards the city, I heard music in all the public gardens; all the world was out among the green, budding trees. Spring is, indeed, come; the trees are almost in full leaf; you seem almost to see the grass and the flowers springing; birds carol from every bough. Music swells in loud strains through the fresh leaves of the English Garden, the Spring Garden, the Garden of Paradise. The Prater, and twenty or thirty other gardens, are crowded with happy, merry people, sitting beneath the trees, drinking coffee and beer, and listening to music.

It is quite extraordinary what time Munich people spend in this way, and quite as extraordinary what quantities of beer are drunk. Alas, *that* beer! — it is one of the unpoetical features of Munich life; it gives that heavy, sleepy, stupid look to the lower classes, and I fear, also, to the citizen class, which is so at variance with the spirituality and the intellectuality of all this Munich art!

CHAPTER XXV.

SCHWANTHALER'S CASTLE OF SCHWANECK.

BEFORE me lie a quantity of wild flowers drooping their poor weary heads over a quaint little terra-cotta vase. Both the flowers and I are just come from a long delicious ramble. An hour ago I was nearly as drooping and weary as the flowers, but a cup of tea has refreshed me as much as I hope the water in the little vase will refresh the flowers — even now I seem to see their heads visibly pricking themselves up.

I have been to Schwaneck, the Castle of Schwanthaler.

At nine o'clock, I met, by appointment, Baron von H., merry little Marie, and Signor L., on the other side of the Sendlinger Gate; and having passed the old Munich Cemetery, with its rows and rows of crosses rising above the low walls, and the new Cemetery inclosed by its imposing walls of dark red brick, built in a singularly beautiful manner, and its solemn round arched gateway surmounted by two simple, earnest statues, we were out upon the plain within sight of the Alps. It was a lovely morning, the larks carolling over our heads; we all felt gay at heart, yet still our conversation turned upon horrors, perhaps, from the charm of contrast. Baron von H. told of an 'interesting murder;' how the daughter of a French gentleman living in Munich, who was very handsome and just married, was murdered by the soldier servant of her husband, because she would not give the wretch money to redeem his master's uniform which he had pawned; how he cut off her head, then quietly took the money, went and paid various debts which he had contracted in the city, and decamped! And how the poor old father and her husband were nearly broken-hearted when they discovered the tragedy. And various equally lively histories did we relate, till our conversation resembled a series of short chapters out of the Neue Pitaval; I relating, as my share, the history of Casper Hauser, which Signor L. and Marie had never heard, embellishing it with explanations out of a certain prohibited book which I once had read on the subject; and then, being in the midst of a horrible history of a woman near Magdeburg, who has just been imprisoned for having kept a little child of her own three years upon bread and water, in a cask in a cellar, till the poor little creature was crippled body and mind, — we found ourselves upon one of the steep banks of the Isar; below us a picturesque large white-washed house, its walls stained with innumerable fading frescoes.

It was a large public-house, and its garden, filled with benches and tables, was already sprinkled over with groups of towns-people come out this lovely summer morning. Peasants streamed along the road below us, which skirted the river and wound round the inn-garden, bearing in their hands little brooms of willow catkins, and mistletoe, and holly. They were bringing them from some church, where they had been blessed, as it was Palm Sunday, and these catkins were, as by the children in England, called *palms;* but why holly and mistletoe should be bound up with the palms I cannot tell: at Christmas here these plants have no significance.

Having sat down on the warm dry grass of the very

steep bank, and admired the distant view of Munich, and listened to the rush of the river and the singing of the larks, we pursued our way. And now we were in a birch-wood; heath was in crimson bloom in the open parts of the wood; soft elastic moss beneath the trees; here and there a group of birches gleaming out like trees of silver; and sprinkled over a steep, mossy bank shining out among those red fallen birch-leaves, what can be those myriads of azure stars! blue hepaticas! our dear old English garden hepaticas! In myriads they rose from the mossy ground, staring up through the grey, leafeless branches of the birch-trees, with wide open blue eyes, into a heaven as deeply blue. How lovely they are, and the whole woods are now brilliant with them! I shall love my blue hepaticas, as Wordsworth loved his host of 'Golden Daffodils.'

The Baron and Signor L. were deep in a discussion about 'high pressure,' and about 'what the Englishman had said on the subject;' and when I held up in triumph my handful of flowers, I fancy they thought me rather gone out of my mind.

And now, though we were in the midst of the wood, and close upon the steep bank of the river, we came upon a large house, or rather a group of buildings; one very like a quaint chapel. This was another *Wirthshaus,* with scores of benches and tables placed beneath the trees, with a pavilion for dancing, with rows of old-fashioned summer-houses, or rather booths, along the edge of the river-bank for the distance of some hundred yards. The ground was undulating and very sylvan. Baron H. said that last May he witnessed a village fête here, which produced a capital effect among the trees; all was dancing, music, beer-drinking, shooting, that day; now all was silent as death, or rather sleep, — a most peaceful sleep. The sun showered down beams as warm as in an English June. We were soon seated at a little table on the very edge of the steep Isar bank, the river murmuring as it rolled lazily over its sandy bottom, amid long, gravelly shoals. In front of us was the Alpine chain, rising as though abruptly from the wild precipitous river-bank opposite, and mingling its jagged peaks with the silvery mountain-like clouds which crowded the heavens.

We hungry pedestrians saw a vision remarkably attractive upon the table before the bench on which we sat. Ham, bread, butter, delicious butter, and wine, capital Rhine wine, for my companions; and for me, of course, *eternal coffee!* And thus most pleasantly refreshing ourselves in sight of the Alps, the conversation naturally turned upon Italy, seeing that one of the gentleman was an Italian, and Baron von H. had spent many years there. First Mariotti's new book was discussed; Signor L. defending Silvio Pellico warmly for the sake of all he had suffered in his youth. He spoke altogether so earnestly and eloquently about his unhappy, beautiful land, with a cloud of real grief ever and anon passing across his face, that I set him down as a good, worthy fellow — different to some disgusting, dandified Italians I saw the other day, who made me almost wish that an Austrian bullet would put an end to their useless lives!

Pleasant and interesting as it was, sitting on this river's bank, listening to descriptions of laurel and orange groves, and of noble suffering patriots, still it was necessary to proceed to Schwaneck. We bade adieu, therefore, to this hamlet or inn, whichever it be, of Heselohe, and once more lost ourselves in the birch-wood. But first I might mention, that being decidedly of an exploring turn, I had dived into those booth-like summer-houses, and found to my astonishment a number of old English caricatures of the time of George IV., pasted upon the walls; several of the summer-houses were papered with prints, mostly from illustrated papers. There was also a number of most absurd French caricatures of the English, as intolerant in their spirit against us as the English were against the French and the Italians! No one can imagine how out of place these absurd and vulgar caricatures seemed in the midst of this sylvan solitude! I hope some prints of the World's Fair in Hyde Park will soon get pasted up there as an antidote to this antiquated poison.

But now to return to the pleasant *green* wood, I was going to say; but *green*, except under foot, it certainly was not, seeing the month was only April. But my fancy clothed the woods with leaves and made the month May or June, for I was recalling the painter's description of the Artists' festival, and I heard with my mind's ear the music sounding through the wood, and saw with my mind's eye the procession with gay banners winding along through mossy, odorous paths; and when we came suddenly upon the little castle itself, I was prepared to see the knight himself on its walls, as on that memorable occasion.

The castle, to my surprise, is a modern castle. It is a tiny castle built by the sculptor himself; but he was not destined to rejoice long in the fulfilment of one of his youthful dreams, for his many years' illness dated almost from its completion. It is a rude, simple little castle, scarcely more than one lofty tower; but the situation is capitally chosen. It stands upon a sort of small headland where the Isar winds in a bold sweep between its precipitous banks; and hence its name *Schwaneck*, or *Swan-point*, as it may be translated.

On one side the birch-wood extends even to the little moat; on the other side is the plain, and in front the river sunk between its wild, picturesque banks.

Having presented our card of admission, and waited until a barking, deep-mouthed hound was secured, we found ourselves within the small court-yard. The first thing that struck us was an effigy of a knight, let into the castle wall; it looked as if brought out of some quaint village church; it was rudely painted, or rather stained, with red and blue: upon his shield and helm he bore a swan; it is the monument of the knight Schwanthaler, erected by his cousin and fellow-sculptor, Xavier Schwanthaler. In another part of the castle wall is inserted a tablet bearing in black-letters the following verse: —

'So stehe denn hier in Gotteshand
Der Thurm am felsigen Uferrand
Gebauet nicht um eitle Ehr;
Zu Trutz nicht oder Waffenwehr;
Nur früher Jugend shöner Traum,
Soll steigen empor im trauten Raum.
Der Blick in die Berge, die Luft so klar,
Vom Flusse das Rauschen wunderbar.
Der Freunde, Wort, und Sag und Sang
Erfrische das Herz im Lebensdrang.'

Upon a door we saw nailed an astonishingly large tawny and black owl, its extended wings measuring considerably more than a yard across: its talons, which were full two inches long, looked as if made of the sharpest and most highly tempered steel. This owl, we were informed by the woman who showed us over the place, had been caught in a trap on the tower only fifteen days ago. 'And most truly glad am I,' said she, 'that the wretch is gone, for every night this winter did the big thing come moaning round the tower with its doleful cry.' For my part a strange pity filled my heart for the fate of this magnificent creature, the life and voice of which must have been so in harmony with the solitary tower, the wild winds of winter, and the moaning of the deep river below.

The interior of the little castle is as rude and unpretending as its exterior. With the exception of the figures of two grim, armored knights, placed one on either side, above a little balcony which overhangs the river, there are no traces here of Schwanthaler as the sculptor; but every stone speaks of Schwanthaler as the lover of the quaint and the mediæval. Schwaneck is a development of the little *sanctum sanctorum* in Schwanthaler's house in Munich, with its grotesque drinking cups and armor. There are but four rooms in this little castle, and they are small in size, and furnished in the most primitive manner; there are no carpets, no easy-chairs, and but one sofa, which looks as though covered with tapestry, though it is not; it is coarse, heavy, and primitive. A few rudely carved chairs, a few massive and rough tables, tall porcelain stoves of olive-green, bearing upon them the heraldic swan, armor, and chivalric trophies, and strange-looking sacred pictures of the very early German school, and with the rafters of the ceilings painted in vivid contrast of the brightest colors; — such are the furniture and adornments of Schwaneck.

The sleeping-room, or rather cell, of the great sculptor contains a simple, oaken bedstead, covered with a red and black quilt. Above the bed, a large and perfectly plain gilt cross is let into the wall; a couple of rude, wooden chairs, and an odd looking-glass, suspended above a much odder table. This table is supported by a pedestal formed of the crooked stem of some tree, which probably grew in the neighboring wood, its rough bark and moss still remaining upon it.

The banqueting-hall is at the top of the castle, so as to command the view. It is the largest, and, by far, the most important room in the castle. A long, heavy oaken table, running across the hall, supports a row of goblets, fantastic enough for an enchanted palace; the walls of the room are papered, up to a certain height, with a dull crimson paper stamped with the same heraldic swan. This paper suggests the idea of tapestry hangings; above the paper, and upon the white-washed walls are arranged coats of mail, shields, swords, and escutcheons; the rafters of the roof are gay with heraldic colors and shields, producing a fine barbaric effect. On one side of the hall, revealed by half-drawn curtains of crimson and gold-colored stuffs, standing in a recess, you see a large, old, gilded shrine. The other sides of the room are rich in windows commanding a variety of views.

'How beautiful!' we all exclaimed, on stepping towards one particular window. Far below us rolled the river, its murmur pleasantly ascending to us; right opposite gleamed forth the snowy Alps, a vast plain extending from the precipitous Isar bank to their very feet; a plain as I have so often said, of some fifty or sixty miles. And, far as the eye could reach towards the right, wound in bold curves, the wild banks of the river, rocky and woody; here crowned with a castle; there, in the far distance, a patch of pine-forest. The effect of the whole scene was heightened for us by an approaching thunder-storm, which cast dark shadows over the horizon.

Of course we ascended to the top of the little watch-tower, which runs up one side of the castle; but, though more extensive, I question whether the view, on the whole, is so striking and effective as seen through the windows of the banqueting-room, or from the balcony overlooking the ruins.

Our survey of Schwaneck was soon at an end, but not so soon our delight. I cannot describe, in words, the peculiar charm of the place, which consists in its perfect unpretendingness, and rude, savage completeness. You forget that it is not a genuine bit of the middle ages, in your satisfaction in it, as the tower of the Knight Schwanthaler.

We somewhat varied our walk home, by returning, part of the way, through a wood, close upon the margin of the Isar, below the precipitous bank; and a still more beautiful path we found it. At one spot, the wood widened out considerably, and the trees of splendid growth reared their tall, smooth, grey boles and branches solemnly into the air, measuring their height with the steep bank behind them. How quiet, dreamlike, it was! the ground carpeted with fallen leaves, among which again bloomed the lovely hepaticas, with mezereon in great luxuriance, a kind of fumitory, both snow-white and dull crimson, a small yellow aconite, and a tiny, but lovely yellow squill. Imagine my joy in finding these flowers! and in such abundance too. I gathered a bouquet worthy of an English garden; and in a little brooklet running through the wood gleamed out, like sunshine, large, golden king-cups, amid their rich green leaves. They seemed a voice from English meadows.

Coming out upon the uninteresting road, Signor L. chanced to say something about a pedestrian tour which he had once made in Elba, whereupon I said, 'Do tell us all you can about Elba, — what you saw and what you did; describe all, for there is a great charm in verbal description of strange lands and new scenes; people thus describing often give one vivid and graphic touches which one never gets in books.' He described, graphically, his visit to Napoleon's country-house, with its lovely gardens, with its saloon adorned with Egyptian views, painted in fresco upon the walls, and with a refreshing fountain playing in the centre of the black-and-white marble floor. He described such old, old fig-trees and vines, such orange groves and hedges of aloes, such solitary convents, such a primitive peasantry, such hot noontides, such views of Corsica, such stretches of sea and sky; he called up so vividly before my imagination the little island of Monte Christo, and the rock out in the sea which Napoleon visited daily, standing solitarily upon it, gazing towards France, as he is so commonly represented in pictures, that I felt at once transported into Elba, and forgot we were wending our way towards Munich! All at once, however, Signor L. interrupted his narrative by exclaiming, 'Ah, no! not even in my own beautiful Italian have I ever been able to express what I feel most strongly — no, I cannot describe this wild, wondrous sea as it breaks over the rocks!' And with this exclamation his beautiful descriptions ceased, for looking round us, we perceived that Baron von H. had long before escaped out of Elba, and was posting away far ahead of us, and that a black thunder-cloud was rapidly coming up behind us. Baron von H., and Marie, had hastened on to order coffee at a wayside *Wirthshaus*, which we reached just in time to escape the storm.

Whilst the rain descended, we amused ourselves with watching a group of regular German *Handwerks-burschen* playing at nine-pins under a shed. Every now and then a long-haired and velvet-coated student, with a great length of pipe in his hand, came to the door to inspect the state of the weather, the game of nine-pins, or the visitors. I had not seen such a genuine set of Burschen since we left

Heidelberg. Here, in Munich, the students seem lost among the other inhabitants.

Fortunately the storm soon cleared off, and at length I reached home, but very tired and very muddy from the wet roads. Before parting, we all agreed, that having enjoyed our April excursion so much, we would certainly, when May arrived, celebrate her advent by another excursion — perhaps go to Starnberg for a day, and make a trip with the little steamer upon the lake — the new little steamer which everybody talked about, and which would be launched in May.

CHAPTER XXVI.

THE MODEL PRISON OF BAVARIA, AND THE MODEL WORKS OF SIGNOR S——.

April 28th.—I have just returned from a visit to the *Zucht-Haus* in the Au, the Model Prison of Bavaria. As yet I feel my curiosity anything but satisfied. I must obtain some official Reports regarding this wonderful prison, that I may understand the working of the system, and facts connected with it, more thoroughly than I could from conversation with the gentleman who went through the wards with us, intelligent and most obliging though he was.

The prison is a large building, situated in the Au Suburb, not far from the lovely Au Church. It has, outwardly, no appearance of being a prison; has windows of various picturesque forms, gazing in great abundance out of its yellow and white-washed walls. It is a cheerful-looking place, in fact, and if it stood among trees would look very like a *château*. But on entering the vaulted and white-washed hall, with long vistas of white-washed passages leading from it, with a soldier standing at the door, and here and there other soldiers in the distance, something of a prison-feeling sank upon me.

Having been politely received in his little bureau by the Director of the Prison,—an extraordiaary man, from all accounts, and famed throughout Europe for his management of this prison, and for various works which he has written on prison discipline, — we were conducted through the establishment by a grave, intelligent little man, the *Haus-Meister*. All the people we met in the passages, whether prisoners or not, had an intense gravity impressed on their countenances.

The first room we entered was filled with men employed in spinning. This is the first employment given to the prisoners on their entrance, and when their capability for learning has been ascertained during the spinning-period, it is decided to what trade they shall be henceforth devoted. A long row of men of all ages, in coarse, grey jackets and trowsers, some with chains round their waists, which were attached to their ankles, sat down the middle of the room, busily spinning from their tall distaffs. Along the bare walls were rows of wholesome-looking beds, with coarse but white sheets neatly turned over their quilts; rows of tin cans were seen to hang in one corner of the room against boards nailed to the walls. A large crucifix was placed conspicuously upon another wall; the windows were large and cheerful; the room was cheerful. But that row of distorted, uncouth, malformed, and but partially developed heads; those white, sallow countenances; those eyes glancing furtively towards you, or sunk in a stupor upon the unceasing slender threads drawn from the distaffs by *manly* fingers; those heavy chains, and the perfect silence, save of the wheel and the little treddle, were not cheerful. It was the first time I had ever been in a prison, or looked upon any great criminals; at least, knowing them to be such. The first sensation, therefore, was very strange: here were men guilty of enormous crimes, men who had murdered in diabolical ways, at liberty as it seemed. There was no unlocking and locking of doors; you saw there men moving about as though they were ordinary workmen. The unusual occupation of spinning for men *did* strike you, it is true; the ill-formed faces struck you, and the chains, when you caught sight of them; but you had to remind yourself that on each of these souls lay the weight of some fearful crime.

One man passed out in his grey jacket, and with the chain round his waist. 'He,' said the gentleman with us, as we walked down the gallery, 'is one of the men who murdered a priest two years ago; he is confined here for life.'

'But how,' asked I, 'can you trust that man to go about unattended? — how is it that these doors are all unlocked and unbarred? — what is to prevent their escaping? The walls are not high in the court-yard — all seems open; excepting for a few soldiers, there appears no obstacle to their escape. Do none make their escape?'

'Now and then,' replied he, 'but very rarely. This is a prison; and, of course, where is the man who would not escape if he could? But they are always overtaken; we have blood-hounds trained for the purpose. Such cases are very rare.'

We saw room after room filled with prisoners: now they were making shoes; now they were tailoring; now weaving table-linen; now cloth: — now we went into a dye-house; now into a carpenter's shop. All were silently, busily at work; all had the same grave look; all, with but two, or at the most three exceptions, had countenances of the most coarse description. There were youths, and old men, and middle-aged men, but all worked apparently at perfect freedom, often with wide-open doors, often in the open court-yard.

It was a startling thing to see murderers wielding hammers, and sawing with saws, and cutting with sharp-edged tools, when you remembered they *were* murderers, and how some tyrant passion had once aroused the fiend within them, though now again he seemed laid to rest by years of quiet toil.

Our guide informed us, that very rarely did any disobedience or passion show itself among the prisoners after the first few months, or the first year of their imprisonment. The constant employment from early morning to evening; the silence imposed most strictly during their hours of toil; the routine, the gradual dying out of all external interests and anxieties, seemed to sink them into a passive calm, until industry became their only characteristic. Each prisoner has his daily task of work given to him, which must be completed. For extra work he receives payment, — half of which he may immediately consume, the other half being reserved for him, by government, until the expiration of his sentence. This is equally the case with such as are condemned to life-long imprisonment, there being always the possibility of a reprieve existing for them. On Sundays, they are allowed to read books out of the prison library, and to play at dominoes, and enjoy various simple recreations. There is a school for the younger criminals, and a hospital for the sick, of course. The only punishment for disobedience to prison rules is a longer or shorter period of solitary confinement in a small room, which was shown to us, containing a hard wooden bed, very like a low table, on which the prisoner can both lie and sit, a stove, and a closely grated window, which is darkened while the prisoner is in his cell: he has his allowance of food shortened, and is left there to his own reflections.

We saw a prisoner in his chains putting the loaves of prison bread into a large oven to bake; prisoners in white caps and aprons were preparing the prison supper in the large clean kitchen: one group was sitting and silently picking the leaves of vegetables to flavor the soup, which was boiling in large caldrons, and was stirred by other prisoners with huge ladles; all moved gravely about, apparently without being overlooked. In each room, however, was a kind of prisoner monitor, whose office was to report upón the conduct of his companions; and this species of mutual watchfulness, kept up by the prisoners themselves, seemed, according to the report of our informant, to answer remarkably well.

In some rooms you saw prisoners turning huge wheels which worked the cloth-weaving machines below, whilst the machines themselves were fed and tended by other prisoners. The whole place was a great manufactory and series of workshops, where, from five in the morning in summer, six in the winter till seven at night, no sound was heard but that of the machinery! After work-hours they were permitted to talk.

I regret not having asked at the time whether there is any visible sign of moral amendment in these poor unhappy wretches — whether friendships spring up among those condemned to spend their whole lives together in this prison — whether traits of kindness were shown among them — what was the average result of this mode of punishment — and various other questions, which now suggest themselves to me.

I was curious to know whether the prisoners were quick in acquiring a knowledge of the different trades carried on in the prison; and, as a rule, our guide said very much so. There were criminals, it is true, who did not seem to have the power of learning anything; but these were the exceptions, and that generally it was surprising in how short a time a trade was learned, which, with an ordinary apprentice, is a matter of years. Here it was the *one* object; it became the only interest, and was unceasingly worked at day after day.

The prisoner who has been longest in this prison has been there thirty years; many are in for life; many for twenty years. There are between five and six hundred at present in the prison. The number of female prisoners is very small in comparison with the men. We found the women busy washing in their wards, — a long row of very tidy-looking women, in the whitest of borderless caps, with white handkerchiefs pinned over their grey dresses. Their countenances, as a whole, were much more cheerful than those of the men: we actually saw smiles!

Here and there, however, was a heavy, uncouth countenance. At one particular washing-tub stood four women. Our conductor spoke to one of them, this being a sign to us to notice them. Two looked up, and fairly beamed with smiles; one, a tall and very handsome young girl, continued to wash away with downcast eyes. I felt a sort of delicacy in staring at her, her looks were so conscious and modest. A fourth, a fat ill-looking old woman, also never looked at the visitors. The two who smiled had remarkably agreeable faces; one, with good features, and a very mild expression; the other, a small woman, and though with bloom on her cheeks, a certain sad, anxious expression about her eyes and mouth. Of which of these four women were we to hear a fearful history related? The only one who looked evil was the fat old woman.

As soon we were in the court, our conductor said, 'Now, what do you say about those women?'

'Three out of the four,' we remarked, 'are the only agreeable faces we have seen in the prison; and, judging from this momentary glance at their countenances, we should say could not be guilty of much crime; perhaps the fat old woman may be so; that tall, young girl, however, is not only handsome, but gentle-looking.

'That tall young girl,' replied our guide, 'was the one who, a year or two ago, murdered her fellow-servant, and cutting up the body, buried it in the garden; the little woman next to her, some two years since, murdered her husband; and the handsome, kind, motherly-looking woman who stood next, destroyed her child of seven years old. The fat old woman is in only for a slight offence. So much for judgment by physiognomy!'

I cannot express the painful impression produced on me by the remembrance of this group. As I returned home, all the faces I met in the streets seemed to me, as it were, masks. I saw faces in expression a thousand times more evil than the countenances of those three unhappy women. How was it? Was it alone that some unusually painful and frightful circumstances had aroused passions in them which only slept in the breasts of hundreds of other human beings who wander about free and honorably in the world; or was *expression*, after all, a deception? In these three women, at the moment we saw them, at all events, the expression was really good and amiable. I cannot give an idea of the strange sort of distrust which seized me. I looked at the ladies who accompanied me, and said to myself — *your* faces are not nearly so good in expression and feature as theirs. I have been looking at my own face, and it seems to me that it, too, might just as well conceal some frightful remembrance of crime.

I was quite glad when a friend proposed that we should go and see a model of Milan Cathedral, made by an old Italian here. I was thankful for anything to banish the remembrance of the three women, and of those round, beautiful hands and arms of the young girl, which had once been stained with blood.

We entered a very handsome house, and soon were in the little room of Signor S——. The room was very small, but bright and cheerful! Flowers were in the bright little window, the glass cabinets were filled with all imaginable knicknacks of glass, china, and various small models; bronze and gilded candelabra filled with tapers stood about upon *consoles;* pictures hung on the cheerful self-colored green walls. In one corner stood a pretty bed, covered with a pea-green silk quilt, and with a snowy pillow trimmed with lace. The little room was, if not 'parlor, and kitchen, and all,' parlor and bed-room: but one gets quite used to such arrangements abroad.

And there was the little Signor himself, all smiles, and speaking in his beautiful Italian, and so honored by the ladies' visit. And there was the most ingenious model of the far-famed Milan Cathedral, standing on its raised stand of satin-wood on a table in the centre of the room. It was a beautiful model, of cream-colored card-board, and with the tracery of the windows, the bas-relievos, the capitals of the columns, the Gothic work of the pinnacles, the many thousand statues, all moulded in bread! You saw the painted glass in the windows, and as the trembling hands of the clever old Signor removed various portions of the model, you looked into the interior, and beheld altars, pictures, gilding, tesselated pavements. Little, tiny people were walking about in the church; everything was there, even to a statue of San Carlo Borromeo himself, concealed behind the high altar. And see! the delighted Signor pulls out a drawer in the satin-wood base; and there is the crypt, the Chapel of San Carlo, the tesselated pavement, the winding staircases descending into the chapels, the altars — everything!

Well, it *was* wonderful! 'Yes, it was vastly admired, said the little Signor; 'architects had come to see it from far and wide; and all pronounced it wonderful!'

And now we began to look at other models which stood

in the glass cases; many were wondrous buildings of his own creation, and if they proved that he had no accurate architectural knowledge, as he himself declared, they proved, at all events, that he had a great deal of fancy, and was decidedly an undeveloped architect.

'And now you must admire my china and curiosities,' he said: 'they are all my own making — all of paper!'

And so they were. The gold tea-spoons, the blue and gold cream jug, full of cream, the plate covered with the heap of biscuits, the dish of oranges; those elegant vases, that pipe and hammer, lying in singular juxtaposition with those elegances and dainties, all were of paper; but so capitally made, that you felt quite deceived even after you had taken them into your hand and felt how light they were. 'And I hope you admire my pair of new boots!' said he, laughing: 'they are of paper; and my blue and white vases up there, they are of paper also! and my candelabra, they are of paper!'

Yes; those massive bronze, and black, and gold candelabra were of paper, and the tapers also of paper — even those that were half-burnt! I began to have suspicions about everything; I expected the little Signor to say next, 'Well, I hope you admire me, for I am of paper!'

Among the various models was a small one of a grave, with its garlanded cross. 'That,' said the old gentleman, 'is the model of my wife's grave: she died two years ago; she was a Milanese; she died in that very corner where the bed stands. I've had my bed placed on the spot where she died; that is her miniature hanging above the bed beside the crucifix.'

I observed that above the bed also hung a print of Paul finding the corpse of Virginia upon the sea-shore. No doubt there was a sentiment of true poetry in the old man's heart when he hung up that picture also. I was glad to recall his hearty laughter but a few minutes before, and to think how, by his ingenious amusement, his beloved hobby, he could banish the sad, though beautiful, ghost which, no doubt, haunted his little room.

I have heard, since our visit, that the old Signor is an entirely self-educated man; that he realized a comfortable little competence before he reached the age of thirty, and that later in life, finding time hang heavily on his hands, he began to make these paper models, which, in their way, are works of genius as well as ingenuity.

CHAPTER XXVII.

THE MAY-FESTIVAL AT STARNBERG.

May 12th.—The May-Festival at Starnberg has been this year especially attractive to the inhabitants of Munich, from the circumstance of a small steamer having been launched upon the little Starnberg Lake the day of the Festival, and making then its first trip. To fully appreciate the excitement of this event, you must bear in mind that steam-boats, in Bavaria proper, are by no means as common as upon the Rhine, the Danube, and the Elbe.

Instead of the Festival being held upon May-day, as was originally intended, it was deferred until Sunday the 11th, people fervently hoping that the day would be fine. And a gloriously beautiful day it proved,—a day of golden sunshine, from early dawn till the soft evening, when the waxing moon rose into the clear warm sky, and the night seemed even more lovely than the day.

I had heard astounding accounts of the crowds who would throng to Starnberg, rendering it next to impossible to find a conveyance either there or back again, and next to impossible, if ever you did arrive at Starnberg, to procure food. For were not King Max and the young Queen, and their court, to be there to sail in the steamer, to witness illuminations and then hold a court ball? and were not the artists going to hold their annual festival? and were not all the gentle-folks, and all the common-folks, of Munich to be at Starnberg upon this eventful day? And were not all the peasants in the neighborhood sure to be there, to wonder at the steam-boat, — and would not there be music on all hands, and a regatta, and a citizens' ball as well as a court-ball? And had not people, for weeks before, hired all the fiacres and carriages that were to be hired in Munich, — and had not all the places in omnibuses been taken days beforehand? Such, at least, were the tidings I heard as soon as I began thinking seriously myself of going to the Festival.

I applied, therefore, to my indefatigable friend, Baron H., claiming his promise, given in April, of accompanying Marie and myself to Starnberg.

The morning of the Fête saw us departing in a stell-wagen from a certain little inn called the *Stackhus Garten.*

Pleasant was the morning, pleasant the road, through its poplar avenues and across the plain, and through the long, monotonous, dreamy pine-woods, which, in fact, are the Royal Park, — and where, said Baron H., you may come upon a herd of fierce wild boars; and pleasant was the view of the Alpine chain, which appeared ever slowly to approach us, though of course it was we who slowly approached it: and pleasant were my reminiscences of Clare's and my expedition to Ober-Ammergau, of which Starnberg had been the first stage: and pleasant was the lively discourse of Baron H., and the smiling rejoinders of the pretty Marie. But pleasantest of all was our glimpse of the Starnberg Lake, gleaming out in the morning sunshine as we descended a gentle hill towards it!

There below us lay the lake, encircled with softly

sloping banks, clothed in the tender May verdure of young beech-woods and of luxuriant grass. The white buildings of little Starnberg, its church, its handsome hotel of semi-Tyrolean architecture, its town-hall, greatly resembling a convent, and commandingly situated upon a low hill, its pleasant villas embosomed in woods and gardens, and its sprinkling of grey Tyrolese cottages, shone out invitingly, illumined by the clear beams of the brilliant morning. And round the verdant shores of the lake, at remote distances, gleamed forth other villas and hamlets and church towers; and the background of our picture was the Alpine chain, its snowy peaks piercing the clouds, and its feet, apparently bathed by the waters of the lake, which stretched away as far as the eye could reach in one direction, a broad, calm, gleaming mirror. The illusion is perfect, although many miles lie between Starnberg Lake and the first range of the mountains,—there is the shadowy line of distant shore, and then abruptly rises the mountain chain.

All houses in Starnberg were decorated with flags, and wreaths, and draperies. Close by the shore of the lake lay the little steamer, which had been launched already, and a crowd of wondering people swarmed around it, some in boats, others on the new pier, others on the shore. Stell-wagen, private carriages and vehicles, many of a singular description, had we seen upon the road, and numbers we now noticed arriving in the little town, or drawn up before the hotel: some way, however, they were not in the swarms which I had been led to expect. But then it was quite early,— not yet half-past nine.

We walked down to the lake to inspect the new steamer as our first pleasure. Men were busy decorating it with garlands — some of the garlands still lay upon the shore, half hidden in the deep rich grass and flowers. We had looked at the steamer — at the crowd, which was composed entirely of peasants, gay in their holiday best — at the new pier, and at the spruce little steam-packet office just erected upon the shore — and then perceived Signor L. pacing up and down the meadow. He looked very handsome and summer-like in his broad-brimmed, low-crowned, straw hat and grey linen coat. I rather surmise that Marie expected this vision at Starnberg of our old acquaintance, although she expressed such pretty surprise.

Soon we were all four being rowed in a little boat across the lake to the hamlet of Lione. We considered that our best plan was to enjoy the lake until we could ascertain precisely what the programme of the festival would present us with. There was the spectacle of the embarkation of royalty, we knew, promised as one pleasure, but we did not feel inclined to await this pleasure a couple of hours. Before reaching Lione we began most seriously to anticipate breakfast, luncheon, dinner, or whatever you may choose to designate a meal at such an hour and under such circumstances. By eleven o'clock we had grown so unromantically hungry that without waiting to breakfast at Lione, as had been our intention, we besought our boatmen to put us on shore at the very first place where food might be procured; and we disembarked at a hamlet bearing a less romantic name than Lione, but where our boatmen assured us an equally good meal might be made.

The gentlemen went into the kitchen to investigate the state of the larder, and Marie and I strolled up into the pleasant garden, or rather wilderness, which surrounds the little inn. Steep, gravelly, winding paths, led among deep grass and flowers up the hill-side, and were shaded by beech-trees just clothed in the exquisite tender verdure of their young leaves. At every lovely spot commanding a view of the sunny lake, a bench had been placed. And a table generally stood before the bench.

Marie and I determined to select the most beautiful view and the shadiest and pleasantest spot in the whole garden as our breakfast-parlor; and behold the most beautiful and convenient had already been selected by a group of students, who were drinking beer and smoking in the loveliest of lovely rustic arbors, with a glorious view of the lake and mountains lying below them: it really was too bad being defrauded of the most beautiful spot in the garden by young fellows who were smoking and beer-drinking; but as they formed a picturesque group with their scarlet caps and white shirt-sleeves, for they had flung off their coats, the day being hot, I gradually forgave them. The second best seat in the garden we discovered was as much infested with ants as the other had been 'infested with youth'— to use the expression of an old Englishman; therefore we were forced to content ourselves with the third best breakfast-parlor. Marie seated herself under the shadowy beech-trees, whilst I, to beguile my impatience for breakfast, began gathering a nosegay. First I plucked cowslips and grasses; but, behold! there were flowers here to be gathered, to my English eyes, far more precious than cowslips; there were tufts of the small Alpine gentian, with its peacock blue so gorgeous in the sunlight; there was the trolius with its ball of gold; there were oxlips and a little plant creeping over the dry turf with a cistus leaf and pea-shaped orange and cream-colored blossom — an entirely new flower to me — and another plant yet more beautiful, and equally un-English, its blossom resembling a blue verbenum, but its leaves soft and of tender green and oval-shaped, growing close to the earth. It had a faint, delicate perfume, such as our greenhouse primulas have. I noticed during the course of the day this lovely lilac flower growing in the greatest profusion in the rich grass around the lake. Marie, I fancy, thought me scarcely less childish in my joy over my odorous bouquet of wild flowers than her good old uncle and Signor L. had done when I discovered the host of blue hepaticas, in the beech-woods near Schwanthaler's castle. Marie, it seemed, did not trouble her memory with the names of flowers; which was an unlucky thing for me.

It was well for us all that our spirits were unusually gay this morning, else they might have been somewhat depressed by the uncomfortable *dejeuner à la fourchette* which was in due course spread for us beneath the tender beech-leaves. It consisted of indifferent coffee, sour wine, boiled beef like India-rubber, flabby veal, and miserable potato-salad. Nobody, however, seemed put at all out of humor by the unsatisfactory viands, and the little inn seemed to be particularly attractive to hungry souls — or rather bodies. The garden became quite animated; first one group after another arrived and dispersed themselves about, and waiters and waiteresses ran madly hither and thither.

A much pleasanter object than the breakfast was the expanse of water, which lay beneath and before us; boats with their blue and white pennons were seen traversing it in every direction, and the white sails of a small yacht belonging to an Englishman resident at Munich were discerned across the lake like the wings of some large bird. And real white wings of birds, the wings of gulls, dipped ever and anon into the sunny waters, and then soared joyously into the sunny sky. But cannon booming across the lake, we hastened down to the shore, intending to await the approach of the little steamer. But upon nearer inspection we found that she still lay a moveless black mass in the distance; and King Max not bearing as punctual a character as our Queen Victoria, we pursued our little voyage.

The programme of the Fête, which we had procured at the inn, informed us that there would be 'Music at Possenhofen;' and to Possenhofen consequently we would go, calling at Lione by the way. Possenhofen is on the opposite side of the lake to Lione.

But our boatman had disappeared! No great loss, however, for he was a surly fellow. Whilst the gentlemen were hunting about for another boat, one came towards the landing-place filled with students and rowed by a woman! 'That's a curious sight to English eyes!' thought I to myself. As the boat put to shore for the students to land, we perceived that this boat-woman was very handsome. 'Let us sail with her!' we all exclaimed: and soon we were seated in her little boat on our way towards Lione.

Signor L. wanted to row: but the girl laughed saucily at him, and seizing the heavy oars with stalwart arms and vigorous strokes, she pulled away.

'*You* know how to row!' she exclaimed in her broad dialect: and her lovely grey eyes laughed merrily beneath her black head-gear, and her rosy lips showed the whitest set of little teeth. How handsome she was! Large of frame, with round, well-developed arms and hands, which were seen to advantage as she plied the oars; the arms and hands were burnt a ruddy brown by the sun, but in form they were perfect. Beneath the black handkerchief which she had arranged hood-wise over her head, and which threw her face half into shadow, and the orange and crimson-striped handkerchief which was crossed over her bosom and tucked into her black boddice, you saw a round snowy throat. Her countenance was of a graceful oval contour, the features delicately chiselled and full of strength, animation, and character, peculiarly charming. How pleasantly she laughed and nodded to her old father when he passed us rowing another boat! he had a brilliant scarlet waistcoat on, which contrasted vividly against his white shirt-sleeves and the blue sky beyond him. She formed a very beautiful picture, our boat-woman, seated there towards the prow of the boat, with the sunshine showering down upon her, and bringing out in marvellous brilliancy her figure quaintly attired in its peasant costume of blue woollen petticoat, bright blue stockings, and heavy shoes, black boddice, pink sleeves tucked up above the elbow, and showing a piece of scarlet lining, orange handkerchief and black head-dress; and behind her the azure and silver Alps rose into an azure and silver heaven, her vigorously plied oars dipping meanwhile with a pleasant monotony into the clear sunny green waters. Thus our little bark, propelled by our beautiful boat-woman, glided past the greenest of beech-woods and the grassiest of meadows, starred with myriads of delicate, brilliant flowers: sounds of distant music swelled voluptuously upon the gentle breeze, whilt ever and anon some gay festal party with a white and blue pennon at the little boat's prow, and a wreath of flowers drooping gracefully from it into the water, would pass us, or was seen in the distance slowly progressing along the lake like some large water-beetle.

We paused at Lione only long enough to imagine how pleasantly a whole summer's day might be spent among its woods and meadows, or even a whole summer, your abode being in a quaint little Tyrolese cottage. At Possenhofen, — where is a small *château* belonging to some Duchess, with pleasant gardens coming down to the water's edge, — we found a group of peasants crowding the pier, of course on the lookout for the steamer. Stepping on shore I saw a lovely bit of Munich artist-life. Upon a tiny promontory which jutted out into the lake, amid deep lush grass and lovely flowers, reclined two young painters. Painters at the first glance I knew them to be, from an unmistakable air about them. One wore a blouse of dark green, the other a blouse of dark brown. They leaned upon their elbows in the cool herbage, the warm sunshine falling upon them, and the soft breeze blowing through their long hair, their felt hats, and a large botanical case, lay beside them on the ground. Behind them were the twisted and gnarled trees of an old orchard bursting into the tender beauty of pear and apple-blossom, and through the checkered shadows of the orchard wandered a gaily attired old peasant woman in her fur cap, leading by the hand a child dressed as quaintly and gaily as the old dame herself, only that instead of a fur cap the child wore a little kerchief tied over her round head. On one side of the young painters rose a screen of tall dry reeds, through the grey stems of which gleamed the sparkling lake, a lovely mirror reflecting the blue of heaven; and above the reeds towered the distant mountains, of a fainter and more ethereal azure, with snowy peaks scarcely to be distinguished in the glare of noontide from the silver of floating clouds.

On we rambled, past old orchards, and through grassy meadows as brimful of flowers as the meadows through which Angelico da Fiesole's rejoicing angels lead the blessed spirits of redeemed mortals. People were seen everywhere streaming along in happy groups, looking almost as full of joy as though indeed these were the fields of heaven instead of earth, along which they passed. Truly, this day at least, we were all redeemed from earth's cares and sadness, and were led along by

God's angels, — Spring, and Beauty, and Peace, through fields of Paradise. Would to Heaven that we English as a nation yielded ourselves up more universally with simple worshipping hearts to the guidance of these angels!

All ranks, all ages, — old and young, rich and poor, parents, children, friends, acquaintance, lovers, citizens, parents, painters, poets, philosophers, — all streamed along, celebrating by their rejoicing hearts God's glorious gifts of May and Nature.

On our way up into the woods we passed a small chapel standing close to the road. It was so small a chapel that it appeared scarcely more than a way-side shrine. It had a tiny belfry, was white-washed, and there was painting of pale sea-green about the belfry lattice-work windows. A large pear-tree grew close to the little chapel, and this pleasant May Sunday the pear-tree was like a tree of ordorous snow, so covered was it with blossom. Bees hummed about the pear-tree, the sun showered down its warm beams upon tree, chapel, and murmuring bees, and from the open door came a low monotonous chant. I looked in through the open door; the little chapel was full of peasants, about twelve women on one side kneeling, about twelve men kneeling on the other side: the men chanted in their deep bass, the women took up the chant with their shriller voices; and when they paused you heard the bees hum, and over all, within and without, was the breath of May and the blessing of God.

Higher up in the woods, too, how pleasant it was! People arrived ever faster and faster: there were parties in carriages, with servants and grandeur; there were parties on foot — the gentlemen with wreaths of ivy or stags'-horn moss twisted round their straw or felt hats, with gentians, cowslips, and those lovely primula flowers stuck into their button-holes—the ladies and children grasping great bouquets in their hands. Here were whole families, and little knots of friends; there were parties of University students, of Academy students, of lads from the Gymnasium. Now I recognised one well-known Munich painter and his family, now another — and friends greeted friends, and fresh tables and seats were brought out from the near rustic inn, and groups sat upon benches on the grass, talking, laughing, eating, drinking, and being right merry. Some, like ourselves, having greeted their acquaintance, and seen what was going on, returned to the lake.

We found our boat and its handsome mistress awaiting us, and soon were landing upon a certain little island which had temptingly invited us all the morning, its trees and bushes seeming to rise out of the very water. But 'distance in this instance had lent enchantment to the view.' The island was in a very chaotic state, King Max having also thought the island attractive, and preparations being made for the building of a small royal villa, and for the laying-out of gardens. The only thing we discovered worthy of remark was a cowardly bull-dog, who, with much violent manifestation of anger and loud barkings, opposed our landing, but who, perceiving our bold determination and undaunted firmness, put his tail with craven air between his legs, and fairly ran away! — never, certainly, was such a *bully* of a bull-dog seen before!

We returned to Possenhofen just in time to witness the reception of the steamer there, as she gaily passed with flying steamers, garlands, and royalty, on board. Very brilliant, indeed, she looked, with a bevy of elegantly dressed ladies walking about the deck beneath an awning, and with the young King and Queen, and Prince Adelbert, graciously replying to the shouts and wavings of caps, hats, and handkerchiefs, from the shore. The King's voice was heard to say something about '*Lebe Hoch Starnberg!*' and on the little steamer passed. And now we in our boat, steered by our beautiful pilotess, followed in the wake of royalty towards Starnberg and — dinner.

But it would be a weariful history were I to describe all our first futile attempts to procure refreshment at the great inn with the semi-Tyrolean architecture. Suffice it tó say, that finding we might wait there till Doomsday apparently — though capital dinners were being devoured on all hands — in despair and hunger we decamped to a smaller inn. And truly now I began to be satisfied as to the crowds which would flock to the Starnberg Festival; and more than satisfied! In this little inn, fearing lest if we sat in the garden far away from the kitchen we might be forgotten, we took up our station in a room which was decorated for the evening's ball. There we waited and waited, devoured with hunger and impatience, amid clouds of tobacco-smoke, and bushels of beer-tankards, and emptied coffee-cups, enduring martyrdom for the sake of procuring dinner — some time. People would accuse me of exaggeration were I to say how long we waited; therefore I will content myself with saying 'ages.' The only pleasant sight upon which my eyes rested this weariful time, was a group of Academy students, who entered the smoky room, carrying long ivy-trails in their hands, and with ivy wreathed picturesquely round their broad-brimmed hats and Raphaelesque caps. What a group of happy life and nature-enjoying youths they looked! — their young, earnest faces, burnt and ruddied by the hot sun, and their keen painter-eyes sparkling with joy which intense worship of nature, such as the painter alone knows, had sent welling up from their hearts.

As I sat looking at this group, my soul sang a hymn

of thanksgiving for the glory which Art may and does so frequently cast over life. In holiest colors the whole joy of the painter's life, and especially of the Art-student's life, rose up before me, — that life of aspiration yet of humility, the more blessed through this humility! that life of eager endeavor, of hope, and of onward progress — that life where the duty is to yield up the soul to the love, worship, and understanding of the beauty created by the Divine Artist; and, when clothed in the neophyte's robe of purity, the glories of the holy temple of nature are gradually unfolded before the astounded, worshipping eyes! It often seems to me that the life of one of these young German painters might be a life as nearly approaching perfect beauty and bliss as any human life is permitted to be; at all events, there are many elements of beauty in it. These painters live much less fettered by conventionality than the same class with us; they live in a country where the symbolism of art everywhere surrounds them; where the sordid cares of life usually press less heavily upon them, and where a spirit of peculiarly noble aspiration and grandeur in art floats through the land. As a woman, and therefore only seeing this art-life in the Germans from a peculiar point of view, and by not mingling in it except at certain beautiful, poetical moments, I may draw a picture in my imagination only of its brightest, noblest phase; but that phases of intensest loveliness do adorn it, is as true as that divinest poetry fills the world.

But to return to a commoner, though at the moment a very engrossing interest. Dish after dish did we see borne past us to other guests, who doubtless were also famishing; but our dishes never arrived, though they were each time promised 'immediately.' One old gentleman especially excited my envy, as I saw a capital roast fowl carried up to him.

'Don't envy *him*, Fräulein!' observed an acquaintance of Baron H.'s, who had joined us whilst we had been waiting in this detestable apartment; 'don't envy him, poor soul! he has been waiting ever since two o'clock for that fowl, and it is now five! I have waited for coffee ever since three! Be thankful if your dinner arrives before the ball commences!' And verily I believe we might have waited until the ball supper itself, had not this benevolent acquaintance volunteered to rush into the kitchen and lay violent hands upon the first dish he encountered. Soon after his return, enter, amid looks of triumph on the part of our 'friend in need,' fowl, coffee, and salad! I do not, however, believe it had been through physical force that we had obtained our dinner, but through the influence with the Kellnerins of his remarkably handsome face.

During all this waiting we had lost the Regatta: but the sequel of the Regatta we did not lose. Musicians ascended into the orchestra, which at first we supposed was the forerunner of the ball, but this was simply that as the name of each successful candidate in the boat-race received his prize, the musicians might trumpet forth his triumph. A man with a white cockade on his coat read aloud the names of the successful boatmen, and from a crowd of weather-beaten men standing at the opposite end of the room, one by one, with bashful mien and delighted faces, they approached and received the prizes and decorations. Of course, much of the company from the garden crowded into the room to see this spectacle.

Thankful indeed was I when Marie and I, leaving the gentlemen to enjoy their cigars, emerged from the room, stifling with its mingled fumes of tobacco and dinner, into the fresh evening air. Without all was animation : people were arriving for the ball ; people were laughing, chatting, and drinking — of course that eternal beer and coffee.

Evening was sinking calmly over the lovely landscape, and Baron H., and his two friends, joining us, we strolled down towards the lake. All looked so exquisitely beautiful in the sunset light, that again we said, 'Suppose we take a boat?' The mountain peaks glowed with tints of rose and lilac, the pearly sky was flecked with crimson and brilliant orange: on one hand rose the moon, whilst on the other the sun sank behind the sloping shore, which was now turned to a dull olive-green in the approaching twilight. Moon and sunset-clouds were reflected in the peaceful waters; now one star came forth in the translucent heavens, now another, just above the darkening mountains, and seeming to rest upon a jagged peak. Silence sank dreamily over all things. The delicious hush alone was broken by the gentle plash of the oars, and the singing of my companions: they sang several of Mendelssohn's Volks Lieder.

A fire suddenly bursting forth on the shore, its ruddy flame reflected in the lake's mirror reminded us of the illumination, and we hastened our return. Doubtless from the lake itself would have been the most effective spot from which to have viewed the bonfires and fireworks, but we thought of damp, of fogs, and of consumptions, and prudently returned to *terra firma*, where, as we set foot, we were greeted by a loud chorus of frogs, which far outcroaked the sounds of merriment proceeding from the little town. Lights shone forth from the hotel windows, telling of the merry doings within. Crowds filled the streets, crowds filled the garden of the inn where we had dined: the Pavilion in the garden, which contained the ball-room, was like a huge lantern. We looked in. The ball had not commenced, but the supper had; ladies, not in ball-room costume, but without their bonnets, and some wearing flowers in their hair, and gentlemen who, doubtless, had smartened themselves up a little after the fatigues and dust of the day, were seated at long tables, in a kind of gallery, in front of the ball-room. I had been curious to know the class of people who remained for the dancing, and to see what a rural ball of this description was like. And now, although the dancing had not commenced, I was quite satisfied, and could picture the waltzes, polkas, and cotillons, which would be danced in the still empty ball-room, of which we caught a glimpse through the open door, all gay with its blue, scarlet, and white festoons of drapery, supported by gilt anchors.

Report of cannon told that the fireworks were about to commence, — and people hastened out into the meadows towards the lake. Uprose a rocket like a long fiery serpent, and fell into a shower of lilac stars over the water. Another, and another, rose! Then suddenly the monastic looking Town-hall, standing upon its hill, gleamed out magically through the soft gloom of the May night, illumined with a warm rose color, now with a pale yellow green, as though it were built of tinted light. And the little church across the lake, crowning the hill above Lione, gleamed forth a pale spectral sea-green, as if replying to the Starnberg signal. And villas, churches, and villages exchanged their spectral greetings across the lake, whose placid mirror ever reflected them. From the shores shot up, in rapid succession, long, red tongues of flame, like wild sacrificial fires burning upon pagan altars: the flames rising steadily on the unruffled waters, whilst smoke curled in white volumes ruddily illumined by the fires. Above all shone the quiet broad moon, smiling down through the May night, and reflecting her calm face in a rivulet which murmured through the meadows. The moonlight gleamed like frosted silver upon the ripple of the streamlet and upon the long grass which, in places, grew in the stream, and was carried along by it, just covered with the waters. All else was a transparent, murmuring gloom: whilst, with the most marvellous delicacy, sharp, black shadows were cast across the frosted silver from the sprays of foliage and long grasses growing upon the bank. This little bit of Nature's illumination was the most magical and beautiful of all the illuminations of this lovely May Festival.

In the midst of these illuminations, divine and human, the steamer, hung with lamps and garlands, was once more to sail forth upon the lake. But this we did not stay to witness, for now we mounted into our omnibus, very happy but very weary, and jolted back to Munich; the moon shining down among the old pine trees in the Royal Park, and showing us, not only the trees and the long procession of royal carriages, with six horses each and postilions and fiery-lamps rushing past us, but groups also of deer feeding quietly by the road-side. At one spot I saw a milk-white doe — the ghost of a doe it might have been — and as she heard the noise of wheels she fled, like a spirit, into the dark glades of the wood. About two in the morning we found ourselves returning to our homes through the deserted moonlit streets of Munich, the houses in the Dult Platz looking as if built out of a gigantic box of Dutch toys, with their closed, sleeping windows, and their stiff rows of clipped acacia-trees rising up before them.

CHAPTER XXVIII.

FUNERAL OF THE DUCHESS OF LEUCHTENBERG. — THE SENDLING BATTLE AND OLD MUNICH.

May 18*th.* — That poor old Duchess, who looked so magnificent at the *Landwehr* Ball in her satin and jewels, with her hat sparkling with diamonds and her cheeks brilliant with *rouge*, and whom this spring I have constantly seen driving out of her handsome palace in her handsome coach, is dead! She died after a very short illness. Every one is relating beautiful things about her. She was King Ludwig's sister, and widow of Eugene Beauharnais, and was related to a number of crowned heads and grandees; and was the possessor of the celebrated Leuchtenberg collection of paintings.

To-day the poor old corpse, as it lay in state, has been visited by all Munich — by all the *bourgeoisie* at least. I observed a crowd before the gates of the Leuchtenberg Palace, and stopped to see what was going on. Presently the huge gates opened, the crowd made a rush, and half of the people were received within the gateway. I found myself in the foremost rank of the remaining half of the crowd, and closely pressed up against the re-closed gates. There we waited a full hour, and the crowd was a detestable crowd. There did not seem a particle of awe or reverence for the spectacle they were about to witness. I stood squeezed up against the bronze gates, fearfully expecting to be precipitated head foremost by the crowd behind, whenever the gates should open, or to be crushed, whilst waiting, against the embossed ornaments upon the gates. Luckily, however, no such accident occurred.

But if the crowd had behaved in an irreverent manner outside the house of death, within they behaved even worse ; rushing up-stairs, laughing, and making a terrible hubbub. I was well pleased that gendarmes, and solemn servants, at the head of the staircase, stood ready to rebuke them. Passing through one or two rooms where furniture stood about in desolate disorder, the crowd crushed into a small room hung with black cloth and escutcheons, and lighted brilliantly with numerous waxen tapers. In the centre of the room, upon a high couch draped with black, decorated with blooming flowers, and surrounded with tapers burning in tall golden candlesticks, reclined the corpse ; it was arrayed in black velvet. The pale brow was crowned with a tiara, from which fell, half concealing the figure, a long veil of white lace. There was rouge no longer upon the white cheeks. You were more than ever struck with the commanding profile, and peculiarly arched eye-brows. There was something very solemn and affecting in the face.

Round the room knelt her court-ladies, shrouded in long black veils, and several gentlemen in brilliant uniforms. On one side of the room rose a small altar, where, at certain periods of the day, mass was celebrated. To-morrow is to be the funeral.

The Duchess is said to have been singularly beautiful in her youth. It was related to me by Fräulein Sänchen, that when in Italy, the peasants fell down and prayed before her, believing her to be the 'Madonna.' This seems to be a popular legend here.

May 19*th.* — At four o'clock this afternoon the grand funeral took place. I went to a house in the Theatine Strasse to witness the procession. Already at two o'clock, whilst I was at the studio, I heard the tolling of the Church bells. But funeral bells toll here in a much less mournful way than the English *Passing-bell.* As I crossed the Odeon Platz, at one corner of which the Leuchtenberg Palace is situated, I noticed a number of soldiers in their blue and white uniforms, drawn up before the palace. Close to the doors of the Theatine Church stood a knot of priests, with a tall crimson banner leaning against the wall. Soldiers were drawn up on either side of the Theatine Strasse.

The house from which I viewed the spectacle is opposite to the abode of the Russian Ambassador. The Theatine Strasse is one of the old streets, and full of picturesque detail, which considerably enhanced the effect of the procession as it approached. Of course the street was thronged with people standing in thick rows behind the soldiers who lined the causeways. Of course, too, all the windows were crowded. Opposite to us at a window in the principal *étage* of the Ambassador's house was a knot of ladies in black. There at a window close by was the picturesque head of a priest of the Greek Church to be seen.

A long train of servants belonging to the nobility headed the funeral procession. They bore burning torches with them; their liveries were of all descriptions and colors. One man was especially remarkable from wearing a gorgeous Hungarian costume of scarlet and light blue trimmed with silver lace; he wore a high cap which had a deal of scarlet about it, and a tall stiff feather. He was an unusually tall man, and this cap made him look gigantic. These were the servants of King Max and of the other royal and ducal households. The dead Duchess's servants, all wearing crape upon their arms and streaming from their cocked hats. The smoke rising from their torches hung in the air above the procession like a funereal veil.

Next came the different Brotherhoods attached to the churches, and who always give great picturesqueness to the processions here: the old men bare-headed, and monotonously chanting as they followed the banners and crucifixes, which were borne by men and boys wearing white linen and the colors of their banner and crucifix canopy. Scarlet, blue, amber, violet, green, and russet, made the street most brilliant in coloring. All was gay to the eye, but mournful to the ear from the monotonous murmur of the old men's voices. Next followed in equal number, trains of priests in black and white, many of them singing, and some preceded by a crucifix. There was the small band of Franciscan Friars, wearing linen robes above their brown frocks, the picturesque cowls hanging over the white linen. There were the priests of the Hof-Kapelle, with broad violet ribbons suspending a small golden cross around the neck. And there were priests in violet and scarlet preceding the Archbishop, who advanced slowly along, a mass of gold embroidery, — his golden robes supported on either hand by golden-robed priests: he bore a rich silver crosier in his hand, and upon his head a rich white mitre.

And now came on the hearse, surrounded by the court-pages, in blue and white. The coffin lay upon a throne covered with a black velvet pall, emblazoned with the Leuchtenberg arms. A black canopy shaded the coffin; decorations and diamond stars glittered at the foot of the coffin. Lions veiled with crape appeared at the foot of the throne, as if guarding the royal dead.

The funeral car was driven by the deceased Duchess's old coachman, and drawn by six of her beautiful horses caparisoned in trappings of black and gold.

The hearse was followed by the Royal Princes and the principal Bavarian nobility, all walking; by the members of the various royal households here, by ambassadors from foreign courts, by the chief officers of the Bavarian army, by the Professors of the University wearing their rich colored robes, and by the Magistracy. The Militia terminated the procession. Trumpets brayed forth, and the dull sound of muffled drums was heard as the train passed along; the soldiers presenting arms as the hearse rolled by. And thus the body of the widow of Eugene Beauharnais was conveyed to the Church of St. Michael, to repose beside the ashes of her husband.

Rain began to fall, much to the discomfort of the pro cession. It returned straggling and drenched through the wet streets; the military bands breaking forth into joyous music.

Mr. von D. told me last evening the history belonging to the huge grave in the Sendling Church-yard, which, together with the frescoed battle-piece upon the walls of the little church, and the small monument erected upon the mound by a certain Philip v. Zwackh 'in memory of the slain,' has long interested my imagination by its mournful poetry.

It was in the year 1705, the year after the great battle of Blenheim, when Europe was devouring her very heart in contests about the 'Spanish Succession,' that the Bavarian peasantry rose *en masse*. They were smarting under the bitter vengeance of the Austrian government, who visited the sins of the princes upon the people; they were ground to the very dust by imposts and cruelty, and had already in public assembly addressed the diet of Regensburg, declaring that 'necessity forced them to arms.'

Two students, Plinganser and Mendl, placed themselves at the head of the peasant insurgents, and were everywhere victorious. Various of the nobility joined them; but this in the end only led to the betrayal of the peasants. On they marched victoriously towards Munich, whither the Imperial General Kreichbaum had been dispatched with reinforcements.

The Vorstadt-Au was already in full insurrection. The giant mountaineer, the Smith Baltes or Sibaldus of Kochel, with his two sons, led on the excited people with the cry of 'Save the children!' a rumor being afloat that the young Bavarian princes were to be carried out of the land. One of the city gates was forced, Sibaldus with his '*Morgenstern*' slaying an Austrian sentinel; and a bloody and fierce conflict ensued.

The peasants, relying upon aid from the nobles within the city who had joined their side, fought long and bravely, but no succor reached their little band: fighting on foot, and between the fire of the Austrians from the city and of General Kreichbaum in their rear, they fled towards the village of Sendling, where, rallying round the little church, these peasants fought like lions; old Sibaldus and his sons falling among the slain. It is said that five hundred perished. The wounded were carried back to Munich, and exposed in the streets during the rigor of the Christmas night. The battle was fought upon Christmas Day.

Misery fell, of course, with only tenfold bitterness upon the peasantry; beheadings, drawings and quarterings, mutilations, grievous fines and imprisonments, being the sole wages received by the survivors of the conflict.

Historians tell us that 'the ringleaders were beheaded:' but the popular voice relates a termination to Plinganser's history which rings in one's heart like a lovely ballad of Uhland.

Long years after this battle fought upon the Christmas Day around the church, the Bavarian Elector was hunting in a wood at some distance from Munich: he encountered an old beggar on his path, — an old man clothed in rags, and having lost an arm and leg.

'Who are you, my poor man?' demanded the Elector; 'and where did you lose your arm and leg?'

'I am Plinganser!' proudly replied the old beggar; 'and I lost my arm and leg fighting for Bavaria against Austria!'

Down from his horse alighted the Elector, took the beggar by his one remaining hand, mounted him upon his horse, and bare-headed walked beside him; and thus with music triumphantly sounding before them, he conducted the brave old man back to Munich. Through the city-gate he led him where the conflict had raged so fiercely, and on towards the old Palace, where the Electress and her ladies were summoned forth to receive the old man. The bells rang out from all the churches; the cannon boomed; the beggar was led into the Palace; the Elector himself took off his rags, clothed him in fine linen, washed his feet, combed his hair, and seated him at his right hand.

And not alone, says the voice of the people, was this the honor of a day, but as long as the hero lived he dwelt in the palace as a beloved and cherished brother of the Elector.

Mr. von D. says, that some years ago a Munich poet wrote a drama upon this incident, and that his play had an astounding success. It was acted fifteen nights running, the audience coming to the theatre in Tyrolean costume, and bursting forth into long shouts of applause at each expression of liberty, and contempt of Austria. So great was the excitement, that the Austrian government remonstrated, and after fifteen nights' success the play was not only withdrawn from the stage, but all copies of it destroyed.

To withdraw the memory of the Sedlinger Battle from the hearts of the people would be no such easy task; it is their Thermopylæ. Not alone do peasants from the mountains visit the grave of Sibaldus and his followers, repeat prayers before it, sprinkle it with holy water, and then with awe-struck looks regard the fresco; but Philip von Zwackh instituted a mass for the souls of the slain, and each autumn a pilgrimage visits it from the Au suburb, 'to pray for the souls so suddenly departed from among them.' And the Guild of Carpenters pilgrimage each summer to the far-famed 'Maria Eich,' there to pray for these patriot souls.

I was told another little incident, which, although of an entirely different character, has also a touch of ballad romance in it. It related to a certain old Electress, who, all her lifelong, had been selling her soul for gold, and strange rumors of whom yet cling around the Maxburg and the old Residenz. Returning from Austria in a heavy coach, attended by her gentlewoman, and bringing back money in an iron chest, — her revenue, as an Austrian Princess, which she had been to fetch, — the coach was upset, and she crushed to death beneath the iron-chest containing her treasure.

I have been seeking in vain for some work on Munich which shall quench my thirst after the old histories and legends haunting the older portions of the city. A little book, the '*Münchener Hundert und Eins*,' (A Hundred and One Things about Munich,) is, as yet, the nearest approach to what I require: but, being bare of detail, it does little more than strengthen my craving after these old memories.

Still I have discovered that an effigy of a 'Wurm,' a dragon-like serpent to be seen upon the corner house of the Wein-Strásse, as you enter the Schrannen-Platz, is placed there in memory of a certain *Wurm* which dwelt, in old times, near Munich — perhaps upon the shores of the *Wurm-See.* This *Wurm*, flying over Munich, is said to have caused, by its venomous breath, the earliest of the great plagues which have at various epochs ravaged the city. The author of the '*Hundert und Eins*' avers that the legend told to his childish ears was, that upon the Schrannen Platz *this terrible Wurm alighted, and was shot dead by one of the cannon planted there.*

I have also discovered that one of the tall red towers of the Frauen Kirche, which, with their dome-like termination, give a character so peculiar to distant Munich, is *haunted ;* and that from the other a love-lorn damsel flung herself at the end of the last century ! I read also of terrible persecutions of the Jews, of old customs, of which the *Metzger Sprung* and the *Schäffler Tanz* are remnants ; of gateways and Towers, similar to the *Falken Thurm* — one of which was the Torture-Tower — having been destroyed within the memory of man. I read of the Emperor Ludwig the Bavarian's Munich, traces of which may still be discovered by earnest seekers ; of Munich of the Middle Ages I read ; of Munich in the desolation of the Thirty Years' War, when Gustavus Adolphus pronounced her 'the golden saddle upon the lean horse ;' and of Munich in the age of Prince Eugene. But diving down into the oldest portions of the town, where frescoes, bleached by the sun, winds, and rains of centuries, are fading on the walls — where heavy browed archways reveal mouldering stairs leading up into the tall many-storied houses — where the walls, and tall roofs and desolate towers, are black with age — and where, beneath low arches, rush dismal, rapid streams; of all these I find no detailed chronicle. And when, as the other day, visiting the Mint, I found myself standing within the old court-yard, encircled with a double gallery of noble rounded arches, and asking its history and purport, was told 'here were held the Ducal tournaments in old times,' — then do I feel the spirit of an antiquarian awake within me, and an unappeasable longing after old memories and traditions seize my imagination.

As I have already observed, Old and New Munich are fraught with an entirely separate poetry, and present totally different aspects. The character of the people in the streets is different — the gaily attired peasants thronging the quaint old streets, market-places, and covered passages; and their primitive wagons, and the heavy brewers' drays rumbling and jolting along the uneven pavements; whilst, in the newer city, elegantly attired ladies and gentlemen aristocratically saunter about, or roll along in their carriages, with every now and then a royal carriage dashing past.

But different in aspect as are these two portions of Munich at the first view, upon nearer investigation one proves but to be a modern development of the other, as King Ludwig is only a fuller development of the artistic germ which is implanted in his race.

This new Munich proceeding from the brain of the artist-souled king, who, as it has justly been observed, 'could abandon his crown, but could not abandon his art,' with its Glyptothek, its Old and New Pinakothek, its Kunst Ausstellung, its Sieges-Thor, its Feldherren Halle, its Basilica, its Hof-Kapelle, its Au-Church, its Rhumes Halle, and Bavaria with its two splendid new wings to the old Palace, with its noble Ludwig Strasse, containing the Royal Library, Blind Institution, Damen Stift, University Jesuits' College, and Ludwig's Church; this New Munich, I repeat, enriched with innumerable great works in fresco — historic, poetic, religious — of Cornelius, Kaulbach, Schnorr, and Hess, with its statues of Schwanthaler, Thorwaldsen, and Rauch, with each important event in the Bavarian annals chronicled in painting, sculpture, or architecture, is indeed a wonderful little city, and unique in these modern days. And when we reflect that King Ludwig has called around him such men as Von Klenze, Gärtner, and Ziebland as architects; Cornelius, Schnorr, Kaulbach, and Hess as painters, to create and adorn this city, giving them glorious scope in which to develope their various genius, and has in every possible way fostered and encouraged art in all its branches, — has founded the Glass and Porcelain painting establishments, and the Bronze Foundry, and has led to the revival and perfection of fresco and encaustic painting, and to the discovery of Sterrio-chromie, — one is inclined to regard him as the sole art-monarch of his race.

Looking, however, back into the history of the old city, — first we have the Emperor, Ludwig the Bavarian, as the beautifier of Munich, — the Emperor whose triumphal entrance into Munich after the Battle of Mühldorf, King Ludwig, with reverence, has had chronicled in fresco upon the Isar Gate, by which he is said to have entered the city, — the gate itself being built, by King Ludwig's command, in exact imitation of the one dating from the Emperor's time.

Then we have Duke Sigismund, the builder in the fifteenth century of the Frauen Kirche, and the diffuser, through this and other works, of a strong artistic spirit and activity among the people; Albert V., a century later, assembled around him men of learning as his counsellors of state, and summoning painters, sculptors, architects, and musicians to his court, for the adornment of his capital and the delectation of his private life. Among these foreign artists came Orlando di Lasso, whose statue King Ludwig has had erected, together with that of Gluck, born in Rhenish Bavaria, in front of the Odeon, and who, in Albert's time, filled the churches of Munich with sweet music. And there is the Elector Maximilian, spite of the horrors of the Thirty Years' War, building the old Resedenz, one of the architectural marvels of his century. And all working earnestly in the direction of art, — blinded at times, it is true, by the grossness of the age in which they lived, but working earnestly according to their lights!

It is a pleasant thought, this artistic link between the Old and New Cities of Munich, — between King Ludwig and his predecessors.

Here occurs a break in the diary of a few months, occasioned by a visit to England.

CHAPTER XXIX.

RETURN TO MUNICH.

November, 1851.—I am again here. Of our journey I will not speak, until we reached Heidelberg. It was about one o'clock in the day. The sun shone brightly, and cast lovely passing shadows across the beautiful chain of hills, as we rushed across the plain by railway from Manheim. And now we were rattling from the station in an omnibus, between the rows of trees skirting the Botanic Garden. How beautiful did all look beneath the autumn sun, and gay with autumn tints! 'Isabel, look!' exclaimed I to my present companion, who was now in Germany for the first time; 'do you see that blue roof of a summer-house up in the vineyard? There, below it, is our old house with the bright green roof! Isabel, this is the old Manheim Gate! Is not this street old-fashioned, and is not the whole town old-fashioned? Do you see that odd cart and those lean horses, with their bells and pointed collars? And do you see those young men? those are students!'

And now we are at the Badenischen Hof, where we only stop to see our rooms, and then hurry out to look about us. It was the time of the October Fair; and in the Parade Platz was the Dutch woman in her picturesque costume, and with her pretty doll-like face, baking and selling 'Waffeln.' All was just as of old, and we walked through it, for Isabel to have a peep at a German Fair, and then on to the Castle. I leave you to imagine the beauty of the scene from the Castle terrace, where we watched the sunset. The town and plain, and winding river, and distant Haardt mountains half veiled by violet haze; the castle rising from amid the gorgeous autumn tints of coral and gold which sobered the red tone of the castle into a warm grey, and telling dark against the sunset sky, which was crimson and amber and lemon color gradating into pale azure, and flecked with sombre clouds of dusky grey and dove-color. I never saw the castle look more magnificent; and all was solemn and gorgeous, and full of a mournful poetry.

As we returned through the town, Isabel had a peep through a window into a students' *Kneip*, where we saw them all jollily drinking and playing at cards, with statuettes of Goethe and Schiller, and other poets, arranged round the room. It was a capital bit of German student-life!

We were advised the next morning not to go up the Neckar in the little steamer; but I was obstinate, and we went. It was a dull morning, and the silence, the gloom, the mournfulness of the day, harmonized wonderfully with the scenery. Those round, swelling hills, crowned with their forests, now gorgeous with autumn coloring,— that swollen river up which we slowly progressed,—the absence of all human and animal life on the banks,— had a solemn influence upon the mind. I could have believed that our spirits had flown back into long past ages, and that this was the day on which Siegfried was stabbed whilst hunting amid these hills; that his sad, beautiful corpse yet lay beneath some of the old oaks with crimson and yellow leaves falling upon it, or was borne mournfully by his friends home through these solitudes upon its bier of branches, and that the trees, and the sky, and the rivers — all nature mourned over the hero. Never was a day a greater contrast than this to my last sail up the Neckar: then all nature was full of fresh life; the trees clothed in their earliest leaves, the most luxuriant flowers and foliage dipping their beautiful sprays and festoons into the clear green waters, birds singing, the sun showering down his beneficent beams upon the forest and the hills and little towns and hamlets, and upon the pleasant groups of peasants busy upon the river banks: but my own soul was sick with an unspeakable anguish. This time all nature seemed to mourn, all human life to have vanished from the shores; and yet within me I had an assurance of happiness, such a delicious peace, that the very mournfulness was a sort of solemn repose to me.

Isabel was much delighted. But the day was a long and fatiguing one; when it grew dark we retired to our little cabin, but though we had it all to ourselves, we were anything but comfortable. We were heartily glad, after fourteen hours on the Neckar, to find ourselves in a tolerable inn at Heilbronn.

But poor Isabel was really ill when we arrived. Who does not know how the change of scene, and the diet, and the excitement of everything, and the smells and the dirt, and the hurry of travelling, always affect one on first going abroad? She has not even yet recovered her taste, and says she feels all taste, all body, till she hates herself. She wishes she had no sense of smell or taste. But the quiet of our rooms, a dinner which an English acquaintance cooked yesterday, some wholesome bread from our old baker here, and a cup of real English tea, have done her good. For myself I was very hungry all the way, and ate and drank to Isabel's astonishment.

From Heilbronn we started at six in the morning by railway for Süssen, where we arrived by nine o'clock. I saw a Stell-wagen waiting for passengers to Nördlingen, and of course supposed it to be the same by which I had so rapidly travelled in the spring from Nördlingen to Süssen. Our luggage was immediately piled on the top, and in we mounted.

'Isabel, dear, put that shawl round your feet; let us arrange ourselves comfortably,' said I.

'It is not of much consequence, as we shall get out again in a few minutes,' returned Isabel.

'In a few *hours* you mean,' said I.

'*Hours!*' exclaimed Isabel, who had felt unwell all morning.

'Yes, for six hours, poor Isabel,' said I, full of compassion; and added, addressing a fellow-passenger, 'Not more than six?'

'*Twelve* at least,' was the reply.

Imagine our looks of horror. Yes, and so it was. The omnibus, now that the Great Exhibition was over, had returned to its old slow ways. It crawled up hill and down; no longer were horses waiting ready harnessed at the different post-stations, and the omnibus rushing on without more than a minute's pause. We alighted several times in the course of the day, and remained at wayside inns, miserably devoured with impatience, whilst the driver guzzled beer and the passengers devoured sour-kraut and sausage. Up, up we slowly ascended bleak, wild, desolate hill-sides by interminable winding roads; the woods ceased; higher and higher we ascended, till we reached a desolate, wild plain which stretches on, and on, and on. It is the *Hochebene,* the elevated plain on which stands Munich; but we were yet many a mile from Munich. Here and there was a melancholy village, or solitary, dilapidated castle or tower! Now you passed through a birch-wood, where were charcoal burners' huts, and where from the black pyramid of charcoal rose curling through the leafless trees a slender column of blue smoke into the mournful, leaden sky. Now you came to a shepherd tending his flock upon a damp, spongy common, where the horizon-line was only broken by a solitary, tall cross; now we rattled into a village, — snow half-melted lay on the roofs, the street was ankle deep in sludge, the bell tolled mournfully through the damp air. It was All Saints' Day; the peasant-women, dressed in their quaint head-dress of long black ribbons, and with their black and striped petticoats; the men in their long blue coats and cocked hats were hastening through mud and damp with garlands to decorate the graves of their friends, and pray for their souls in the church.

We alighted at a wretched inn. Isabel was half choked by the bad air of the one common sitting-room, which was the only place we could enter. There was a huge, quaint iron stove making every corner of the room warm; peasants were drinking and smoking near it; two travellers of a somewhat higher grade were sitting at a table covered with a white cloth, devouring soup, and there were plates laid for us. It was very dirty, and very close, and very poverty-stricken; but very picturesque. Light fell through a checked blind of a dull pink into the nook behind the screen. A shrine, containing a hideous Madonna and dead Christ, hung in the corner upon the white-washed wall. Children with plaited hair and short petticoats were playing on the uneven boarded floor. The landlord, a man resembling a tadpole in figure, with large head and spindle legs, all the more spindling because cased in black velvet breeches and black worsted stockings, joked and served beer to the jolly, loud-talking peasants.

Once more we stopped for half an hour at a village just before dusk. There, happily having the coupé at last given up to us, we wrapped ourselves in our cloaks, looking like a couple of hooded friars curled up into either corner. What a journey that was! On, on, on! Rattle, rattle! rumble, rumble! We nodded, — we slept, — we started up, cramped and cold!

'Isabel, how are you?'

'So weary! Anna, how are you?'

'*So* weary!'

We nod and sleep again! Rattle, rumble, rattle! The driver, in his blue blouse and with his cracking whip, duskily grows into a frightful phantom. All seems a nightmare! On, on! A desolate horizon of dull heath dimly seen by a baneful moonlight — patches of snow *grinning* here and there with fearful, cold distinctness.

'*It is* a dream!' exclaimed Isabel, in a weak voice. 'I feel *so* strange, quite hysterical, and as if I could scream a loud scream!'

'Don't do that!' exclaimed I, and laughed heartily! but to my astonishment my laughter ended in a violent burst of tears: not that I was in the least unhappy or low-spirited, but from sheer fatigue and weakness. At this Isabel was all right in a moment; and so was I, for I was quite alarmed by my own tears.

'We must soon be at Nördlingen!' we exclaimed. And soon we were. And when we were seated at a very large, well-spread table, near to a large warm stove, with two comfortable, soft, white beds looming out of the distance, our desolate journey seemed truly a mere dream.

We slept deliciously; and as the train for Munich did not start till half-past ten we had plenty of time to rest. We had a fire lighted in our stove before we got up, and were so luxurious even as to order the chambermaid to bring us our breakfasts ready made to us; and thus we lay and rested. Suddenly we heard from the neighboring church-tower a most melancholy blast of wind-instruments: the most soul-touching strain — the very essence of lament and sadness. We started up!

'Isabel, listen!' I exclaimed; 'how beautiful, how touchingly mournful! what can it be?'

Isabel listened with her eyes swimming with tears.

'What is it?' I asked from the maid.

'It is the dirge for the dead; some one must just have died; and then they always blow from the tower.'

I cannot tell you how beautiful this seemed to us, coming suddenly in this manner, like a lament breathing down from heaven upon the little, old decaying town.

'Do you wonder, dear Isabel,' exclaimed I, 'at my love of Germany, when such little poems are ever coming across us? Does one not forget all the bad smells, and all the coarseness of common things, in the existence of a living poetry such as this?'

We were soon at Munich; but we seemed to be travelling into the polar regions: snow, snow, snow! One vast expanse of snow, only broken here and there by dark fir-woods. At Augsburg we stopped and had a good dinner, so as to be prepared for an empty larder at the Werffs.

At about a quarter to four o'clock we reached Munich. I felt only as if I had been on a little excursion, and were returning to a home. I did not feel at all excited, only very happy.

'Look, Isabel, out there! Don't you see the giant arm of the Bavaria, rising with its wreath above that building?'

But we were at the Station before she could notice it.

'Never mind! never mind, dear Isabel!. We are at Munich!'

'What a beautiful Station!' exclaimed Isabel, as she looked up to its rich ceiling of mosaic work of inlaid woods.

'Yes, it is a fit entrance to an Art-City. But look there! Don't you see an old Franciscan friar, with his hood drawn over his head? Is he not picturesque? But now, jump into this *fiacre* and let us drive *home!*'

'No. 57, Neue —— Strasse!' said I to the driver. Bang went the door, and away we rolled through the slush of melting snow, and with snow driving around us, along back streets to the Neue —— Strasse. Out I sprang, ran up stairs, pulled the well-known bell! The door opened; —there was Madame Thekla!

'*Ach mein Fräulein! Ach Herr Je! Herr Je! mein Fräulein!*' and she stretches out her arms like a big bird flapping its wings. 'You never wrote the little letter to tell us when you were coming, and we have been so uneasy;—but two letters are come for you! And we have not lit the fires!'

'Never mind that, dear Madame Thekla; come down to my cousin; tell me what I must pay the man, and just see to our luggage!' And down I ran again, and then up again, rushing against dear old Fräulein Sänchen, whom I kissed with a most hearty kiss.

'And now let me have a fire and coffee, and give me my letters!'

The day after our arrival, taking a droschke, one of the new public conveyances which are just introduced at Munich,—and elegant, convenient little carriages they are, with their well-dressed and polite drivers,—away we drove, so that Isabel might have an idea of the good city of Munich. It was a beautiful afternoon, cold and clear, the air sharp, but the sun shining gloriously, and gleaming upon the snow which lay upon the roofs of the houses.

We drove through the old part of Munich, up the Residenz Gasse, which was all astir with the corn-market, and where the old women were as busy as ever in their little booths among their quaint earthenware, and through the old gateway of the *Rath-Haus,* and along the street called the *Thal,* which leads down to the Isar Gate, and is always crowded with long shambling wagons heaped up with casks and huge beer-barrels going to and fro from various great breweries which infest that neighborhood. Isabel felt inclined to be one continued *note of exclamation,* — so many strange, old-fashioned, foreign sights did we see.

Now we rattled through the Isar Gate, and Isabel turned round to observe the effect of the fresco-procession of the Emperor Ludwig of Bavaria; now I pointed out to her the Great Government Pawnbroking Establishment, where during Carnival time such extraordinary properties accumulate, — beds, spoons, cradles, clothes, — all for the sake of Carnival jollity; now we passed the barracks of the Cuirassiers, who wear the white cloaks which I so much admire; now we crossed the long Isar Bridge, and glanced up and down the river winding in the sunshine between its shoally banks; and we passed the *Volks-Theater*, and were in the midst of the Au suburb. Isabel looked everywhere around her, and was vastly amused at the queer little shops, the grotesque shrines, the fir-trées stuck up before little public-house doors, and the skeleton-like carts and lean horses, and the men in big cloaks, which everywhere met her eye. And now, driving across the open space where stands the Au Church, we alighted at one of its portals.

Isabel felt the whole spirit of those lovely, clustered stone columns which rise up in long rows like a grove of lofty palm-trees; their branches parting and petrified into a noble Gothic roof. Surveying all this beauty, we spoke of the fate of Ohlmüller, who died when scarcely forty years of age, before he saw this one great work of his brought to completion; and how he had offered up to it health and life itself, ascending the spire with incessant zeal, — he who had been a martyr from his boyhood to asthma. But may not this have been a type of the man's spirit, this undaunted aspiration which willingly would yield up life itself to ascend towards heaven? She looked round with delight upon the rich windows, through which the sunlight falling reflected rainbow tints upon the cold, grey, severe columns; this radiance of heaven glorifying earth, and turning its duskiness and hardness into gorgeousness and light! To Isabel it seemed as if the children, and youths, and old, old women, who were praying in the church, must certainly have come there as part of the picture prepared for our edification, so quaint and picturesque were they.

As we stood in the church we saw two women advancing from a door close to the high altar. One was a lady handsomely dressed in a white satin bonnet and large Cashmere shawl; she was followed by a nurse, bearing before her a little baby lying on a cushion and covered with a long white lace veil. It was evidently a christening. They passed on to a side altar, where, amid flowers and golden candlesticks, and gold and azure tracery, stood a figure of the Madonna and Child. The little infant, on its cushion, was placed upon the altar before the Virgin; the lady and the servant knelt together and prayed. It was a beautiful little scene.

Leaving the church we went to the Au Theatre. It was half-past three, and the performance was just beginning. It was a strange sensation that of stepping out of the fresh keen air and sunshine into the darkness and noise and hot atmosphere of the little theatre. We had the most aristocratic places, in a box where I have seen the royal princes before now; and for these we paid eightpence each. To see so good an audience at so early a performance would in England have been singular; such numbers of men, too, who with us would have been busy at their work till at the earliest six or seven o'clock. The piece was 'The Musketeers of the Quarter-Master's Lady,' or '*Wart a bisle.*' It was very droll and very capitally acted; and though, of course, Isabel understood hardly a word, she was greatly amused.

We drove home in the moonlight at six o'clock, and on reaching home found that Isabel's piano had arrived, so that there was another pleasure for us; and whilst I prepared tea she tried her new instrument.

CHAPTER XXX.

A MOURNFUL WEDDING. — AN INCURSION OF GERMAN TEACHERS. — THE STUDENT.

THE other evening, having called on Frau Amsel, whilst I sat talking with her a young lady came in almost out of breath, saying, 'Put on your bonnet, my dear, gracious lady, and let us go to the Basilica; there is a wedding there!'

'I will go with you,' said I, 'for I have never yet seen a Catholic wedding.'

We saw numbers of people crowding into the Basilica. It was growing dusk in the large church. A throng of spectators surrounded the space railed off round the high altar. Upon the marble steps leading up to the altar, and on either side, stood ladies and gentlemen belonging to the wedding party. The altar was decorated, as well as the flight of steps, with orange-trees, and palms, and flowering shrubs: but few candles burned upon the altar, and the lamp suspended from the roof, containing the ever-burning flame, seemed only to make the gathering twilight more perceptible. The white-robed priests, the bride and bridesmaids in their white muslin dresses, the tall black figures of the bridegroom and his friends looming out from the top of that long flight of marble steps; the monotonous voice of the priest droning forth his marriage homily; the damp raw air of a November evening striking to the hearts of all; the mighty figures of prophets, and angels, and martyrs upon the golden walls of the church, were shrouding themselves in duskiness and gloom; the feeble light of the tapers from the altar, illuminating nothing in the whole cold and solemn building save and except a huge golden crucifix, and farther off a lesser cross which gleamed out harshly and severely, and startlingly, as though the type of anguish, and suffering, and sacrifice, were to be the sole idea of life and marriage. All formed one of the most mournful scenes I ever witnessed, and quite haunts me even now when I recall it.

The priest prayed and joined their hands, and placed the rings upon their fingers; and one heard the money clink through the cold darkness, as the bridegroom, according to Roman Catholic custom, endowed his bride with his gold and silver, and his worldly goods. And whilst the priest still prayed, a tramp of feet, a sort of hushed roar, was heard through the church; and across the broad marble pavement came a train of black and white garmented priests, bearing funeral wreaths and banners: — they were returning from a funeral!

The bridal train descended from the altar, and as they moved onward towards the sacristy, preceded by priests, we caught a glimpse of the bridegroom and bride, who, by this cold light, looked as rigid and cheerless as the whole scene: two elderly ladies who followed were, I noticed, dressed in black, as though it were a funeral! And as they went on through the church, they passed the mourners of the other ceremony, who were praying in their weeds, and burning small tapers; and yet farther on, and still more in the gloom, and only revealed by a white cloth thrown over his face, as he sat in his confessional, they passed a priest shriving some poor penitent.

Was not this a cheerless wedding?

November 11*th.*—We have had an incursion of German teachers, in reply to Isabel's advertisement in the '*Neuesten Nachrichten.*' The time mentioned in the advertisement was nine o'clock on Monday morning. But on Monday morning, long before nine, the incursion began. We had just sat down to our little breakfast-table, and were about to enjoy our first cup of tea, when Madame Thekla popped her head in at the sitting-room door, saying, in her usual mysterious and hoarse whisper, 'that if we pleased, a lady was there asking if we wanted a German teacher!'

Isabel and I, sitting grandly upon our sofas, side by side, with the untasted breakfast before us, see a young and prepossessing girl enter very modestly,—we push the table aside, offer her a seat, and commence the necessary inquiries. We think she will do, and take her address; still we will not decide until we see who else offers.

'Let us only make haste and finish our breakfast!' cry we; but ring! ring! ring! we hear at the door.

'Isabel, we are in for it now!' exclaimed I; and before the words are spoken, Madame Thekla's head once more mysteriously appears in the doorway, and behind her looms forth a gaunt figure, wrapt in a long black cloak. The figure enters. The usual inquiries are made; we ask at what hours she could give the lessons, and she informs us 'It *muss* be afternoon,—I much to do in the *keetchin* morning,—I much to do,—I get marry in few weeks.' She would not do.

Ring! ring! ring! Great talk in the passage: the door opens for the *keetchin lady*, and a vision of bonnets looms once more in the distance in the shape of a queerish old mother and a pretty but coquettish daughter. Ring! ring! ring! We are aware of German teachers seated in Madame Thekla's kitchen, in Madame Thekla's little parlor, in Madame Thekla's passage, — of teachers standing upon the stairs!

We grow quite bewildered by nice faces and ugly faces, round faces and thin faces, red faces and sallow faces; by faces in pink bonnets and black bonnets, in blue bonnets and grey; by faces with curls and with bands, with hair *à la Chinoise;* by teachers who speak good English, and *small* English, and no English at all; by high terms and low terms; by certificates from Educational Establishments, and laudatory letters from learned professors; by accounts of lessons given to the ——, and the ——, and the ——; by conceit and affectation, and with touching poverty, and meekness, and gentleness. And now a slight pause came in the succession of applicants. We agreed that really we must put an end to the incursion. Among those we had already seen we must have found the right one. Madame Thekla must tell those who were yet arriving that the English lady had met with a teacher.

Then turning a deaf ear to all future ringings at the door, and to all chatterings of Madame Thekla, we drew a long breath after our exertions, and once more prepared our unlucky breakfast, by boiling fresh water over our spirit-lamp, and making a second edition of tea.

There was something affecting, in no slight degree, to us, in this rush to obtain a few Gulden a month. One could have grown quite sentimental over it, had not many of the ladies, old and young, giving themselves considerably absurd airs, informing us of what excellent and high-born families they were, and how their *real* reasons for answering the advertisement was, to practise their English. Perhaps it might be so!

Our feeling inclined still towards the young girl

who had first applied, — her sweet manner, her shabby dress and intelligent face, spoke loudly in her behalf. But the mother of another candidate contended with the sweet girl in our good will. Both Isabel's heart and mine had instantly warmed towards this lady; her face was such an anxious, kind face, and her voice had such a sad echo of sorrow in it, — it seemed to breathe sighs. Although we had conversed in German, and Isabel did not understand a word of what had been said between us, she had understood the tones and looks, and instantly agreed to suspend the decision until we had seen this lady's daughter. She was to call at half-past twelve.

At twelve I went out, leaving Isabel to see the young lady. On the stairs I met an ascending teacher, and, at the front-door, two more entering. I imagined every young lady I encountered in our street must still be a teacher.

November 14th. — There is now deep snow, but as I wanted to secure a model for Monday, and also to purchase tracing-paper, I went out immediately after breakfast, at an hour when most people are scarcely out of their beds in England, and quite enjoyed the walk, — all looked so exquisitely pure and calm. The cold here is much less difficult to bear than the cold of England, because of the dryness of the atmosphere. I went out, as I said, to buy tracing-paper, having come to the end of the supply I took with me, and I found it extremely dear. How strange it is that tracing-paper, which is so much used in Munich, should be so expensive!

You cannot think how picturesque the streets looked in the snow; snow covered the ground, pure as in the country: snow lay heavily upon the house-tops, and upon the different statues in the public squares, and drifted on carts and the roofs of carriages. People were wrapped up in the warmest of cloaks and coats, many with hoods picturesquely drawn over their heads; little lads were busy with their little wooden sledges; most quaint objects, many of them, in their hooded cloaks, looking like little grey, and brown, and black goblins. I greatly enjoyed my snowy walk; and it rejoiced my heart, in all the cold and winterly weather, to see the signs of busy industry which met me in the streets; I mean the signs of busy learning and study, which were quite in harmony with my frame of mind. First, there were lots of little boys and girls rushing out of a public school with their slates, and knapsacks, and bags; then there was the train of students returning from some lecture in the University, — handsome vigorous youths and young men, with their portfolios under their arms, and their faces full of intelligence and animation; — then, as I passed the *Conservatorium*, the Musical Academy, a loud sound of chorus-singing burst upon my ear, and from a door came forth a troop of boys, several of them very young and small, carrying their violin cases; — they had been learning.

What a beautiful thing, what a beautiful state is that of the student, after all! the very aspiration, endurance, patient labor, and uncertainty of this phase of human life, engendering faith, and hope, and love, and humility, throw a peculiar halo of beauty around it. I have often felt this, but never more strongly than to-day. It seemed to me that the acquiring, the accomplishing, was, as far as the soul itself is concerned, really more than the acquisition, — than that which is accomplished.

CHAPTER XXXI.

THE BOISSERÉE GALLERY IN THE PINAKOTHEK.

Accompany me this bright, frosty, winter's morning to the beautiful Munich Picture Gallery — the Pinakothek. The trees, and shrubs, and grass in the gardens, and lining the roads, as we approach the Gallery, are glittering with hoar-frost, and look as if molten in frosted silver. We have scarcely emerged from the streets of the newer portion of Munich. There rises the yet unfinished building of the New Pinakothek, destined to contain pictures of modern schools. Two frescoes of Kaulbach's series of designs illustrative of modern German art, already arrest your eye upon its external walls. The grey wooden booths, clinging as it were to the upper portion of the building, swallow-nest-wise, conceal the artists at work upon the other frescoes of the series. Divided from the New Pinakothek by a broad public road, and standing in a garden inclosed by slight, low, iron railing, we see the Old Pinakothek. It is built of pale yellow brick, and in the style of a Roman palace, after the design of Leo von Klenze. The long centre picture gallery is lighted by sky-lights of violet-colored glass, which give a very peculiar character to the whole building. The statues of five-and-twenty artists, from designs by Schwanthaler, Van Eyck, Memling, Dürer, Holbein, Schön, Rubens, Van Dyck, Velasquez, Murillo, Claude Lorraine, Poussin, Francia, Angelico da Fiesole, Masaccio, Leonardo da

Vinci, Perugino Ghirlandajo, Michael Angelo, Raphael, Titian, Bellini, Andrea del Sarto, Correggio, and Domenichino, keep watch and ward, — an immortal band, standing around the treasury of their works, and ennobling with a poetic thought the broad parapet of the Pinakothek.

We ascend a low flight of steps guarded by lions couchant; the tall portal opens as by magic, and we stand in the presence of a giant — a mild giant clad in the blue livery of the Bavarian court: a broad crimson and white band crosses the gigantic breast, huge top-boots adorn the gigantic legs, a peaceful smile beams over a placid giant face, — the celebrated giant porter of the Pinakothek nods us a morning greeting, and we hasten up a flight of broad, grey, marble steps, beneath a tinted roof, and catching on our way through a spacious window an expanse of this cloudless Munich heaven, against which rise in sharp relief the white artists' statues in long perspective line.

We enter a room hung with full-length portraits of Bavarian kings and electors in their royal robes: they are King Ludwig and his ancestors, who have gathered together the treasures preserved in the Pinakothek. King Ludwig comes of an art-loving race. In this room loiter the attendants and servants of the Pinakothek; and here you can buy a catalogue if you like; but we have already one with us — a very well-worn copy — an old friend: so we pass on into the next room, the first hall of the gallery, and containing the works of Albert Dürer, of his master Michael Wohlgemuth, and of Albert Dürer's disciples and imitators.

But not even here will we pause long this morning; you must come with me into this gallery of cabinets, which runs parallel with the central gallery of halls, and which said cabinets principally contain the famous pictures of the Boisserée Gallery.

This Boisserée Gallery is interesting from many points of view. When Napoleon had rifled Italy and Germany of their most precious works of art, and assembled them in the Museum at Paris in a grand exhibition in the year 1803, there might have been seen three young Germans day after day, week after week, month after month, studying these art-treasures, and studying especially certain quaint old pictures by an early German master. These youths were Sulpiz and Melchior Boisserée, together with their friend Johann Bertram, — all three from the good old city of Cologne. These quaint pictures in the Paris gallery reminded the three friends of certain pictures of a similar character which they remembered to have seen hanging in their childhood dim and forgotten in dusky side chapels and cloisters in their native city. These memories inflamed their imaginations, whilst their taste and understandings were being daily developed by the study of the noble works of art assembled in Paris, and by intercourse with Frederick Schlegel, then resident at Paris, and who delivered private lectures on philosophy and belles lettres to the three youths. A deep interest thus awoke within them for this early and almost forgotten school of painting — an interest which deepened gradually into an absorbing passion, and became the one object of their lives.

Returning to Cologne after a nine months' sojourn in Paris, and accompanied by Frederick Schlegel, they commenced an earnest quest after the old paintings which lingered in their memories like dreams.

Great changes had of course taken place in Cologne upon the suppression of the monasteries under Napoleon's rule; and the revolution occasioned among pictures was not the least of the revolutions. Strange tidings reached the three youths and Schlegel, of paintings used to patch dove-cotes with; of paintings turned into table-tops, and into screens; of paintings sold at auctions as make-weights, with 'lots' of old iron and other rubbish; and of paintings burnt for fuel. But upon nearer inspection these proved to be generally pictures of but little value, and of a much more modern date. The real old pictures were mostly still hanging in the dusky cloisters, or were concealed in garrets and vaults. A legend of their great intrinsic value lived yet in the popular mind, keeping them sacred, although the very existence of such works was forgotten by the *virtuosi* of the last century.

Several pictures of value also had been purchased by two art-lovers at Cologne, the Canon Walraff and the Merchant Lieversberg. But the glory of preserving and rescuing the greater number and the most valuable of the treasures was reserved for the Boisserées. We are told that one day meeting a hand-barrow in the streets of Cologne among a heap of lumber, the brothers discovered one of the gems they were in search of; this they purchased, and it became the nucleus of the gallery now bearing the brothers' name.

Wolfram of Eschenbach, one of the latest of the Minnesänger, sang, in the 13th century, in his romance of 'Parcival,' of the glory of certain wonderful painters of Cologne. Old chroniclers told of certain wonderful painters, Master Stephen and Master Wilhelm of Cologne: what now remained of their works — who knew more of them except a legendary renown? Yet even the works of these old masters were brought to light through faith, and love, and zeal. Strange old pictures they are with their gold grounds, revealing the fact that German as well as Italian art springs from Byzantine origin, and that Germany has had her Cimabues and Giottos.

Picture after picture thus came forth from its dusky

nook — Madonnas, saints, martyrs, burning in rainbow tints upon their golden grounds; years passed on in zealous labor, in journeys made into the Netherlands in quest of pictures, in research of all kinds: gradually the Gallery grew and grew. Goethe, Tieck, and Schlegel entering into the Boiserées' enthusiasm, a universal interest was excited throughout Germany for this early art, whose history was yearly emerging from its obscurity — link after link revealing itself in the almost forgotten chain. And how bright and clear are these links! First, these old semi-Byzantine masters of Cologne, with their disciples, the precursors by two centuries of Albert Dürer and his school; then the Cologne school transplanted into the Netherlands, the school of the Van Eycks, Hubert, John, and their sister Margaret; — these noble, fine Van Eycks, with their beautiful domestic attachment, their wonderful industry, their strong originality. John Van Eyck, the perfecter, if not the originator, of oil-painting; Margaret, the pupil and zealous assistant of her brothers — that steadfast woman 'who,' says an old chronicler, 'declined many offers of marriage with noble gentlemen for love and devotion to her art.' Are they not a noble trio? Then we have Hans Memling, the '*Memlino*' of the Italians, whose master he was in landscape painting, influencing Perugino and Raphael also. He is a beautiful vision in this art-history is Memling, with his exquisite tenderness and refinement, and his singularly romantic life — a mingling of the painter and the soldier. Now he is painting his St. Johns and Madonnas; now he is fighting for the Duke Charles of Burgundy; now he is lying sick and wounded in the Hospital of St. John at Bruges; now he is painting for the good monks who have tended him in his sickness the exquisite works which are yet preserved in the Hospital at Bruges as its greatest treasure.

Then we have Roger of Bruges, Hugo van der Goes, and others; Israel van Meckenem; Jahn de Mehlem; Quintin Matseys, of whom everybody has heard; Lucas van Leyden, that extraordinary man, a painter at twelve years of age, the admired friend and rival of Albert Dürer, and who died, it is said, of poison, administered to him by a less generous rival whom he had entertained upon his artistic and almost princely progress through the Netherlands; and so we come to Mabuse and Van Orley, and the Italianizers, and to the death of early Christian art in the Netherlands. Yes, it is a beautiful chapter in the history of art, is this early German and Flemish school, especially connecting it also with Albert Dürer and his school.

And to me one of the pleasantest passages in this chapter is the thought of the intense joy which must have transported the Boisserée brothers, as one after another these gems of art were drawn forth into the light, and old names and legends assumed the dignity of history, and this noble gallery was finally brought to its resting-place in this beautiful Pinakothek, purchased by King Ludwig as one of the greatest treasures of his kingdom, and preserved here as a noble monument to all — to the old painters themselves — to the zealous brothers Boisserée — and to the Art-King Ludwig.

But why do we linger at the threshold of these Cabinets? Let us enter and bathe our spirit in the poetry of these old pictures; let us listen to their teachings as though sweet antique legends were read to us in some quaint tongue out of an old missal! What a glitter of golden grounds blazes upon our vision in those pictures of Master Stephen and Master Wilhelm. Solemn, gorgeously robed saints are there leaning upon their attributes of martyrdom, their swords, their crosses, their wheels; they are old men all of them, yet in a green old age, and stand erect and statue-like, within golden niches of richest Gothic tracery.

Then, as we advance farther along the gallery of cabinets, descending nearer and nearer to our modern world, what a flutter meets us of rainbow-tinted wings, whose plumes are stolen from peacocks, doves, and parrots! Now we encounter fabulous scaly, green, scarlet, and azure dragons; but gallant youthful knights and angels, clad in armor dazzling and golden, are at hand with glittering spears and swords to slay the monsters. Ambrosial locks fly in the wind, a vigorous arm brandishes the keen spear, a mailed foot is planted upon the grisly dragon! — he is writhing in his death agony! And how one is bewildered by the stiff embroidered robes of priests, warriors and ladies, — robes gorgeous with every burning tint, and sparkling with every gem — jewel-encrusted are mitres, crosiers, copes and stoles, ladies' stomachers, and warriors' breast-plates. What wealth in golden and crystal goblets, in dagger-hilts and golden crucifixes! In what silent, old, wainscotted rooms do we not repose ourselves — what shady courts or crowded quaint city streets do we not gaze into through round-arched windows, sitting in upon scarlet-cushioned window-seats, and breathing the perfumed breath of some tall white lily rising out of a crystal or golden vase! And do we not hear the soft lisping of saints breathing their prayers as they bend over missals lying open upon carved ebony reading-desks! and do we not even hear the silvery tones from St. Cecilia's golden organ, as she touches its keys with her taper fingers, and tiny angels hover around, wafting her garlanded brow with their small wings and fluttering azure and rose-colored draperies.

And above all, do not our spirits take flight through the

most lovely of landscapes! through scenes such as one alone sees in dreams, or in these old pictures, across the most verdant meadows, where bloom the richest flowers; across broad lakes mirroring the purest of heavens, and where float majestic swans, and sweet large water lilies unfold their chalices. And now we toil up arid mountains, where the grass grows hask and yellow, and where here and there a slender tree quivers its delicate tracery of leaves and branches against a cloudless sky. But if we toil over stones and rocks it is only to command glimpses along vistas of lovely, enchanting, distant country; to overlook plains and ranges of blue mountain peaks; to see quaint hamlets, and castles, and towns, and convents, and fortresses sleeping upon the plains and crowning the mountain heights; whilst saints, and prophets, and warriors, and sages, pilgrimage through the meads and valleys, passing on their martyrdoms and to their glory. And it is ever spring, — clear, pure heavens of spring, — May verdure, May flowers; the very brooklets murmur and dance over their glittering pebbles and sand with a vernal gladness. It is the Spring of Art, with its clear, bright, tints unfaded, unmellowed by the storms and heats of summer. In Titian we have the gorgeous hues of mellow autumn, the scarlets, oranges, and crimsons deepened into solemn glory, by warm, dusky shadows, cast, as it were, by umbrageous groves, and contrasting richly against deeply blue autumnal skies. There is perfected beauty, solemn, gorgeous, yet with a certain pensiveness, as though the Hamadryads sat, with bowed heads, and arms folded over their breasts, amidst the falling leaves. But with these earlier masters it is still spring and childhood. They have the unquestioning faith, the unperfected knowledge, the deep love, joy, and simplicity of children's hearts: thus vernal odors float through their pure skies, thus their birds carol vernal songs, their leaves and flowers sprout and unfold themselves in vernal sunshine.

There are three little pictures of Memling, before which we must especially pause. They are well known by engravings, but without having seen the brilliancy of the color, and the delicacy and purity of the manipulation, but a faint idea can be formed of the peculiar charm of these pictures. In the engravings the quaintness of the drawing alone tells in grotesque harshness, and all harmony is lost.

These pictures are the Adoration of the Magi, and its two wings, upon one of which is painted St. John; upon the other St. Christopher. The Adoration, as usual, is represented as taking place in a singular abode — a mingling of ruined palace, cottage, and stable. A meek Virgin, draped in dark blue, with heavy white drapery falling around her pale face, holds upon her lap a grave little naked Infant Jesus, who stretches forth his tiny arms towards the adoring kings. Behind the Virgin, resting her folded hands upon the back of the Virgin's seat, and standing with modest downcast eyes, is a little waiting-maid. Beyond this group, and seen between slender porphyry columns, is a stable which has a round arched window, supported also upon marble columns. An ass and mule are seen eating in the stable, out of a manger. And one's eye wanders now through the porphyry columns into a farther and much gloomier apartment, where a bright fire burns. This dark room is divided by a low lath-and-plaster partition from the stable; and upon this partition is perched a pair of doves. It is extraordinary the detail of every kind crowded into these old pictures. And through the round arched window of the stable, and through the open door-way of the ruinous abode, we catch glimpses of round hills, green with the rich deep grass of later spring. Upon the summit of the nearest hill rises a beach-tree, spreading its verdant crown against the deepest, clearest, azure sky. A quaint town, of Lombardic architecture, shines out between the hills. Down the grassy slopes descends a train of gorgeously-attired horsemen and men on foot: these are the attendants of Gaspar, Melchior, and Balthasar, three kings, now entering the ruin to adore the meek and heavenly Infant. Gaspar, the eldest of the three, has a wrinkled brow and a benign aspect. He kneels before the Child, his aged hands folded together in quiet prayer. He wears a long scarlet, jewel-clasped, and fur-trimmed tunic, bound round the waist. At his knee lies his violet velvet gold-embroidered cap of mediæval cut. Melchior has sunk upon one knee on entering beneath the roof, and presents to mild old Joseph a rich crystal goblet. Another crystal and golden goblet stands upon a little table near to the Virgin, the offering of Gaspar. Melchior has a noble, manly countenance and bearing; both his face and figure are seen in profile, as he kneels there in his gold-embroidered crimson velvet tunic, which, parting at the side and confined round the waist by a gem-encrusted band, displays a sleeve and hose of deep blue velvet, and a gorgeously-wrought dagger hanging at his side. Crisp, wavy brown hair parts upon his forehead, flowing backward on to the shoulders, and a pointed beard gives a peculiar character to the whole head. The tradition is, that in Melchior, Memling has portrayed his patron and military general, Charles of Burgundy. He is a gallant gentleman of the fifteenth century; and among such must Memling himself have fought and feasted. Balthasar is of a still more youthful figure, and is entering from the meadow, bearing in his hand a third rich goblet. His costume is of violet velvet, and has a decidedly oriental character about it.

Grass and flowers spring up among the ruinous masonry

of a low wall, which divides us the spectators from this brilliant pageant. There is a rose-bush, every leaf and bud lovingly painted with the most delicate care; the dew and perfume seem yet to hang about them. There is St. John's-wort, too, with its pale golden blossoms; there are dandelions with their globes of fairy-down; there is a tuft of delicate-leaved maiden-hair; and a dusky orange snail crawls slowly along the broken, low wall, leaving his silvery, slimy track behind him. How lovely in these pictures are such little bits of nature, connecting us with the ideal of the middle ages through these simple weeds and flowers, and the tiny creatures dwelling among them, which, though human beings have long ago cast off their gorgeous array, yet burn in azure and scarlet dyes, and glitter in burnished coats of mail!

To the right of the Adoration, in its little wing, stands St. John the Baptist. Over his robe of camel's hair he wears a mantle of deep violet. He glances towards us with large, soft brown, eyes, pointing with his meagre fingers towards a gentle little lamb, which lies upon a scarlet-bound volume, supported on his left hand. It is in a meadow of rich grass and flowers where St. John is standing; a tall white lily has sprung up at his feet; before him gurgles a shallow brooklet, murmuring over pebbles and shells, which gleam brightly through the transparent water as they lie scattered over the golden sand. A brilliant kingfisher meditates amid the lush-weeds which overhang the streamlet's banks. Joyous little lizards play and dart to and fro across a sandy, rugged pathway leading up towards a beetling, top-heavy rock, which rises abruptly from the meadow. A similar crag rises again farther off in the meadow, approached by a pleasant pathway, winding up through a young oak-grove. Between these two rocky heights your eye wanders into an enchanting distance. There is a quiet lake lying amid smiling meadows; a quaint city rising upon the farther shore, and far, far away gleam the blue peaks of a mountain-chain. Across the calm lake sails a little boat; and through the pure heavens wing their way a rejoicing flight of birds.

In the other compartment of the little shrine we see St. Christopher approaching us through the transparent, sparkling waves, which are just murmuring into tranquillity after the recent tempest. The uprising sun gilds with warm beams the precipitous, rocky banks — of the Rhine! — Yes; for the Rhine, with its castle-crowned and vineyard-clad banks, has been transported into Palestine by the admiring Memling! The sunbeams bathe hills, rocks, vineyards, castles, and churches; the sunbeams tint with rose and violet the long streaks of retreating storm-clouds; and on through the emerald waves comes patient, old, obedient Christopher, bearing upon his stooping shoulders the little Christ-child, who blesses the whole world with three upraised fingers of his tiny hand. On comes the patient old man, with his dark azure tunic tucked up above his knees, and with a crimson mantle fluttering round him and the tall staff upon which he leans. But words can convey no image of the magic splendor of the tints, glowing, gorgeous, and liquid as the tints of a painted window, or of precious gems; nor yet of each minutest detail wrought out with most loving, delicate care.

How different in beauty to these child-like German pictures is an exquisite little Entombment of Christ, in one of the cabinets, of the early Italian school; yet it is, to a degree, kindred in spirit! It is one of several small pictures of Angelico which the Pinakothek contains, and has always strangely affected me. In Memling and Van Eyck our sympathies with the natural world are especially called forth; here Angelico touches with a spirit's hand our highest spiritual being. It is a very small picture, painted in tempera, and looks like a pale and faded water-color drawing. The colors are tender rose, tender blue, and grey, with golden tints for the hair, and gold for stars, and delicate tracery upon the draperies. The feeling produced upon my mind by this exquisite creation is as of an ecstatic vision seen by saint or martyr.

The figures are of course arranged with perfect symmetry. The lifeless form of Christ, supported behind by Joseph of Arimathea, rises in the centre, pale and stark; the wondrously noble head bowed on the breast, the eyelids with the shadow of death upon them — the whole tender, mournful, beyond the power of words to express. The rich golden hair falls in gentle waves from the pallid brow around the visionary countenance. The lower portion of the figure is draped in very soft, semi-transparent, white drapery, which hangs in perfectly symmetrical folds; the arms are stretched forth, as if upon the cross, but the hands drooping. The right hand is kissed by the Virgin Mary, the left by St. John. They both approach the figure of our Lord timidly, lovingly, half kneeling; their figures and heads are seen in profile; the attitudes are almost similar, and each is garmented in pale rose-colored and pale blue drapery. And how adoring, how tenderly, purely beautiful, are their countenances, filled with an unearthly grace — such grace as alone is seen in Raphael's early pictures, and in Angelico's. A golden star gleams upon the shoulder of the Virgin. Behind the figures rises the grey, formal sepulchre cut in the rock, above which are seen the tops of dark cypresses; dark grass, filled with tufts of formal grey and pale blue flowers, covers the ground; all is unreal, mysterious, symbolic, as if traced by the hand of a seraph rather than by the hand of man!

CHAPTER XXXII.

SLEDGING.

November 22d. — The great feature of this week has been sledging. Last Sunday was the first day that sledges made their appearance. For several days the snow had kept falling and falling, and the sky had continued of a sullen white with unfallen snow.

We felt certain that sledges must soon make their appearance, and talked about the poetry and romance of sledging. We recalled the sledgings in Miss Bremer's novels, and Frithiof, and old King Ring, and Hamilton and Hildegard's sledging adventure in that clever book the 'Initials,' and determined that when we had our drive in a sledge it also should be towards Nymphenburg, in memory of Hildegard and Hamilton's misfortunes.

And on Sunday afternoon we heard from the street a merry sound of bells — 'A sledge, Isabel! a sledge!' cried Anna. In a moment Isabel had rushed to the window, exclaiming in an excited voice, as she looked out, 'Oh, how pretty! how pretty! Come, Anna! *do* look at its scarlet trappings, at its fur lining, at the funny people wrapped up in it!' And Isabel was ready to clap her hands like a delighted child.

On Monday morning, as I entered the English Garden, and was admiring the heavy masses of snow which hung in fantastic forms upon the dark branches of a group of fir-trees, and was enjoying the purity, and silence, and beauty of the whole scene, a sharp, clear sound of bells rang through the frosty air; and skimming along the white smooth road which wound among the trees, came on a bright green and golden sledge, drawn by a brisk black horse, brilliant with scarlet trappings and musical with little bells. It was a peasant's sledge; and wrapt up in his cloak, and with a fur cap drawn down over his brows, and with fur gloves upon his hands, within it sat a burly peasant. So pretty was the whole thing, so gay and fantastic, that a little thrill ran through my nerves, and I was as perfect a child in my joy over the pea-green sledge as Isabel had been the day before.

In the course of Monday, sledges were to be seen everywhere. Sledges were seen standing before doors, without horses, as though people were bringing them forth from their summer retreats and were inspecting their state and condition, whilst others were being pulled along to blacksmiths and coach-builders to be repaired.

Gentlemen's carriages have begun to travel upon sledges instead of upon wheels — ditto droschkies, ditto fiacres — ditto peasants' carts — ditto laundresses' carts — ditto brewers' carts. Little lads, of course, go to school and return upon sledges instead of upon their own legs. Water-tubs and buckets, and milk-jars, or rather the wooden pails, hooped with brass, in which people here carry their milk about — all travel on sledges. Things and vehicles moving upon wheels or legs, one begins to consider very much out of fashion! Together with the droschkies and fiacres now put upon sledges, you see upon the stands sledges-proper — two-and one-horse sledges — green, blue, and yellow, grand, elegant, and shabby; and these sledges you see driving about in all directions, with their heavily cloaked and be-furred drivers generally standing up behind, *à-la-Hansom-cab*, and cracking their long lashed whips till the streets resound again. You see a couple of students in one sledge; — a whole family, father, mother, and a crowd of children, in a family sledge — you see a lady and gentleman alone — you see, perhaps, as I did last night, two fat citizenesses, one driving, with a couple of round-faced rosy children peeping out from under the apron of the sledge, and seemingly quite close under the horse's heels. You see a couple of Munich '*gents*,' — for there are such animals here — with big-buttoned coats, jaunty hats, and cigars in their mouths, driving a lean shambling horse at a furious rate, whilst they themselves seem ready to be *spilt* from their slight sledge any moment; and you see numbers of well-to-do big-boned peasants, rapidly skimming along in their sledges, which all bear a striking resemblance to each other, being green, often of painted wicker-work, and quaintly adorned with gilt tracery-work, which looks as though it were of iron gilt.

In order to see as much winter life as possible, I have varied my walk to the studio these last several mornings, by going down through the Hof-Garten, where, by the by, three days running, at the same hour and upon the same spot, I have encountered, buttoned up to the chin in his warm furred coat, his Majesty King Max, taking his morning walk, and then I have wended my way down an old street which leads to the St. Anna Vorstadt. And upon these walks I have not only seen all these varieties of the *genus* sledge, but also soldiers emptying out of long heavy carts loads of snow into the branches of the Isar, which flow through the town, and met processions of laundresses which have vastly amused me. In the early morning they were entering the city with clothes-baskets and bundles, piled up ever so high upon wooden sledges, which they both drew along and pushed. The sledges were not few in number, and the procession was rendered yet more fantastic from gay-colored dresses and white petticoats, borne aloft like pennons upon long poles ! All bright and fresh in the clear winter's morning, their comely faces glowing with exercise and the sharp air, their gowns and gay handkerchiefs as clean and bright as their faces, these laundress-maids and matrons looked wondrously attractive. Just picture to yourself this train winding along through the old street, white and crisp with its snow, and tell me whether, together with a pea-green sledge rushing along here and there, and every now and then a group of peasants, men and women, cutting up wood before the houses, the scene was not quaint and pleasantly foreign ? These groups of cutters of wood are very amusing. The man — for the group usually consists of one man and two women — the man in a chocolate or pale pink cotton jacket, black velvet breeches, and black top-boots, chopping away upon a heavy block which he has placed upon the causeway; the women in pink or blue cotton boddices, with large wadded *gigot* sleeves, and scarlet or green, or scarlet *and* green mixed, woollen petticoats, and with black or white kerchiefs tied over their heads, one sawing pieces of wood in a skeleton-like sawing machine, the other carrying away, in a wooden basket on her back, the cut and sawn pieces of wood through the heavy arched door or rather gateway of the house.

But to return to sledging and to *our* sledging. On Tuesday afternoon the sun shone out gloriously, and casting long gleams on the studio floor through the high windows, my eyes glanced up and encountered, smiling through leafless branches flecked with snow, such a lapis-lazuli heaven that I forthwith put away my drawing, and some twenty minutes later stood in our little sitting-room, startling Isabel with my exclamation of 'On with your cloak! quick! quick! we will go in a sledge to Nymphenburg! — Hurrah for Hamilton and Hildegard, we will honor their memories by the self-same drive, on the self-same day!' Isabel was much pleased with the scheme. Fräulein Sänchen was dispatched to bring us the handsomest sledge she could find on the stand, with *two* handsome horses. We made a hasty dinner, whilst the good old soul bustled off, wrapt ourselves up in all our warm things, and were ready by the time musical and significant jingling of bells was heard beneath our windows. Our sledge — I grieve to record it — was a bright yellow! I am sorry for this, seeing that a bright yellow vehicle of any description is an eyesore to me. However, we will regard it as a *golden* sledge.

Our horses were very wild — at least in appearance, — our driver a perfect monster, in his dark blue cloak, edged with brown fur at the sleeves and round the deep cape. Our trappings were scarlet, the lining of our sledge dark blue. We, ourselves, you may picture in thick veils and furs, and black hooded cloaks. Away we started; the long whip cracked again and again in artistic flourishes, its echoes resounding through the quiet streets, and, together with the horses' bells, making a tremendous riot. Isabel was quite alarmed because everybody in the street stopped to look after us.

'Of course they do, Isabel, of course; — don't *we* stop and look after every sledge as it dashes past? — it is only proper respect to the early sledges of the season.' And on we dashed.

The sun shone upon the long lines of delicately tinted houses, pale pinks, stone colors, greens, and salmons; the tall roofs were dazzling with snow; the sledges and groups of people we passed in the streets looked brilliant patches of colors, contrasting against the whiteness of the road, and shone upon by the bright sun. We drove out towards the vast plain; the sun was beginning to sink slowly into an abyss of molten gold, which revealed itself behind a gigantic range of mountain-like clouds of lilac and amber; the tall obelisk burnt in the rays of the setting sun till it appeared a mighty tongue of fire leaping up into the azure heavens; the sun-beams lay upon the broad doors of the Glyptothek, gleaming like flame; the statues, the columns and pediment, both of the Glyptothek and of the Corinthian Temple facing it, were tinted with the warm light, and rose from the expanse of snow beyond, in sharp outline, and of the most exquisite, creamy hue. And before us lay the plain, — dreamy, dazzlingly white, — with long shadows falling across it of delicate azure, with trees and villages in the middle distance of ethereal greys, and so tender, so unreal in their coloring, yet, at the same time, so distinct in their contour, that one was transported with delight.

We passed beneath one of those long beams suspended across the roads, painted with winding stripes of the Bavarian colors, which are seen here in lieu of turnpike gates — entered a road lined with trees on either hand — ascended a slight hill — breweries and wayside beer, and coffee-houses and small villas skirting the road, and having again reached the level ground, were in the Nymphenburg *Allée*, as it is called.

But behold! a mist, dense, blue, and cold, approached us! We could not see a hundred — nay, not fifty — not twenty yards before us. Yet, behind us, lay Munich in the clear sunshine. Mist rose rapidly and stealthily from the snowy plain. To the right hand and to the left mist blocked up the avenue. How strange! There was nothing for it but immediate return, — there was no Nymphenburg that day! The pedestrians, horses, drivers, and riders of various degrees who approached us, or passed us on their way towards the city, presented a singular appearance: beards, hair of man and beast, and the fur of their cloaks and trappings, were covered with a white rime, — they appeared suddenly to have gone grey.

As rapidly as possible we returned to Munich, where all was still so pleasant in the evening sunshine, that we continued our drive. We drove past the Basilica, across the Dult Platz, and through the most frequented streets till we entered the Ludwig Strasse, which, in winter, is the great afternoon parade of Munich. People, as usual, were promenading up and down the noble street, and sledges and carriages were rapidly driving to and fro. All looked most bright and gay. As we glided along, we both decided that the Ludwig Strasse was wearing an extremely handsome face that day. Now we skimmed past Duke Max's palace, past the Royal Library, where the colossal statues of Aristotle, Hippocrates, Homer, and Thucydides, throned aloft, looked more than usually solemn and venerable from the snow-hoods and draperies fallen upon them; past the Ludwig's Church, the white slender towers of which cut boldly against the pure rosy evening sky; past the *Damen Stift*, the University, the Jesuits' College, the now silent fountains, and emerging beneath the Triumphal Arch, found ourselves in the long poplar avenue leading to Schwabing.

We had just time to drive as far as Schwabing for Isabel to have a dim and dreary glimpse of the Church, where is the picturesque Overbeck gallery, and of the house where dwells the little old woman with the throng of children, and of the yet more distant church with the pea-green spire: but all was now cold, snow, ice, and icicles, — so away we sped home again to our comfortable tea-table, our driver cracking his whip yet louder and longer, and in one of his evolutions nearly carrying off poor Isabel's nose. And this was the more unkind, as I discovered that this day happened to be her birthday!

November 26th. — To-day we had another holiday, thanks to the attraction of sledging. Isabel was overjoyed when once more Anna suddenly returned from the studio proposing a fresh attempt to reach Nymphenburg. Fräulein Sänchen was again dispatched for a sledge, — the very handsomest she could hire, — and for Anna's new bonnet from the milliner's; for Anna, *at length,* was going to relieve her conscience by making a call, only too long due, at Madame de ———'s.

Sledge and bonnet arrived in due time, and well had Fräulein Sänchen executed her commission: she clapped her poor old bony hands with satisfaction and joy, the good old Fräulein! as she ran into our sitting-room all crimson-nosed from the frosty air, and bidding us to look out of the window at the magnificent sledge which she had brought. It was a magnificent sledge which we had greatly admired on the Odeon Platz, — large and white, lined with scarlet cloth, and covered in with a leopard skin, — two tall golden ornaments in the front, crowned each with a golden bunch of grapes,—but the supreme grandeur of the whole were plumes of white and blue feathers, which nodded upon the horses' heads! The driver and his horses were in keeping with the sledge — was it not magnificent indeed? A fit equipage to convey ladies to an ambassador's house?

But ah! the Russian lady, the Frau Oberstin, who lives at the end of our street, and who, unluckily for the hard-working English girls, has taken a great fancy to them, she and her six little boys! — also had thought the sledge magnificent! The elder two of the six little fellows, going to their afternoon school, had met Fräulein Sänchen as she returned in the sledge, and had, after setting up a shout of recognition and admiration, besought leave to mount 'into the glorious sledge just for a tiny drive,' — but the burly be-furred driver had cracked his long whip unfeelingly, and sped past the 'little grey goblins,' as hand-in-hand they stood upon the pavement, with the hoods of their grey cloaks drawn over their heads, gazing after the departing glory with big round brown eyes. But as the handsome sledge dashed round the corner of —— Strasse, the portly figure of the gay Frau Oberstin had appeared among the ivy-wreaths of her window, the casement had flown open, and the good-humored face of the lady, and the golden locks and rosy cheeks of a third child had leaned out into the sunshine, and a clear little voice had rung through the frosty air, reaching Fräulein Sänchen's purposely deaf ears, with the cry of 'We come, we come!'

And assuredly they did come! Anna, listening to the old Fräulein's description of the Frau Oberstin's sudden apparition at the ivy-wreathed casement, gave a violent jerk of vexation to the strings of her new bonnet, when in burst the smiling, uninvited guest, brilliant in an elegant *toilette*, with the golden-haired Adelbert springing around her, and his blue and white plumes bobbing about like mad things.

'Here we are, my dear young ladies, you see; come to drive out with you in the splendid sledge, — you know you couldn't possibly drive out by yourselves — it does not look well! and it's just what I've been wanting all day. I was terribly moped; and Adelbert, my *Würmchen*, didn't you want a drive in the beautiful sledge? Oh!

we'll have such a charming drive, won't we, dear young ladies!' exclaimed the good Oberstin, with the most delightful self-assurance.

A cloud passed over our brows; but the Frau Oberstin wore such an elegant blonde veil, and little Adelbert was so blinded by his curls and his feathers, that probably neither of them could see the dark looks of their proposed companions.

'We are going to make a call upon Madame de ———,' observed Anna, in a cold voice.

'Oh, never mind that, Fräulein *Ovitt;* never mind *that!* We'll sit in the sledge whilst you call.'

'I fear you will scarcely find room in the sledge, Frau Oberstin,' observed Isabel.

'*Not room!*' ejaculated the portly dame. '*Not room!* my dear Fräulein; it's the largest sledge in all Munich! there would be room and to spare for all my six boys! And, by the by, I dare say we may meet Ludwig and Max returning from school when we return from our drive, or the nurses somewhere with Luitpold, Otto, and the baby; and you wouldn't mind — now would you? — though you always *do* pretend to say you are not lovers of children, — to take some of the dear *Würmchen* for a drive. It *is* such a beautiful day, and *such* a large sledge!'

It was certainly not agreeable to have your sledge forcibly taken possession of by uninvited companions. But out in the sunshine, when the handsome lady, seating herself in the best seat, with every possible grace arranged Adelbert between Isabel and Anna, demanding from them 'whether, now, they really did not think it was a very splendid thought her going with them?' they were forced to relax in their vexation, and smile.

Madame de ——— was not at home; so leaving cards,

away we dashed past the little house with its golden balcony formerly inhabited by Lola Montes, but not in the direction of Nymphenburg! The Frau Oberstin had already decided that our drive must be to the Au-Meister in the English Garden, — had given, in her loud tone of command, directions to the driver, — and away to the English Garden we were now speeding.

Away we dashed through the streets, every body turning round to admire the splendid sledge, across the Odeon Platz, where stand the statues of Gluck and Orlando di Lasso, which to-day in the sunshine looked extremely well, as you caught the gleam of their tawny bronze against a back-ground of dazzling snow and a heaven of summer blue; and through the archway of the Arcade we dash into the Hof-Garten. All looks especially gay this winter's afternoon: people walking under the arcade; people walking about over the crisp trodden snow beneath the formal rows of leafless trees which fill the square. On one hand stretches the garden-front of the Palace, its pediment crowned by the allegorical figures of the different provinces of Bavaria, and its façade gay with decorations in a style to my taste too much resembling French plumb-box ornament; but which, nevertheless, looked bright and cheerful in the wintry weather. Before us lies a long, white, many-windowed building, with steep and dormer-windowed roofs — a barracks. Behind us, and to our left hand, the arcade, the frescoes and dull scarlet walls, and groups of statuary which shine out, from beneath long rows of rounded arches, pleasantly enough, as you catch transient glimpses of them between the leafless trees. This Hof-Garten fresco decoration one might give as about the worst specimen of Munich art; but truly to-day the *effect* was good. Among the promenaders in the Hof-Garten, — it is of course a great resort of nurses and children, — we found one of the Frau Oberstin's nurses, — the one who wears the pretty Munich costume. The baby was asleep on a pink cushion laid upon a little wooden sledge, and sleeping he was drawn over the beaten snow. Fat little Luitpold was toddling beside the picturesque nurse-maid.

The Frau Oberstin instantly catching sight of the group, had Luitpold transferred with lightning rapidity from the snowy ground to the warmth of the grand sledge. There would have been no use in remonstrance from us, could we have hardened ourselves into sufficient ungraciousness. And when the little fellow shouted with glee, and hid his little hands under the leopard-skin, seeking with much merriment to catch hold of his brother's hands, and their blue and white plumes danced together as gaily as the plumes upon the horses' heads, we gradually called forth our latent amiability.

'Surely,' observed the complacent Frau Oberstin, 'to-day we shall meet the Royal sledges; they are a fine sight! And *we* look so handsome, with these dear children, that really I should not object to it!'

But we did not meet the Royal sledges.

We met, however, troops and troops of people streaming out of the English Garden, as though it had been summer. And summer it might have been, judging from the sunshine, and deep, clear, joyous sky above us. Of a truth the day was a delightful blending of the beauty of summer sky and winter landscape.

Now we swept past some grand old beech-tree, whose mossy boles and venerable twisted roots, still strewn with ruddy leaves, rose green and sylvan from amidst the expanse of spotless snow; now past a clump of shrubs whose crimson twigs and stems were a flush of warmth; now we greeted with delight fantastic bowers of clematis which festooned the forest-trees, and bore upon their myriad entwined and slender fingers wreaths and masses of snow, beautiful and soft as clustering blossoms.

We might have been travelling through an enchanted forest, such lovely gems hung from the branches. Here rich bunches of the scarlet dog-wood berries mingled with black berries of the privet — coral and jet; a golden leaf fluttering here and there; and ever and anon a slender pendant icicle catching the sun-beams, flashed out from an over-hanging branch like a diamond dagger.

We met many sledges so bright in color, that if one has compared the berries and icicles to gems, one is tempted to call these sledges flowers which have come out in winter to adorn the pleasant garden. That large flaunting sledge, yellow 'picked out' with red, must be a tulip; that comfortable, compact little 'turn-out' certainly is a ranunculus; here we have a deep blue larkspur, and there, in the modest, quaint peasant's sledge of green and gold, we have the pleasant, common, golden buttercup, half buried in its rich green leaves! And we, too, with our scarlet cushions and our azure plumes, we must be a bouquet of lovely lobelias! No, it would have been more correct to liken sledges to brilliant birds, or to gorgeous, swift, and cheerily singing insects, for all have their sharp clear chime and jingle of bells, as they sweep along! Our bells were silver, — a gradation of bells, and, therefore, of sound. The bells were hung within a steel bow which was arched above either horse's neck! Pleasant and gay was their ringing in the enchanted forest!

We have passed the round temple-like pavilion standing upon its high mound, and which always in summer, when seen amid leafy trees and across an expanse of flowers, reminds me of the Temple of Hymen as depicted in valentines, and towards which a very yellow-haired and rosy-cheeked Cupid is conducting a blue-coated swain and a bashful maiden in white frock and pink sash. We have passed various pretty rustic bridges spanning branches of the Isar which dash and foam over mossy stones, — we have passed the lake, now one sheet of snow-covered ice, over which a crowd of skaters is careering, — we have passed various disconsolate looking and deserted summer-houses and coffee and beer resorts, where now snow lies in thick piles upon tables and benches; and now we are in a part of the Garden which is quite new to us. Here and there among the trees we notice little wigwams made of grass and reeds: have we reached, then, the abode of woodland elves? Ah! there are the elves, crimson and green, with brilliant sparkling eyes peeping at us from out the underwood, and flitting across our path.

The little boys are enchanted, — we are in the Pheasantry! Now we have arrived at the Au-Meister!

'What *is* the Au-Meister?' asked we, full of curiosity.

'Only a little Wirthshaus!' returned the Frau Oberstin.

'Very good coffee at the Au-Meister! gracious ladies!' observed our big, jolly driver, turning round with a face red and circular as the sun which was setting behind the wooded horizon; — 'And very good beer too!'

But neither attraction persuaded us to alight from the splendid sledge; and our driver turned his horses' heads towards Munich with a very dissatisfied countenance when commanded so to do by the Frau Oberstin's strong voice.

CHAPTER XXXIII.

A STUDENTS' TORCH PROCESSION.

December 1st. — Frau v. Amsel brought us word to-day that there would be this evening a torch-procession of the students in honor of one of the favorite professors of the University. It had been extremely foggy all day, and it was feared this might interfere with the effect of the spectacle. The mist, however, seemed to be driven away by the torches as they came up the broad Ludwig Strasse like dancing fiery tongues, hundreds and hundreds of them, in two long lines, up either side of the magnificent street, casting their ruddy glow upon the parapets, statues, Byzantine mouldings and arches of the noble buildings. Every object was illumined with a burning glow.

We had taken our station upon the broad flight of steps of the Damens Stift, which faces the Ludwig's Church; and thus commanded a good view up and down the street. The students assembled in front of the University, which is at the lower end of the Ludwig Strasse, nearly filling with their numbers the wide space between the University and the Jesuits' College. There the torches were lighted, and then each student bearing his torch, the procession — preceded and followed by a band of musicians, playing marches alternately — advanced along the street.

Imagine these two approaching streams of torches, borne in the hands of youths and young men quaintly attired in hooded cloaks, or in black velvet coats, and each student wearing a small tricolor skull-cap of the colors of his corps, and with his corps-band crossing his breast. As the torches burned down, the youths, to refresh the flame, struck them on the ground, leaving as they marched along streaks and sparks of fire behind them. Here and there, at certain distances up the centre of the broad street, between the lines of torch-bearers, strode the signors of the different corps, one by one, in full costume of black velvet coat, with a broad tricolor scarf crossing the breast, with white leather breeches and huge black shining boots, which reached above the knee, with spurs and jingling sword-sheaths ringing upon the frosty earth, and bearing in their hands gleaming naked swords.

Up the centre also slowly progressed, here and there, an open carriage, in which sat students wearing their tricolor corps-caps, but otherwise dressed as if for a ball, in black coats, white waistcoats, white cravats, and white kid gloves. These were the students deputed to wait upon the favorite Professor.

The ruddy torch-light flared upon the groups of spectators crowding the causeways; upon the sepctators leaning from windows; upon the broad portals and white façade of the Ludwig's Church, bathing in warm light the rounded arches, the sculptured saints and capitals, whilst the two slender towers faded away gradually and mysteriously into the upper darkness and coldness of night. The torches with their columns of ruddy smoke swayed to and fro, here leaping up and casting their crimson glow upon some fair-haired and delicately featured youth, or upon the gigantic stalwart corps-signor who strode beside him, and whose brawny proportions, closely-cropped red hair and burly beard, and gleaming broad-sword, showed forth wildly in the unearthly light like those of some old German knight of the middle ages. Further down the street the torches flitted and danced like hundreds of fire-flies.

Leaving the Ludwig Strasse and crossing two or three squares, we found the fiery tongues flitting through a grim old gateway, which leads into the older portion of the city. They cast their red illumination upon many a heavy balcony, upon many a quaint old-gabled house, upon many a dingy frowning portal, upon many an antiquated shop. Their red light flared also upon a house with a long row of high windows running along the ground-floor, and which were defended with iron stanchions, quite prison-like. It was a great school of boys; and all these windows were crowded with animated boyish faces, rosy, pale, plump, meagre, handsome, plain — illumined with eagerness as well as by the torch-light. You saw how the little fellows burnt with desire for the time when they, no longer prisoners, should, as free, jovial, and admired '*Musen-söhne*,' march gallantly through the streets with music, torches, and loud shouts of 'Victoria, Bavaria!' At length the procession paused; the musicians arranged themselves on either side of a somewhat humble-looking house. The corps-signors grouped themselves in the centre of the street opposite.

Was this small, almost mean-looking dwelling, then, the home of the beloved and learned professor, in whose honor the whole University had come forth in such gallant array? Or must not the professor rather live in one of the two lofty antiquated and imposing mansions which rose to the right and left of the humble abode? Yes, the professor probably would come forth and address his pupils from that heavy balcony of fantastic iron-work which adorned the larger of the two imposing mansions. But no! there is no festive look about the great houses. About the little house there is an expectant air. Lights shine through the four windows of the middle story. In one window burns a taper; another window is open.

Soon the students who have arrived in carriages descend and enter the house; they may be seen in the lit-up room conversing with a grey-headed gentleman. The two bands of musicians greet the great professor with music. One of the students calls forth a congratulation from the street; the grey-headed gentleman leans out from the open window, and in a low voice, whose tones scarcely reach us where we stand, addresses a few words to the crowd below. The signors clash their swords together; there is a loud but brief hurrah! the music bursts forth once more; again the professor bows from his window, and a lady gazes down upon the crowd from the window where burns the taper. A glimpse is caught of the student-deputies drinking wine within the professor's lighted rooms; and the train of torches once more moves along.

The procession again wound through the picturesque streets, passed beneath another grim old gateway, and emerged upon a large square. Here the torch-bearers forming into a vast ring, the quaintly-attired corps-signors, with their brandished swords, stood in the centre, with the musicians on either hand. The voices of the many hundred students burst forth like the murmur of the ocean into the solemn *Guadeamus Igitur*. Then, clashing their swords, the signors shouted a loud 'vivat!' for their University and Academic freedom, and at once hundreds of burning torches were flung whirling and flaming through the air; then falling, formed two pyres, where they burnt down gradually, and smouldered; first, however, sending up vast masses of red flame and columns of dusky crimson smoke, which cast a fantastic lurid glare upon the rapidly departing crowds.

December 2d.—Isabel is bending down over her slate, writing various profound questions out of Ollendorf's Grammar about 'Have you my ass's hay? No, I have not your ass's hay; but I have the hay of my neighbor's ass.' She is everlastingly puzzling her brain with such questions, till I wonder that she does not go quite crazy, and frequently startles me with the interrogation, 'Has the baker's dog got the fine golden collar? No, the dog of my brother's tailor has the fine golden collar.'

Apropos of dogs and dog-collars. To-day I asked what had become of my old friend Carlo, that beautiful dog which, in the statuette of Kaulbach, lies at his feet looking up lovingly into his face; and I learned—what I had feared would happen—that the poor, old, handsome beast, with his blind eye, was *dahin*—had disappeared from the surface of the earth! 'Ah! he was done for at the last dog-examination!' was the reply.

'Dog-examination?' asked I, forgetting for the moment how the dogs here are looked after and examined by the police as though they were human beings.

'Yes! he was condemned by the police to die at the last examination, and he exists no more.'

I told Isabel, when I returned home, of poor old Carlo's fate; and after dinner, when in a very lazy mood we were lying each upon our sofa, and had commissioned Fräulein Sänchen to prepare our coffee, we began questioning her about these public 'dog-days,' whilst she stood superintending the boiling of the milk over the spirit-lamp. She told us that each quarter of the town is summoned to present its dogs upon a certain day, twice a year, to the police; and that then, the state of health of each dog being ascertained, every dog in good health receives a little ticket, which is hung round his neck. Fräulein

Sänchen was surprised that we had never noticed these little metal labels. Any dog found without his label is liable to be killed by the police. All dogs pronounced dangerous, ill, or very old, are destroyed, and buried at a certain spot near Sendling, which is the grave-yard of all the dogs and horses of Munich.

'Fräulein Sänchen,' said I, much interested about this horrible spot, 'is it there that the public execution of criminals takes place?'

'No, gracious Fräulein! people are beheaded on the Theresien Wiese.'

'Have *you* ever, Fräulein Sänchen, seen a beheading?' I inquired with a shudder, knowing that most Munich women of her class hasten to witness executions as an ordinary excitement.

'Certainly,' she replied: she had witnessed the executions of two criminals often spoken of in Munich — the soldier-servant, who murdered the young wife of his master and her maid; and the man who had killed an old priest two or three years ago.

The accomplice of this man I had seen in the Au Prison, where he is confined for life. It is seldom that the law of capital punishment is carried into execution in Bavaria. I understand that King Ludwig had a peculiar horror of signing a death-warrant; and this accounts for so many murderers being confined in the Au Prison. There are rumors of a law being now in contemplation by which the execution of criminals in Bavaria shall be closed from the eye of the public — shall alone be witnessed by certain deputed officials. And when one meets with instances of women, usually tender-hearted, such as Fräulein Sänchen, hastening to witness one public execution after another with *gusto*, one desires that the law were already passed. From Fräulein Sänchen I derived the following ghastly picture.

Early in the forenoon the condemned criminal is conducted from the prison to the Stadt-Gericht (Court of Justice), in the old portion of the city. The unhappy man is bareheaded; his hair and beard are cut quite close; he is clothed in a grey or black blouse of woollen stuff; upon both breast and back is hung a placard, setting forth the particulars of his crime; he is seated in a peasant's wagon; two priests attend him,—Catholic, if he be Catholic,—Lutheran, if he be Lutheran. Gendarmes follow the wagon; a dense crowd presses around. The procession halts before the windows of the Court-house. The solemn judge appears; he reads the condemnation of the criminal; he breaks a staff. 'The staff is broken—the words are spoken!' he exclaims. There is a death-like silence. The criminal looks up towards his judge. The bells of all the churches begin to toll; the procession moves onwards; the multitude grows and grows.

What a mighty ocean of spectators are awaiting the procession upon the Theresien Wiese in the midst of this soft May-rain! There rises a tall scaffold. Upon the scaffold is a chair; behind the chair stands a man in black; beside the chair is a bier; and beside the bier stand gendarmes. The criminal, in his grey frock, and with his staring labelled breast and back, ascends the scaffold. The man in black comes forward, beseeching pardon from the miserable man for the deed he is about to perform. The criminal's eyes are bound with a handkerchief; he is led towards the chair; he is placed in it. The man in black with his long sword strikes a terrible blow from behind, through bone and muscles and arteries! Two — three blows, perhaps, he strikes! — such things have been. Forth spouts the crimson life-blood like a hideous fountain, — there is a rush of people with handkerchiefs to be steeped in the warm gore, as charms against sickness and misfortune, — and the spectacle is over!

CHAPTER XXXIV.

STREET-MUSIC. — THE ANTIGONE.

December 11*th.* — Yesterday morning, Isabel heard for the first time mass performed in the Hof-Kapelle: those grand chants pealing through the golden and frescoed galleries affected her imagination as much as I had expected. After we came out of the chapel we did as the rest of Munich did, went to hear the military band play at 12 o'clock, beneath the Feldherrn-Halle, as it is called, — a beautiful portico which terminates the Ludwig Strasse, at the end opposite to the Sieges-Thor. This portico is very beautiful, built by Gärtner, upon the plan of Orcagna's Logia dei Lanzi at Florence. Three noble round arches, rich with sculptured devices, rise upon slender columns from a flight of broad steps. Two bronze statues, designed by Schwanthaler, are placed within the portico: they are of Tilly and Prince Wrede.

Beneath the Logia the military band of the Haupt-Wach plays every day at 12 o'clock, and as they play remarkably well, and choose good music, it is a great resort of the Munich people, especially on Sundays.

As we disliked the gossiping crowd in the street, we posted ourselves at a window of a public gallery in the palace, which overlooks the scene. Imagine now a military band ravishing our ears with strains from 'Norma' or the 'Zauber Flöte,' and imagine the street — square, almost one must call it — the Ludwig Strasse having widened out here into the Odeon Platz — crowded with motley groups. As to-day happened to be very cold, with snow lying upon the ground, the crowd principally consisted of gentlemen. This fact, however, did not prevent the scene being very gay in color, and picturesque in cut of garb. At these twelve-o'clock concerts, the students of the University always muster in great numbers. Their scarlet and green, and white and crimson caps, and caps also of three colors combined, tell out very gaily. Many of them also wear *Bernouses*, lined with blue or crimson like a woman's cloak; those who wear neither *Bernouse* nor mantle will have a bright-colored scarf twisted round their throats, deep-blue, or green, or parti-colored. Their bright youthful faces increase greatly the effect of their fantastic array, and as their long beautiful hair floats back from their brows in the wind, an onward look of 'Excelsior' is given to many a face. But all the students' countenances are not beautiful, or filled with an eager aspiring — there are numbers of ordinary and of 'devil-may-care' faces.

There, too, assemble 'Philistines' as well as students — to use student phraseology. Here are Munich Exquisites in light kid gloves and spruce hats, and with gold-headed canes daintily held in their well-gloved hands, and more picturesque specimens of 'Philisterium' in felthats of every shape and hue, and with brigand-looking cloaks; here are lean and burly and bloated citizen-folk — here are officers and privates from every Bavarian regiment, and here is also a sprinkling of Tyroleans. That is a very picturesque group now crossing the square. Three men and one woman, all handsome, with clear eyes and bright complexions; the men have short curling beards, and wear tall hats of black felt, adorned with heavy gold tassels; they have broad green bands crossing their scarlet waistcoats, dark green coats, and black velvet breeches. The woman looks most demure and modest, following the men, and never raising her eyes from the ground: she is very gay in her costume also. She has a tall black felt-hat, with a gold tassel, a black boddice, and gorgeous pink sleeves and petticoat.

As it was such a cold day, many ladies had taken refuge, like ourselves, in the gallery of the Palace, and the row of gallery windows being lined with female faces, caused many looks and smiles to be directed up towards the windows from the crowd below. And these eyes and these smiles no doubt caused many other smiles and some blushes to pass over the faces at the windows. We noticed a very pretty blush pass over a pretty face encircled by a pink bonnet standing just before us.

But the musical quarter of an hour was over! The music suddenly ceased: the soldiers descended the steps of the portico, and first having deafened us with their frightful drumming, marched past the Theatine Church, which faces this side of the Palace, and which, with its domes and heavy *renaissance* architecture, formed our background to the motley crowd. The soldiers turning the corner of the Odeon struck into a lively march, — as usual disturbing the sermon of good Mr. Smith, preaching, in a room of the Odeon, his good sermon to the good respectable congregation which constitutes the English Church at Munich.

I must confess we had felt rather wicked as we encountered on our way to the Hof-Kapelle all the good English folks wending their way thither; — English embassy in its carriages, all bright, and respectable, and solemn — English of lower degree on foot, all recognisable from solemnity, respectability, and by what the Frenchman called 'mutton-chop whiskers.'

The crowd dispersing from the twelve o'clock music, usually betakes itself on Sundays to the Kunst-Verein — Art-Union Exhibition, which is open all the year through in rooms over the Hof-Garten Arcade. Each week the pictures are changed, or at all events if *all* are not changed some of them are; and Sunday is the first day of each new weekly exhibition. There critics and artists, students and connoisseurs and non-connoisseurs, criticise, admire, and gossip. To-day nothing particular struck us there. We saw a few clever *genre* pictures, a lovely Tyrolean landscape or two, some clever sketches made by an artist upon an Italian tour; but nothing especially worth chronicling.

December 18*th.* — We were present the other evening at the second performance of 'Antigone,' which has been revived here to do honor to the King's Name-day. We were lucky in obtaining excellent seats just close to one of the Royal boxes, where Isabel, who has not yet become as much accustomed to the sight of royalty as I have, had the pleasure of watching King Ludwig's elbow just beside us as he propped his head upon his hand and leant forward. King Max and his Queen, and Prince Adlebert, occupied a box in the centre of the theatre, commanding a full view of the stage. In fact, so many princes and princesses, and grand people, were present, that it might have been the gala night itself. These old Greek plays are much the fashion in Germany since the King of Prussia revived them at Berlin.

The stage was arranged as much as possible after the antique model. There was a lower stage upon which the Chorus appeared and disappeared, and grouped themselves round an altar which rose in the centre, and was hung with wreaths and votive chaplets, and an upper stage, approached by a flight of steps, where the play itself was performed. A screen rose between the two stages, and when we entered the theatre hid the higher and farther stage from sight. When the screen sank, we saw the front of a Theban palace, which remained throughout the tragedy ; for there was no changing of scenery, and only one single pause in the performance, when for a few moments this screen again rose.

Until the orchestra breathed forth Mendelssohn's foreboding strains, and whilst the musicians were tuning their instruments, and the sole female performer was silently passing her fingers over the strings of her harp, we beguiled our impatience by reading the argument of the tragedy as it stood in the programme.

According to historians, the epoch of the tragedy is about 1230 before Christ. It has been prophesied to Lagos, King of Thebes, that his future son shall be his destroyer. Thus when his wife Jocasta bears him a son, Œdipus, Lagos has him exposed upon a rock to perish. The child, however, is saved, and grows up into a youth. Œdipus, accidentally meeting his unknown father, slays him, and having solved the enigma of the Sphynx, is raised by the Theban people to the throne of his slain father, and then marries Jocasta, his own mother. Four children are born to them, Eteocles and Polynices, sons — Antigone and Ismene, daughters. The soothsayer, Teiresias, revealing these fearful relationships to Œdipus, Œdipus puts out his eyes, and wandering forth in his misery, dies. Jocasta hangs herself; Eteocles and Polynices contend about the government of Thebes. Civil war ensues — the brothers slay each other, and the whole land is overwhelmed with a great distress; Creon, brother to the dead Jocasta, seizes upon the sceptre. At this point the drama of Sophocles commences. Creon has issued a command that no one shall inter the corpse of Polynices, the betrayer of his country: this, according to antique feelings, being the greatest insult that could be offered to the dead. But Antigone, driven by a sister's love, buries the body, and is condemned herself to death by Creon.

The wailing, portentous strains of the overture have now died away, and the screen sinks. A noble, white-robed female figure is seen leaning against the columns of the Palace. The figure raises her white face, when another female form glides forth. This second woman is of a slighter, gentler mould; she is not arrayed in spectral white, but in a rich orange tunic and sweeping azure mantle. They are Antigone and Ismene. Antigone, in low, earnest tones, hoarse with emotion, beseeches her sister to disregard the commands of Creon, and to aid her in burying the beloved dead. Ismene is full of fear — refuses, and leaves her sister. Antigone, with a stern white face, and proud bearing, raises a golden ewer upon her head, and slowly descending the steps from the upper stage passes off. A troop of old men, wrapt in their ample mantles of sombre hues, with heads and locks hoary with age, and steadying their steps with tall staves, appears on the lower stage to the right and left of the altar. They are the chorus of aged Thebans. They sing in lamenting accents of discord, war, misery, and of the hapless corpse lying unburied. They wave their aged arms, and their plaintive voices rush howling and whistling like a sorrowing wind through a drear, wintry forest.

Slowly the portals of the Palace swing back upon their hinges, and, attended by four white-robed youths, Creon appears, majestic. A heavy mantle of rich Tyrian purple sweeps around him; his glossy black curls are compressed beneath a simple circlet of gold; his nervous, white arm gleams like polished ivory as he grasps a tall golden wand. He sternly commands the chorus to watch over his behest regarding the body of Polynices. His accents are few and stern.

A messenger arrives in haste. He ascends the flight of steps; he pauses, leans on his spear, and speaks — the body has been interred!

Creon, mad with rage, issues his command that the offender guilty of this great crime be sought after and punished with fiercest vengeance.

The old men raise their warning voices in loud appealing chorus.

Antigone, her face rigid, white, and stern, is dragged forward by a soldier. She is accused; she declares her deed, and her readiness to suffer for it. Creon, transported with his rage, implicates Ismene. Antigone proclaims her sister's innocence of all participation in the deed, refusing to listen to Ismene's prayers, as she beseeches permission to share her sister's death of ignominy. Then, in a fit of human weakness, Antigone bewails her miserable doom, and the awful destiny of her whole race: her 'Woe! oh, woe!' moans around. She is led off by guards. Two youths follow her, bearing water in a golden ewer, and bread in a basket; for she is condemned to be thrown into a cavern, there to perish with hunger. Passing the altar, she flings herself before it, clasping it with her arms, pressing her pallid brow upon its steps. The guards cover her with a black veil. She shudders beneath it, rises, and with bowed head slowly passes away.

In solemn dirges the chorus laments her fate, and the fate of her race.

But now up the steps flies a youth towards the palace. He is clad in a rich white tunic, bordered with a deep hem of gold; he wears golden sandals upon his feet, a golden sheathed sword swings from his girdle. He pleads with the stern King by eloquent words and gestures: but the King remains unmoved. The youth, concealing his face in his mantle, retires. He is Hæmon, — the betrothed of Antigone, the son of King Creon.

A very aged man, with a child guiding his faltering steps, ascends towards the King: it is the soothsayer Teiresias, who comes with tidings of evil from the gods. The gods must be appeased, says the venerable seer — the body must be interred; Antigone must be released. Creon relents.

The chorus rejoice, crowning themselves with garlands, and hymning praises to Bacchus, the tutelary god of Thebes.

Again a messenger! He demands Queen Eurydice. The Queen, attended by her ladies, comes forth from her palace. It is to learn that Hæmon, her beloved and beautiful son, has burst into the cavern in search of Antigone, has found her dead by her own hand, and has then destroyed himself!

The miserable Queen is borne forth by her attendants.

Slowly, slowly, and most mournfully, now approaches a strange group, and creeps silently and slowly up the flight of steps. Creon, divested of his golden diadem, his face haggard and woe-stricken, aided by mournful attendants, is bearing home his dead son. He has wound the stark corpse in his royal mantle; the long rich hair of the dead sweeps the earth and marble stairs as the head droops over the miserable father's arms. Gently they lay down the youth wrapt in his father's mantle. Creon bows over the corpse. He is no longer the haughty monarch, but rather seems some miserable spectre bending there in his white garments; all the pomp of royalty has fallen from him; all that remains is the agonized human being. His face is white as the face of the dead; he presses his son's head to his breast in convulsive agony, covering it with kisses and tears. The attendant youths avert their faces.

The palace-gates slowly once more swing widely open. There in her royal robes dies Eurydice — dies by her own hand. Creon staggers towards her like one in a bewildered dream. The gates again close — the aged men raise their voices — the drama is at an end.

Such is the plot of Antigone. Meagre in detail, awful through its rude simplicity, it creates a breathlessness such as is felt in presence of the Elgin marbles.

To complete the artistic effect of the whole, the draperies were of richest colors, of most harmonious arrangements, and, made of soft fine woollen, fell in folds of serene and purest beauty. The draperies had been arranged by Kaulbach.

CHAPTER XXXV.

VISIT TO THE GREAT BRONZE FOUNDRY.

December 19*th.* — We have been to the great Bronze Foundry to-day. This Foundry is situated on the outskirts of the city, in the road leading to the Palace of Nymphenburg. I took with me a card of introduction from Dr. F.; for I had a desire to see, and have some conversation with, Ferdinand Miller the inspector, and the man through whose patience and energy all those great and difficult works have been accomplished.

Approaching the workshops standing in their desolate inclosure, you see before you, near one of the entrances, a huge bronze lion, fellow to the one sent to the Great Exhibition. A black-handed artisan coming forth from one of the workshops, I presented to him Dr. F.'s card, and he turning back with us we entered one of the two buildings in the inclosure.

The first room into which we were led contains two other of the four Lions destined for the car of the Bavaria upon the Triumphant Arch in the Ludwig Strasse. These grim gigantic beasts, gazing down with their large bronze countenances, seemed the tutelary gods of the place, and the hum and metallic vibration which filled the air, the hymning of their worshippers. Workmen were busy filing and polishing their colossal forms, smoothing their vast sides, and rasping their golden manes. Workmen were filing and polishing portions also of other statues. Here was a diademed colossal head of Charlemagne; there a bust of Goethe; there a mail-clad arm — a fragment of rich drapery; there a golden lyre and wreath; leaning against the wall stood two circular shields, gleaming like gold, — the shields of Victories in the Bohemian Valhalla. What a rasping and filing! what a murmur and metallic vibration! Keen-eyed, dexterous-fingered men and youths bending over their masses of golden metal, — light falling from lofty windows upon their picturesque heads and forms in broad gushes, — presented a scene striking and peculiar. One was instantly reminded of the earlier designs in Retzch's Illustration to the Song of the Bell: there were the same groups, the same heads, the same attitudes, and added to these, color, light, shade, and motion.

The man who attended us was an excellent guide. I told him that we had seen the Colossal Lion in London, and inquired after it; he said it was now at Cologne on its way home, and that it must remain there until Spring, when the Rhine steamers recommenced running.

I told him how, a few years ago, I had seen the Bavaria in progress here, when the mighty clay mould stood beneath its wooden tower, and how fortunate I considered myself to have witnessed last year its great day of triumph; and when I said how deeply I respected and admired the exertions of the 'Herrn-Inspector,' and spoke of the interest which both I and my companion took in all these mighty works, the man's face lighted up with a smile of pride and intelligence.

Now we stood in a lofty room whose high bare walls were intersected by long windows, and in the centre of which rose a huge brick furnace, and before the furnace was a deep pit. This was one of the smelting and casting rooms; but neither smelting nor casting was just then going forward. The workmen were busy preparing for a casting of a large portion of the Bavaria which is intended for the Triumphal Arch, and which will take place in about a month. The preparation of the various moulds, and their numerous portions, is a long and difficult process. Here in this room, lay open, side by side, portions of the various moulds for the head and arms of the Bavaria and for the Lions, — the great work now in progress. Here was the mould of her head and face, which have just been cast; there, in the pit, lay what our guide called the '*Kern*' or kernel of her head, — the mass of clay which is introduced into the centre of the mould, so as to render the casting hollow. A heap of unsuccessful castings lay in one corner of the room; masses of dark metal in which some traces of beautiful form were yet conspicuous, — an heroic helmet, or a nobly formed and sandalled foot.

But the most interesting casting-room is contained in the second and larger building, before the door of which stands the huge Lion. It is in this atelier that the great Bavaria was cast.

This room contains two furnaces, and is consequently very lofty and of great extent; so large and lofty, in fact, that the plaster casts of various colossal statues standing about appear only of an ordinary size. There is the plaster cast of the statue of Gustavus Adolphus, — the statue that was wrecked some few weeks since off Heligoland on its way to Sweden. We learned, however, that on this very day Ferdinand Miller had received tidings of its rescue from the waves, and that the brave old hero had been fished up again after infinite trouble, having lost, however, in the salt water, all the golden glory of his bronze. He had come up, as perhaps befitted one who had just paid Neptune a visit in his submarine haunts, a hero clothed in garments of green, the salt water having oxydized the metal.

In company with Gustavus Adolphus stands Herder the poet; and the musical composer Orlando di Lasso, leaning on his lute, the Poet of Melody, (*Ton Dichter*,) as he is designated in the inscription on the pedestal of the statue. A gigantic cast of the beckoning hand of the Bavaria hangs against the wall; it is covered with a red dust, which, telling warmly in the shadows, relieves it strongly from the cold, grey wall behind. Heaps of red earth, plaster, and clay bestrewed the floor, mingling, to the eye of the uninitiated, in chaotic disorder with gaping moulds and fragments of models and portions of finished castings which lie and stand around.

Here were, again, Retzch-like groups. A young man was bending over the clay-model of a door preparing for the Au Church, and which represented Ohlmüller the architect, and other artists connected with the decoration of this lovely church, presenting their designs to King Ludwig. The skilful hands of the young man delicately moulded and smoothed the wreath of oak leaves and acorns which encircled the design; whilst bearded and grave-visaged men anointed and joined the moulds for the forthcoming statue of the Bavaria.

We looked around, thinking of the many spectacles of interest which these grey and begrimmed walls had witnessed. Schwanthaler, and Stiglmayer, the departed, had been here; here, no doubt, beneath that bust of himself garlanded with dead leaves had stood King Ludwig and his artists to witness the triumphant casting of the Bavaria's head; here, too, occurred that mighty anxiety of mind, when, through the sultry summer days and nights, Ferdinand Miller, and his no less anxious wife and toiling workmen, watched the smelting metal for the casting of the Bavaria's chest and shoulders, — the largest portion of the Colossus; and where, in the midst of their breathless watching, fire burst forth, and only through the bravery and coolness of mind of Ferdinand Miller were the casting, and the smelting-house saved! How many hours of patient labor, of wearing anxiety, of bodily fatigue, of accomplished resolve, and of glorious triumph, have passed away between these high, grey, dreary-looking walls!

Such scenes were passing before my imagination, when I saw a man, of a broad strong make and a resolute countenance, approaching us from among a group of talkers. He was scarcely better dressed than an ordinary workman; but there was the stamp of education upon him, and the determined look of energy and command which distinguished him from the others.

That genial, resolute face, begirt with its bushy light brown beard, I remembered to have seen at the May-Festival at Starnberg.

'Have I not the happiness and honor of addressing the Herrn Inspector, Ferdinand Miller?' said I, — with doubtless an expression of that earnest enthusiasm and respect on my countenance which I felt in my heart.

'Yes; I am Ferdinand Miller,' said he, raising his cap and glancing at Dr. F.'s card of introduction, which he held in his hand; and forthwith we found ourselves talking of the Bavaria Festival, — of Schwanthaler and his fate, — of the memories, beautiful, sad, yet poetical, connected with this great Foundry.

I told him of the deep interest with which I had read of the anxious nights and days of watching over the smelting for the great Bavaria's casting, and of the fire. He pointed up towards the blackened rafters above the furnace, before which we happened to be standing, saying —

'There it burned and smouldered whilst we watched below; yes, it was a time never to be forgotten — a fearful experience!'

Of this and many other things we talked; and all ended by our receiving an invitation to be present at the casting of that portion of the lesser Bavaria, for which, as I have already said, preparation is now making, and which no one can witness except invited by the great master himself!

CHAPTER XXXVI.

CHRISTMAS-DAY — A CHRISTMAS-TREE IN A BEAUTIFUL HOME.

Christmas-Day, 1851. — Someway a strange fear seemed to have possessed me this beautiful Christmas-day, when such rumors of revolution are abroad — a fearful despondency lest the power of evil were about for a time to attain awful ascendancy. Had not again and again in the world's history, the good, the pure, the noble, the refined, fallen beneath the hoofs of the brutal, the cruel, the strong? — did it not seem as though nations must endure martyrdom as well as each individual human soul? Was not even now a deeper, sadder tragedy preparing slowly, stealthily for Europe — sadder perhaps than aught else the world had witnessed!

What had Christmas availed in the world? what real earnest hold had Christ's blessed words upon the world? The masses were brutal and superstitious; the few were faithless. What blood had been shed in vain! what anguish been endured in vain! and again and again must be shed in vain, before the mighty victory be achieved!

Such was the sad under-current of my thoughts as I walked along through the snowy streets, with many another questioning, which the reading lately of old Catholic legends has suggested. But of Christ's own pure, blessed words there were *no* questionings.

Thus pondering in a vague despondency, a peal of trumpets vibrated through the frosty air, sending a quick gush of joy through my heart; and, scarcely knowing how I came there, I found myself standing in the small chapel of the Franciscan Monastery. It is very small and octagonal, with light falling from windows close to the ceiling. It is in the vile renaissance style — all scroll-work, gliding, and flutter. Round the walls, in each of the eight compartments where were no shrines or altars, are arranged large oil-paintings illustrating the life of St. Francis. All the ornaments are vile, judged by one's standard of purity, beauty, and simplicity; still this morning the effect was poetical: the chapel seemed a gorgeous grotto — an incrustation of gold and bright-colored objects: the very priests kneeling there robed in stiff crimson velvet and gold brocade, rich and stately as the priests in Van Eyck's marvellous little picture in the Dudley Gallery, seemed a portion of the barbaric ornament.

The cold early morning light fell in slant rays through the oval windows upon the clouds of incense which floated upwards, and through which glittered the golden stars which spangled the azure roof. Incense filled the whole chapel, meeting one on entrance as if with a bodily presence; and music from a concealed choir flooded the chapel, — such delicious sweet music as of angels' voices; now in soft, solemn chorus; now bursting forth into wild hallelujahs; now hushed into deep, mournful murmurs, as if ever a sense of sadness and foreboding mingled with ecstatic joy, — yes, even when hymning praises to God and celebrating the birth of a Saviour.

I felt my spirit bow in worship with that ignorant crowd of poor people who filled the chapel. Ah! how beautiful, how holy, was faith! though I might be as ignorant, as superstitious, as the most ignorant peasant there, what mattered it? Better love a phantom than nothing; to be without love was to be without faith or joy.

The spirit of God had spoken in that music as it spoke of old to Saul when David touched the golden strings of his harp; all the demons of doubt had fled, and I *could* alone believe in the strength of goodness!

On my way back I met two priests coming through the snow from the Monastery, bearing the host to some sick person. They were clothed in white robes embroidered with gold; the one in front carried a light burning in a large lamp shaped like a lantern; the other reverently bowed his head above the sacred wafer, and the wine which he bore upon a linen napkin, the whole covered with a crown of massive silver like a royal diadem. A lady in her silks and satins, and a little ragged urchin, as the priests came on, paused, knelt in the snow, and crossed themselves! I paused also, longing almost for the faith which taught them to believe that the body of Christ had really passed before them, making sacred the very air through which it moved.

The snow fell in thick flakes, in most excellent Christmas fashion, upon the fur-collar and warm blue over-coat of our droschke driver, as he drove us through the snowy streets and snowy English Garden to the house of our kind friend the Frau Hofräthin von ——. We were invited upon this evening of St. Stephen's Day, the second Christmas holiday, to witness the re-lighting of the Frau Hofräthin's splendid Christmas tree.

The Frau von —— and her bevy of sweet-looking daughters — a group worthy of Miss Bremer's 'Home' — welcomed us in the heartiest manner in the fresco-painted saloon, in the centre of which rose the tall fir-tree loaded with its fruit of sweetmeats, nuts, tapers, and strings of glittering beads of glass. The tapers were not yet lighted, and we were told not to pay much attention to the tree, in order that we might be all the more struck by its perfect beauty when it should be lit up.

As we might not as yet admire the tree, we admired various lovely trinkets and books which the mother and daughters had given each other, and also a grand set of toys representing Wallenstein's Camp, which had been given to little Hugo, the youngest of the family, — 'the idol,' as the mother called him — a rosy, blue-eyed, long flaxen-haired little fellow of three years old. Little Hugo, together with a brother some year or two older, also flaxen-haired and blue-eyed, formed a very pretty picture in the beautiful saloon, dressed in their little quaint black velvet tunics. Now they were clapping their hands and peeping round the lovely mysterious tree; now they were clinging to their mother.

Whilst we were admiring the presents the door flew open, and the eldest son of the house entered, followed by nine youths with swarthy faces, black eyes, and scarlet *fezes*. They were the nine noble Egyptian youths sent over by the Pacha of Egypt to study at Munich. There was Salem Salem Awad, son of a great philosopher and poet; Prince Murad Ibrahim, son of Pascha Amurad; Prince Hassan Hassan, son of an Admiral and Pascha; Prince Jussuph Katschador, son of a Bey; and five other equally noble Egyptians, with names equally worthy of figuring in the 'Arabian Nights'; and the nine noble Egyptians, as if they were a corps of ballet-dancers, moved gracefully towards the lady of the house, who rose, together with her fair daughters, to receive them: and smiling, they pressed their right hands upon their hearts, their lips, and brows, — saluting the ladies with the oriental *salaam*.

We two foreigners were introduced to the Egyptians; and again nine pair of dark eyes glittered, and nine scarlet *fezes* bowed, nine right hands pressing breast, lips, and brows.

Again the door opened, and more company arrived, — it was the Baron and Baroness D——, the care-takers of the Egyptian youths during their sojourn in Munich, and their children.

Hildegard, the eldest daughter — the 'artist daughter,' as she is called in the family — now summoned us to coffee in an adjoining room; — I must tell you, that Hildegard, this evening being somewhat an invalid, and fearing the cold, had wrapt a soft pink gauze scarf round her sweet pale face: she resembled a delicate blush-rose. Coffee was handed round to us by the mustachioed servant, whilst one of the five daughters presented to each of the company most delicious cakes, which were heaped up in a perfect mountain upon a rich silver salver. It was a very pretty sight, these nine noble Egyptian youths standing in line along the room, each with his scarlet fez upon his head, and with his coffee-cup in his hand, and those sweet young girls with their fair hair and dark blue eyes, in their blue dresses and green dresses, and Hildegard with her soft pink halo around her, flitting to and fro: surely the noble Egyptians must have believed they were *houries.*

During this coffee-drinking, behind the folding-doors which divided the two saloons, the Christmas-tree was being lighted by Heinrich von ———, and all the small children in the company forgot their coffee in a state of delightful excitement. At length the doors were flung open — everybody set down their coffee-cups and moved to the door-way: there burnt the magical tree as if descended from fairy land. A tall tree it was, pyramidal in its form, and had been cut down among the Tyrolean mountains; its lowest branches rested upon the polished white floor of the saloon; its tapering topmost branch touched the arabesqued ceiling; its every twig and bough loaded with fruits and cakes, and gilded *bon-bons*, its hundreds of bright tapers, like flowers of fire, glittering and gleaming, and casting a brilliant illumination upon the frescoes by Kaulbach, and the luxuriant festoons of flowers and leafage by Neureuther, which decorate the walls, upon the divan of scarlet silk which runs along one side of the saloon, upon the nine Egyptians, upon the stately fair-haired mother and her five fair daughters, upon the little boys in their black velvet tunics, and upon the other groups of guests. There was a universal exclamation of delight.

And the smiling blush-rose, Hildegard, presented to each guest a graceful little present from the tree; one received a gaily-gilt case of *bon-bons* tied with red ribbon; another a queer little fishing-basket filled with chocolate fish; and so on.

People had subsided into conversation, when a gentleman, short in stature, but with an extraordinary fine head and strongly-marked features, entered the room. Heinrich von ———, who was talking with Isabel and myself, suddenly started up, and with much *empressement* conducted him to his mother.

'Do you know who that is?' asked he, returning to us.

'No,' we replied.

'It is,' pursued our friend, 'the great traveller Fallmerayer, the man alone second to Humboldt; he is Knight of the Bath, and possesses almost every decoration from almost every court in Europe, but to-night he only wears one decoration — did not you notice it suspended round his neck by a scarlet band? That decoration was bestowed upon him by the Grand Sultan: three decorations of this order alone exist: the decoration is a golden full-moon surrounded by a circle of diamond stars. The Egyptians have been burning with desire to see the great man for these months past, and to-night my father has arranged their meeting with him.'

The company seemed now pretty nearly to have all assembled. The Frau von ——— suddenly stood before Isabel and myself, holding by the hand a very amiable-looking gentleman,—'The Father!' said she: and we were most kindly welcomed by the master of the house.

'Wilhelm!' exclaimed the eldest son of the house, to a young musician who had just arrived among the other guests, 'thou art an artist; seat thyself at the piano, and let us have our mother's dance round the tree!—and you, Hildegard, Emilia, Rose, Hugo, Angelo, come, all of you join hands; let us dance our mother's dance round the tree—she must have her Christmas circle!' And the five sisters and the three brothers—from the womanly, calm Hildegard and the heavenly-eyed Emilia, down to the fair-haired children, Angelo and Hugo—formed a wide circle, joining hands, and slowly to the sound of music moved round the tree. The father and mother stood side by side in front of their guests, looking on.

'But ah! there is *one* wanting in the circle,—my beautiful Ludmilla!' half whispered the mother, with a low sigh, and tears swam in the clear eyes of the sisters. A portrait of the beloved and departed one hung in the adjoining saloon. It was the portrait of a golden-haired young creature with clear eyes, and with an unusually spiritual grace about her. Last Christmas she had been among them. The sisters talked much to us about her in the evening; they said she had been from her childhood the most richly-endowed of them all; and with the tenderest love they pointed out to us her portrait when a child, painted upon the wall by Neureuther, and looking forth pensively from amid the rich festoons of foliage which surround her.

With Isabel, Emilia talked much about this beautiful Ludmilla; she also told her many interesting and curious things regarding her own sojourn in Milan, where she had gone to study music under a celebrated composer; she told her how she had, when Christmas came round, decorated a Christmas-tree for a number of Italian children, who had never before seen such a wonder. The tree was laurel, and not pine; — but whether the tree be laurel of Italy or pine of Germany, when glittering with fruit of sugar and flowers of fire, little children, she said, will always clap their hands and shout with glee! Much that was very strange about the outbreak of the revolution in Milan, which Emilia had witnessed, she also told.

I, meantime, was talking with certain of the noble Egyptians. 'I have heard in England much about the Egyptians studying in London,' said I to one of the youths; 'are they friends of yours?'

'Oh, our beloved brothers! our beloved comrades! Do you know them? How is it with them? tell us how it is with our beloved comrades!' exclaimed the excited lad. 'The lady — the English young lady, knows our beloved brothers in London!' cried he eagerly to the other Egyptians; and soon a knot of scarlet fezes had assembled round me.

'I myself do not personally know your brothers in London,' said I, with regret, as I saw their excited dark eyes beaming upon me; 'but they often visit at the house of a friend of mine; my cousin, too, the young lady in the lilac dress, sitting there in the corner of the divan, has seen and spoken with your brothers at this friend's house; the tutor of your brothers is also a friend of my friend — thus I can learn for you how it is with your brothers, and convey any message. Shall I do so?'

'Yes; our affectionate brotherly greetings. We want to know if it is well with them. And oh! is it well with our other brothers in Manchester — with our three brothers in that dark, smoky Manchester, where there is no blue sky, and no sun as in Egypt? we are very anxious about our brothers in Manchester! They write now and then, but not much: we cannot make out whether it is well with them — whether they are content with their guardians. It is well with our dear brothers in Paris — very well; they have horses to ride, and much money. But is it well with our brothers in Manchester, where there is no sky — only smoke?'

I promised that I would learn all I could for them; and this promise diffused around me universal satisfaction. The remainder of the evening, until supper was announced, glided away in pleasant talk: mine was principally with Hildegard. We began with Art, of course, and then wandered away to the Alps; and in spirit we ascended these Alps, so dear to both of us, gathering on our way the loveliest bouquets of Alpine flowers — golden, lilac, peacock, azure, and crimson; we ascended from the rich pasture valleys up through solemn pine forests, till we gathered, at the risk of losing our lives, the wonderful *Edel-weiss*, (noble-white,) which alone blooms amidst eternal snow. God has lovingly clothed its stalks and its petals in a garment of white wool: it is a little flower of flannel!

The Blush-rose gave me a bouquet of this Edel-weiss, which I wore all the evening.

Isabel and I have been invited by this kind family to visit them in their beautiful mountain home. What a paradise will our visit be! and what rainbows of real, not imaginary, flowers will we gather!

The elegant and abundant supper was served in a dining-room on the ground-floor. The room was hung with oil-paintings of the lakes and mountains around their mountain-home. All was bright and sparkling with delicate china, snowy damask, and glittering silver. Different, however, in many ways from what a supper-table in England at Christmas-time, in a family of equal consideration, would have been: it was much less sumptuous and costly, and there was no decoration of one's well-beloved old holly; but the hospitality, the grace, and the refinement, might have vied with the most hospitable, the most refined of English homes. How talkative and merry was everybody! How gay those nine scarlet fezes made the supper-table look, seated alternately with the blond-haired, blue-eyed sisters! The swarthy oriental countenances, contrasting with these delicate complexions and golden hair of the north, would have rejoiced old Etty's heart, and made him, had he seen them, paint more crowds than ever of swarthy heroes and golden-haired, blue-eyed nymphs.

The little sons of the house, Angelo and Hugo, were entertaining their guests at a supper-table in an adjoining room. The 'Mother' rose once or twice from the head of the table during supper, and glided into the children's apartment, from which, as the laughter and hum of voices in the grown-up banqueting-room sunk ever and anon, we heard children's shrill gay laughter and a chorus of merry little voices. Once, as the 'Mother' passed the Blush-rose on her return to the supper-table, the Blush-rose pressed the 'Mother's' hand, laid it against her cheek, and mother and daughter exchanged a momentary glance into each other's eyes of the tenderest love.

People seemed as though they never could leave the enchanted circle ; — and who willingly would have left it? At last, however, adieus were made ; there was a hum of voices — a wrapping-up in hooded cloaks and shawls — and away we were driving once more through the snowy streets.

CHAPTER XXXVII.

STREET PICTURES. — 'THE FRANCISCAN IS THERE!' — WE REACH NYMPHENBURG.

January 10th, 1852. — To-day, going and returning from the studio, I saw several beautiful pictures in the streets. I often see such; and could — so brilliant are they in coloring — fill a sketch-book with them, calling them prismatic colors from the streets.

Here is a picture *à la Mulready;* a group of peasants is setting out in a sledge homewards from a little inn. The inn is quaint and heavy, standing at the corner of a street. The warm obscurity of a heavy archway, through the gloom of which loom forth tubs and barrels, forms a picturesque and quiet background to my brilliant group. The road is of a tawny brown, from up-trampled, though still crisp snow, with pure snow only seen here and there, close up about the door-posts, and flecking the walls. But there is no expanse of snow to form a broad light in my picture. The tone of the whole picture is warm and rich. The sledge is a queer old sledge; its body is of basket-work, a deeper shade of tawny-brown than the snow on the road; the horse brown — approaching to a purplish-black; he is very lean and shaggy, and harnessed with rope; an old, stained, yellow-green cloth is flung over his back. A very old woman with much ado is settling herself in the sledge. She is leaning forward, so that her face is quite in shadow. Her head is bundled up in a brilliant crimson handkerchief, her body is bundled up in a cloak of the richest ultra-marine. On this side of the sledge, standing with her back turned towards me, her face looking up at the old woman, is a peasant-girl. Her head is covered with a dark olive-green handkerchief, bordered with orange; the ends are tied behind her head, and fall upon her shoulders, which are clothed in a rich, full violet-colored jacket. Her petticoat is dull crimson, striped with black. On the other side of the horse, and arranging the harness, stands a peasant-man, whip in hand; he wears a dark fur cap, black velvet jacket, and high black boots. The brilliant color and harmonious richness of the whole group was inconceivable.

I saw another picture when I was turning into the studio. The morning sky was bright and clear — a shower of sunshine glittering upon the crisp white snow and upon the frosted trees. A young and beautiful peasant-girl, attired in a pink jacket above an indigo-colored petticoat, and with a brown handkerchief bound tightly across her brow, in the curious fashion worn by the women in Munich, and which leaves the shape of the head gracefully seen, was seated in a pensive attitude upon a huge, heavy, primitive wooden sledge. A lesser sledge, but equally rude, was attached to it; and both were drawn along by a couple of mild, cream-colored oxen. Rough pieces of timber were heaped up behind the girl, upon the larger sledge. She sat leaning her oval face upon her beautifully rounded hand; she appeared to see nothing around her; her gaze was introverted; the oxen were unguided by hand or voice, and slowly, with bowed heads, proceeded on their way. My eyes followed them along the snowy road, slowly winding between the glittering trees, until they disappeared behind a quaint group of houses:

but as long as they were in sight the girl never raised her head.

Returning home late in the afternoon I encountered a group worthy of some modern Van Eyck. There is a great school-house close to the Franciscan monastery which I have already referred to. As I passed the school to-day a crowd of little maidens came trooping forth; rosy-cheeked, bright-eyed little maidens, bundled up in warm cloaks and funny little fur-trimmed hoods. A cheery-looking Franciscan was passing at the same moment as myself. I had walked side by side with him for a minute or two, and had remarked to myself what a pleasant countenance his was. The children seemed to know the pleasant face well enough, for the instant they caught sight of the friar one and all ran skipping towards him, and a dozen little fat hands, one after another, were thrust into his hand, and a dozen chubby faces, as of a dozen cherubs in an old religious picture, were raised towards his kind, beaming countenance. I smiled as I passed, looking the good man full in the face; and he, smiling half at me and half at the little ones, exclaimed in a clear voice: — 'Nay, nay, my children! Surely this is enough!'

It was a group such as might have been painted for St. Nicholas with his children.

I have been two afternoons this week sketching a quaint bit of a room in one of the houses near the studio. When I went to-day to complete my sketch, I saw a curious little feature of Catholic life. The first day when I had entered, the old mistress of the little abode exclaimed: — 'Ah, I thought the gracious Fr ulein was the Franciscan!'

This was because I had knocked at the door before entering, I found. Her neighbors never knocked; but the Franciscan did, it seems. Whilst I sat sketching, I heard the word 'Franciscan,' 'Franciscan,' again and again on the lips of the old woman and her gossips, who were everlastingly dropping in, either to talk with her, or to stare at me! 'Franciscan' was about the sole word I understood of their jargon; for speaking among themselves, their German became something very different to that in which they addressed 'the gracious young lady.' Yes, there were several other words which fell upon my ear—'cold,' 'wood,' and 'clearing up.' '*Abräumen*' seemed the great word of all. '*Jo, jo, abräumen; Den Hof kehren*,' those were the great subjects of conversation with a silly-looking, pale-faced little woman, who had big round eyes, big round gold rings in her ears, and a white cloth tied over her head. It was also the staple of discourse with the burly, fat, gruff-voiced woman who possessed a dirty face, and had a crimson 'kerchief tied over her head; as well as with the pink-cheeked, soft blue-eyed old woman, who looked like a gentlewoman, she was so clean and sprightly. But 'Franciscan' was the word most of all current in their discourse.

This morning entering the court-yard of the house, I encountered the pink-cheeked old lady; and smiling, but somewhat in a mysterious voice, she said to me:—'Oh, Fräulein, please to wait a moment; the gracious Franciscan is there!'

I smelt even upon the threshold of the house a delicious odor of incense. I longed to go in and see what the mysterious Franciscan, with his delicious incense, could be about. However that never would have done—it would have been far too impertinent. I waited, therefore, outside the house until he should take his departure. Every now and then I caught a glimpse of a priest's head and white robe between the large, green arum-leaves which half filled the window of the little sitting-room. Soon I saw a Franciscan, with a white robe over his brown frock, coming down the steps of the house. A boy was with him, carrying a censer. The lad had put a great-coat over his white robes, as the day was very cold. The Franciscan read out of a book. They both paused beneath the old wooden gateway; the boy swinging his censer; the Franciscan turning over the leaves of the book, and muttering; and then away they went.

The little room, when I entered, was sweet with incense. The old man was putting on his great cloak, and taking up his wood-saw, preparatory to going out to his work; the old dame — and a wooden-faced, heavy-featured old dame she was — was scraping large radishes, which lay on the table. There was no look of ceremony about the place. I began my sketching.

'May I ask why the Franciscan has been here?' I asked after a little pause, during which the old woman had scraped and I had drawn.

'It is the custom for the Franciscans to go about during the Festival of the Three Kings, to burn incense and pray in the houses. They pray in every house; and write upon the door the date of the year and the Three Kings' names — Gaspar, Melchior, and Balthaser.'

I find, upon inquiry, that the custom is confined to the suburbs of Munich, not prevailing in the city.

There were signs yesterday of the departure of the snow, after these many weeks of frost.

Isabel pleaded so hard for us to have one more afternoon's sledging together, that I could neither resist her entreaties nor the invitations given by the blue sky! Therefore we set out to choose the sledge ourselves this time, determined that no one should be tempted to force their company upon us by the sight of our sledge.

We arrived at the stand of sledges upon the Odeon Platz in time to witness two sets of people just mounting into the only two sledges remaining upon the stand.

'How provoking!' cried Isabel, with considerable vexation: 'how very disagreeable!'

'Never mind, Isabel,' returned I, with a natural perversity, feeling sweet-tempered and patient just because my companion was a little ruffled in her temper — 'we can take a droschke!'

'A *droschke*, indeed! A droschke! Who cares for a droschke! No, it's a sledge we want. We must — we *will* go in a sledge!'

'But where *is* the sledge?'

'Here it is! here it is!' cried Isabel; and up dashed our grand white and scarlet sledge, with the blue and white plumes and the burly driver.

In a moment I have darted across the Platz, in fear lest any one else should snap up the wondrously beautiful equipage. But behold, the burly driver is seen rolling over in the snow! Away dash the horses, and bolt up into Tambosi's coffee-house — or at least seem to do so! Up jumps the burly driver again, his broad back white with snow; and away after the sledge rush droschke-drivers and gentlemen. There is a shouting — a bustle; gentlemen rush to the windows of Tambosi's; the horses are caught; a crowd collects.

Isabel watches all from the other side of the square; and she sees me walk into the crowd, look at the sledge, say a few words to the burly man, who has by this time shaken the snow off him, and mended his grand white reins, which have been broken in the adventure, and then mount into the sledge.

Isabel is immediately at the side of the sledge, and prepares to get in. 'Help the lady in, help the lady in!' cries a gentleman among the crowd; but no one seconding him, he helps the lady in himself. People stare open-mouthed. 'Sophien Strasse!' cry we; and away we dash at full speed. Our breath is gone, so swiftly fly the horses.

'Only think if we should be upset!' we both exclaim.

'Of course we shall be upset; Hildegard and Hamilton were upset, and we are only imitating their drive to Nymphenburg.'

I will not pretend to say that we were not both of us a little frightened, although we laughed.

'How beautiful that sledge is!' I exclaim, as a lovely sledge dashes past us filled with officers, the handsome horses' heads crowned with plumes of scarlet feathers.

'That is young Baron S.'s *private* sledge,' observes Isabel, astonishing me with her knowledge of Munich people.

And now we paused in the Sophien Strasse, where the Amsels live.

Meta and Lina, however, could not accompany us. 'They were in great trouble,' said their maid. 'The young Baroness Heideck was suddenly dead; so very suddenly! She was to have gone with her young ladies that very night to the ball; and now Fräulein Lina and Fräulein Meta were gone to order flower-wreaths for the Fräulein Baroness's coffin!'

As we came out on the plain, and whilst I was pondering upon this sad death, I heard Isabel talking about 'blue — oh, so blue in the distance!'

'Blue! blue! What do you mean, Isabel?'

'Oh, it is so blue there — the clouds are so blue!'

And looking in the direction in which Isabel pointed, I exclaimed, —

'The Alps, the Alps, the delicious Alps, Isabel! Why this is the first time you have seen them, I declare.'

Isabel's face flushed crimson — tears rushed to her eyes.—'Oh, Anna! *my first view of the Alps!*'

And there they rose, blue, blue, blue — dazzlingly blue; the jagged peaks cutting against a pale streak of orange sky; their fissures seamed with snow, their rugged sides fretted with patches of snow and ice; and a vast snowy plain reaching from them to us. You have seen masses of cobalt in its mineral state: imagine, then, a jagged mass of this mineral streaked with silvery ore, and then you can imagine how blue the Alps looked. And as far as the eye could reach, these wondrous blue mountains skirted the vast, dreary plain.

Never had I seen them look more poetical, more sublime, than yesterday, when after two months' veil of haze they burst upon Isabel's astonished sight. With our eyes riveted upon the glorious mountain vision, we sped along for some time in silence. At length we began to notice a peculiar jolting motion in the sledge.

'Have you any *particular* business, ladies, in Nymphenburg?' demanded our driver, slowly turning round, and staring at us fixedly with his little brown eyes out of his big, round, red face.'

'No *particular* business,' returned I.

'Because,' remarked he, still very slowly, and fixedly staring — 'because the roads are bad, and —'

'*You* don't want to go to Nymphenburg,' I returned; or rather completed his sentence.

Isabel and I laughed.

'So again, a third time, we shall be frustrated in our attempt to reach Nymphenburg; but this time we will go. Drive on.'

'Good,' mumbled the man. Away we jolted.

We jolted through villages, where there were gaunt farm-houses covered with very queer frescoes, and where quaint pumps and dove-cotes adorned ghastly farm-yards; and where churches with very quaint towers, crowned with little red domes, rose amid gaunt crosses; and at length we entered a noble avenue of limes.

The leafless branches interlaced lovingly, forming overhead an exquisite, rich tracery; and the stems and twigs looked richly brown and ruddy amidst the snowy landscape. There is a similar avenue also, skirting a frozen canal; which canal, in fact, divides the two avenues. At the end of each avenue is seen a view of the Nymphenburg Castle in dim perspective. Huge blocks of ice, of the most delicate tender blue and green, lay in chaotic confusion upon the canal banks; the ice made a lovely foreground. And across the expanse of snow the blue Alps shone ever towards us — the streak of orange still resting behind them, and a dark stretch of gloomy pine-forest extending across the middle distance. A peasant-woman in a fur cap and pink boddice and scarlet petticoat came towards us across the snow. What a beautiful, peculiar little picture it formed.

Along the avenue we jolt, till we find ourselves entering a semi-circle of the most singular aspect. It is a semicircle of huge Dutch toy-houses — white houses with rows and rows of ugly straight windows, with tall, red roofs, and dormer windows and clock-towers. The centre house is higher than the rest; a double flight of steps leads up to it; the windows are more ornamental. Soldiers parade before the entrance. This is the palace itself; and what *can* all the other houses be? What a semi-circular, unaccountable village of palaces, or of palace out-buildings it is. Out-buildings they certainly *must* be, for manure-heaps grace certain doors. I must not forget to tell you that in front of this semi-circle were frozen ponds, ending of course in the canal.

Our driver asked us whether we wished to see the interior of the castle; but we assured him that on such a cold day we preferred the warm furs of his sledge to the cold splendor of the palace; which, however, might attract us, perhaps, when summer should come. Until then we would now bid adieu, therefore, to Nymphenburg, with its wonderful gardens — of which we caught a shivering glance — where rows of naked statues, and vases and urns filled with snow, made us feel yet colder than before. And then, listening to our driver's narrations of fountains, and grottoes and baths, and of how he had one summer, every evening, at eight o'clock, driven out an Englishman to Nymphenburg to see the sunset-light reflect itself in the magnificent fountain, we, or rather the horses, made the best of their way back towards Munich.

We were very cold, and somewhat disappointed in the external charms of Nymphenburg. But we had *been* there; and that was something. Some day, when the leaves are come, and birds are singing in the Linden avenue, I may have pleasanter things to chronicle about this royal château.

CHAPTER XXXVIII.

A GREAT FIRE AT NIGHT.

Last evening, sitting quietly writing letters, we heard a most singular drumming in the street — not the usual nine o'clock change of guard, but the quick discordant beating of a drum. Up to the windows we started, and opening them, looked out into the glorious moonlight, which sparkled and gleamed upon the snowy street. Other casements flew open; people were seen rushing out of the houses. There was a sound of tolling of bells, — the sound of trumpet calls. A ruddy glow suffused the dark blue heaven. 'It is fire! fire!' resounded through the street.

I called to Fräulein Sänchen. I hurried on my cloak, and leaving Isabel leaning out of the window, prepared to set out, accompanied by the ever-willing old soul, to see the conflagration. It was impossible at so late an hour to find a droschke, however desirous of expedition we might be. Away, therefore, we hasted along the slippery streets, I leaving the poor old Fräulein panting behind me. On we posted, the silent streets bathed in the clear moonlight, which glittered upon rows of resplendent icicles depending from the eaves of the tall roofs; lights flitted from window to window; doors banged heavily to and fro; dark-cloaked figures were seen like ourselves hurrying along. Now we overtook a group of students leaving a *Wirthshaus* in quest of the fire; now a heavy cart rumbled and jolted and rattled away past us, turning out of some gloomy, heavy-arched court-yard, on its way to the scene of action; now marched on a body of soldiers; whilst a gendarme galloped at full speed through the echoing street.

As we entered the great thoroughfares of the city the crowd increased. All the world was in the streets, or looking out of their windows. Soldiers, summoned by the trumpet-calls, went tramping on in dark compact masses; officers were wildly hurrying to and fro; and high up into the intensely blue sky rose the ruddy illumined towers of the *Frauen Kirche,* from the belfry windows of which swung cressets like brightly burning stars. From the St. Peter's Church, and from the other old churches of the city, swung other cressets, the dread signal of fire; and from their belfries bells were wildly tolled and horns blown.

Fire-light glowed upon spires and turrets, and upon the steep snowy roofs of the quaint houses, tinting them with a rosy blush, as if they were Alpine peaks at sunrise; and down upon all smiled the broad calm moon, casting long fantastic shadows across the snowy streets.

The fire was at a brewery, in one of the oldest parts of Munich, in a little lane leading out of the Sendlinger Strasse. I saw no fire-engines hurrying madly along, as would have been the case in London. I saw, however, heavy clumsy drays conveying water in large tuns, jolting and jingling along, the lean horses urged on by shouting men, who clustered round the tuns. The engines were already on the spot, and these tuns were on their way to supply them with water.

Now we are close to the scene of excitement. Soldiers with glittering swords and bayonets are posted everywhere. The fire is in the rear of the brewery; the malt-house is burning; the flames have just burst through the roof. We have found a capital standing-place within the wide court-yard of a conventual-looking building, and one which commands a view of the burning premises. Here we stand in safety from the crowd in an open space, with a snow-covered garden stretching out before us, a snow and ice-covered fountain in its centre, around which grow fruit-trees, their leafless branches now rising black and gaunt against the burning crimson of the sky. Right opposite to us is the house in flames; — keen tongues of fire flickering and panting through the windows, through the chimneys, through the roof; — clouds of sparks hurrying across the night sky like a dust of stars; — volumes of red smoke ever and anon obscuring everything. Amid the shouts of men, the neighing of horses, and the rush of the flames, you hear the shower of pattering tiles, as they rain down from the roof; the flames hiss and dance and curl like mad fiery snakes; the air grows warm, and the snow melts from the burning roofs, running off in streams. Why are no engines at play on this side of the burning pile? Why do the flames here conquer all before them unopposed?

There is a shout of 'The Engines! the engines!' and soldiers drive away the crowd out of the court-yard — us among the number. In thunder the fire-engines, followed by heavy drays with their tuns of water. People willing to aid in pumping are allowed to re-enter the court.

I had met Lina and Meta Amsel, with their man-servant, in the crowd, and joining their party, sent home poor old Fräulein Sänchen to inform Isabel that I should probably not return till the morning, as we were intending to see everything that was to be seen, and it appeared probable that the fire would yet last for hours. The poor old Fräulein was most thankful to be dismissed, as the grief over her cloak, which the crowd had despoiled of its cape, had for the last hour quite overpowered all her interest in the fire.

The Amsels and I had fled into the corner of a narrow flight of steps which overlooked the court-yard; and here we stood watching the fate of the burning house for nearly an hour. Every now and then came a rush of people with more water; now we were startled by the sudden raining down, from above our heads, of a host of fire-buckets, which had doubtless hung for years idly upon the ceiling of the court-yard gateway.

I greatly desired to see people handing along the bucketfuls of water in a mighty line, as I had read of. I had both heard and read how the police might press any one into this service, men, women, children — the very noblest in the land, if necessary. Willingly would I myself have worked in the chain, so strong grew my anxiety about the fire. Soldiers ever and anon shouted, 'Out! out with you! Those who won't work must out!' But still we were not pressed into the service; neither did we see anywhere the chain of water-carriers.

And the flames of heat increased and increased. The long rows of windows in the conventual building glimmered as if of molten copper. There was a cry that it also was on fire. An excited officer, spurring his horse madly through the gateway, shouted, 'It is a government building! — it must — it must be saved!' To which the crowd answered with a laugh. A gentleman talking with the Amsels, hearing this cry of fresh alarm, suddenly exclaimed — 'Heavens! Desshardt lives here: I must be off and help him to remove his things;' and away he rushed. And more soldiers and more water — more water and more soldiers — arrived. We were driven forth from our shelter upon the steps within the gateway, and the heavy gates of the court were closed upon us.

We were now out in a street, but not in the street where stood the burning brewery. Nevertheless, what a confusion was there! People were flying with their children and goods hastily collected together, in awful alarm, and snatched from the fury of the devouring tyrant. A stream of bewildered folk hurried along through the middle of the street; they heeded nothing as they blindly pressed forward between the rows of stationary spectators. Here came a man in his dressing-gown, his cap drawn over his face, a hunting-pouch crammed with the most heterogeneous articles slung round his shoulders, and in either hand a terrified little girl. Here a husband bore along in his arms his sick wife, her fainting form wrapt round with a large cloak. Now a young girl ran along, wringing her hands and crying aloud. Beds and bedding, tables, chairs, wardrobes, pictures, baskets of books, clothes, papers, umbrellas, are borne past. Here comes a cart of cheese; here come again beds and bedding, *ad infinitum.* Here comes a little lad carrying with care a canary, which flutters wildly in its pretty cage; here come two students with their music books, a violin, a mass of manuscript, learned-looking books and swords, laid upon a little sledge. Here comes an easel, here a huge canvas, here a baby in its cradle, here an old blind woman led by a little child; here again comes bedding, bedding, bedding! Now huge, splendid mirrors, now kitchen utensils, and now a wagon loaded with sofas, chairs, boxes, heaped up madly! All is confusion, bewilderment. There are heaps of furniture piled up in the streets; there are carts and there are drays with huge tuns rolling, thundering along; there are shouts, murmurs. 'The whole quarter will be burnt down!' cries a man in a hollow voice. The heavens flush and glow; sparks fly around in thick showers. We try to approach yet nearer to the burning houses, but again are driven back by the soldiers. Again we enter the court-yard which I have already mentioned. The *Staats Gebäude* (Government building) is untouched, but the roof of the brewery has fallen in with a tremendous crash; the gables stand up like golden gables; the white roofs of some lower buildings gleam ghastly white, with an orange glare behind them. Men are seen standing on walls and parapets, pouring torrents of water from the snake-like pipes of the fire-engines; but those slender streams of water seem impotent compared with the raging fire: those pipes look no more than so many leeches crawling over the roofs. Nevertheless the flames are abating. The great danger, thank God! is past. Gradually the fire ceases to rage, to destroy.

Under the escort of two officers, acquaintance of the Amsels, we were passed along through sentinels and the crowd till we approached within a few yards of the burning brewery; but even here, on account of the narrowness of the lane in which the brewery stood, the view was not complete. A mass of engines filled the little street. We were now in the midst of the long pipes which extended in all directions, like enormous serpents, across the street, and ran up steep walls and over precipitous roofs, where men, telling as black shadows against the fiery glow, plied their whole strength in deluging the flames. There were no women here except ourselves. There were soldiers and busy workers, whilst the corporation, with silk scarfs tied across their breasts, superintended the operations. All worked earnestly, eagerly; the flames sank and sank; the neighboring church-spire, which had risen above the conflagration illumined with orange and scarlet light, seeming at times, surrounded with flames, and with its burning cresset, like a martyr crowned with a celestial star, and rising towards heaven from a bed of fire, now paled into an ordinary church-steeple, shone upon by an ordinary moon. Moonlight again triumphed; all grew gradually calmer.

Crowds, however, yet lingered around the glowing ruins; flames yet fitfully leaped and flickered; smoke yet arose in heavy volumes. Soldiers yet stood guard in the plashy discolored snow, amid a wild disorder of carts, engines, heaps of furniture, charred beams, and trailing pipes, which intersected the streets and walls. But all danger was past.

At three o'clock in the morning we wended our way, with exhausted frames, to Mrs. Amsel's, wondering where all the unlucky fugitives of the night had found shelter.

The next day nothing was talked of but the fire. Seven-and-twenty years ago, it is said, this brewery was burnt down, the brewer having in both cases made himself unpopular, by raising the price of beer. People blessed their stars that half Munich was not consumed, — that the fire did not break out in the dead of night, — that the weather was calm, — and that there was a thick covering of snow. It is said, also, that Prince Luitpold aided in extinguishing the fire.

CHAPTER XXXIX.

A VISIT TO THE DEAD AND TO THE NEWLY-BORN.

January 12th. — This afternoon there was a regular thaw; nevertheless I set out from the studio to the Cemetery, which is precisely at the other end of Munich. It was all sunshine over head and all sludge underfoot. It was a deplorable day for so long a walk; but my reason for choosing to visit the Cemetery to-day was because the corpse of the young lady, the friend of the Amsels, who died so suddenly, was lying at the Dead-House: and as I had heard a sad history regarding her death, and had long determined to pay a visit to the Dead-House, I went this afternoon spite of the mud.

Walking up the long pathway of the burial-ground, between the hundreds of crosses and monuments crowding thickly upon each other, with the bells tolling solemnly meanwhile from the Cemetery-chapel, I felt how, now entering the city of the dead, the joyous activity of the old part of Munich through which I had just passed stood forth in strange and striking contrast. Yet people thronged the broad pathway; crowds were hastening along, — men, women, and children, rich and poor. Whither were they bending their steps this miserable, dirty day? Now a funeral train encountered the throng, and the people stepped aside upon the spongy graves as it passed, bowing before the upraised crucifix.

When I neared the cloistered wall which separated the old from the new burial-ground, I perceived a still denser crowd. What could be the attraction? At once it flashed upon me that the attraction was the Dead-House, — the living were come to visit the dead!

And such was the case. Large windows, or rather doors, open out of the Dead-House into the cloisters. Here people congregate and gaze in at the corpses. I know not whether upon every day of the year the populace of the good city of Munich flocks to this awful spectacle. At all events, to-day there was a great crowd; and I do not believe that any corpse of extraordinary interest was exposed. I observed a considerable number of students among the crowd: as I pushed my way beneath the cloisters I found what had attracted them.

Jostled up against by men, women, and children, lay two corpses in their open coffins supported upon biers. I suppose they had been brought out for burial. However, there they were. One was the corpse of a student. He lay in his coffin dressed in his best clothes; his black dress-coat, black trowsers, patent-leather boots; a white cravat tied round his throat, white kid gloves upon his hands; he seemed dressed for a ball: but oh! his face — that statue-like expression upon the marble brow, the sunken white cheeks, the heavy eyelids darkened by the touch of death, the thick golden moustache curling over the livid lips! His tricolor corps-band crossed his breast. His hands were folded together, holding upon his heart a large bouquet of fragrant flowers, together with a small cross of black wood. Whilst I looked at him, a peasant-woman dipped a brush into a vase of holy-water standing near the coffin, and sprinkled the poor dead face with it.

The other corpse was of an old lady. No one seemed to pay much attention to her. She had no flowers, not even a wreath of artificial ones. She lay stiff and stark in a black silk dress; a prim lace cap was fastened around her rigid, old face; her feet poked out of the coffin in a pair of stuffed shoes tied on with broad sandals. There was something unusually affecting to me in these poor, aged feet attired in the old-fashioned shoes; they evidently were the shoes she had saved up as her holiday shoes, her shoes for feasts and festivals, — and now they were going down with her into the grave to the feast of worms. No one but myself cast more than a glance at the poor old lady, — all eyes turned towards the handsome student; she was but a withered last year's kex; he was a vigorous young tree fallen in a sudden storm.

The crowd jostled and pushed and talked and made itself very comfortable, greatly enjoying the spectacle.

'Eh! eh! that's a fine corpse!' remarked a jolly red-faced woman, wearing a golden swallow-tailed cap upon the very back of her curly black head. 'But he does not look so handsome — does he, Lina? as when —'

The 'when' was lost in a whisper into Lina's ear, and the jolly woman and smart girl passed on.

'Ach! and this is what we shall all come to sooner or later,' moralized a ragged, shrivelled old man, with a blue nose and very wheezy voice.

'Only nineteen years of age! poor thing! poor thing! and she a *Braut* (betrothed girl), too!' sighed a gentle, motherly-looking woman, who might have been a baker's or miller's wife, gazing in through the window.

'Poor Marie!' spoke another voice: 'to think of her lying there in the very ball-clothes in which she was to have danced with her bridegroom at last Thursday's ball!' And the speakers thrust their faces up to the window where many other faces were thrust.

On either side of the window hung a kind of 'table of

contents' of the corpses lying behind the glass. The 'table of contents' was framed, and decorated with emblems of mortality. The eager spectators consulted its columns with deep enjoyment, muttering to each other names, ages, and causes of death.

When a space at the window offered itself, I also looked through it. I breathed, or fancied I breathed, as I neared the window, the clammy, soul and body sickening odor of death, — that fearful odor which once breathed can never more be forgotten. Looking within, I saw a solemn room where various corpses were arranged upon biers, and where many empty biers were awaiting corpses

In the centre of the room lay the statue-like figure of a young girl — the 'Marie' of the speakers, and the Amsels' friend, I imagine. Her face had the pale yellow tint of ivory upon it; her brow was wreathed with myrtle — she was now the bride of death. She lay as if in a trance; her hands were crossed upon her breast; a delicate gauze veil flowed over her, down to her feet. A grove of greenhouse flowers bloomed around her pillow, which was trimmed with exquisite lace; flowers bloomed in her hands; flowers bloomed at her feet, and tall waxen tapers rising out of bronze candelabra burnt and twinkled amid the leaves and blossoms.

There was a second dead woman's face, which was affecting and beautiful. The head lay slightly turned aside; the lips were crimson; the cheeks, scarcely sunken, were flushed in patches with a bright crimson tint, which looked rather of life than death. Her hair was jet black, and parted with the nicest care over a broad, low white brow. She also was covered with flowers: tender sprigs of passion-flower and fern drooped over her. Close beside her in its little coffin lay an infant. And beyond these there were other rigid faces, old and young and middle-aged, glaring with a ghastly white from distant biers, all with stern profiles set towards the ceiling; all with the wondrous print of death impressed upon them.

And without, the crowd murmured and crushed upon each other, and went and came in active enjoyment. Some very few might have real sorrow within their breasts; some very few might be touched by this vision of solemnity; but to the mass it was simply vulgar excitement and pastime. I felt a real sense of relief in the thought that, dying in England, no such curious gossiping crowd would gaze upon my corpse, or upon the faces of the dead dear to me. My very soul revolted and sickened at such desecration of the solemnity and the silence of death. If we have dead-houses in our new English cemeteries, surely admission to them will be alone granted to the friends of the deceased! The remembrance of this crowd of the living troubles my imagination far more than the remembrance of the calm, holy corpses. I cannot endure the thought that, when the hour of death arrives for —— or ——, crowds of gossiping idlers will gather before the dead-house to gaze with unsympathizing eyes upon the deserted temples of these great spirits! Such crowds assembled around the body of Schwanthaler, when it also was laid here.

I passed out of the burial-ground, by the lofty portal which is crowned with its solemn statues, and walked along the banks of the Isar, looking up into the clear sky and listening to the rush of waters just released from the chains of ice which have bound the river for weeks. The waters rejoiced with glad voices, as if hymning their triumph in renewed life, and the sky had the word Immortality written upon it; but it was long before I could dismiss the painful impression which my visit to the dead-house had left upon me.

January 15*th*. — About a week ago a baby was born in this house; and to-day was the christening. Isabel was curious to see the ceremony, and mentioning her curiosity to Madame Thekla, Madame Thekla mentioned it to the nurse, the nurse mentioned it to the lady, and the lady, through Madame Thekla, sent us an invitation. This lady is the Frau Majorin von Schwerdt. She, her husband, and children, we know very well by sight, but our acquaintance went, until to-day, no farther than bowing politely to each other when we met on the stairs. Thus you see that our invitation to be present upon the occasion of the christening was somewhat peculiar.

This afternoon at three o'clock, festally attired, and attended by Madame Thekla, we descended to the *étage* below us, which is inhabited by the *Frau Majorin*. The man-servant, all in his best, opened the door to us — the women-servants standing about in the passage, were all in their best, and the drawing-room was filled with an assembly of relatives, also all in their best. Major v. Schwerdt in his blue uniform, with crosses and orders glittering upon his breast, received us as we entered the saloon. All the gentlemen were in uniform, and one old officer, with snow-white hair and moustache, was resplendent with decorations. The ladies in their elegant light silk dresses, and rich lace falls and caps, stood in a semicircle; and within the semi-circle was a table covered with white linen, and upon which a crucifix and burning tapers were placed. Before this altar stood two old priests in white robes.

Now a lady presents to the elder priest the little infant lying within its pretty curious little chrysalis of pink satin and lace. And the priest blesses the infant, laying it in its chrysalis upon the altar before him, and reads the Latin service out of his missal; and the godmother repeats the responses for the little babe, the little Emma Maria Theresa — and the priest breathes upon the infant's brow in token of spiritual life being breathed upon her, and lays his hands also upon her, claiming her as God's own; and marks her with the cross in sign of her having taken upon herself the cross of Christ to bear until the end of all things. And the priest lays salt within her little lips that she may love the taste of wisdom, and that God may preserve her from corruption and the foulness of sin. And the priest denounces the devil; and the priest anoints the little breast and shoulders with oil: on the breast, in order that she shall be strengthened to combat against the devil, the world, and the flesh; upon the shoulders, that they may bear with ease the yoke of Christ; and the priest changes his blue stole for one of white and gold, laying it over the little infant in sign of her state of sinfulness being exchanged for a state of purity. And the priest pours water three times over the uncovered head of the meekly submitting babe, to typify the three days during which Christ rested in the grave, arising from death upon the third, as this infant shall arise from a spiritual death into a spiritual life. And the priest anoints her with the holy chrysm, anoints her as a Christian, as a partaker of Christ's royalty, as a sacred being; and a lighted taper is held close to her little hand to show that she has come forth from the darkness into the light, and how with love in her heart burning like this taper, she shall go forth to meet her heavenly bridegroom, and that 'her light shall shine before men;' and thus in the name of the Father, the Son, and the Holy Ghost, is she baptized and received into God's fold.

The old priest delivered, after these ceremonies, a short address to the little assembly upon the significance of the rite; then bowed to the father Major v. Scherwdt: a hum of conversation was heard, and the little brothers of the newly christened Emma Maria Theresa ran about the room in unrestrained glee.

We returned our thanks to the Frau Majorin's mother for the pleasure we had received through witnessing the ceremony, and begged she would present our compliments to her daughter. The Frau Majorin, she informed us, was in the adjoining room, and would we not enter and speak to her ourselves?

Of course we did so, and found that the sick lady had watched the ceremony through the open door-way. As we stood beside the invalid's bed, the priests entered, together with the Major, and the nurse carrying the infant in its pink chrysalis, and the pink chrysalis was laid upon the mother's lap. The old priest made the sign of the cross, and so did the *Frau Majorin.*

The inferior priest held a burning taper which shed a pale golden glory over the white peaceful countenance of the mother, over her quiet white brow, which looked doubly white from contrast with the black hair which lay in heavy waves beneath the lace border of her cap; the golden glory fell upon the snowy lace-trimmed pillows which propped her head and shoulders, upon the snowy sheets and snowy bed-quilt; all was pure, spotless, and calm. The superior priest prayed in a quiet voice for the mother and child, and then blessed them. Tears filled the mother's eyes, swelling gradually and rolling over her cheeks whilst he prayed; and she folded her delicate white hands in prayer, the thick golden rings of her betrothal and marriage gleaming in the rays of the taper. The Major, in his decorated uniform, leant over his wife's pillow, and the little infant had fallen asleep within its rose-colored chrysalis.

We returned to our little abode in the upper *étage,* feeling a new interest in our neighbors.

CHAPTER XL.

THE CASTING OF THE SEIGES-THOR, BAVARIA.

January 22*d.*—At eleven o'clock this day, the casting of the principal portions of the *Seiges-Thor*, Bavaria, took place.

We set off in good time, and as we proceeded along the Nymphenburg road, towards the foundry, several other droschkes were speeding on likewise, and troops of gentlemen were walking beneath the trees which line the road. All were bound like ourselves for the foundry; all turned down the *Erz-giesserei*, from one of the lofty chimneys of which, thick black volumes of smoke were vomited.

Carriages drew up before the gate; people alighted; people entered the court-yard, many of them stopping, as we also did, before passing through the open door of the building, to notice a fire-engine standing in front of the huge grim bronze lion, and its long snake-like pipe stretching up to the huge roof of the casting-house, where it lay in watchfulness near to the lofty vomiting chimney.

All within was stir and expectation. I have already described the interior of this casting-house; the pit sunk in the ground; the rudely raftered roof; the windows placed high in the walls; the huge furnace, open at top, and rising like a low windowed tower at one end of the vast desolate hall, which is supported by many square brick-work piers.

A rude stage was erected opposite the furnace, in which were congregated a number of people, principally ladies. But before we take our stand there, we will inspect the furnace somewhat more closely. Wild orange-colored flames roared through its narrow niche-like windows, leaping and rejoicing in savage glee; from its top hurried thick volumes of lurid smoke, and columns of dazzling dancing sparks sprang up into the mysterious gloom which hung above the furnace. Sunk into the pit in front of the furnace lay the earthen mould, built into it in fact, with a narrow channel left round it, into which the molten metal was to flow. Three long chains of ponderous links descended from the dusk void, the orange and scarlet glare flashing and resting upon them; two-thirds up the three chains seemed lost in a murky vagueness, dark as Erebus; low down, on either side the furnace, was a small door, which the workmen opened ever and anon to feed the raging flames within with fresh metal, or else to stir them up with long poles. I thought, as these doors opened, of the children cast into the fiery furnace, and how their figures might have gleamed forth through such openings, flitting past in awful safety amidst the whirl of flame, accompanied by the fourth august white-robed form. I thought of the horrible death of Robert in Retzsch's designs for 'Fridolin,' and again recalled the foundry scenes in the same artist's illustrations of the 'Song of the Bell.' There was the very group he has given us at the furnace-mouth, its impressiveness heightened tenfold by color and by Rembrandtesque light and shadow.

Up rises the furnace-door; forth rush curling waves of fire, with fiery surf scattered around; blinding, glaring, orange light broadly falling upon the dusky workmen, who, shading their averted faces with their gloved hands and slouching hat-brims, excite and teaze the devouring element with their long poles. And Ferdinand Miller is ever near to the gaping jaws of the furnace, directing and superintending; his face glowing in the intense heat, his brow beaded with sweat. The rough walls of the furnace rise duskly in the lurid haze; crimson and orange light glares from the windows in wondrous gradation up the walls, until lost in cold darkness, where, through dimly discerned rafters and scaffolding, gleam two long narrow streaks of daylight. The fire-glow glares and burns like ruddy gold upon the quaint forms and eager faces of the groups of workmen, who toil with their long poles before the furnace mouth; and long grotesque shadows are cast flickering behind them upon the ground and walls. The fire-glow glares upon the knot of earnest spectators surrounding the furnace and the pit, and assembled upon the stage, or leaning against walls and brick columns; it illumes them with a magic brilliancy, which is rendered at certain points yet more wonderful, from cool blue daylight striking upon their brows, whilst the cheeks are flushed with the reflected light of the flames. And above the crowd of living figures rise colossal forms of armed warriors, and peaceful poets, and sceptred monarchs; these glowing crimson; those standing calm and pale in the cold light of day.

A glowing heat meanwhile fans our faces; and we hear the rush, rush, of flame, the cries of the workmen, the commands of Ferdinand Miller, and an answering far-off voice dropping down out of the mysterious darkness above us.

Much had to be done ere the imprisoned molten metal could be released. Now burning cinders are placed around the mould within the channel, to heat it in preparation for the scalding metallic stream; now workmen, with delicate care, remove the plugs which have stopped up certain air-holes upon the surface of the mould, and brush away the dust; now the cinders are removed, and the holes in the channel for the entrance of the metal into the mould are opened, and after much passing to and fro of workmen in their slouched hats, and with their leathern aprons fastened behind with brass chains and clasps, and who carry high above the heads of the crowd long bars of iron red-hot at their tips, or gigantic ladles glowing of a vivid vermilion; now, after an hour of expectation, Ferdinand Miller proclaims in a loud voice that the casting is about to commence.

'May I beg of you all here,' he exclaims, 'to remain perfectly quiet, whatever may happen. All necessary preparations for safety are made; should any danger occur I will inform you; but keep quiet, I pray you all. By all means we must avoid a sudden current of air.'

Workmen approach bearing a tremendous bar, with which to burst open the tiny aperture in the blank wall of the furnace, above the pit, and through which the metal is to flow. Ferdinand Miller stands as yet upon the mould; his men surround him upon the borders of the pit. With a burning flambeau held before him, he once more examines the air and metal holes. The bar is suspended to the three chains. Ferdinand Miller leaps from the mould; the men stand ready beside their bar; there is a momentary solemn pause, in which the constant rush, rush of the flames imprisoned within their citadel falls monotonously on the ear; the besiegers of the citadel pause solemnly beside their battering-ram; they pause in prayer. Heads are uncovered; heads are bowed; and there, within the forbidden circle of the workmen, near to his friend Ferdinand Miller, stands Wilhelm von Kaulbach, his head bare and bowed to his breast — his fine, calm profile illumined by the fiery glow.

A moment's pause, and the battering-ram strikes! Forth from the aperture streams liquid, golden, quivering metal; down, down, down it streams, filling the channel around the mould; lurid smoke darts from the air-holes, and forth leap, springing into the air, golden, burning, quivering jets of molten metal; golden, burning, quivering stars shower around, falling amid the workmen, and even to the feet of Ferdinand Miller and of Kaulbach. I feel the people around and behind me fall back in a haste of momentary terror.

'The casting is accomplished!' shouts Ferdinand Miller.

Caps and hats are waved in the air; a thrilling hurrah bursts forth, and is swelled by a sudden blast of trumpets sounding forth from the upper darkness.

'A vivat for King Ludwig!' he again exclaims. Another hurrah and burst of music.

'And yet another!' cries a workman, flinging up his cap into the air; and there is a third deafening acclaim.

The golden molten metal hardens within its channel; workmen try it with iron bars, and then cover up the glowing mass with sheets of iron.

People crowd with congratulations around Ferdinand Miller; more daylight streams into the building; the furnace is illumined with a wondrous, hazy violet light; the rushing of the flame is lost amid the rejoicing of human tongues.

Thus passed over in happy accomplishment the casting of the largest portion of the *Sieges-Thor*, Bavaria.

CHAPTER XLI.

THE ARTISTS' MASKED BALL.

On Saturday, in all the grandeur of our fools' caps, we proceeded, under the escort of Dr. F., to the Artists' Festival. We seem to have winter back again in full force, for the streets are once more deep in snow, and the frost is bitterly keen. And now on this cold evening, when all looked colder from the twilight gloom falling upon the street, the warm glow of lights which gleamed from the long rows of windows in the Odeon welcomed us with a delicious hospitality.

It might have truly been a London train of carriages that extended from the Odeon afar up the street, so long and closely packed was it. And as we eagerly looked out of our frosted carriage windows, the scene was exciting. It was absurd to think of taking up our position in this train; we therefore drove back again and round to the opposite entrance of the Odeon, where, consenting to walk a little distance through the snow, we were enabled to enter. The staircases were hung with rich tapestries, and orange-trees and myrtles were arranged upon the steps in two thick rows, and up between them streamed a crowd of maskers.

But what a magic vision bursts upon us when we enter the ball-room itself! In the centre rises a pavilion, stolen certainly out of Fairyland! Graceful and slender Byzantine arches of white and gold, and with delicate vermilion tracery upon them, cluster together, supporting tall figures symbolical of former Artist-Festivals, and, crowning the whole, a graceful, youthful figure of Joy holding his cup. Ivy and vine cluster around, and festoon the graceful arches; tall, golden tripods rise, heaped up with flowers; wreaths of fresh greenery, and golden tambourines and pipes and flutes, hang around the base of the pavilion in joyous symmetry; beneath the pavilion, nestling amid a grove of odorous shrubs and flowers, four magical swans, with white and golden plumage, arch their necks and pour from their open bills ruddy streams of wine! The fairy vision towers to the very ceiling of the lofty Odeon Hall, where, from a wreath of roses red and white, spring forth long silken streamers of white and pink, extending like a vast umbel over the whole hall, each streamer attached at its farther end to a smaller chaplet of roses hung upon each capital of the grey marble columns which support the galleries of the hall.

These grey marble columns are also gay with decorations — hangings of crimson with a simple diaper pattern of gold clothe them up one-third of their height, and from pillar to pillar swings a wreath of foliage and roses; thus color and flowers encircle the whole hall. Beneath the orchestra-gallery rises a low carpeted platform, which is approached by two flights of steps, where stand, as guards, two masked figures in mediæval costume. In the very front of the platform rises a grand towering group of trophies — the trophies of painting and music.

The heavy white emblazoned banners of the two societies of Munich painters fall in brotherly harmony with the smaller banners of two musical societies who have lent their aid for the festivities of the grand night. Beneath the banner-folds hang clusters of palettes, brushes, strings of bladders of color, architects' rules, compasses — a glorious array of artistic tools. Ivy sprays, and wreaths of pine and moss, bind all together, uniting them with the musician's trophy, a cluster of musical instruments, trumpets, violins, flutes, clarionets, and drums! Beyond the platform is a partition of dark green drapery, with garlands hung symmetrically upon it.

We stood completely bewildered with the magic of the scene which was increased a thousand-fold by the marvellous crowd collecting.

Every lady and gentleman had been requested by the Artists' programme to assume a fool's cap for the evening, in case they did not come in masks or fancy costumes. Thus every head presented a brilliant bit of color. The gentlemen received their caps with their tickets, and these caps were simple enough in form, but of two most vividly-contrasting colors, — green and scarlet, yellow and pink, blue and orange.

The ladies' fools' caps were much more extraordinary; varying from a quaint, tiny jester's cap of mediæval cut, covered with gold and silver bells, embroidery, flowers and feathers, to an ordinary evening head-dress rendered Carnivalesque by bells fastened to the ends of the ribbon trimmings; there were pointed witches' hats; tiaras; shepherdesses' hats; jelly-bag caps; there were caps trimmed with lace, with gold, with silver, with ostrich feathers, with peacock feathers, with cock's feathers; there were caps of scarlet, of blue, of amber, of pink; there were parti-colored caps, and tri-colored caps; and caps of velvet, of lace, of gold, of silk, of gauze, — of every hue, texture, and fashion, in short; all, more or less, developments of the jester's cap of the middle ages. There were hundreds and hundreds of these caps surmounting faces of every age and every expression; there were hundreds and hundreds of costumes — costumes, it would seem, of every era and every country beneath the sun!

Here comes a solemn Arab Sheik and his wife; their swarthy faces, their golden bracelets and anklets upon their dark limbs, their ample woollen mantles of creamy white, or striped with sober violet and brown, all breathing of the desert! Here tumbles through the crowd, whirling his club of jingling bells, a dwarf of the middle ages, clad in scarlet. Here mince along, in their high-heeled shoes, a courtier and lady from the Court of Louis XIV. Here comes a jolly English tar in his red shirt, with his low-crowned hat, and a pipe in his mouth. This must surely be Albrecht Dürer himself! Look at his mild, calm face beneath that beetling black velvet cap! look at his short fur-trimmed cloak of chocolate color and at his leathern pouch, slung at his side and mounted with rich steel ornaments. Here are Americans, Armenians, Turks, Portuguese, Italian peasants, Venetian senators, knights and ladies of the German legions; here are pilgrims, knights, troubabours, savages, and devils. Here are whimsical beings with huge silver ram's horns, with golden ram's horns, with huge, flapping, pointed ears, with beaks and false noses! There is the chorus of singers, with beaked noses, and queer, big spectacles, looking like a flight of extraordinary birds: — and only listen to their low chirp! chirp! they are birds surely, and not men! There are caps with peacock feathers towering yards high above the crowd; here comes a whole peacock's tail! Here a gigantic butterfly nodding at the end of a long wire, which no doubt is fastened to some strange cap, could we only see it in the crowd! Here is Mrs. Bloomer herself, and there the favorite sultana! Here are two gigantic ladies in gigantic yellow silk hats, with gigantic bouquets and fans in their hands, and black masks over their faces. There is a terrible old man who is always winking his eyes and wrinkling his brow, who has a mane of powdered hair, a monstrous shirt-frill, and a false nose! Here is a band of courtiers with the heads of gigantic cocks and hens! look how they open their long beaks, and snap right and left as they move along.

Wilder and wilder, madder and madder grows the scene; louder and louder wax the laughter, the squeaking, the crowing, the flapping, the whispering, the piping; louder and louder, madder and madder!

But a hush falls suddenly upon the multitude, gentlemen in golden fools' caps make a pathway through the crowd; and towards a seat prepared for them at the right of the platform proceed the two Kings, the two Queens, and their Court. They wear no fools' caps: the Kings carry their black hats in their hands: the Young Queen has exquisite diamonds in her hair and on her bosom; the old Queen wears a very quiet head-dress; the Court ladies, wreaths of ivy and natural flowers. How quiet and simple they all look!

The Court take their seats; the musicians sing a joyous welcome; there is a Vivat for Bavaria; the King Ludwig, the Artists' King; for German Art! The musical director, a singularly handsome man, in a singularly handsome dress of black velvet, all covered with scarlet rosettes, gives a signal to the orchestra, and suddenly down drops the drapery beyond the platform, and forth leap, spring, tumble, screaming, yelling, and whirling their arms and their clubs, a mad troop of fools, scarlet, yellow, white, in their quaint, whimsical, mediæval dresses, with long ears and pointed sleeves, and ribbons, and scallopped jerkins flying in the wind! They fling bon-bons among the crowd, they fling humorous mottoes, they jingle their bells, they rattle their wooden clappers! They leap, tumble, spring from the platform down among the multitude!

How mad, how mad they are! And look! look! On comes a wonderful crowd across the platform, a crowd of South American Indians! Look at their dusky forms clad in jaguar skins! Look at that noble figure clad in gold tissue, and crowned with a tiara of orange and scarlet feathers! They are representatives of the various Mexican tribes; their black locks are confined within glittering silver diadems; their noses and ears are pierced with feathers, golden rings, and porcupine quills; strange plates of brass hang upon the breast of one; another carries his barbaric weapons. Here, too, come Spanish-Mexicans; here negroes with their hoes; here the planter in his broad straw hat and loose white trowsers and white coat! Ah, that planter is Rugendas, the painter of strange Mexican scenes and people, — Rugendas the painter and tropical traveller! These Mexican costumes are those which he brought with him as artistic spoil. And a wonderfully arranged Indian procession it is.

But on, on, come yet other strange forms: a band of hunters and warriors of the far-off Niebelungen time. It took one's very breath away with surprise, as warrior after warrior marched along in his wondrous helmet, upon which rose the lovely, expanded wings of hawk, and owl, and heron; the helm wreathed with ivy-sprays, frequently, also, covered entirely with fresh green moss, till it looked a portion of the old primeval forest. Sometimes, between the wings, rose the head of a hare, a fox, or other sylvan creature; sometimes, instead of wings, the helmet was crowned with branching antlers; sometimes the head was covered with a hood which fell in simple folds around the face, or tightly wrapped itself around the throat, but ever these old Germans wreathed their brows with ivy or pine twigs. Their whole garb was of a sylvan character; their short jerkins, bound round the loins with jewelled girdles, from which depended daggers and hunting pouches, were green as the summer woods, or russet and orange as the woods of autumn; orange, or grey, or russet were their hoods; their tight hose were white, or grey, or scarlet; their boots of untanned leather or scarlet. On their backs were slung huge horns, spoils of the *Auer-Ochs,* from which to quaff mighty draughts of mead. In their hands some bore long hunting spears, others quaint primeval musical instruments, violins of marvellous slimness, with a most small allowance of strings, and which made strange, sweet, small music, tiny flutes and wondrously constructed drums, all murmuring and muttering of long-departed ages.

The processions descend and mingle with the crowd. Suddenly the band of fools, who, I believe, by the way, were all young painters, dash, whirling their clubs, and leaping, and shouting, through the multitude, who part before them, and thus a narrow circle round the room is formed, and dancing commences. And marvellous were the whirling couples who flew around the circle, and marvellous the antics of these merry mad fools, who had constituted themselves masters of the ceremonies. Men of the nineteenth century are they no longer, but the merriest of Merry Andrews who have ever dwelt in Emperors' palaces or Barons' halls. Mad, jocose, impertinent are they; yet chivalrous withal. Behold a group of them leaping upon each other's shoulders, and climbing up towards the enchanted pavilion to catch, in a tall goblet, the ruddy wine falling from the bills of the magic swans. Behold, a fool having caught his heel in a lady's train, flings down his club, flings down himself also before the lady's feet, and with an arch, imploring gaze, and mock distress, beseeches her pardon! And look at that scarlet fellow nursing his legs as he sits upon that flight of steps, and swinging his body backwards and forwards, whilst he carols a merry song.

But dancing was not the whole amusement of this festive evening.

Once more there is a bustle upon the platform. A large golden wheel fixed upon a frame is brought forth. This is the Wheel of Fortune.

Each lady on entering the hall, has received an elegant card, printed in gold, upon which, together with a grotesque group of Carnival figures, is a list of the dances for the evening, and a certain number written in one corner of the card. This number is her number in the lottery. The wheel is turned. To the sounds of trumpets the number of the prize is called forth. Away dashes the troop of fools in mad career through the ball-room, and the supper-rooms, in search of the fortunate lady. After a merry search she is discovered, and led in triumph to the platform, where seated, she receives her prize with much ceremony; a graceful vase, or book perhaps, or basket filled with flowers. A document of complimentary, humorous, and appropriate verses, adorned with sketches, she also receives upon a cushion; the verses, I should observe, being first read aloud to the company. Many a picturesque group was thus formed on the platform. Let us take the first group as an example. The band of fools have led up a bright-faced maiden with large, laughing blue eyes, golden hair, and a complexion 'red as the red, red rose,' so covered is she with blushes. Her dress is of blue velvet, cut square at the bosom, in the old German style, and bordered with a stiff band of rich golden brocade incrusted with jewels; a jewelled girdle, to which depends a quaint pocket, is clasped round her waist; her arms and bosom are covered with sleeves and a deep tucker of white lawn; and a blue and gold embroidered tiara surmounts her blonde locks. She is a veritable *Burg Fräulein.* It is a Provençal troubadour, who kneeling before her, presents a fragrant mass of flowers; his face is a gallant, poetical face; his hair curls in thick clusters around his compact head. His dress is of pink and white silk, pink and white alternating; a little hood, pink one half, white the other, hangs upon his shoulders; roses, pink and white, adorn him; there are roses on his breast, roses upon his sleeves, roses upon his hose and upon his shoes; roses encircle his jerkin; his very face looks a rose! He seems the very embodiment of romance, of the Romaunt of the Rose; perhaps he may be. But whether he is or not, he is, at all events, a well-known historical painter, and an officer to boot.

Many were the picturesque groups, and that not alone during the drawing of the lottery, which this evening produced. I look down from the platform upon which I am now standing: not, however, by any means because *I* am the lucky drawer of a prize. And half hidden by the Painters' Trophy, his figure shewing beneath the cluster of musical instruments, sits crouching a Bedouin in his long, spectral bernouse; he props his dark face upon a dark arm, and looks up into the face — not of another Bedouin — *that* would have been too real for so fantastic, delirious a night! — but into the face of a Niebelungen hero — of Siegfried himself, perhaps: the winged, ivy-encircled helmet, the orange fur-trimmed doublet, the hunting-spear glittering in his hand, the huge, grey, silver-mounted hunting horn slung upon his back, the short hunting-boots upon his feet, how strangely they contrast with that dark Arab in his spectral bernouse!

Everything is so genuine, so exquisitely beautiful and appropriate in the costumes, so thoroughly artistic, that the groups seem groups not of maskers, but of beings summoned by an enchanter's spell from far-off regions and long-departed ages. One's imagination bewilders itself in a perplexing romance, so striking, fantastic, whimsical, are the contrasts on every side!

The Cotillon is now being danced. From our position upon the platform, the spectacle is very extraordinary. In the centre rises that fairy pavilion with its flowers, its swans, its heroic statues, its undulating radiation of silken streamers, through which, looking upwards, your eye rests upon the bright frescoed hues of the ceiling. The grey marble columns of the hall, draped partly with crimson, are our horizon. A mass of quaint, gorgeously-attired human beings fills the hall; they rise in brilliant tiers beneath the columns; they rise, a low, human pyramid, upon the steps of the pavilion; they fill, as with waves of scarlet, orange, violet, green, and crimson, the whole body of the vast hall. An open, but narrow, space surrounds the pavilion: here whirl the dancers in mad career. They are dancing beneath tall hoops of blue and white, which are held above their heads by the scarlet, and orange, and parti-colored fools, standing opposite each other, at certain distances within the circle. The chandeliers, with their hundreds of starry lights, gleam and fling down their bright radiance over the gorgeous, glittering scene. The music wildly peals and pants; and ever and anon some merry laugh, some mad shout, rises above its harmonious voices, and the voice of the whole assembly, — that murmuring, strange, united voice of the crowd!

Was not the whole scene like the dream of a fevered brain! — a scene likely enough to return, if ever one should wander into the mysterious land of delirium.

But the Cotillon is over. Hark! a march bursts from the orchestra! Yes; and behold how through the crowd winds a procession of hunters: they bear garlanded torches in their hands, together with their spears and bows. The musicians, with their primitive musical instruments, lead the way, piping and playing on their simple pipes and upon their tiny violins. What an old-world feeling they carry with them! Forth they march. And now behold a hideous monster, with a head looking each way, makes his appearance. A hurried chase of him commences: his heads are chopped off and borne in triumph round the circle, to the sounds once more of merry, small music.

Again there is dancing; again the musical societies burst forth into song: the merriment seems ever on the increase; the fools are for ever careering round the circle in unwearied antic mood. Now they encounter the celebrated Neureuther, whom one has long since recognised as the author of the Fairy-pavilion; they hoist him on their shoulders; they bear him round the hall with loud acclaim. Now there is a hue and cry after some other well-known name. The great artist has disappeared. 'Where is ———?' shout the fools; 'we have lost ———!'

'He has fled into the gallery! Don't you see him high up aloft?' shouts a voice, and the hall rings with laughter.

And thus the night wore on in full embodiment of the painters' motto emblazoned on their decorations and upon their cards:

'Tages Arbeit; Abends Gäste!
Saure Wochen! Frohe Feste!'

Never, surely, was there a more joyous festival, or one more graceful, and fantastic, and poetic, than this *Künstler Bal* of 1852. Long lives and merry ones to the joyous artists! let us cry: and long, long life and a glorious immortality to the joyous, genial German art! A right hearty — *Lebe Hoch für die Stadt München, für Münchener Kunst und Künstler!*

At half-past four o'clock, as we alighted at our house, through the dark blue sky of this February morning the holy sound of bells fell upon our ears; — they rang for matins.

Isabel has sent me a description of the Artists' Festival of February, 1853, an extract from which I here give.

'The device for the Artists' Ball this year was the same as last — fools and fool's caps, — all looked very much the same; but, as a little variety, instead of Mr. Rugendas's procession of savages, there was a band of fifty young girls, each one assuming in her costume the character of a flower. This procession was led by the king of the fools up the steps of the platform on which was placed his throne; and here they all stood round him after he had taken his seat. The room was crowded, much more even than last year, and the jolly, noisy, mad-cap fools were seated upon ornamental scaffolding placed half-way up the lower pillars of the hall. From these eminences they by turns addressed witty speeches in verse to their king; and after a variety of funny things had been said, one fool at last asked the king which of the lady flowers then present was the rarest, the fairest, and altogether the most worthy of honor? The king at first seems much puzzled what answer to make: he gazes round on the fifty blooming maidens standing by; — there was Miss K. in a zone and wreath of moss roses; Laura F. wore a gold trellis-work, over which ran pink roses; another artist's daughter, a tall, noble-looking girl, wore a water-lily, which sat like a star upon her forehead; another the blue fleur-de-lis, the delicate long leaves of which hung gracefully from the back of her hair over her white shoulders; there was a brilliant head-dress of vivid mountain-ash berries; little, or rather large, turrets of ivy, the trails of which fell over round and lovely arms, and encircled tiny waists; there were two heads powdered as white as any snow-wreath, overtopped by a mass of nodding snow-drops: besides these there were magnolias, violets, and many others, formed according to the character of the flowers into very tasteful, though somewhat large head-dresses, and otherwise decorating the attire of the wearer.

'Considering the native wit of a "fool," the king appeared somewhat *foolish*, in the ordinary sense of the word, and most horribly perplexed did he contrive to look, being all the time mocked and jeered at unmercifully by his wicked subjects: they uttered unearthly shrieks, and, as further signs of impatience, flapped their wooden clappers with a perfectly stunning din.

'At length the king arose, saying that he believed he could now guess their riddle: Was not the *Edelweiss* the fairest and rarest flower that grew? And instantly, as if impelled by a magical impulse, at one bound, making their thousand bells dance and ring, the Fools sprang to their feet upon their stages, and sang,—

'Wie im Alpen Rosen Kranz
  Edelweiss vom Felsenthrone,
Also in des Festes Glanz
  Strahlet als e? Frauen Krone,
Leuchtet als die Herrscherin,
  Bayerns holde K??igin!'

'As 'mid Alpine flowers and snow,
  Rock-throned Edelweiss is beaming,
So amid the festal show,
  As the crown of noble women,
As the monarch, is she seen
  Our Bavaria's gentle queen!'

'The pretty little queen, seated beneath her crimson velvet canopies, appeared quite affected, and almost ready to weep. King Ludwig, who sat beside her, clapped his hands, and smiled, and bowed, and seemed most highly delighted. The young Queen wore in her tiara of diamonds a sprinkling of *Edelweiss,* which at a distance produced the effect of pearls. This secret of the royal toilette had evidently been betrayed beforehand to the fools. The lines are said to be the composition of the Painter Teichlein ; the music was by Baron Perfall — the handsome Musical Director of last year's Artists' Ball.'

CHAPTER XLII.

SPRING PICTURES.

THIS last week has been Passion-week; and as usual all Munich was rushing from church to church: but this year I did not rush with them — I only went to two churches with Isabel, when she had no other companion.

This year, someway, all looked faded and weariful to me. The only thing that I saw which I did not see last spring was a group of peasants in the Basilica, kissing the wounds of a frightful crucifix, which was laid upon the altar steps. Never was anything more disgusting.

This morning I went with Isabel to hear high mass performed in the Hof-Kapelle, as the music is very fine there on Easter Sunday. The robes of the priest, all gold, rose-color and green, were beautiful; and the troop of elegant court pages in their blue and silver, bearing their burning tapers, and gracefully bending their handsome little silk-stockinged legs, was pretty; but that was all. I feel as though I had had enough of Romish pageantry for some time to come.

April. — There is no denying now that Spring is at hand; yet as I am still far from ready to bid adieu to Munich, I am inclined to close my eyes to her signals, which each day greet me on my walks through the English Garden. Dog's-mercury and the lovely glossy arum leaves are rapidly revealing their vernal beauty. I see pale oxlips nodding here and there upon mossy banks, and bunches of them lie withering upon the pathways, gathered farther on in the Garden by children's hands, and then dropped. At times, as the sense of rapidly approaching spring forces itself upon my unwilling eyes, most ungratefully do I long that the beautiful unfolding leaves would, for a short, short time, pause in their unfoldings — would curl themselves up again in their gummy buds and their delicate silky spathes; for all will have burst in fulness of beauty, and will be over, before one's heart has recognised and rejoiced in it, and another tender, beautiful spring will be vanished away, like a swift dream, out of one's life.

But it is not alone through leaves and blossoms that Spring announces her advent in the English Garden; she announces it in many ways, and in none more lovely than by her gulls. Do not say I am *gulling* you when I talk of *gulls* in the English Garden. The other morning, as I neared the little bridge crossing the rushing branch of the Isar, opposite to Prinz Carl's Palace, not many hundred yards from the town, and below the very palace windows, I saw a number of large, white-winged birds, careering about wildly in the air, just over the little bridge. The Garden resounded with their shrill cries. There must have been about a hundred of these birds, at the very least. Now they flapped their broad white wings, till they gleamed and glanced dazzlingly in the sunlight; now they poised their quivering grey little bodies in the deep blue sky, or balanced themselves upon the sparkling green waves of the rushing water; then again darted up, up, up away high into the sky — whirling among the distant leafless trees, like a cloud of white butterflies — their wild cries echoing joyously, vernally, through the lawns and groves of the wild, park-like Garden. It was a lovely, joyous bit of poetry.

I understand that these birds come at a certain time each Spring, for a few days, to particular spots in the English Garden, and then again disappear entirely. They come in search of a peculiar kind of food. They fly many miles from a lake among the mountains; each night returning to roost in their Alpine home.

The other evening, upon this same bridge, I had another pleasant peep into the lives of small woodland creatures. A brisk squirrel suddenly dropped down from a tree before me — glanced at me with his roguish black eyes — set up his tawny, bushy tail — paused for a moment, as if gazing at, and meditating upon the slavery endured by the poor sentinel, pacing with glittering bayonet before the ducal palace; then sprang nimbly up again upon the tree, disappearing in the network of branches.

The *gardeneresses* also announce that Spring is at hand. Coming suddenly upon a group of these the other day in the English Garden, I was considerably staggered for the first moment with regard to their sex. All wore hats — broad-brimmed and narrow-brimmed — slouch hats Tyrolean hats, straw hats, and felt hats and beaver hats — green, grey, black and brown. All wore handkerchiefs tied beneath their hats — red, orange, blue-and-white, striped, spotted and checked. All wore very short, thick petticoats, and very clumsy shoes — some even big boots — and many wore coats — great-coats or jackets — drab, brown and black. All had rakes in their hands, and were raking away heaps and heaps of dead leaves as fast as they could rake. Their faces were the faces of old men, not of women.

Never, certainly, did I encounter a more astounding company of *odd-fellows.*

Smiling to myself, I passed this group of gardeneresses, and crossing the rustic bridge, which spans a second branch of the Isar flowing through the Garden, I beheld approaching the bridge over which I leaned a small raft, formed of a few huge pine-tree stems, come rushing along with the current. The water dashed over the little raft, swilkering between the mighty stems, and drenching the great leathern boots of the men who guided the raft. And what a calling of cheery voices there was! what a brushing past of overhanging trees and shrubs! what a clever management of the long rude helm!

And a fresh raft was seen to shoot forth from behind a bend in the little river's bank; and there was more shouting, and more clever steering; and then gliding beneath the bridge, upon which I stood, the two rafts danced merrily along towards a second and still more picturesque rustic bridge farther down the stream, and above which soared a whirling crowd of my favorite gulls. And again came a third raft — and another, and another!

Doubtless these huge pine-trees, felled among the Alpine solitudes, were now departing, after their winter's sojourn in the Royal Munich Wood-yard, on their long voyage to Vienna — or, it might be even farther; perhaps they would float onward and onward — the rafts joining together as the stream ever widened, till they approached Turkey.

Baron H., I recollect, once described to me an excursion which some students he knew had made to Vienna on a raft. In description, at all events, it sounded very delightful. The floating so dreamily along the solemn Danube — the peculiar life among the raftsmen — the pausing for the night with the raft at old-world villages upon the banks — villages far away from the beaten path of ordinary travellers — the glimpses of a quaint, fresh, peasant life, opening out before you in the talk of the raftsmen and of the villagers — all this, I well remember, most pleasantly affected my imagination. I remember, also, that a sort of little sigh for a moment heaved itself up in my heart as he described it, — 'Oh, if I were but a man, then would I voyage with a raft!'

But, thank God! such silly sighs as this do not often heave themselves up in my heart; for the longer I live the less grows my sympathy with women who are always wishing themselves men. I cannot but believe that all in life that is truly noble, truly good, truly desirable, God bestows upon us women in as unsparing measure as upon men. He only desires us, in His great benevolence, to stretch forth our hands and to gather for ourselves the rich joys of intellect, of nature, of study, of action, of love, and of usefulness, which He has poured forth around us. Let us only cast aside the false, silly veils of prejudice and fashion, which ignorance has bound about our eyes; let us lay bare our souls to God's sunshine of truth and love; let us exercise the intelligence which He has bestowed on us upon worthy and noble objects, and this intelligence may become keen as that of men; and the paltry high heels and whalebone supports of mere drawing-room conventionality and young ladyhood withering up, we shall stand in humility before God, but proudly and rejoicingly at the side of man! Different always, but not less noble, less richly endowed!

And all this we may do, without losing one jot or one tittle of our womanly spirit, but rather attain solely to these good, these blessed gifts, through a prayerful and earnest development of those germs of peculiar purity, of tenderest delicacy and refinement, with which our Heavenly Father has so specially endowed the woman.

Let beauty and grace, spiritual and external, be the garments of our souls. Let love be the very essence of our being — love of God, of man, and of the meanest created thing — LOVE that is strong to endure, strong to renounce, strong to achieve! Alone through the strength of love, the noblest, the most refined of all strength — our blessed Lord Himself having lived and died teaching it to us — have great and good women hitherto wrought their noble deeds in the world; and alone through the strength of an all-embracing love will the noble women who have yet to arise work noble works or enact noble deeds.

Let us emulate, if you will, the strength of determination which we admire in men, their earnestness and fixedness of purpose, their unwearying energy, their largeness of vision; but let us never sigh after their lower so-called *privileges*, which when they are sifted with a thoughtful mind are found to be the mere husks and chaff of the rich grain belonging to *humanity*, and not alone to men.

The assumption of masculine airs or of masculine attire, or of the absence of tenderness and womanhood in a mistaken struggle after strength, can never sit more gracefully upon us than than do the men's old hats, and great coats, and boots, upon the poor old gardeneresses of the English Garden. Let such of us as have devoted ourselves to the study of an art — the interpreter to mankind at large of God's beauty — especially remember this, that the highest ideal in life as well as in art has ever been the blending of the beautiful and the tender with the strong and the intellectual.

But I have wandered away in thought far from the Royal Wood-yard, which I was just about to enter after leaving the English Garden and rustic bridge, and where, this pleasant spring-tide, I am constantly observing things striking and peculiar to my English eyes.

I confess to an unaccountable sort of affection for this wood-yard; it is not beautiful or particularly quaint, but someway it has seized hold of my fancy, and it is just one of those spots which, in after years, when my head reposes on its English pillow, will often rise up dreamily before me, and in fancy I shall again and again be walking along the raised pathway beside the rushing green mill-stream — with softly turfed banks sloping down, and then the acres of wood-yard stretching away on one hand, whilst the water rushes on the other. I shall see the heaps and heaps of carefully stacked wood piled up for royal consumption; I shall hear the distant sawing and chopping of workmen; I shall see their little grey huts and houses sprinkled here and there. Perhaps it is mid-winter, frost and snow lying on the ground; in through the huge grey gates rattles and jolts a long grey wagon, drawn by four beautiful horses, upon one of which is mounted a man in the royal livery: it is a royal wagon, come to fetch the royal wood for burning in the royal stoves; and another long wagon, drawn by equally handsome horses, soon follows it: men begin instantly piling the wagons with wood, and a wagon already laden making its appearance from the more distant part of the inclosure, rattles with its four mettlesome horses and blue-liveried postilion bravely away through the great gates. A splendid piece of timber tumbles off from the royal load as the wagon sways through them; but the royal servant and royal horses never deign to stop for a piece of lost wood, and rattle still bravely up the road.

A poor shrivelled little old woman, with a kerchief of orange and blue tied over her shaking head, and shading the grotesque features of a thorough '*Märchen-Frau,*' comes tottering along over the frosty ground, and perceives the mighty prize. She darts upon it with sudden agility, she casts furtive glances around, she wraps it up in her crimson stuff apron, and quietly pursues her way. Poor old *Märchen Frau!* I will not tell of your little theft to the watchers in the wood-yard; I know as well as you do, although your blear eyes can no longer read the words, that nailed up upon these very gates are official denunciations against all thieves, purloiners, and smokers of pipes or cigars within the precincts of the Royal Inclosure; nevertheless, pursue fearlessly your way home to your wretched dwelling, miserable little old woman! for you are no great sinner after all: muttering confused words about 'cold' and 'the dearness of wood,' you had come tottering across the rich wood-yard, and never had reached your hands towards the tempting stacks of the King's wood; and when at the very threshold, out in the road, lay a fine piece of timber, surely it must have been flung down for you by the loving hands of the Angel of Mercy!

But now in fancy, I see quite a different scene going on in the wood-yard! The snow and ice have vanished from the earth—there is a vernal freshness in the air, a softness, an awakening life; water is pouring in from all the sluices of the mill-stream, the green mill-stream itself is dashing and tumbling about like a mad thing. All the wood-yard is transformed into a small lake, intersected by the raised pathways which cross it here and there; and tumbling over each other, and hurrying, and pushing, and scrambling, and pitching, come hosts and thousands of small pieces of timber, carried along by the rushing waters. The little lake is covered with a navy of many thousand pieces of wood.

Men are running to and fro with poles, pushing along

stranding pieces of timber, or inspecting the flow of water, the dykes, and dams, and locks. It is a very animated scene, and the children of St. Anna suburb know this, and all the day through, groups of children may be seen watching and shouting with merriment as the waters continue to flow along, bearing upon their small green waves these miniature navies!

But gradually the waters fall and fall — dry land appears, and the thousands of stranded pieces of wood are carefully piled up into the innumerable large stacks which adorn for the greater portion of the year this Royal Wood-yard.

Or again, I see a singular operation going on — the waters have vanished from the mill-stream. Its course over moss-grown piles is laid bare; instead of clear rushing waters through which, looking down in autumn, you had watched with delight the brilliant leaves fallen from the over-hanging trees lying there like gorgeous gems of scarlet, and gold, and amethyst, imbedded in richest green velvet, you only now see slimy ugly brown tresses of water mosses and weeds. Men are busily at work in the water-course; the old moss-grown piles gradually disappear, and fresh ones are being driven in. And what an extraordinary process this is of driving in the piles! In early morning, late in the afternoon, and all day long, you hear the monotonous and peculiar cry of the workmen, as they, standing together in a ring, each holding a cord in his hand attached to a rough machine within the circle, tall poles acting as a fulcrum, they raise by their united power a tremendous weight, letting it fall again upon the head of the pile; then by repeated blows driving it in. There is the short monotonous cry of the men — then the dull heavy fall of the huge weight upon the pile — then again a pause — once more the monotonous cry, the dull blow, and the pause — and this with a strange uniformity all the long day through, continuing even often for weeks at a time.

It is as monotonous to watch the driving in of these piles as it is to listen to it. The men move as if portions of some marvellously quaint machine — not as if they were men; their pink and chocolate and dark blue cotton jackets and blouses, with here and there a scarlet cap or green Tyrolese, in the distance, forming a motley mosaic.

But the pleasantest scene of all in the Wood-yard is when the bell for noontide prayer sounds from the near Franciscan chapel: the tolling of the bell comes fitfully across the trees upon the balmy April breeze — the turf is studded with golden ficaries and dandelions and trefoil and silver daisies — round-faced children from the neighboring suburb have strayed into the Wood-yard, they are making little nosegays and garlands with the flowers — they are a group to delight the heart of Ludwig Richter, the Dresden artist: away above the stretch of the grey acres of stacked wood rises a line of noble trees, the frontier trees of the English Garden, and above them sweep the azure spring heavens with streaks of cirrus-cloud enhancing their loveliness. In the foreground, before a carpenter's shed built of grey weather-beaten planks, and its open doors revealing heaps of shavings and a carpenter's bench, stands a group of workmen — youths and old men, and men of middle age; their dress is quaint, and with dashes of rich color about it; here a scarlet cap, there a deep maroon or indigo jacket. They are standing close together.

As the first toll of the monastery bell swells on the breeze, each head bows itself upon the breast: the silver locks of the old artisan, — the crisp dark curls of the youth, — the scanty grizzled hair of the man in middle life — are uncovered to the sun. A dull murmur of prayer breaks from their lips, and they cross themselves devoutly upon breast and brow.

The children have flung their flowers upon the grass, and pray also.

Easter Sunday. — This afternoon the Werffs apparently have been rendered somewhat choleric by eating meat after their long fast. Although it was meat blessed by the priest — and, therefore, holy meat — they have had a grand quarrel!

Poor old souls! I cannot avoid smiling when I recall the scene, — or rather the sounds. For two whole hours we had heard talk! talk! talk! and that too in the loudest of voices. I supposed at first that this was merely some Easter visit they were receiving, and thus also explained why Fräulein Sänchen had never made her appearance for the removal of our dinner cloth.

I opened the door, — so very extraordinary waxed the sounds; and I then heard the voice of Madame Thekla at its highest pitch proceeding from her little sitting-room, interspersed every now and then with a short scornful laugh. At the same time, out of the kitchen, Fräulein Sänchen poured forth another torrent of words with ditto laugh, — scouring away meanwhile vehemently; yes, scouring away, although it was Easter Sunday afternoon. Scouring is her joy and consolation, I verily believe!

Perceiving how matters stood, I broke in with a loud ringing of our hand-bell.

Having arranged her features into becoming calmness, the poor old Fräulein made her appearance.

'Have you had company, Fräulein Sänchen?' I asked: 'what a tremendous talking there has been in your kitchen!'

'No! no! SHE's angry!' replied the old creature, removing the table-cloth, and uttering the words with such a comically black thunder-cloud look — with such an irresistible nod and then a wink — that had she only been a comic actress she would have made her fortune.

'*Ja! Ja!* SIE *ist böse!*' And this was all she would vouchsafe about the grand quarrel. When she comes in she nods, and when she goes out she winks, and between the two wears the thunder-cloud upon her brow. To-day she had put on, for the first time since Lent, her favorite string of blue-glass beads round the thinnest and most yellow of poor old necks. Pity is it that Dickens never saw her, for then, of a truth, she would have been immortalized, with her oddity, her faithfulness, her good-nature, and her crossness.

This winter the exclamations each evening of '*Immer so fleissig! Immer so fleissig!*' have by no means lessened; and my nervous dread of them has only increased in a tenfold degree. Our rule has become to put aside any occupation we may be engaged upon just before the expected advent of the good Fräulein, which is always about nine o'clock, after which she and her sister lock themselves into their rooms for the night, good early souls! The best plan to escape the nerve-torturing '*Immer so fleissig! Immer so fleissig!*' is to lie upon the sofa with your head buried in the pillow, as if asleep. Alas, dear old Fräulein, how often have we been forced to practise this innocent deceit! and as thy dear old feet have trod with hushed and stealthy steps across and across our room, arranging anything that might be out of its place, and with anxious silence thou hast set down upon a distant table our wondrous 'tea-machine,' — our portable *kitchen*, in fact — by means of which we often prepare a cup of chocolate or boil an egg for our suppers; yes, as we have listened, smiling with shaded faces, to thy stealthy footsteps, how have our hearts smote us for even so small a piece of hypocrisy towards one whose heart was full of such sterling goodness as is thine!

But if, however beguiled by interest in our occupation, we have forgotten the flight of time and the arrival of the 'tea-machine,' then woe betide us! Often have I more than once heard Isabel stop short in some sweet *Volks-Lied*, which she was singing for my especial delectation, and rush into some ear-piercing exercise, or rattle over the keys of the piano, in order to render it impossible for our innocent tormentor to gain a word from her. Still would she remain conscious of eyes fixed upon her with a gaze of admiring astonishment, — of a face held most pertinaciously upon one side, — of a pair of poor old bony hands crossed patiently over the pit of the old Fräulein's stomach; and the words '*Immer so fleissig! Immer so fleissig!*' would pierce to Isabel's nerves spite of shriekings or thunder of piano-keys.

As for Anna! her resource in such extremities is intense abstraction; if she is writing letters, how intolerably fast does her pen scratch over the paper — often words of utter nonsense! Her head is never raised, yet her eyes see, as if by *clairvoyance*, that droll old visage ogling her across the room, and she hears, above the scratch of the pen, the '*Immer so fleissig! Immer so fleissig!*' dropping from her lips. And thus will the two continue, — the one to scribble in frantic haste with unraised head, the other gazing at her from a distance with eyes of humble wonder mingled with rising ill-humor — until the old Fräulein flounces off in a huff, remaining black as a thunder-cloud for the next four-and-twenty hours; or Anna is fairly vanquished, and raising her face smiles! and is repaid by a ten-minutes' martyrdom of exclamations over her '*Fleiss*,' and over her extraordinary correspondence, and of inquiries after every '*Herr*,' '*Frau*,' and '*Fräulein*' member of her 'much respected and highly well-born family'—unlucky Anna! Or if Anna is drawing, then is the martyrdom somewhat varied. 'Ah, when,' says the loquacious soul, 'will people learn in their youth to spare their precious, dear little eyes? Ah! she knew well—that she did—what it was to over-work the eyes—yes, yes! she knew well enough the temptation of the *Fine Arts!* Had she not worked bell-ropes, and smoking-caps, and pocket-books, on the finest, finest canvas? Did not she know what it was to do fine work? Had not she embroidered flowers, and scrolls, and landscapes, in silk, wool, and cotton? That she had! Had she not when in the convent embroidered and fine-sewn, together with the other young ladies, a whole set of baby-clothes for the daughter of the Electress? That she had, indeed! And had she not got up by peep of day to embroider? and had she not sat up late at night and embroidered? That she had! And had not she knitted two dozen pair of finest-patterned stockings for her lady sister? That she had, and she would show us them, too!—(this for about the twelfth time) and the bell-rope, also, in the next room, was her work. There was no bell, certainly: but the bell-rope of such fine work was hers! That it was! Yes, yes, we might think that our eyes would not fail—but she knew better, that she did! and she knew what the Fine Arts were! And her hands, too! we might think *they* never could have held a delicate needle! but, yes, indeed they had: but old age! old age, and scouring, and washing, and cooking, they spoilt any hands! Ah, if the dear Fräulein would but take warning, and not ruin their dear little eyes over the Fine Arts!'

Alas! dear old Fräulein, after many such a gossip as this, repeated for the twentieth time, often have I thought how that neither thou nor Anna had yet attained to the practice of the truest and most difficult of all the Fine Arts ever taught or studied, — the *Art of Living with Others:* and often have I wondered, as I have felt a struggle between compassion, love, and irritation contend within my spirit, whether this Art ever *is* attained in this world to perfection. But truly alone in the New Testament do we find the teachings of this Fine Art; as, I believe, also may be found teachings for all other Fine Arts. Yes, even for the Fine Arts, so called, *par excellence.* But I cannot now branch out into this theory of mine, which at times has risen up before me with an especial loveliness.

CHAPTER XLIII.

CARTOONS.

April. — In Kaulbach's studio, this week, there is a drawing which has especially struck me with its beauty. It is a design in charcoal, but finished with exquisite care, — one only of the vast number of designs which this great man is ever creating, with inexhaustible fancy and imagination.

It represents Mercury announcing to Calypso the command of Jove that Ulysses shall depart. Calypso is seated beneath a rural alcove, in a languid dream. The luxuriant foliage of a southern clime clambers up the stem of a palm-tree growing beside the alcove, and wreathing lla with beauty. The hot noontide sun flings clear broad shadows from the tangle of leaves and blossoms across the front of the bower, where sits the lovely enchantress. The upper portion of her figure is thrown into shadow by the luxuriant foliage, her beautifully rounded figure revealing itself through her softly clinging drapery; her hand is listlessly resting on her lap, and holds the shuttle of the loom which stands beside her. Her beautiful face is raised with dreamy listlessness towards young Mercury, who, standing out in the broad sun-light, his winged feet just alighted upon earth, points with extended arm and caduceus towards the mournful Ulysses, who, with bowed head, is seated far out in the glare of sun-light, beyond the rustic alcove, upon the margin of the sea.

Gentle little waves roll in towards the mournful Ulysses; but he heeds them not. An extended flight of migratory birds — the key-note of his thoughts — stretches itself across the sky, winging its way over the ocean, as he sits mournfully, with bowed head, in the sunshine.

At the feet of Calypso, in a chafing-dish, burn fragrant woods and gums, the soft smoke curling up among the rich foliage of the bowery alcove, and across the goddess's antique lyre, which leans against the palm-tree stem. Doves flutter and coo among the palm branches. All is as soft, tender, and full of an enchanted languor, as Keats's poetry, yet strong withal as old Chapman's Homer.

The small cartoons and studies for color for the completion of the New Pinakothek frescoes have been made this early spring by Kaulbach.

The principal one of these designs represents the Artists' Festival in Munich in 1845; the other designs are simply single whole-length portraits of the great German painters whose works will be contained within the New Pinakothek — Cornelius, Schnorr, etc. — with decoration of garlands upborne by lovely children — graceful, of course, but in no way especially remarkable.

The Artists' Festival of 1845 is a link in the series of frescoes illustrative of the history of modern German Art, to which I have already referred.

It introduces us into the very heart of the whimsical and picturesque jollity of German artist-life. The groups are as if suddenly transferred from the Artists' Masquerade to the canvas. In the centre of the composition rises Schwanthaler's statue of King Ludwig arrayed in his royal robes. A bevy of fair maidens crowned with flowers surrounds the statue, binding garlands of flowers with which to adorn it: one, seated upon an upturned rustic basket, leaning slightly back from the group, hangs a wreath of roses upon an emblazoned shield presented to her by a page.

Upon a slightly raised platform beyond this group stands, in semi-circle, a marvellously comic array of singers — a dash of Kaulbach's Hogarthian satire. The gravity and quaint distortion of the countenances and attitudes are irresistibly droll. That huge stout man with the ear-rings, and with the bearing and countenance of a Friar Tuck, sending forth with deep complacency the most sonorous of bass notes from his broad ponderous chest, and whose tidily smoothed hair is adorned with a garland of vine-leaves, is a wondrous contrast to the meagre, excited, yet withal most earnest countenances of several of the other singers, and to the calm dignity of the musical director.

Above the singers hang festooned insignia of the festival, bound together with gay streamers and garlands, and slung from golden and richly wrought columns; and on either hand of them presses on a group of Munich painters, wearing their gorgeous and whimsical array. Here is a gathering of slashed sleeves, glittering chivalrous armor, ermine-lined mantles and embroidered doublets. There behold the grave and noble costume of Albert Durer; a workman from the Bronze Foundry in his leathern apron; and again slashed sleeves, garlanded brows, and caps of mediæval cut.

Meanwhile, to the right of the bevy of fair damsels who are calmly binding their fresh garlands, and below the platform, an extraordinary war is being waged. Sir Fresco and Sir Oil — mad urchins upon hobby-horses — are tilting at each other; their lances are mahl-sticks, their shields are palettes. Sir Fresco is unhorsing unlucky Sir Oil, whose mahl-stick is broken, and whose visor is being pierced by his antagonist's lance. The little Monk of Munich (*Munchen*, the crest of the city taken from its name) is laughingly bending forward, about to crown the victor.

The counterpart to this merry episode is a group of mad fools.

When the delicious May had returned, and the whole land was once more redolent of spring, — when in early mornings the English Garden was filled with a very concert of eloquent blackbirds and thrushes, and in the balmy evenings with soft strains of wind instruments floating through the freshly opened leaves and blossoms, Isabel and Anna said to each other, Now will we take a delicious holiday after the long days of winter industry; now will we set forth for a whole week of happiness to the neighborhood of Starnberg. Anna all day should sketch quaint and lovely bits of nature, and architecture, and weeds, and picturesque peasants, to her heart's content. Isabel should study her German among fresh leaves and flowers and beneath a cloudless azure sky, and gather up old melodies and songs to sing in her English home, with her sweet clear voice. Yes! such a holiday should be enjoyed by them as never before had been enjoyed by any two female students!

And later, too, on in the warm summer, they would pay that long talked-of, long dreamed-of visit to the kind Von ——s, in their beautiful poetical home among the mountains; and there Isabel, beside lore of German and mountain melodies, should gather up much knowledge in the stately kitchen from the sweet artist-sister, — the

'Blush Rose,'—as celebrated in the family circle for the mystic preparation of certain celestial viands as for her Art,—viands so lovely to the eye that all artist-souls mourn over their demolition.

Anna said, 'Thank God, at last my soul will steep itself in the deep joy of those Alpine peaks,—of those clear deep green Alpine waters, of those rare and gorgeous Alpine flowers!' Anna already felt her spirit 'seated upon an Alp as on a throne.'

But, although May was come, the Great Painter was still in Munich, and at his studio, and would not yet, for several weeks, depart on his usual summer journey; and so long as he, the Priest of the Art-temple, remained, the 'Art-student' would remain, also, a faithful recipient of the food of knowledge which his gracious words scattered around him. Thus Anna always said, 'When the Great Painter is gone,—then will we take our holiday, then will we go and see —— and —— and ——'s studios; then will we go *really* to Nymphenburg, walk in the stately gardens, and see the far-famed fountains play; then will we visit the decaying palace of Schleissheim, and discover in its gallery Wilkie's 'Opening of the Will;' then of a truth will we have a long day's enjoyment at the much-vaunted Menterschwaig; then will we witness the arrival of a pilgrimage up among the woods at the chapel of Maria-Eich; then will we inspect a great Brewery; then will we fairly exhaust the 'lions' of Munich.

But all must remain unseen, unenjoyed, till after the departure of the Great Painter;—to desert the studio until then could not be thought of.

But letters arrived for Anna, which suddenly put to flight all these day-dreams.

Various of her beloved ones from the dear old home in England were setting forth upon a long voyage; they were setting forth to Australia for a season. When Anna read these letters the words swam before her eyes; she was like one in an astounding dream. She rejoiced with a great joy that her beloved ones should visit this marvellous Australia, should experience the poetry of a great voyage and of a new land; but the Alps, the glories of German Art, the beauty of her own and of Isabel's calm life, seemed to fade before her. An immense yearning after the beloved departing ones filled her soul, and nothing but setting forth immediately for England could satisfy her or calm her.

Then came a strange time of adieus, and of packing up clothes, books, and drawings in all haste. Then came the last hour in the beloved old studio, — the last hour in the dismantled sitting-room of the dear little home, with Isabel declaring that when Anna was gone, and had carried off her drawings and prints from the walls, all would look so changed that she could not endure to remain in the same house, although it was with the good old Werffs. And at last came the final moment at the railway, when Anna, seated in the corner of a carriage, waived her hand to dear Isabel, as she stood beside Fräulein Sänchen, who was crying into her big white pocket-handkerchief, and to various friends come to bid a last adieu.

And then the steam-whistle shrieked through the air, and away dashed the train. Yet, as hour after hour removed the Art-Student from the beautiful little Art-city of Munich, only the more noble did the Art there and the artist-life rise up before her, as if transfigured in her soul.

THE END.

BOSTON, 135 WASHINGTON STREET.
OCTOBER, 1854.

NEW BOOKS AND NEW EDITIONS

PUBLISHED BY

TICKNOR AND FIELDS.

THOMAS DE QUINCEY'S WRITINGS.

CONFESSIONS OF AN ENGLISH OPIUM-EATER, AND SUSPIRIA DE PROFUNDIS. With Portrait. Price 75 cents.

BIOGRAPHICAL ESSAYS. Price 75 cents.

MISCELLANEOUS ESSAYS. Price 75 cents.

THE CÆSARS. Price 75 cents.

LITERARY REMINISCENCES. 2 vols. Price $1.50.

NARRATIVE AND MISCELLANEOUS PAPERS. 2 vols. Price $1.50.

ESSAYS ON THE POETS, &c. 1 vol. 16mo. 75 cents.

HISTORICAL AND CRITICAL ESSAYS. 2 vols. $1.50.

AUTOBIOGRAPHIC SKETCHES. 1 vol. Price 75 cents.

ESSAYS ON PHILOSOPHICAL WRITERS, &c. 2 vols. 16mo. $1.50.

LETTERS TO A YOUNG MAN, AND OTHER PAPERS. 1 vol. Price 75 cents.

THEOLOGICAL ESSAYS AND OTHER PAPERS. 2 Vols. Price $1.50.

ALFRED TENNYSON'S WRITINGS.

POETICAL WORKS. With Portrait. 2 vols. Cloth. $1.50.

THE PRINCESS. Boards. Price 50 cents.

IN MEMORIAM. Cloth. Price 75 cents.

HENRY W. LONGFELLOW'S WRITINGS.

THE GOLDEN LEGEND. A Poem. Just Published. Price $1.00.

POETICAL WORKS. This edition contains the six Volumes mentioned below. In two volumes. 16mo. Boards. $2.00.

In Separate Volumes, each 75 cents.

VOICES OF THE NIGHT.
BALLADS AND OTHER POEMS.
SPANISH STUDENT; A PLAY IN THREE ACTS.
BELFRY OF BRUGES, AND OTHER POEMS.
EVANGELINE; A TALE OF ACADIE.
THE SEASIDE AND THE FIRESIDE.
THE WAIF. A Collection of Poems. Edited by Longfellow.
THE ESTRAY. A Collection of Poems. Edited by Longfellow.

MR. LONGFELLOW'S PROSE WORKS.

HYPERION. A ROMANCE. Price $1.00.
OUTRE-MER. A PILGRIMAGE. Price $1.00.
KAVANAGH. A TALE. Price 75 cents.

Illustrated editions of EVANGELINE, POEMS, HYPERION, and THE GOLDEN LEGEND.

OLIVER WENDELL HOLMES'S WRITINGS.

POETICAL WORKS. With fine Portrait. Boards. $1.00.
ASTRÆA. Fancy paper. Price 25 cents.

BARRY CORNWALL'S WRITINGS.

ENGLISH SONGS AND OTHER SMALL POEMS. Enlarged Edition. Price $1.00.
ESSAYS AND TALES IN PROSE. 2 vols. Price $1.50.

NATHANIEL HAWTHORNE'S WRITINGS.

TWICE-TOLD TALES. Two volumes. Price $1.00.

THE SCARLET LETTER. Price 75 cents.

THE HOUSE OF THE SEVEN GABLES. Price $1.00.

THE SNOW IMAGE, AND OTHER TWICE-TOLD TALES. Price 75 cents.

THE BLITHEDALE ROMANCE. Price 75 cents.

MOSSES FROM AN OLD MANSE. New Edition. 2 vols. Price $1.50.

TRUE STORIES FROM HISTORY AND BIOGRAPHY. With four fine Engravings. Price 75 cents.

A WONDER-BOOK FOR GIRLS AND BOYS. With seven fine Engravings. Price 75 cents.

TANGLEWOOD TALES. Another 'Wonder-Book.' With Engravings. Price 88 cents.

LIFE OF GEN. PIERCE. 1 vol. 16mo. Cloth. 50 cts.

JAMES RUSSELL LOWELL'S WRITINGS.

COMPLETE POETICAL WORKS. Revised, with Additions. In two volumes, 16mo. Cloth. Price $1.50.

SIR LAUNFAL. New Edition. Price 25 cents.

A FABLE FOR CRITICS. New Edition.

THE BIGLOW PAPERS. A New Edition. Price 63 cents.

EDWIN P. WHIPPLE'S WRITINGS.

ESSAYS AND REVIEWS. 2 vols. Price $2.00.

LECTURES ON SUBJECTS CONNECTED WITH LITERATURE AND LIFE. Price 63 cents.

WASHINGTON AND THE REVOLUTION. Price 20 cts.

JOHN G. WHITTIER'S WRITINGS.

OLD PORTRAITS AND MODERN SKETCHES. 75 cents.
MARGARET SMITH'S JOURNAL. Price 75 cents.
SONGS OF LABOR, AND OTHER POEMS. Boards. 50 cts.
THE CHAPEL OF THE HERMITS. Cloth. 50 cents.
LITERARY RECREATIONS AND MISCELLANIES. Cloth. $1.00.

GEORGE S. HILLARD'S WRITINGS.

SIX MONTHS IN ITALY. 2 vols. 16mo. Price $2.50.
DANGERS AND DUTIES OF THE MERCANTILE PROFESSION. Price 25 cents.

HENRY GILES'S WRITINGS.

LECTURES, ESSAYS, AND MISCELLANEOUS WRITINGS. 2 Vols. Price $1.50.
DISCOURSES ON LIFE. Price 75 cents.
ILLUSTRATIONS OF GENIUS. Cloth. $1.00.

R. H. STODDARD'S WRITINGS.

POEMS. Cloth. Price 63 cents.
ADVENTURES IN FAIRY LAND. Price 75 cents.

BAYARD TAYLOR'S WRITINGS.

ROMANCES, LYRICS AND SONGS. Cloth. Price 63 cents.
POEMS OF THE ORIENT. Cloth. 75 cents.

WILLIAM MOTHERWELL'S WRITINGS.

POEMS, NARRATIVE AND LYRICAL. New Ed. $1.25.
POSTHUMOUS POEMS. Boards. Price 50 cents.
MINSTRELSY, ANC. AND MOD. 2 Vols. Boards. $1.50.

GOETHE'S WRITINGS.

WILHELM MEISTER. Translated by THOMAS CARLYLE. 2 Vols. Price $2.50.

GOETHE'S FAUST. Translated by HAYWARD. Price 75 cts.

CAPT. MAYNE REID'S JUVENILE BOOKS.

THE DESERT HOME, OR, THE ADVENTURES OF A LOST FAMILY IN THE WILDERNESS. With fine plates, $1.00.

THE BOY HUNTERS. With fine Plates. Just published. Price 75 cents.

THE YOUNG VOYAGEURS, OR, THE BOY HUNTERS IN THE NORTH. With Plates. Price 75 cents.

GRACE GREENWOOD'S WRITINGS.

GREENWOOD LEAVES. 1st & 2d Series. $1.25 each.

POETICAL WORKS. With fine Portrait. Price 75 cents.

HISTORY OF MY PETS. With six fine Engravings. Scarlet cloth. Price 50 cents.

RECOLLECTIONS OF MY CHILDHOOD. With six fine Engravings. Scarlet cloth. Price 50 cents.

HAPS AND MISHAPS OF A TOUR IN EUROPE. Price $1.25.

COUNTRIES I HAVE SEEN. A new Juvenile.

MARY RUSSELL MITFORD'S WRITINGS.

OUR VILLAGE. Illustrated. 2 Vols. 16mo. Price $2.50

ATHERTON, AND OTHER STORIES. 1 Vol. 16mo. $1.25.

DRAMATIC WORKS. (In Press.)

MRS. CROSLAND'S WRITINGS.

LYDIA: A WOMAN'S BOOK. Cloth. Price 75 cents.

ENGLISH TALES AND SKETCHES. Cloth. $1.00.

MEMORABLE WOMEN. Illustrated. $1.00.

MRS. JUDSON'S WRITINGS.

ALDERBROOK. By Fanny Forester. 2 Vols. Price $1.75.

THE KATHAYAN SLAVE, AND OTHER PAPERS. 1 vol. Price 63 cents.

MY TWO SISTERS: A Sketch from Memory. Price 50 cts

POETRY.

ALEXANDER SMITH'S POEMS. 1 vol. 16mo. Cloth Price 50 cents.

CHARLES MACKAY'S POEMS. 1 Vol. Cloth. Price $1.00.

CHARLES KINGSLEY. The Saint's Tragedy and Poems. (In Press.)

LEIGH HUNT. Complete Poetical Works. (In Press.)

ROBERT BROWNING'S Poetical Works. 2 Vols. $2.00.

HENRY ALFORD'S POEMS. Just out. Price $1.25.

RICHARD MONCKTON MILNES. Poems of Many Years. Boards. Price 75 cents.

CHARLES SPRAGUE. Poetical and Prose Writings. With fine Portrait. Boards. Price 75 cents.

THOMAS W. PARSONS. Poems. Price $1.00.

BAYARD TAYLOR. Poems. Cloth. Price 63 cents.

JOHN G. SAXE. Poems. With Portrait. Boards, 63 cents. Cloth, 75 cents.

HENRY T. TUCKERMAN. Poems. Cloth. Price 75 cents.

BOWRING'S MATINS AND VESPERS. Price 50 cents.

GEORGE LUNT. Lyric Poems, &c. 1 vol. Cloth. 63 cts.

PHŒBE CAREY. Poems and Parodies. 75 cents.

MEMORY AND HOPE. A Book of Poems, referring to Childhood. Cloth. Price $2.00.

THALATTA: A Book for the Sea-Side. 1 vol. 16mo. Cloth. Price 75 cents.

PASSION-FLOWERS. 1 vol. 16mo. Price 75 cents.

MISCELLANEOUS.

MRS. MOWATT. AUTOBIOGRAPHY OF AN ACTRESS. 1 vol. 16mo. Cloth. $1.25.

WENSLEY: A STORY WITHOUT A MORAL. Price 75 cts.

AN ART-STUDENT IN MUNICH. BY ANNA MARY HOWITT. Price $1.25.

ESSAYS ON THE FORMATION OF OPINIONS AND THE PURSUIT OF TRUTH. 1 vol. 16mo. Price $1.00.

WALDEN: OR, LIFE IN THE WOODS. By HENRY D. THOREAU. 1 vol. 16mo. Price $1.00.

LIGHT ON THE DARK RIVER: OR, MEMOIRS OF MRS. HAMLIN. 1 vol. 16mo. Cloth. Price $1.00.

THE BARCLAYS OF BOSTON. BY MRS. H. G. OTIS. 1 vol. 12mo. $1.25.

NOTES FROM LIFE. BY HENRY TAYLOR, author of 'Philip Van Artevelde.' 1 vol. 16mo. Cloth. Price 63 cents.

REJECTED ADDRESSES. By HORACE and JAMES SMITH. Boards, Price 50 cents. Cloth, 63 cents.

WARRENIANA. A Companion to the 'Rejected Addresses.' Price 63 cents.

WILLIAM WORDSWORTH'S BIOGRAPHY. By Dr. C. WORDSWORTH. 2 vols. Price $2.50.

ART OF PROLONGING LIFE. By HUFELAND. Edited by ERASMUS WILSON, F. R. S. 1 vol. 16mo. Price 75 cents.

JOSEPH T. BUCKINGHAM'S PERSONAL MEMOIRS AND RECOLLECTIONS OF EDITORIAL LIFE. With Portrait. 2 vols. 16mo. Price $1.50.

VILLAGE LIFE IN EGYPT. By the Author of 'Purple Tints of Paris.' 2 vols. 16mo. Price $1.25.

DR. JOHN C. WARREN. The Preservation of Health, &c. 1 Vol. Price 38 cents.

PRIOR'S LIFE OF EDMUND BURKE. 2 vols. 16mo. Price $2.00.

PALISSY THE POTTER. By the Author of 'How to make Home Unhealthy.' 2 vols. 16mo. Price $1.50.

WILLIAM MOUNTFORD. THORPE: A QUIET ENGLISH TOWN, AND HUMAN LIFE THEREIN. 16mo. Price $1.00.

MRS. A. C. LOWELL. THOUGHTS ON THE EDUCATION OF GIRLS. Price 25 cents.

CHARLES SUMNER. ORATIONS AND SPEECHES. 2 Vols. Price $2.50.

HORACE MANN. A FEW THOUGHTS FOR A YOUNG MAN. Price 25 cents.

F. W. P. GREENWOOD. SERMONS OF CONSOLATION. $1.00.

MEMOIR OF THE BUCKMINSTERS, FATHER AND SON. By Mrs. LEE. Price $1.25.

THE SOLITARY OF JUAN FERNANDEZ. By the Author of Picciola. Price 50 cents.

THE BOSTON BOOK. Price $1.25.

ANGEL-VOICES. Price 38 cents.

SIR ROGER DE COVERLEY. From the 'Spectator.' 75 cts.

S. T. WALLIS. SPAIN, HER INSTITUTIONS, POLITICS, AND PUBLIC MEN. Price $1.00.

MEMOIR OF ROBERT WHEATON. Price $1.00.

RUTH, A New Novel by the Author of 'MARY BARTON.' Cheap Edition. Price 38 cents.

LABOR AND LOVE: A TALE OF ENGLISH LIFE. 50 cents.

MRS. PUTNAM'S RECEIPT BOOK; AN ASSISTANT TO HOUSEKEEPERS. 1 vol. 16mo. Price 50 cents.

EACH OF THE ABOVE POEMS AND PROSE WRITINGS, MAY BE HAD IN VARIOUS STYLES OF HANDSOME BINDING.

☞ Any book published by TICKNOR & FIELDS, will be sent by mail, postage free, on receipt of the publication price.

Their stock of Miscellaneous Books is very complete, and they respectfully solicit orders from CITY AND COUNTRY LIBRARIES.

www.ingramcontent.com/pod-product-compliance
Lightning Source LLC
LaVergne TN
LVHW020912110826
845150LV00004B/652

* 9 7 8 1 4 2 5 5 5 6 1 9 8 *